MANAGING CORPORATE LIFECYCLES

ICHAK ADIZES PH.D.

PRENTICE HALL PRESS

Library of Congress Cataloging-in-Publication Data

Adizes, Ichak.
  Managing corporate lifecycles : how to get to and stay at the top
  / by Ichak Adizes.
      p. cm.
  ISBN 0-7352-0057-2 (cloth)
  1. Organizational change. 2. Corporate culture. 3. Organizational
  behavior. I. Title.
  HD58.8.A343 1999
  658.4'063.—dc21   98-52210
                                                                     CIP

Printed in the United States of America

10 9 8 7 6 5 4 3 2

ISBN 0-7352-0057-2 (cloth)

PRENTICE HALL PRESS
Paramus, NJ 07652

On the World Wide Web at http://www.phdirect.com

This book is dedicated to the memory of my best friend, Marco Naiman.

Acknowledgments

I want to thank all my colleagues at the Adizes Institute for their help in writing this book.

My associates have debated with me for years, have sharpened my thinking and enabled me to make the improvements presented in this revised, enlarged edition. Outstanding among them are Carlos Valdesuso of Brazil and Aurelio Flores Ysita of Mexico.

Dr. Sara Cobb provided all the references and end notes that appear at the end of each chapter. I could not have done it by myself.

Dr. Patrick Griffin prepared the bibliography at the end of the book.

The editor, Elyse Friedman, helped rewrite this book many times. If it were not for her patience, understanding, and editorial brilliance, it would have not been as readable.

My assistant, Dakota Bayard, kept it all together and worked on the illustrations and the accuracy of the manuscript.

Last but not least, I want to thank my wife Nurit who let me be by myself for weeks in a row. Although she missed my company for many, many weekends as I labored on the manuscript, she supported me without a fuss. Without her love, this book would not have been written.

To all, thank you!

About the Author

Dr. Ichak Adizes, founder and director of professional services of the Adizes Institute in Los Angeles, California, is also the Dean of Studies of the Adizes Graduate School for Organizational Transformation at the Institute. He developed the diagnostic and therapeutic methodology for organizational and cultural transformation that bears his name. Dr. Adizes has applied his methodology to organizations employing as few as 30 people and as many as 150,000. The Adizes methodology for organizational therapy has helped organizations in a variety of countries including the United States, Malaysia, Israel, Spain, Mexico, and Norway achieve results and gain leadership positions in industries ranging from banking to food services, and in organizations as different as churches and government bureaucracies. Twelve hundred pages of manuals and hundreds of hours of video and audio tapes document the methodology. As of today, more than 1,000 companies around the world have applied the methodology, and more than 200 Adizes-certified practitioners serve organizations in a dozen countries. A noted speaker and author, Dr. Adizes lectures in four languages, has been the keynote speaker at numerous professional conferences and conventions, and has addressed corporations in more than 35 countries. *Fortune, Business Week,* the *New York Times,* the *London Financial Times,* and the *Public Broadcasting System* are a few of the media outlets that have featured Dr. Adizes and his work.

Dr. Adizes, whose books have been translated into 22 languages, is the author of *Industrial Democracy* (Initial publication: New York: Free Press and Columbia University, 1971); *Self Management,* with Elisabeth Mann Borgese (Initial publication: Santa Barbara, CA: ABC CLIO Press and the Center for the Study of Democratic Institutions, 1975); and *How to Solve the Mismanagement Crisis* (Initial publication: New York: Dow Jones Irwin, 1979). (Subsequent editions of these books have been published by Adizes Institute.) His other books include *Corporate Lifecycles* (Englewood Cliffs, NJ: Prentice Hall, 1988); *Mastering Change* (Los Angeles, CA: Adizes Institute, 1992); and *Pursuit of Prime* (Los Angeles, CA: Knowledge Exchange, 1996); and numerous journal and magazine articles. He has held a tenured faculty position at the Anderson Graduate School of Management, UCLA, as well as appointments as visiting professor at Stanford University, Tel Aviv University, and the Hebrew University in Jerusalem. He lives in Santa Barbara, California, and Caesaria, Israel, with his wife Nurit and their six children.

Contents

Chapter 8
The Aging Organizations: Aristocracy   *153*

Chapter 9
The Final Decay: Salem City, Bureaucracy, and Death   *171*

PART II
Analyzing Organizational Behavior
187

Chapter 15
Structural Causes of Aging   *307*

Part III
Raising Healthy Organizations
329

Chapter 16
Organizational Therapy   *331*

Part IV
Appendices
403

Introduction

In this book, I present the theory of organizational lifecycles and the principles for leading organizational change that I have developed and practiced over the past thirty years. This theory and these principles allow us to discriminate normal from abnormal problems in organizations and to apply the appropriate interventions that lead organizations to their Prime condition. Both the theory and principles explain why organizations grow, age, and die, and what to do about it. They describe and analyze the usual path organizations take as they grow and the optimal path they should take to avoid the typical problems of growing and aging.

What Is New in This Revised and Enlarged Edition?

This revised edition complements the two books I've published since the first edition of *Corporate Lifecycles* was published ten years ago: *Pursuit of Prime* discusses how an organization should be managed depending on where it is on the lifecycle; *Mastering Change* presents the theoretical underpinnings of the methodology for transforming (treating) organizations. Thus, for this revised edition, I have not repeated the material from the first edition that is handled better and in more depth in *Pursuit of Prime* and *Mastering Change*. For clinical training on how to make therapeutic interventions, I direct the interested reader to the degree and certificate programs at the Adizes Graduate School for Organizational Therapy, which has been licensed and initiated since the first edition was published. That means that this edition focuses more on the descriptive, analytical parts; the interested reader who wants more depth on the prescriptive parts should study the additional two books.

Another point. After I had finished writing the first edition of *Corporate Lifecycles*, I realized that something was wrong. I asked myself, if organizational integration is so important, why is it low at the growing stages and high in the aging stages? At the time, I could not answer that question. It has taken me ten years to resolve that dilemma, and I report my findings here. I have learned that although it remains true that entrepreneurship causes growing and a lack of entrepreneurship causes aging, Integration is the factor that precedes entrepreneurship in predicting organizational growth and aging. This factor enables the creation of the nurturing environment for entrepreneurship and, thus, for organizational growth. Integration also allows organizations to treat aging problems more proactively—that is, earlier. Because this factor is subtle, it is commonly ignored and neglected in the pursuit of growth. That neglect is what causes organizations to take the typical path—with all its pains—on the organizational lifecycle.

My research has illuminated several additional factors that enhance the existence, or cause the demise, of enterpreneurship in organizations. These factors further explain the pains of growing and what we used to understand as the inevitability of organizational aging.

Once we better understand the interplay among the factors that cause growing and aging, we can accelerate an organization's progress to Prime, the most favorable stage of the lifecyle, and keep it there longer. Ten years ago, to rejuvenate an aging organization and at least point it toward Prime used to take three years. Today, with better understanding, presented and explained in this edition, we can achieve the same results with even bigger organizations in less than a year. Thus, I have discovered that organizations need not experience the growing pains I described in the first edition of this book. There is an optimal path, presented here, which although it generates other problems, they are preferable to those on the typical path because they bring an organization to Prime faster and can keep it there longer. Furthermore, the problems on this path are rarely pathological, i.e., they do not endanger the existence of the organization.

The first edition described only the typical path. How to reach Prime faster and without the problems of the typical path—via the so-called optimal path—is a new addition, making it an enlarged edition.

Purpose, Methodology, and Organization

This book is directed to consultants and organizational leaders who are responsible for managing organizational change.

It is not a collection of case studies nor is it based on rigorous statistical analyses. Neither is it a literature survey, although this book provides footnoted references. Rather, this is a progress report on my thirty years of experience with organizations, the patterns of behavior I have observed, and the approach I have taken in treating them. The Adizes Institute, headquartered in Los Angeles, California, has associates worldwide who are full-time trained practitioners of the methodology, and this book reflects their experiences as well.

The book's examples are collages of the many companies we have worked with over the years. Some of them are publicly known—through books and/or articles, as will be referenced later—as users of the methodology. Otherwise, names of clients of the Institute are kept confidential.

Domino's Pizza is one of those publicly known, as described in Tom Monaghan's book, *The Pizza Tiger*.[1] Domino's practiced the methodology and grew from $150 million to $1.5 billion in sales in seven years. Another of the better known clients, the Bank of America—at the time the second largest bank in the world with $120 billion in assets and 90,000 employees—had reached a point in its Lifecycle where it was no longer growing and used the methodology to revitalize.[2]

We have also used the Adizes methodology to help such non-profit organizations as the Los Angeles Department of Children's

Services, the largest children's welfare organization in the world.[3] In Ghana's Ministry of Health, I facilitated the establishment of the Health Delivery Planning Unit, which the World Health Organization considered at the time a model for third-world countries.[4]

I have used the methodology and consulted with the prime ministers and/or presidents of Sweden, Greece, Brazil, Macedonia, Yugoslavia, Israel, and El Salvador, mainly lecturing on how to rejuvenate governmental bureaucracy and the political machinery. My associates and I have been involved in using the methodology to resolve some sensitive policy issues that remain confidential.

But not all clients are huge corporations or government agencies. We have worked with churches, a worldwide missionary organization, and TV channels. I can say with confidence that the Institute has tested the methodology repeatedly under a variety of conditions, and we can replicate results regardless of organizational culture, size, and technology. The one variable that can affect the efficacy of the methodology is the CEO, who must be committed to implementation, and there must be positive chemistry between the CEO and the Adizes-certified associate who is leading the process.

While this book focuses primarily on corporations, it also points out similarities to marriage, the personal process of growing and aging, and the process of change in civilizations, biological systems, and even religions. Obviously, such comparisons are necessarily superficial, and I admit that I wouldn't be surprised if they are even totally wrong. But life has taught me that everything is related to everything. If we do not see a relationship, it is only because we don't understand it yet. Still, we must try to pierce the veil of separation. We must strain for at least a glimpse of the universality and the rules that govern this universality.

I have organized this enlarged and revised edition of *Corporate Lifecycles* into three parts. Part One describes what is going on. It describes the typical behavior of organizations through the lifecycle stages on the typical path organizations take, from Courtship up through Prime and aging to the end of the organizational lifecycle, and the normal and abnormal problems they encounter on that path. Part Two, the analytical part, provides tools that explain why organizations grow and age. Part Three provides a short description of the interventions necessary to bring an organization to Prime, and this is the part that is complemented by *Pursuit of Prime* and *Mastering Change*. It also includes the principles of guiding an organization along the optimal—faster—path and describes how an organization behaves on that path. This is necessarily short because we have had insufficient experience with this path. It is a subject for further work and will be subsequently reported.

My hope is that this will not soon meet the fate of what Samuel Johnson gave as a review to a literary aspirant: "Your manuscript is both good and original; but the part that is good is not original, and the part that is original is not good." Nevertheless, I had fun writing it and hope you will find it thought-provoking.

I learn from the experience of others and encourage you to communicate your ideas—whether critical or supportive, theoretical or experiential—through the *Adizes Institute Journal for Organizational Transformation* or communicate to me directly by e-mail at Adizes@adizes.com. I furthermore welcome you to visit our web page: www.adizes.com

Ichak Adizes, Ph.D.
Santa Barbara, California

Notes

1. T. Monaghan, *Pizza Tiger* (New York: Random House, 1986).

2. See M. Johnston, *Roller Coaster: The Bank of America and the Future of American Banking* (New York: Tichnor and Fields, 1990); also, R. Salsman, *Breaking the Bank* (Washington, DC: American Institute for Economic Research, 1990).

3. I. Adizes, R. Chaffee, and Y. Hasenfeld, *Revitalizing Child Protective Services.* School for Social Services (Los Angeles, CA: UCLA, 1988). (Also prepared as Adizes Institute Working Paper #22.)

4. I. Adizes and P. Zukin, "A Management Approach to Health Planning in Developing Countries," *Health Care Management Review* 2, 1(1997): 19–37.

PART ONE

What Is Going On?

CHAPTER ONE

Change
and Its Repercussions

Change has no precedents.
NICCOLO MACHIAVELLI

The Perpetuity of Problems

It might not be news to you if I were to say that we all experience change and change is a phenomenon that exists for as long as we can perceive anything.

Change gives rise to events that can be opportunities or problems.[1] When we encounter changes, we need to make decisions and do something different because we face a different phenomenon. Think of walking down a street. When we come to an intersection—a change from what we have been experiencing—we confront a problem or an opportunity: Should we turn right, turn left, turn around, or continue straight ahead? We need to decide and act, and whatever we decide to do is itself a change that leads to new problems.

Every problem or opportunity introduced by change generates a solution, which causes more change, and we face a new reality and a new set of problems or opportunities.[2]

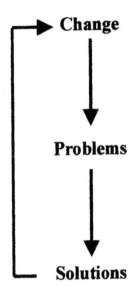

Figure 1-1: Change–Problems Cycle

Thus, as long as there is change, there will be problems and opportunities.

Nothing endures but change.
HERACLITUS

And the corollary is:

*Since change is here to stay, problems are here to stay
... Forever!!!*

I was surprised when I reached that conclusion. After all, bookstores are full of books promising that if only we follow this or that recipe for success, our organizational problems will disappear. Many political ideologies and religions make the same promises: Follow these rules and you will inherit salvation or earn a place in heaven.

I suggest that those promises cannot be realized because change is life, and as long as we are alive, we will have problems.

Consider the saying, "Life's a bitch; then you die." What's more, the "livelier" we are, the more problems we will have.

Take, for instance, a software company with which I consulted. The managers complained about the magnitude of the company's problems. The company had taken less than two years to grow from zero to $180 million in annual revenues. "What do you expect?" I asked. "When will you have no problems? Only when there is no change. And that will happen only when?" They knew the answer. "When we are dead," they replied.

If change is life and we have no problems only when we are dead, then slowing down the rate of change—one way to reduce problems—is tantamount to committing suicide. The dinosaurs did not adapt to change, and neither do many large corporations that currently rule the world. If they want to stay alive, they'd better learn to manage and *lead* change.

There is an old joke about two guys who went on a walking safari. They saw a lion approaching them. One of them started putting on his running shoes. "You can't outrun the lion," his companion said. "I'm not trying to outrun the lion," the first guy responded. "All I need to do is outrun you!"

As change accelerates, the challenge to survive becomes more complex.[3] Who survives? Those who make the right decisions the fastest and implement them the fastest.[4]

It is not the strongest of the species that survive, nor the most intelligent, but the one most responsive to change.

CHARLES DARWIN

Making wrong decisions quickly and implementing them quickly is a prescription for disaster. You end up with worse problems than those you were trying to solve. Nor will you thrive if your competition can make the right decisions faster than you can, or if in spite of making the right decisions promptly, you take more time to implement them than the competition.

My observations are not comforting, but the truth is that solving one generation of problems does not mean clear sailing forever. Your solutions only give rise to the next generation of problems. I don't know about you, but I admit that I still catch myself in the middle of the night wondering when my problems will all be over. And I know the answer: Never. I will stop having problems only when I stop being alive.

Growing up does not mean getting past all problems. Growing up means being able to handle bigger and more complex problems. Once I sent a New Year's greeting card to my clients that said, "I wish you bigger problems next year." And at the bottom of the card, I added in very small letters, "that you can handle easily."

Each of us is as "big" as the problems we handle and struggle with. "Small" people deal with small problems: the kind of car they own and the quality of their neighbor's kitchen wallpaper. "Big" people struggle with such problems as the quality of their children's education, the environment they will leave behind, and the quality of life in their communities. Having fewer problems is not living. It's dying. Addressing and being able to solve bigger and bigger problems means that our strengths and capacities are improving. We need to emancipate ourselves from small problems to free the energy to deal with bigger problems.

What's new? It's not change itself. Change has existed for billions of years. The news is that the rate of change is accelerating.[5] More and more problems are confronting us at a faster and faster rate. We can become "smaller and smaller" people focusing on the more and more trivial, or we can grow to deal with what really counts for *life*.

I attend many executive committee meetings where people discuss necessary changes, and more often than not, someone will interrupt the proceedings to say, "Slow down. We are running with too many balls in the air." But how can they slow down if the competition is putting on its running shoes?

Change is stressful. We all know that. People are stressed. Organizations are stressed. Societies are stressed. Psychologists have devised a way to measure stress, assigning a certain number of points to each of various life events: divorce, changing jobs, even going on vacation.[6] What is the common denominator in each of those stress-inducing events? Change.

So, should we slow ourselves and our companies?

Yes, if all the companies in our industry agreed to slow down. But even that wouldn't work unless society as a whole also slowed down. But that would work only if the entire world slowed down. That is too much to ask. The solution cannot be to slow change. The dinosaurs tried that. The purpose of this book is not to show you how to slow change or how to survive it. Rather, my purpose is to show you how to accelerate finding and implementing the right solutions with a minimum of stress.

From Prediction to Acceleration

That which can be foreseen can be prevented.
CHARLES H. MAYO

For a blind person, every obstacle is a sudden surprise.
ANONYMOUS

I learned from my two young sons how to speed up solutions. When they were small, they would make me take them to an electronic arcade. Once there, they spent most of their time with their favorite game: racing cars. I realized to my surprise that although neither of them had ever driven a car in his life, they were always able to beat me in the race. The secret was that they had played the game so many times they knew the computer program by heart. They knew when a car would pass and where the turns were. They could drive proactively. Because I didn't know what was coming next, every turn presented a crisis. I crashed. I tumbled. Not knowing the road ahead, I drove reactively, slower than their proactive driving. The game reminded me that when I drive in a foreign city I drive much slower than the locals who beep at me and make rude gestures. It's not that they can drive better. They simply know the road ahead. They can afford to drive faster than someone for whom each and every inter-section is a crisis that demands a new decision.

When we know the road ahead, we can drive faster because we drive proactively. Likewise, if we can predict change, we will know what is ahead for a corporation, and the problems will not surprise us. We will deal with them promptly because rather than being unexpected crises, they will be events for which we have planned and prepared ourselves.[7]

I have discovered that I can predict change. I can predict future problems. It's a lot like raising children. With the first child, every problem is a crisis. The fifth one grows almost by himself. Having seen the problems before, one is less likely to panic. Grandparents, because they've seen so much, often are more lenient than parents. "Leave the kid alone; he'll grow out of it," they advise. Like a grandparent who has experienced many children, I have worked with hundreds of companies. I concur with others who have studied dynamic systems. Problems appear in predictable patterns and have common causes.[8]

The Common Cause

First, let us identify the common patterns and later we will identify the causes and discuss what to do about them.

Let's think about predictable patterns. What happens when a car gets old? It falls apart. How about an old house? It also falls apart. An old person? Falling apart.

What are the common denominators here? First, let us realize that a system does not need to "breathe" to be alive. Everything has a lifecycle; people, plants—even stones.[9] A geologist will tell you that one stone is young while another is old. And astronomers refer to stars as young and old. Granted, lifecycles differ in terms of length: A butterfly's lifecycle is one day long. A star's lifecycle may last millions of years. Organizations, too, have lifecycles: They are born and grow, and, unless management knows what to do, they age and die.

The second common denominator is that when systems change, they fall apart. They disintegrate. And to fall apart and disintegrate, they do not need to get older. Young people commit suicide; young systems disintegrate, too. Whether a system is young or old, what causes its disintegration is change, and the faster the change, the faster the disintegration, which is manifested in what we call problems.

Problems are manifestations of disintegration caused
by change.[10]

I challenge you to consider this: Each and every problem—your car runs badly, the bathroom plumbing is backing up, your boss and you don't get along, your neighbors are difficult, or you and your spouse argue continuously—I suggest, stems from something that is falling apart. The successful diagnosis of every problem is the correct identification of what is falling apart, and a successful treatment or therapy is the integration of those parts into a new whole.[11] That new whole, if it is healthy, is, by itself, capable of keeping itself together, and able to create a new self when it experiences new change.[12]

None of this should be news to anyone. When we are worried about someone, we say, "This person is falling apart! He is coming unglued!" And on a larger scale, we say, "This family, community, or country is falling apart." By the same token, when we are impressed, we say, "This person, family, or country has it all together."

The role of leadership is to lead the necessary change that creates new problems, reintegrate the organization to solve those problems, prepare it to be changed again, and have new problems.

The challenge of leadership on any level—individual, family, organization and society—is to change continuously and, nevertheless, always remain together!

The false assumption is that the way to prevent a system from falling apart is to prevent change. That is tantamount to committing suicide. It is the ultimate "falling apart." In other words, if you do not assume responsibility for breaking the system the way you want it broken and then integrating it to a better plateau, it will break by itself to a worse plateau. So inaction does not save you; it gives the power of your demise to outside forces. The way to remain healthy is to take charge of your destiny by changing that which needs to be changed.

The best way to cope with change is to help create it.
BOB DOLE

The role of leadership is not to prevent the system from falling apart. On the contrary, it is to lead change that causes the system to fall apart and then to reintegrate it into a new whole.

When leadership can neither cause the necessary change nor bring the system together, it's time to call in those whose profession it is to provide this service. It's easier to perform that leadership function if one knows the road ahead: what to expect, which problems are normal, which are abnormal or pathological, what causes those problems, what to do about them, and when to do nothing about them.

The lifecycle theory of organizations presented in this book gives such tools to those who take responsibility for leading change.

Lifecycles and the Nature of Problems

I have suggested above that every system—breathing or not—has a lifecycle. We know that living organisms—plants, animals, and people—are born, grow, age, and die. So do organizations.[13] As they change, progressing along their lifecycle, systems follow predictable patterns of behavior. At each stage, systems manifest certain struggles—certain difficulties or transitional problems—they must overcome. Sometimes a system doesn't succeed in resolving its problems on its own. It requires external intervention, importation of external energy with different qualifications to emancipate it from its predicament.

For several thousand years, the medical sciences have been developing diagnostic and therapeutic tools for treating physiological systems. The tools for diagnosing and treating an individual's psyche have a more recent history, and the tools for diagnosing and treating organizational behavior—to change organizational culture and consciousness—are in their infancy. This book is my contribution to this emerging field.

Normal vs. Abnormal Problems

Whenever an organization makes the transition from one lifecycle stage to the next, difficulties arise. In order to learn new patterns of behavior, organizations must abandon their old patterns. When an organization expends energy to make effective transitions from old to new patterns of behavior, I consider its problems normal. If, however, an organization expends energy inward in futile attempts to remove blockages to change, it is experiencing abnormal problems which usually require external therapeutic intervention. If the abnormality is prolonged and threatens the organization's existence, its problems are pathological, requiring a different intervention— not therapeutic, but "surgical" in nature. Such intervention is beyond the scope of this book.

An organization can solve its normal problems with its own internal energy, setting processes in motion and making decisions that will overcome the problems. An organization cannot avoid those normal problems because it needs to learn and develop its capabilities. Like a baby, it has to fall to learn to walk. An organization has to learn how to budget resources, how to set discipline, and how and when to make decisions. It has to develop an organizational memory of experiences in order to advance to the next stage of its life.[14]

Managers of many young companies complain about how difficult it is for them to make and live within a budget. I tell them they are lucky to have those problems to solve while they are small and young. They have the opportunity to learn while the cost of making a mistake is not so critical as it would be if the organization were much bigger and the stakes were higher. One executive compared the process to tracing a trajectory to a point in space. In the beginning a small deviation is inconsequential. If, however, you allow that deviation to continue, later, when you are far from the starting point, the costs of correction will be enormous. If one allows the normal problems of childhood to go untreated, in adulthood they can become abnormal or even pathological.[15]

Normal problems are transitional in nature: You encounter them, solve them, learn from them, and readily move on. Abnormal problems are cul-de-sac problems. You "drive around in circles," seeing your problems repeat themselves over and over again. You keep encountering problems you thought you'd solved, but they continually reappear in a new version or in a new manifestation. Management's attempts to resolve them only produce other undesirable side effects. Abnormal problems cause unnecessary pain and slow organizational progress, retarding an organization's ability to develop. They frustrate and entrap it in a particular stage of the lifecycle. The organization, like a middle-aged person with unresolved problems of adolescence, is "stuck." In abnormal situations, management feels incapable and helpless to resolve the issues by itself. Soon the organization loses trust in its leadership.

Organizations with normal problems don't require external intervention. Solving normal problems is the task of their leaders. Organizations with abnormal problems, however, require periodic external interventions that can lead them to Prime and keep them there. Organizations with abnormal problems need interventions from extensively trained organizational therapists who can help them overcome the cycle of repetitious problems that block their progress.

Pathological problems are distinguishable from abnormal problems by their gravity and their chronic nature. Those are problems that, because they were not treated in time, now threaten the organization's ability to survive. The most obvious examples of pathological problems are: uncontrollable negative cash flow, continuous emigration of key human resources away from the organization, unresolved quality problems, rapidly declining market share, tremendous drops in the company's capacity to raise financial resources, and so forth. Organizations with those problems can't afford therapy because therapy takes time, and time is a resource those organizations do not have. Instead of an organizational therapist, the board should hire an organizational turnaround specialist who can temporarily take on the chief executive officer's role, and perform whatever "surgery" is necessary. As I said before, treatment of pathological problems is outside the scope of this book.

To be successful leaders, to focus our energies and diagnose organizational ills, we must learn to distinguish normal problems— those transitions an organization *should* experience in order to move to the next stage of the lifecycle—from abnormal problems it need not experience.

The Typical vs. the Optimal Path

Most organizations follow a typical path. On that path, they encounter problems that exist because the organizations have yet to develop certain capabilities. By solving those problems, they develop the capabilities they need to advance along the lifecycle. On the usual, or typical, path, organizations develop capabilities one at a time. We will talk about those capabilities—how they develop, the sequence in which they develop, and how they help solve predictable organizational problems—in Part Two of this book.

Since I published the first edition ten years ago, I have learned that organizations may take a shorter path to Prime, the state in the lifecycle in which function and form, flexibility, and self-control are all synchronized. An organization in Prime can change in a controllable way, achieving optimal results and sustaining that performance over time. Taking that path, an organization can and should develop all the capabilities simultaneously.

In this edition, I describe both paths. First, I present the typical path, analyzing why problems occur at each stage of the lifecycle. Next, I discuss the optimal path and its repercussions.

For the purpose of illustration, let us consider examples of three different organizational problems.

It's perfectly normal for start-up businesses to find themselves short of cash. They see it coming and predict it. In its earliest stages, a company's need for cash to finance growth far exceeds its ability to generate it. That is a normal problem on the typical path. But this normal problem can be avoided altogether if a company follows the optimal path. A well-managed company should be able to overcome that problem with good financial planning. If its business plan makes sense, and its leadership and its industry are trusted and respected, money will come pouring in. Thus, while shortage of cash on the typical path is a normal problem, on the optimal path it will be considered abnormal because it did not have to happen.

What if a company suddenly found itself short of cash because management, not knowing how to project cash flows, hadn't predicted the problem? That is an abnormal problem on the typical path. Management should have known. A cash crunch is deemed pathological if, even after instituting cost controls and cash-flow planning, the company cannot survive. In such a case, therapeutic intervention could be too little too late. A cash shortage also becomes a pathological problem when management refuses to recognize cash shortage as a problem.

Take, for instance, a company I knew whose founder lived in a fantasy land, dreaming of what *should* happen. People, he believed, should have been excited about his innovative ideas. He was always selling everyone his belief that the cash problem would soon be solved by an infusion of capital from willing—but nevertheless unknown—sources. That pathology is not all that rare. Its tragedy is that the founders honestly believe in what they say, and even at the last moment, they don't know what happened or why their companies failed. Some readers may find this difficult to believe, but I have witnessed such folly more than a few times.

An autocratic management style can also turn from a normal problem into pathology.[16] I've often seen this syndrome in fledgling organizations during the early stages of growth. As I asserted in my book *Pursuit of Prime,* autocratic management is desirable in the start-up stage of development. Parents need to tell their child what to do, and founders need to be in control in order to sustain interest in their creations. The need to control becomes abnormal if that style doesn't change to keep pace with the company's development and maturation. The problem intensifies when the autocratic leader has only two choices: to change his style or to yield the leadership position. The problem reaches pathological proportions when no forces can persuade him either to change his style or to step aside. I have treated several companies where the autocratic, self-centered, ego-driven leaders could not be changed because they owned everything, lock, stock, and barrel. They were either unwilling or unable to change their style even though it meant the demise of their companies.

In a fledgling business, the founder is the biggest asset. If, however, the founder's style is destructive, he or she is the company's biggest liability. Frequently, when such a person dies, the company dies, or the family that owns it loses control within three generations.[17]

Now, let's consider organizational aging. Many of you will find the following surprising. I myself was surprised because, like everyone else, I had considered aging to be a normal predicament. After all, who expects to remain young forever? We wish for everlasting youth, and generations have searched in vain for a vitalizing potion. But having applied my methodologies to organizations worldwide, I have discovered that I can retard organizational aging. That led me to wonder whether it is possible for humans also to retard aging. Yogis look ageless, and they do not die from diseases of aging. They die healthy. They recognize when the time has come to go to sleep and not wake up. Who of us wouldn't like to die healthy rather than suffer from the debilitating diseases of old age? People can retard the aging process. So can organizations. What is the secret?

Rather than steal my own thunder, I'll keep that secret for another chapter.

Organizations can have normal and/or abnormal problems of growing. The problems of aging should all be considered abnormal because organizational aging can be averted with appropriate treatment. To reverse pathological aging requires major sacrifices such as downsizing, which I consider a radical solution to a pathological problem.

Curative treatment at any stage of the lifecycle calls for removing abnormal problems so that the organization can progress to the next stage of the lifecycle and experience a new set of normal problems.

Preventive treatment involves development of capabilities that enhance the company's advance to Prime and sustain it there. Prime is the most desirable state, and it is not necessary to depart from it.

Now that we have defined terms and outlined the purpose and structure of this book, let us proceed with descriptions of the various stages in the development and aging of organizations on the typical path.

Notes

1. See P. Watzlawick, J. Weakland, and R. Fisch, *Change: Principles of Problem Formation and Problem Resolution* (New York: Norton Books, 1974), for a clear description of the relationship between change and problems. These authors note that change and problems are interlinked, and that they arise inevitably together.

2. See B. Keeney, *Aesthetics of Change* (New York: Guilford Press, 1983), for a discussion of the role of language in the construction of problems. He suggests that "reality" is a function of the descriptions that we make of it. Thus problems, as well as the process of problem solving, are a function of our descriptions.

3. M. Eigen, R. Winkler, and M. Kimber, *Laws of the Game: How the Principles of Nature Govern Chance* (New York: Harper Colophon Books, 1981) give a cogent discussion of the relationship between evo-

lutionary processes in nature and the drive to survive in complex environments.

4. For an elaboration on this point, see J. Diamond, *Guns, Germs and Steel: The Fates of Human Societies* (New York: Norton, 1997) for a discussion of sociobiological perspectives on "right decisions."

5. K. Gergen and D. Whitney, "Technologies of Representation in the Global Corporation," in D. Boje, R. Gephart and T. Thatchenkery, eds., *Postmodern Management and Organization Theory* (Thousand Oaks, CA: Sage, 1996), carry on a thoughtful discussion regarding the impact of globalization on rates of change in organizations.

6. L. Holmes and R. Rahe, "The Social Adjustment Rating Scale," *Journal of Psychosomatic Research,* 11 (1967): 213–218.

7. D. Barry and M. Elmes, "Strategy Retold: Toward a Narrative View of Strategic Discourse," *Academy of Management Review* 22, 33 (1997): 429–452, argue that planning is a narrative process that involves developing the scenarios that can adapt to crises as they emerge.

8. S. Kauffman, *The Origins of Order: Self-Organization and Selection in Evolution* (New York: Oxford University Press, 1993), extends the arguments of chaos theory. He makes it very clear that, in the relationship between order and chaos in emerging systems, even in chaotic processes there is a pattern that emerges.

9. E.C. White, "Negentrophy, Noise and Emancipatory Thought" in N.K. Hayles, ed., *Chaos and Order: Complex Dynamics in Literature and Science* (Chicago: University of Chicago Press, 1991), pp. 236–267, discusses patterned cycles present in the emergence of a meaning system which has, he argues, attributes of a living system.

10. See F. Masterpasqua and P. Perna, *The Psychological Meanings of Chaos: Translating Theory into Practice* (Washington, DC: APA, 1997). The authors have examined psychological disintegration using chaos theory. They argue that change brings about chaos, which then results in problems of integration.

11. F. Verela, E. Thompson, and E. Rosch argue in *The Embodied Mind: Cognitive Science and Human Experience* (Cambridge: MIT Press, 1993) that eastern philosophy provides a framework for understanding and enacting integration.

12. S. Kauffman, *At Home in the Universe: The Search for Laws of Self-Organization and Complexity* (Oxford: Oxford University Press,

1995), has a very clear and readable discussion of the relationship between chaos, as disintegration, and order; integration requires, from this perspective, the introduction of new information into the system.

13. Eastern societies have long integrated biological and natural processes into their social thought. In the West, the idea that human societal organizations could be explained by natural organic lifecycles was first articulated by the new historical criticism of the Enlightenment: Montesquieu (1744), *De L'esprit de loi;* Vico, *Scienza nuova* (1744, 3rd ed.); Edmund Burke, and esp. Condorcet, who posited a ten-stage cycle of historical growth, (1794) [Sketch of an historical tableau of the progress of human spirit]. In the 19th century, the modern science of historiography looked in reverse directions (with the possible exception of Hegel and the distinct exception of Russian social critics Belinksy, Herzen, and Chernychevky) to the detail of "fact as fact." In the 20th century, historiography has been more concerned with transcendent historical values than immanent "cycle-like" models of explanations of human organizations, with the exceptions of O. Spengler (*Der Untergang des Abendlandes*, 1919) and the more successful, but also controversial, study of world civilizations on a lifecycle model by A. Toynbee (*A Study of History*, 1946–).

The impetus for studies in the lifecycle of business organizations in the 20th century came from the new social sciences of sociology (Comte's 19th century positivism) and, particularly, from psychology (esp. Piaget, [1954]); M. Klein and the psychodynamics developed by the Tavistock school; and, esp. Erik Erikson's studies on the stages of human growth (often cited by early business writers on the lifecycle). Coincident with this interest in the late 1930s was the introduction of typologies, stages of organization, and managerial dynamics in business writings, esp. J. Schumpeter on the entrepreneurial and bureaucratic: *Business Cycles: A Theoretical, Historical & Statistical Analysis of the Capitalist Process* (New York: McGraw Hill, 1939), and Max Weber and the translation of his 1912 treatise into English as *Theory of Economic Development: An Inquiry into Profits, Capital, Credit, Interest and the Business Cycle* (1932; 1954); D.C. McClelland (1961), esp. his research on entrepreneurship in Indian villages; P. Drucker (1946; 1954); and the sensitivities for further study of organizations created by A.B. Chandler on strategy and structure (1962). The use of the lifecycle in family, marriage and vocational studies also spread partially under the impact of Erikson (P.C. Glick et al. [1955]),

S. Minuchin (1974), and later produced a number of significant family and marriage studies parallel to the organizational lifecycle studies, esp. Carter and McGoldrick (1989).

An early effort to construct a lifecycle model was D. Super et al., in *Teacher's College Record*, 58 (1957), who divided vocational life into five stages from growth to decline. Other early writings in applying the idea to business were E.T. Penrose on biological analogies to the firm (1952); D.H. Thain on stages of corporate development (1969); L.L. Steinmetz on the dynamics of growth and survival (1969); and A. Tanski (1980). A key article in propelling lifecycle studies was L.E. Greiner in the *Harvard Business Review* (1970) on "Patterns of Organizational Change," in which he postulated five stages of growth. In the 1980s and into the early 1990s, there was a spate of lifecycle and "evolutionary" studies; in the July, 1986 *Business Periodicals*, it achieved for the first time a sub-heading in categories of business research and publication. In 1980, J.R. Kimberly, R.H. Miles, et al. drew together a series of articles, *Organizational Life Cycle*, which included contributions by N. Tichy, W. Ouchi, J. Freeman and D.A. Whetten. Other significant studies during the decade included work by: D. Boulding (1974; 1975 on "decline"); D.A. Whetten (1980 and subsequent articles, also on "decline"); J.B. Miner (1982, on "entrepreneurial types" and bureaucratic "stages"); R.E. Berenbeim (1984, on "business families"); J. Freeman (1982, on "natural selection and survival"); P.H. Mirvis (1977); W.G. Dyer, Jr. (1986, on "transitions in family firms"); L.M. Miller (1990, with a six-stage development process); among others.

During the 1980s, several longitudinal studies on the "effectiveness" and "predictability" of lifecycle stages were done by D. Miller, J. Freeman, D. Miner, K.S. Cameron, R.E. Quinn, P.H. Friesen, R. Drazin, R.K. Kazanjian, among others. D. Miller and P.H. Friesen (1983) tested five stages of growth and decline supported by 54 variables with prevalence of "complementaries" at each stage; they had positive results of predictability. R. Drazin and R.K. Kazanjian (1990) used the del procedure for prediction analysis of three separate stage models of "lifecycle imperatives." They found some support. The overall results of such studies have been ambiguous.

In the 1990s, research on the lifecycle theory has changed, giving way to the study of other segmented approaches to organizational development and transformation. The difficulty in many of these early—and revolutionary—studies is that they sought either a mechanical application to the organic realities of life and organization, treating regularities as absolutes; or, they stopped short of pursuing the modifications and subtleties of human interaction. I have had the good fortune to apply my theory to over 500 companies worldwide in the "laboratory of experience," and this lifecycle theory has had constant feedback and modifications from this experience.

14. In his book *In Over Our Heads: The Mental Demands of Modern Life* (Boston: Belknap Press, 1995), R. Kegan develops a model of the stages of evolution of consciousness. It is interesting to consider how managers develop the administrative and relations skills to negotiate, to manage differences, and to work collaboratively. According to Kegan, these are skills that are developed in stages, as consciousness itself develops and grows. This model suggests that good management requires more than an MBA.

15. See A. Maslow, ed., *Motivation and Personality*, 3rd ed. (New York: Harper Press, 1987); of the many works by Erik Erikson, see especially *Childhood and Society*, 2nd ed. (New York: Norton, 1963), *Identity and the Life Cycle* (New York: Norton, 1980), and *Identity: Youth and Crisis* (New York: Norton, 1968).

16. In *Reframing Organizations: Artistry, Choice, and Leadership* (San Francisco: Jossey-Bass, 1991), L. Bolman and I. Deal discuss the role of the leader in framing problems for solution. They note that management style is key to being able to foster effective frames for action that promote creativity and growth.

17. See D. Bork, et al., *Working with Family Businesses: A Guide for Professionals* (San Francisco: Jossey-Bass, 1996) for a description of the complexity of the family business lifecycle, addressing the specific kinds of problems the family business encounters in its evolution, i.e., succession.

CHAPTER TWO

Courtship

The best way to predict the future is to create it.

PETER DRUCKER

I call the first stage of organizational development Courtship. This stage precedes the organization, which has yet to be born. It exists only as an idea.

Courtship

Figure 2-1: The Courtship Stage

Building Commitment

In Courtship, the emphasis is on ideas and the possibilities the future offers. The would-be founder is excited and enthusiastic and "selling" everyone on how wonderfully his idea is going to come out. To whom is he really selling the idea? Whom is he working hardest to convince? Himself!

There is something very important taking place. During this time, the company is like a jet sitting at the end of the runway preparing for takeoff. The pilot is revving up the engines, creating a lot of noise. Why the noise? The jet isn't even flying. The pilot is building thrust and momentum so that once the brakes are released, the jet will take off quickly and smoothly. Likewise, the Courtship stage of development is characterized by lots of talk and no action, but what is happening is critical for the future success of the company.

Lest you miss my point, let me emphasize that *the founder is building commitment.* At the same time that he is testing the idea on others, the founder is building his own internal commitment to the idea. He's wondering what everyone else thinks. Is it viable? The more he succeeds at selling his idea to others, the stronger his own commitment grows. This process is crucial for the healthy "birth" of an organization. Why is it so important?

He who has a why to live can bear almost any how.

Friedrich Nietzsche

I have named this stage Courtship because the situation is not so different from the prelude to marriage. At what point are we really married? Not when we put rings on our fingers. We are truly married when commitment happens, is tested, and survives the test. When are we divorced? Not when the judge signs the papers. Rings and papers are only formalities. The marriage is dead when there is no more commitment to keep it alive. It is commitment that makes any organization—marriage, business, or society—viable.

For a plane to perform the function for which it was designed, it must first take off. To become airborne, it needs forward thrust—the momentum it builds during the engine revving stage. Similarly, for an organization to start performing the function for which it was designed, it needs to undertake risks. No risk is taken without commensurate commitment, and it is during the Courtship stage that founders build that commitment.

If you want to gauge the viability of your organization, you should assess the commitment of all who are related to or associated with it.

You should consider not just your managers. Ask the same questions of your employees, customers, suppliers, and other stakeholders from your community.

Excitement, enthusiasm, emotion, and passion for the subject—coalescing energy to a single point—these are the signs of building commitment. Such a process can generate abnormal or pathological problems. Like lovers building mutual commitment, company founders are given to making unrealistic promises that could cause problems later on. The regrettable promises of Courtship seem almost inevitable. In exchange for vague assurances of support, the excitable founder promises and gives away shares of the future company to family members, lawyers, and friends. At the time, the promises are easy to make. After all, at the Courtship stage the company has no tangible worth. The inexperienced founder doesn't believe he's giving away anything significant, but later on, when the company is worth something, his lavishness will return to haunt him.

Just as in marriage, where love nourishes commitment during Courtship, founders must fall in love with their ideas for companies that will build and sustain their commitment. Later on, when their companies come into being, it is the founders' commitment that sustains their motivation during the difficult challenges of early development—Infancy.

An organization comes to life when the founder's commitment has been successfully tested; that is, when the founder and investors undertake risk. Conversely, if no one shares commitment for an organization, it dies. Courtship needs to build commitment commensurate with the risk associated with bringing the organization to life. The higher the risk, the deeper should be the commitment. As Conrad Hilton said, "If you wish to launch big ships, you have to go where the water is deep."

If we know the weight of the jet, we can tell the pilot how much thrust it will take to lift it off the ground. If we can predict the bumps on the road map of a marriage, we should be able to predict how much commitment will be needed to avoid divorce. If we know how much risk a fledgling company will face, we can tell its founder how much of his and other people's commitment will be required to launch a successful enterprise.

When innovators bring me their new products and tell me they want to start companies, at first I do not listen to *what* they say. I listen to *who* says it and *how* it is said. To create a successful company, one needs more than just a good idea, a market, and the money to back it up. What every new company needs is a committed leader—someone who is willing to lose sleep once the company is born, and who can bring together the idea, the market, and the money.

It's important to test the noise level—the sound of the revving motors. How committed are the founders? Have they made significant financial commitments to their endeavor? The bigger the task, the more zealous the commitment must be. Commitment must parallel the long-term difficulty of turning the idea into a viable business. I base the assessment of the necessary level of commitment on a number of factors: The complexity of putting the business together; how long it will take to see positive results; and the degree of necessary innovation. I estimate the last factor by estimating how many existing "sacred cows" must be slaughtered.

Too many people want to make big money with small commitments. It simply does not and cannot work. If there is inadequate commitment, all the energy will be spent on labor pains, and a stillborn organization is delivered.

We can examine the relationship of commitment to risk on a macro level, too. For example, we can predict the success or failure of a revolution by looking at the commitment of revolutionaries. The task of changing a society is immense. To bring about a significant change, revolutionaries must be willing to die for their cause. Talk and rallies are good for prime-time television, but the magnitude of a commitment is measured by the price people are willing to pay.

Commitment—or lack of it—is what sustains—or
destroys—an emerging enterprise.

Without substantial commitment, organizations break apart when they encounter rough times.

Founder: Prophet or Profit?

When we talk about commitment to undertake risk, we should also ask: What is the source of the founder's commitment? What motivates the founder or product champion? If the founder's motivation is only to make money, that will be insufficient to sustain the enterprise through this Courtship stage. No one knows for sure what kinds of profits a company might produce. When a baby is in her cradle, is her parents' motivation to feed and change her so that when she grows up she will be a doctor or a lawyer who can support them in their old age? It better not be.

The motivation of a founder has to be transcendental; it must exceed the narrow limits of immediate gain. The commitment cannot be strictly rational. First and above all, founders must be emotionally committed to the value of their ideas in the marketplace. The idea should obsess them. Founders should be responding to a perceived need. They can't help but satisfy that need. The profits or money the product or service will produce merely validate their belief in their idea.

In Courtship, the founder's motivating goal should be to satisfy a market need, to create value, to make meaning.[1] Founders should be excited about the needs the product will satisfy; and when challenged, they should defend the functionality of their product and its service. If we were to ask founders to describe their creations five years hence, they should describe companies that service clients increasingly well—that satisfy needs more effectively. If founders speak exclusively about the return on investment (ROI), commitment won't sustain their companies should difficulties arise. Of course, without profits, their companies will die. While poor ROI can kill a deal, the promise of ROI can't make a deal. To make deals you need founders who believe that their products or services serve real needs and that there are live clients who will appreciate what the founders have started.

If a person plans to form a company because he anticipates a good return on his investment, he is like a prophet who speaks because he wants to go to heaven or a woman who yearns for a child because she wants to have a doctor for a daughter. The prophet does not want to go to hell; the woman does not want to have a child who can't hold a job; and, the founder does not want to go bankrupt. Return On Investment is a controlling, not a driving factor. ROI cannot engender an organization, but lack of ROI can eventually bring about its demise.

People who are exclusively interested in money or ROI will get discouraged and quit before profits are realized. After all, business isn't always profitable. Ideas must be made operational, and that process usually involves at least a few mistakes that postpone profitability. A baby requires parents to care for her through all the diseases of childhood. It's not all smiles all the time.

A successful Courtship is one that focuses on issues beyond the potential for profits.

Profitability is like a scoreboard in a tennis match. You can't win by watching the scoreboard. The scoreboard tells you only whether you are winning or losing. To actually win a game, you must hit the ball over the net into the opponent's court. Each volley is another opportunity to improve your performance. Players might not hit each ball right, but each volley is like a new game, starting from zero. When one is learning to play, the score is meaningless. A person must be committed to the idea of learning the game first and to winning it later. The same is true of emerging organizations. Founders must be determined to hit the ball. They must be aiming to satisfy their clients' needs as measured by sales first, second, and third. Only after that is established as being successful will the scoreboard—profits—come into question.

The commitment to client needs is independent of whether or not the client perceives the need. Founders, like prophets, forecast needs as they perceive them—not necessarily as expressed by potential clients. Thus, the founder talks about what the market *should* buy, not necessarily what it *is* buying. If market needs were known, and if the market already had expressed its wishes in high sales volume of the product or service, the innovation and risks would be lower and the project would demand lower commitment. In such a case, we are seeing not a prophet who gives birth to a movement, but a "me-too" exploiter of trends. Even in that case, there must be enough commitment to pay the price that makes that exploitation work.

Entrepreneurs who start companies focused on needs that have yet to be identified or expressed are product-oriented rather than market-oriented. Even they can't easily describe the need their products aim to satisfy. Rather than responding to established needs, they try to educate and change the behavior of the market. They, in a sense, express what *should* be the need of the market. Through their actions, they articulate and operationalize that need. They are more business prophets than business entrepreneurs.[2] And like other prophets, they can be crucified because, in the short run, the power structure will reject them. No one understands their messages until their products prove themselves.

Founders are highly vulnerable to those who promise to help them sell or finance their ideas. In exchange for the promise of marketing and financing, the newcomers are likely to take significant shares of ownership. And the prophets, the founders, whose devotion is more to their products than to control and ROI, end up losing control of their companies to venture capitalists or fast-talking marketeers who get to enjoy the fruits of the innovation, measured in money and recognition, while the founders are frequently ignored or forgotten.

Why, despite any number of marketing courses, are prophet/founders not market-oriented? Prophet/founders focus on what the market *should* want, and they dedicate their energy to developing the product or service that should satisfy that need. Consequently, they must be product-oriented until they can develop products of acceptable quality, capabilities, and functionality. Prophet/founders fight the dilution of their dreams, always speaking of the reality they are trying to create, not the reality they are willing to accept.

Observers accuse many founders of being ignorant of marketing strategies and realities. This phenomenon is normal. To quote George Bernard Shaw: "Reasonable men adapt to their environment; unreasonable men try to adapt their environment to themselves. Thus all progress is the result of the efforts of unreasonable men."

As we will see in the next section, founders' commitments to products they believe the market *should* have rather than to products the market *wants,* and their relatively low commitment to profit, may later become pathological problems for their companies. Founders might not know when to give up their exclusive dreams. They may be too product-oriented for too long. They won't compromise even to get their products or services in the market. They act according to their perception of what *should* be for far too long.

Even founders who progress beyond product orientation might find it difficult to make the transition to profit orientation. That transition requires attention beyond the technology of the product or service. When it's time to focus on client interface as well as financial and human factors, those elements of management may be beyond the founders' experiences. Nevertheless, many founders insist on making all strategic decisions alone—and at their peril.

What is normal at one stage of the lifecycle can be
abnormal in another stage.

Fanatic commitment is necessary for a successful Courtship and its successor, Infancy; but in later stages, it can become pathological. For example, consider a company that is chronically losing money because its product or service is misplaced in the marketplace. It needs to change and adapt to client needs. Founders who fight that reality because of their dreams are like overzealous parents who deny, and thus do not act on, their child's psychological problems because they are blinded by the image of what they believe the child should be. In some cases, the more founders fight reality, the deeper into trouble their companies sink. They hold on to their dreams. Their fierce commitment to their ideas is what sustains their creations through the very early stages of Courtship. At a point in the next stage, Infancy, founders need to know if it's time to let go of their dreams and adapt to reality. That paradox makes it difficult to appraise the qualities of good founders. If founders are committed, can they let go? If they are capable of letting go, are they committed enough?

Investors encounter another problem. Highly committed founder/innovators are highly charismatic, and their commitment can be contagious. They believe in their innovations; they believe in themselves. It's easy to confuse them with pathological liars or con men. Many investors have found themselves caught in the webs of fast-talking, apparently highly committed and enthusiastic innovators who, it turns out, were selling snake oil. If it seems too good to be true, it *is* too good to be true. Investors should check how much founders personally have at stake. Watch out for anyone who uses Other People's Money exclusively.

Healthy founders are highly committed, and, at the same time, they have an eye on reality. They are committed, but they are also willing to learn from experience. A founder should be a reasonably unreasonable person—someone who has fanatically strong beliefs and is still able to listen to reason.

Building a Commitment Correctly

It is normal to have doubts during the Courtship stage. Conversely, to have no doubts whatsoever can generate pathological problems down the road. The founder should be able to answer these questions:

- Why are we doing this?
- Who is going to do it?
- What exactly are we going to do?
- How are we going to do this?
- When should we do it?

Note that the focus is on why-who-what-how-when *we* are going to do, not why-who-what-how-when *I* am going to do.[3] The founder must realize from the beginning that he or she cannot do it alone.

Please also note the sequence of the questions. The most important of those questions are the *why* and *who* questions. Next in importance are those that ask *what* and *how*. Why start a company, or a unit within a company, or even the seed of a future unit by spending resources on a new product or new market?

Is there a need? Can we develop and nurture the need? Do we have the capability to provide and satisfy the new need? Note that I am skirting the question: Is it within our capabilities? That question applies more to an established company. In that case, be careful. The people who answer that question have vested interests and will give a negative response to protect their turf. That is why the personal computer had difficulty growing in the mainframe environment of IBM and Digital Equipment Corp., and the cellular phone got nowhere in AT&T. Later, when AT&T saw the proven market for the wireless, it bought back what it had invented in the first place—for more than a billion dollars. This point will become clearer when we discuss how structure impacts strategy—how structure can age an organization and dampen its capability to innovate and grow.

The *who* question is also critical. Many innovator/founders have difficulty managing money and marketing and promoting their creations. The problem is similar to artists who are ill at ease negotiating the price and, by implication, the value of their own art. They do fantastically well representing others, but they can't negotiate on their own behalf. It's not unusual for an innovator to have difficulty selling his or her own creation. So the new product—even if it's a winner—doesn't easily penetrate the market, and the company suffers from debilitating cash crunches.

To overcome the problems of starting businesses successfully, the government of Israel has funded a number of incubators to nourish innovation and nurture emerging businesses. An inventor who wants help promoting his or her innovation can submit a proposal that describes a new idea or product and demonstrates a need for it. The proposal should also describe other products or services the innovation will replace and provide an estimate of the amount of capital necessary to commercialize it. The experienced executives who serve as the incubator's advisory board review each proposal. If they believe in it, they allocate a sum of money and appoint a project manager to manage the finances. Eventually, they will designate a marketing manager to search for strategic alliances or identify distribution channels. In exchange for all that, the innovator yields a percentage of ownership to the incubator, and the incubator redeems its equity when the new company goes public, is sold, or merges. The incubator never maintains ongoing ownership of the companies it has established. The ROI from successful ventures finances other endeavors. The project manager and marketing manager also get stock. Instead of doing everything on their own, innovators have the support of a complementary team in a nurturing environment.

I have found that answers to the *what* and *how* questions are secondary. *What* exactly we are going to do changes as the company gains experience. The answer to the *how* question is even less reliable. The *how* changes almost daily until success is realized. Nevertheless, from the start, we need to think about *what* and *how*, continually adapting and changing as our experience grows.

Is It Real True Love, or Is It Just an Affair?

Figure 2-2: The Affair

A Courtship that can't withstand reality testing is only an affair. If at the first sign of obstacles, commitment evaporates, it is a Courtship with pathological problems. The would-be founder has fantasies about how things should be, but they are grounded in nothing more than wishes. The idea never progresses beyond the dream.

During Courtship, pathological problems do not look like problems because they don't seem difficult and they cause no pain. Everything is rosy. That is precisely why Courtship's pathology is so dangerous. It can give birth to an Infant organization, but because nobody has tested the idea, the Infant organization will be ill-prepared to deal with reality. There was no reality testing at conception, and now nobody is prepared for the newborn infant.

Compare the formation of a business to the transition from rosy courtship to the reality of marriage. In some cases, it can be quite devastating. It's worth dealing with hard questions at an early stage. The process of writing a prenuptial contract convinces many couples to cancel their plans to wed. Similarly, when we get excited about a business idea, we may start negotiations to form a partnership, but once we work out the details and put everything into writing, it may not look quite so exciting. As the Arabic expression says: "The devil is in the details."

What, then, defines the birth of a company? It's not the signing of articles of incorporation. A company is born when there is some tangible expression of commitment—when the founder undertakes risk. Risk has a number of manifestations: A person quits his or her old job, signs an office lease, or promises to deliver a product on a certain date. When the founder incurs and undertakes substantial risk, the organization moves to the next stage of development, called Infancy.

Problems of Courtship

Normal	*Abnormal*
Excitement, reality tested	No reality testing of the commitment
Details thought through	No details thought through
Realistically committed founder	Unrealistically fanatic founder
Product orientation—commitment to add value	Exclusive ROI-profit orientation
Commitment commensurate to risk	Commitment not commensurate to risk
Founder in control	Founder's control is vulnerable

Notes

1. K. Weick's, "Sensemaking in Organizations: Small Structures with Large Consequences," in J. Murnighan, ed., *Social Psychology in Organizations: Advances in Theory and Research,* pp. 10–38 (Englewood Cliffs, NJ: Prentice Hall, 1993), offers a theoretical framework which addresses the role of communication in creating the vision that generates commitment and enthusiasm. Weick later published this as a book, *Sensemaking in Organizations* (Thousand Oaks, CA: Sage, 1995).

2. J. Schumpeter's ideas were first published in 1912 as *Theorie der wirtschaftlichen Entwickelung* and first translated into English in 1934 as *Theory of Economic Development* (Cambridge: University Press, 1934). In *Business Cycles* (New York: McGraw Hill, 1939): 102–109, is found his most popular discussion of the entrepreneur and entrepreneurship. See also D.C. McClelland, *Motivating Economic Achievement* (New York: The Free Press, 1969) and *Achieving Society* (Princeton, NJ: Van Nostrand, 1961) as key works representative of McClelland's pioneering research in synthesizing economic activity and motivation, which he published in many studies in the 1950s and 1960s.

3. D. Barry and M. Elmes, in "Strategy Retold" (*Academy of Management Review* 22, 33, 1997): 429–452, have an interesting perspective on the role of narrative in organizational processes; they differentiate a collective story, one which elaborates a "we" and operates to create a culture of participation from the story of "I" which autocratic leaders tell.

CHAPTER THREE

Infancy

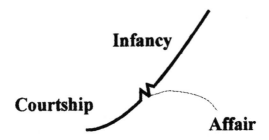

Figure 3-1: The Infant Organization

Product Orientation

Once risk has been undertaken, the nature of the organization changes dramatically. Cash is needed to pay bills. The focus shifts from ideas and possibilities to the production of results. For that, the company has to sell, sell, sell. Now that we want to control risk, we don't need more ideas. We need sales. "Don't tell me any more product ideas. I want to hear how much of our current product line you have sold."

While the founder talks about sales and should be preoccupied with bringing in sales, in reality the Infant organization is not sales-oriented. It's product-oriented. It's busy tinkering with the product, with the technology, with problems in production and performance. Is that normal? Yes! The organization needs to operationalize its product, which it has not done and could not have done in Courtship. If the company developed the product in the garage, it still needs to beta test the product in the marketplace; and, if that is successful, it needs to proceed to mass production. Those are activities that must take place and problems that must be solved before massive sales can begin. Some companies shy away from sales at this stage because they are aware that they cannot deliver.

So where are the financial resources coming from? The founders sell equity to finance the start up. They borrow to their eyebrows, and they endure a lot of sleepless nights.

For many fledgling companies, switching focus from ideas to results is trying. This stage is analogous to the period before and immediately after a wedding. Newly married spouses complain, "The romance has gone out of our lives. Before we were married, we used to talk all the time. Now that we're married we hardly see each other." And, the response to that is, "That's true, but before we got married, we agreed we wanted to have a family and buy a house. All that costs money, which we have to earn."

Infant companies find themselves in a similar quandary. During Courtship, there was time to talk and dream. With the undertaking of risk, there is no time to talk—only time to act.

On a social/political plane, we experience a parallel situation. Once a revolution succeeds, the first people who end up in prison are the idealists who started the movement in the first place. Why? Because the new social order has no need for more new dreams; it needs to fulfill the promises of the dreams that fueled the movement's origins.

At this stage of organizational life, what counts is not what someone thinks but what he or she does. The question founders must answer, and the question they ask their employees is, "What have you done? Have you sold, produced, or accomplished anything?" It's time to shun and discourage the dreamers of yesterday. "I have no time to think" is the typical complaint of the manager of an Infant organization. "There is just too much I have to do."

The Infant needs to sell, sell, sell. Selling is critical because without cash the young company won't survive. Nevertheless, I have found that many Infant businesses are weak on sales and that problem can become pathological if they are preoccupied with the product, but not working to finalize it. They are perfecting it. They are continually coming up with new versions, new ideas. It's a never-ending process—not of continuous improvement, but of continuous perfectionism. The founder is more excited with starting something new than with finishing something "old." He is excited with the possibilities the idea provides and with making it work. Selling takes a back seat, although it should not. This behavior can easily develop into a pathology; the company will run out of cash and out of financial backers, and collapse.

Since the original edition of this book, I have worked with a number of startups, getting a clear picture of what happens up close. Invariably, the sales effort in Infancy is much weaker than it should be. The founder is the only salesperson because he or she knows the product or service better than anyone else, and the founder is also the product's most fervent champion. But founders have no time. They are busy with product design and debugging performance. They have to raise money to finance their companies, and they have to deal with whatever else falls on their desks. So sales gets only a portion of the time it should.

To develop a sales organization and to delegate the effort first requires stabilizing the product, creating sales policies and sticking to them, and developing sales-support materials that accurately depict the company and its product. All that takes time, and the Infant company does not have its time management in place yet. It responds to the squeakiest wheel. It is management by crisis. The true sales orientation does not develop until the company gets to Go-Go, the next stage in growth and development.

If sales orientation is insufficient for too long, the company will go bankrupt. The product is good; the market is there; and even financing could be there if there were sales. The company is a pathological case.

Leadership Transition

Infant companies confront a major paradox. The higher the risk they face, the higher is the requisite commitment to ensure success. In Courtship, the founders must be dreamers who can build commitment to the dream. Once the companies emerge as Infants, however, the risk is large, and they need hard-working, results-oriented founders who are *not* dreamers. The higher the venture's risk, the greater the wake-up shock when the organization is actually born. Not everyone can make the transition from prophet to action leader—someone who can actuate the prophecy. In transformations involving two leaders, there is almost always conflict between them: One clings to the ideal while the second needs to compromise the ideal in order to operationalize it and put it into action.

Consider Moses and Joshua. Moses was a prophet, and Joshua was a doer. The Bible tells us that God did not allow Moses to cross the Jordan River into the Promised Land. I don't believe God was punishing Moses. I suggest it was a reward God gave his faithful servant. If God had allowed Moses to cross the Jordan, Moses would have had to compromise his ideals, becoming a doer first and a prophet second. Rather than being eternally revered, Moses would have suffered the rejection and negation endured by later prophets who tried to bring their prophesies to realization.

Climate

A company in Infancy has little in the way of policies, systems, procedures, or budgets. A description of its administrative procedures easily fits on the back of an old envelope in the founder's vest pocket. Nearly everyone in Infant organizations, including the president, is doing something, usually handling one crisis or another. There are few staff meetings. The organization is highly centralized; it's a one-person show. It rushes ahead at full speed, eagerly ignorant of its strengths and weaknesses. Like a baby who hits instead of touches, Infant organizations have no way of knowing how much pressure to exert. These emerging organizations are prone to making excessive commitments because they are mistakenly confident that they'll be able to honor them. They overbook their schedules, and then they must postpone delivery dates. Nevertheless, they strive to respond to client complaints. Its members struggle to meet clients' needs, usually by working on weekends and holidays.

Infant organizations are very personal. Everybody is on a first-name basis, and there is very little hierarchy. There are no systems for hiring or for evaluating performance. They hire people when the need arises or whenever an impressive candidate appears. New recruits generally start working right away because Infant companies more often than not postpone hiring. And people get promoted for producing results or for knowing how to exert pressure on the boss.

At this early stage in the lifecycle, businesses are like newborn babies. They require frequent feedings in the form of operating capital, and if they have to wait too long, they are very vulnerable. Most of them have no managerial depth. They have no capable leaders to replace their founders. They have no track record or experience, so a mistake in product design, sales, service, or financial planning can have fatal repercussions. Such mistakes have a high probability of occurring: These shoestring operations have no capital for establishing a complementary team that can make well-balanced business decisions.

No organization can remain an Infant forever. For the most part, the time and emotions necessary to keep an Infant alive far exceed the immediate economic returns it offers. If Infancy is prolonged, pride of ownership wanes. The founder/owner becomes exhausted and gives up. In this case, the death of the organization is not imminent and sudden, as in Courtship; it is a prolonged process with the founders' continuously declining emotional commitment and steadily increasing complaints about "how bad it is."

Infant organizations characteristically:

- are action-oriented and opportunity-driven, thus
- have few systems, rules, or policies, thus
- perform inconsistently, thus
- are so vulnerable that problems become crises on short notice, thus they manage by crisis, thus
- the leader who does everything is loathe to delegate authority, and thus
- commitment of the founder is constantly tested and crucial for survival.

In many ways, Infant organizations are like living infants. In order to survive, they require two things: regular infusions of sustenance and parental love and commitment. Deprived of adequate nourishment and care, Infant organizations can develop pathological problems and die.

Undercapitalization

We have to understand fully this need for periodic infusions of cash. Can you imagine inexperienced parents who plan for a nursery, toys, and cradle but forget about the milk? The milk a company needs is the working capital for such purposes as financing, increases in inventory, and covering accounts receivable. Without working capital, the newborn organization can perish.

Some founders underestimate the amount of cash and working capital they will need. That mistake stems from the enthusiasm typical of founders during the Courtship stage. A realistic view of cash needs is incompatible with building fanatical enthusiasm, and fear is not characteristic of Courtship: Faith (often blind) is. So, would-be entrepreneurs project extravagant sales and conservative capital needs. Instead of planning for the worst and hoping for the best as they should, they plan for the best and expect it. Forging ahead, many founders just *hope* that somehow their crying babies will get the milk they need. They rely on miracles. Miracles are part of the plan. They will happen because they have to happen. One can hope, but one must not rely on miracles.

The problem of undercapitalization grows more acute when companies succeed. That's just the opposite of what one might expect. The more a new company sells, the more working capital it needs to finance its receivables and inventory. I know of a retailer who, in order to increase sales volume, started selling on credit. The company did go bankrupt, but it wasn't on account of low sales. It just dried up. A company with sales increasing 35 percent or more annually will have trouble financing its growth from internal sources.

Founders can avoid the pains of undercapitalization during Infancy if, during Courtship, they really analyze what will be done, how it will be done, and who will do it—for both the short and long term.

For a healthy Infancy, there must be a realistic business plan, and cash flow must be monitored on a weekly basis. Cash flow should be the focus of record keeping. Accrual accounting is good for tax purposes and profitability analysis, but it doesn't track immediate survivability. Monitoring accounts receivable and inventory turnover is essential to avoid draining the Infant company's liquidity.

Infant organizations complain of being undercapitalized, and in their efforts to generate cash, they make several basic mistakes:

- They take short-term loans for investments that yield results only in the long run.
- They discount their prices to generate cash, but too often the discounts are so large, the sales don't cover variable costs. Consequently, the more they sell, the more they lose.
- They sell equity to venture capitalists who do not share their visions or interests.

Those mistakes can be serious enough to destroy companies. Initially when those solutions are implemented, the symptoms of the cash crunch seem to disappear. Over the long run, however, those treatments only aggravate the disease. The company ends up in even deeper trouble. And venture capitalists can turn out to be like the wolf from "Little Red Riding Hood." They approach with great big smiles. "All we want to do is help," they say. The real goal of venture capitalists, as it should be, is to earn substantial returns on their investments. Unfortunately, for some it also means: as fast as possible. Such traders put a clamp on a company's growth and eventually destroy a company by squeezing profits prematurely, in the short run. Founders should watch their organizations' cash flow, loan structure, and cost accounting and, if they bring in venture capital, they should make sure the investors agree to be there for the long haul.

Founder's Commitment

The second variable that can cause Infant mortality is the loss of the founder's commitment. Why is the founder's commitment critical?

Most Infant organizations have negative cash flow in the beginning. Their need for operational cash exceeds cash from sales. That creates pressure to be action-oriented, opportunity-driven, highly responsive, and flexible. Founders look for cash at any cost, leaving little space for rules and policies. They are experimenting and trying to define success. Rules and policies at this stage would suffocate the chance of satisfying client needs. Only when they can articulate success can they develop rules and policies to control and repeat that success. Having few rules and policies, and being very flexible and expedient about getting cash, leaders of emerging companies develop bad habits. They make decisions that set precedents.

For Infants, the cost of bad habits is low, but the benefits of getting the cash are high. As business gets bigger, and their client lists grow, the benefits of bad habits are no longer critical for survival, but the cost of bending to clients' demands in order to get the sale, postponing collections to avoid offending clients, and absorbing the cost of clients' continuous product adjustments can all skyrocket. Sales go up, and profits go to the basement. If a company makes too many concessions and bends too much to get a sale, it will run out of money and the founder will eventually lose control.

With few policies and rules, performance of Infant organizations is inconsistent. This is not unusual, but it makes Infant companies vulnerable. Their problems can become crises that turn management into a fire brigade. In an environment of management by crisis, it's not unusual to find very little delegation.[1] And the one-person show has to be the founder's show. When the founder is not committed, problems go unresolved, becoming crises that can annihilate a company. What does a founder gain by being committed? Founders of Infant organizations can expect to reap the following benefits:

- Twelve- to fourteen-hour days, seven days a week for much lower salaries than they would earn as employees elsewhere. The opportunity to make a million dollars is but a dim and distant dream.
- Weekly struggles to make payroll for employees who don't seem at all grateful.
- Getting to work long and hard, only to return home to a spouse and family who resent being "neglected."

Why bother?

During Infancy, the founder reaps few tangible rewards. The only thing that holds many young companies together is their founder's love and commitment to what their companies can and should be: the idea and commitment created at Courtship. Founders cannot let their dreams die. Their self-esteem is on the line. Their fledgling businesses are founders' tickets to immortality. They are their creations, their footsteps on a virgin beach, the monuments that will outlive them.

Infants require lots of work and many sleepless nights. What do they give in return? Even when new babies smile, it's not because they recognize anyone: They have gas. But despite no evident return, parents are committed. The same is true for company founders. In Infancy there is no tangible return. Talking about potential future profits is like talking about what a baby will be when it grows up. It's just talk.

What keeps founders going is the commitment they make during Courtship. If their commitment evaporates, their companies die. The highly focused commitment to their organizations might be so strong that it strains founders' personal lives. Understanding that led me to insist that founders who sign up for my lectures on organizational lifecycles bring their spouses. I present the following analogy: Postpartum women are tired. Some suffer depression. The newborn baby exhausts them. An unsympathetic husband nevertheless wants to fool around. His wife might beg him to leave her alone because she is worn out. If the husband is not empathetic, he might become annoyed and complain, "Ever since *you* had the baby I no longer exist."

When the husband pushes his wife to choose between him and the baby, whom does she choose? No matter where in the world I have asked that question, people always give me the same answer: She chooses the baby.

Founders who have just established their companies feel like those new mothers. They dreamed about their ideas and built their commitment over time, maybe for even longer than nine months. Now that they have taken the risk, they are totally preoccupied with their new "babies." When they come home after a grueling day at work, they are still absorbed in the problems of service and quality. They are preoccupied with anxiety about pressure from the bank. Their spouses want their share of attention. But the exhausted founders can hardly talk. The unsympathetic spouses are furious: "Ever since you have *your* company, you no longer have a family. We don't count. Only your ego trip counts."

If the spouse keeps pushing, who wins, the company or the spouse? Yes, you are right. The company wins, and it's time to call in divorce lawyers. The spouse erroneously perceives the company as a competing lover. The spouse fails to realize that the founder has given birth to a baby.

What does a smart mother do after she gives birth? She shares the baby, and when the husband comes home, he should change, feed, and rock the baby. "It is *our* baby." Similarly, smart founders share their company problems. "It is our company, honey, not just mine."

*Starting a company means putting
your personal life on hold.*

Founders often have to make a choice: the company or the family. An Infant organization requires constant attention. Founders continuously face problems for which they are ill-prepared: dissatisfied customers, lousy suppliers, reluctant bankers, unproductive employees. There are no precedents, rules, policies, or organizational memories to which they can turn. Each decision sets the precedent, and making decisions from scratch requires an abundance of energy. Getting the cash necessary to make ends meet requires more sales, and more sales create the need for more resources that require more cash. The need for more cash renews the need for even more sales. That endless circle means that founders work long days and rarely sleep at night.

The founder of Mexico's Banco de Commercio told a gathering that when he started the bank, his wife asked him why. "To start a business," she said to him, "is like going to sleep young and waking up old." It requires full attention, total dedication, and total commitment. It's like a long dream. To many, it's a nightmare.

In a successful marriage, the husband is supportive of his wife after she gives birth to their baby. By the same token, founders' spouses need to be understanding and supportive during Infant stages of their companies. Prudent founders enlist the cooperation of their spouses, encouraging them to share the joy and pain of creation. Without the support of their families, founders generally have to forfeit either their families or their companies.

A founder's commitment can disappear for more reasons than an unsympathetic spouse. If their cubs have been handled by humans, mother wolves will abandon their babies, leaving them to die. What causes such behavior? A mother wolf rejects her cubs when her scent is no longer on them but someone else's scent is.

Likewise, when an Infant organization is manhandled by outsiders, the founder may no longer identify with the company. Many founders give away shares during Courtship or sell off pieces of their companies to venture capitalists and other external investors in order to secure an adequate supply of capital. If there is continuous intervention from those outsiders' hands and the founder no longer considers the company his baby, he will abandon it. Without the commitment of the founder, the company will languish and die.

That kind of rejection can occur in a larger organization as well. New departments and satellites are like new organizations in that they need high commitment. If every time the "baby" wants to do something new, corporate headquarters requires dozens of forms and formal requests, the new unit's founder may walk away, saying "If you make the rules, you can run the show."

Such external intervention might originate in government, which, through rules, laws, and regulatory requirements, can create an environment in which only large and well-established companies can compete.[2] In start-up companies, founders may be so overwhelmed by the legal and accounting costs of compliance that they become alienated and quit.

When government intervention is minimal, people assume that whatever "is not forbidden is apparently permitted." But with intense external control and governmental intervention, people assume the opposite: "If it is not permitted, it is apparently forbidden." Thus, in societies where the government is deeply involved in regulating economic affairs, the entrepreneur might perceive that he will have to ask permission for everything: It appears as if everything is forbidden. Asking extensive permissions stifles entrepreneurship. Added to the normal risk of starting a business, this factor can destroy initiative.

Swedish law requires boards of directors to include elected employees. Furthermore, it's very difficult to fire anyone. A well-established company may be able to afford the cost of compliance, but for a start-up company that frequently changes direction and continually redefines success, the price of compliance can be prohibitive. It would be so difficult to alter corporate structure or reconstitute a board of directors that many would-be founders anticipate losing control even before they start their enterprises.

Autocratic Leadership Style

Many consultants, spouses, and other observers criticize founders of Infant organizations for not delegating, for working too hard, and being too opinionated. But such behavior comes with the territory of starting a company. For a company to succeed in Infancy, its founder must be enthusiastic, passionate, and resentful of anyone's interference. Such zeal is universal. Have you ever seen movies about the animal kingdom? All animals protect their young, allowing no stranger to approach. As human animals, founders fiercely protect their Infant organizations. They do not delegate. They insist on a one-person show with centralized, autocratic management. According to my theory, this problem is normal on the typical path (abnormal on the optimal path), and it should disappear once the organization outgrows its Infancy. It's abnormal and can become pathological if it continues after the organization has gone beyond the Infant stage of the lifecycle.

There is one more reason why Infant organizations have autocratic leadership: management by crisis. Because Infant organizations are fighting to survive, they cannot postpone decision-making. With no significant experience or track record, there is little organizational memory, and few, if any, rules or policies. Many decisions set precedents, and the company lurches from crisis to crisis. Everyone gets used to thinking, "If it's not a crisis, we have no time for it." In such an environment, it's normal to have only task-oriented employees.[3] Those manager cowboys live by the motto, "Shoot first. Ask questions later." There is no time for planning or thinking because everyone is busy doing.

Those cowboys find the survival mode's hard work and dedication personally exhilarating. Their lights burn late into the night. Their families go for days without seeing them. Singles often marry their coworkers. It's guerrilla war. Only the strongest survive, and those who do, establish close friendships in the high-stress situation.

With no titles, organization charts, or hierarchy, MBAs often have a difficult time functioning in an Infant organization on the typical path. Their questions about job descriptions, structure, strategies, goals, compensation, benefit plans, and career-succession ladders are met with dumbfounded amazement. "Let's see," the founder of an Infant company might answer, "your job is to do anything and every-

thing that needs to be done. As far as career succession, you are starting at the top. The harder you work, the higher you go. Any more
questions? Ask me." The one-and-only.

When I started the Adizes Institute, I was fortunate to get one
of my brightest MBA students as my first employee. Sitting in my
kitchen, he asked me about his career-succession ladder. That was a
reasonable question. I remember teaching him that well-run organizations must have long-range goals and objectives. Company leaders
must translate those goals into specific plans of action, one of which
is career development for managers. But sitting in my kitchen, with
a company that consisted of just him, me, $5,000 in the bank, and no
idea of how the unique and innovative consulting firm would work
out, the question was ludicrous. My response to his question was,
"Henrick! You are standing at the top of the ladder, but that ladder
is underground. You want to rise? Great! Start pumping the ladder
up."

For an MBA who has been taught to make strategic and policy
decisions—that is, to think like a boss—it can be quite discouraging
and depressing to have a "one-and-only" boss. Furthermore, busi-
ness-school skills appear useless in an Infant organization on the
typical path. An MBA's questions about long-term goals and strategy are unanswerable. Infant organizations do not prepare definite
long-range plans and strategies. The Infant lacks the necessary product and market experience. It has a vision, a dream, an intent. But
plans and measurable goals are vague. There is no experience yet.

"If we knew what to do, we would do it. We're still trying to find
out what we actually have to do," a founder once told me. Out of the
new experiences, patterns emerge, and later they will form the basis
for projecting the future and for setting long-term goals and strategies. With no real experience about what works, a detailed plan is
only a frustrating practice in futility. At this stage of the lifecycle, on
the typical path, the prevailing and expected style is management-
by-the-seat-of-the-pants. That style cannot and should not remain as
the dominant style when the company moves to the next stage of the
lifecycle.

Infant companies need to test ideas and gain experience first-
hand. But because they are also likely to be short of cash, they cannot afford to let people learn from mistakes. Good experiences are
achieved with good decisions. Good decisions are based on good

judgment, and good judgment is derived from bad experiences—so-called mistakes. Since their Infant companies cannot afford too many mistakes, founders must keep a close eye on everything. They centralize everything. There is no real delegation of authority, and that's the way it has to be. Subordinates are errand boys or gofers who assist the founder. This is normal. If they delegate, without any system of controls, founders might inadvertently and unintentionally lose control. I once saw a cartoon in the *Wall Street Journal:* Two unshaven homeless men dressed in rags are sitting on a park bench sharing a bottle of wine. The caption says, ". . . and then my consultant told me to delegate."

Employees are usually not so capable as the founders. If they were outstanding leaders who could make decisions of the same high quality, they would be starting their own companies. Often employees of Infant companies are people who joined temporarily and decided to stay. Rather than having been recruited, they wandered in or just happened to be available. After a while, they become indispensable. The founder can't afford to fire them because they know too much, and it would be too much trouble to replace them.

As I showed earlier, zealous commitment is mandatory for a successful Courtship, but it can become a pathological problem in Infancy if the founder does not let go of a bad idea and adapt to reality.

During Infancy, the founder's hard work, refusal to delegate, and focus on short-term results are the crucial elements of organizational survival. Those same traits, however, can become a pathological stranglehold on a company in Go-Go, the next stage in its lifecycle.

If an organization is to develop, its management must also develop. Note that "development" does not imply more of the same. It means change. Development is both qualitative and quantitative. If the founder cannot mature and change his or her style, the organization will need a change in leadership.[4]

Infant Mortality

A healthy Infancy balances growth with cash availability. Founders of healthy Infant companies feel in control of their operations. There is support at home, and none of the daily crises are fatal. They work long hours, refuse to delegate, make every decision and enjoy doing

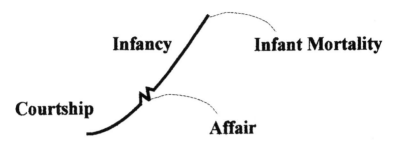

Infancy   Infant Mortality

Courtship

Affair

Figure 3-2: Infant Mortality

so. Infant mortality occurs when founders suffer from ennui, when they are alienated from or lose control of their creations. It also occurs if the company irreparably loses liquidity.

No organization can remain an Infant forever. The energy required for takeoff exceeds the energy necessary for maintenance. One cannot long sustain the energy level required to get an Infant company off the ground. Enthusiasm and commitment wear thin, and the company dies. Time is of the essence. A prolonged Infancy is a sign of pathology.

When its cash and activities reach a level of stability, an organization will emerge from Infancy and move into the next stage of the organizational lifecycle. By relative stability I mean cash flow is healthy; customers start bringing in repeat business; brand loyalty is developing; supplies stabilize; and production no longer presents daily crises. The founder finally has time to breathe. The baby is able to sleep through the night. Once this stabilization occurs, the Infant organization moves into the Go-Go stage of the lifecycle.

Problems of Infancy

Normal	*Abnormal*
Product orientation	Premature sales orientation
Questioning investors	Doubting investors
Commitment not threatened by risk	Commitment destroyed by risk
Negative cash flow	Unanticipated negative cash flow
Sustained commitment	Loss of commitment

Lack of managerial depth	Premature delegation
Few systems	Premature rules, systems, procedures
No delegation	Founder's loss of control
One-person show but willingness to listen	No listening; arrogance
Mistakes	No room for mistakes
Management by crisis	Unmanageable crises
Supportive home life	Nonsupportive home life
Supportive board of directors	Nonsupportive board of directors
Changing leadership style	Unchanging or dysfunctional change in leadership style
Short-term Infancy	Prolonged Infancy
Short-term financing for short-term investments	Short-term financing for long-term investments
Benevolent dictatorship	Dictatorship

Notes

1. R. Stacey, in *Complexity and Creativity in Organizations* (San Francisco: Barrett-Koehler, 1966), makes the point that crises themselves are the result of a failure to adapt; in nonadaptive systems, more centralized control is often the solution for the failure to adapt. Paradoxically, less control and more reflection, Stacey argues, builds adaptive capacities.

2. See R. Axelrod, "The Dissemination of Culture: A Model with Local Convergence and Global Polarization," *Journal of Conflict Resolution* 41, 2 (1997): 203–226. Axelrod demonstrates that cultural drift is a process whereby many smaller systems are, over time, consolidated into two or three big ones.

3. J. Martin, in *Cultures in Organizations: Three Perspectives* (Oxford: Oxford University Press, 1992), notes that cultures that favor task-orientation are less focused on relationships, so there is a greater likelihood that differentiation, over time, will lead to conflict. Thus the task-orientation that is characteristic of organizations in infancy leads quite naturally to increased conflict as the organization moves to create differentiated functions and departments.

4. See G. Fairhurst and R. Sarr, *The Art of Framing: Managing the Language of Leadership,* Jossey-Bass Business and Management Series (San Francisco: Jossey-Bass, 1966), for a description of the management style as a function of the manager's ability to reframe and manage language. From this perspective, the development of the founder is related to his or her capacity to frame contexts in ways that promote problem solving and reduce conflict.

CHAPTER FOUR

The Wild Years: Go-Go

Developing a company is just like planting a tree;
Don't plant it one day and then pull it up next week
and look at the roots to see whether it's growing.

ANONYMOUS

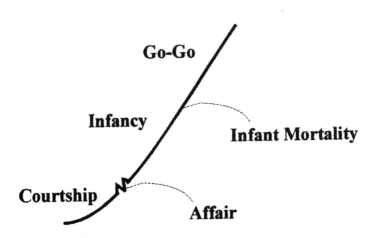

Figure 4-1: Go-Go

What is a Go-Go organization? In Courtship, we see the formation of an idea. In Infancy, committed founders put their ideas to work. Now, the idea is working, the company has good cash flow, and sales are up. The company is not only surviving, it's flourishing, and success makes the founder and the organization arrogant—arrogant with a capital A.

Opportunities as Problems

The greater the organizations' success, the more arrogant their founders.

Some feel they are invincible. Consequently, Go-Go companies get into trouble when they go in too many directions at the same time. Go-Go companies are like babies first learning to crawl. They're into everything. They never see problems—only opportunities. Everything they touch they either want to eat or try to break. Likewise, for Go-Go companies: Everything is an opportunity. On Friday night, the founder of a Go-Go company, a shoe business, goes away for the weekend. On Monday morning, he walks into the office and announces, "I just bought a shopping center." This does not surprise the employees. It has happened before.

"The real estate business? How did we get into that?"

"Well, I got a deal that was too good to pass up. Anyway, what we did for the shoe business we can do for real estate!"

Drawing by McCallister; © 1976, *The New Yorker Magazine*, Inc.

Present success has made the founder forget the difficulties of Infancy. The success of Go-Go is the realization of the founder's dreams, and if one dream can be realized, why not other dreams, too?

Pathologic Go-Gos are mini-conglomerates. They are involved in many related and unrelated businesses. Unfortunately, this diversification usually means that Go-Gos are spread much too thin. The leaders inevitably make the mistake of getting into a business about which they know nothing. The company loses more money overnight on a shopping center than it made in a whole year selling shoes.

In Go-Go, almost every opportunity seems to be a priority. At a meeting of one Go-Go organization, managers each listed the organizational priorities as they perceived them. As a group, the managers listed 173 different priorities: Too many priorities mean no priorities.

When I organize Go-Go companies, I sometimes feel as if I were watching a cat give birth. Just when I think that the last kitten has been born, another head emerges. I always ask managers in a Go-Go organization, "How many businesses are you in?" When they have finished giving me all the details, someone invariably remembers just one more deal, one more business, one more opportunity they are exploring or have already committed to. The founder of the International House of Pancakes described the Go-Go period he went through. He told me, "At that time, I felt the world was on sale." In the Go-Go stage, sales are up fast and easy, so founders become sloppy. They don't plan for results. They simply expect them. Frequently, they pay the price.

Go-Gos have so many irons in the fire, they cannot and do not give attention to each one. And it's not unusual for them to get burned by one or more of them.

Reactive Sales Orientation

In Infancy, organizations are product-oriented, and in Go-Go they turn to their markets. However, turning to the market does not mean there is a marketing orientation. It indicates only a selling orientation. What does that mean? Marketing is the thinking part of selling: deciding what products to sell at what price, through which channels of distribution, and specifying how to promote them. Marketing is a planning and positioning function. It is not only deciding what to do but also what *not* to do. In Go-Go, the arrogance of success is such that a discussion of what not to do is premature; Go-Gos on the typical path consider such discussion almost sacrilegious. Selling is a producing and doing function. Marketing calls for defining and carrying out plans, providing information on the effectiveness of the plans in the marketplace, and reacting to those results with necessary adjustments to the plans.

While Infant organizations are product oriented, Go-Go organizations face the "crowd" and become sales oriented to the extreme. "He would sell his mother-in-law if he could," said one executive about the founder of a Go-Go company. The sales orientation is addictive, and more means better. The organization equates sales with success, and it exploits rather than plans for opportunities. The organization is opportunity-*driven* rather than opportunity-*driving*. Management responds to the environment rather than planning the environment it wants.[1] More means better for a Go-Go, thus the decision to focus on what *not* to do is not very popular—yet. In the rush to get the product to market, people make promises before they know how the company will fulfill them. The company ships unfinished products, without manuals, and with no spare parts available. It's a nightmare for the customer. The company is conducting on-the-road engineering, virtually chasing and fixing the product as it makes its way to the customer. That means engineering never actually releases the product for mass manufacturing. The company sells the product before engineering finishes it and before manufacturing even designs it for manufacturability.

I encounter this problem in almost all start-ups, and I consider it abnormal rather than pathological. It is not pathological because experienced customers apparently are used to it. They complain, groan, and moan, but they plan for disappointment in their projections. It's a game everyone plays, but it isn't normal because it can be avoided.

A proactive marketing orientation calls for identifying new client needs and designing services and products to satisfy them. It's too early to do that in Go-Go.[2] The organization is still captive of and wants to capitalize on the needs already identified in Courtship and developed in Infancy.

The Climate

In the Courtship stage, there is a vision. As an Infant, the organization experiments with the vision of Courtship, working toward a product orientation.

That experimentation carries the organization into its Go-Go stage with a sales orientation. That sales orientation can lead to abnormal outcomes. Some Go-Gos assume a fixed profit margin on all sales, believing that increasing sales automatically mean higher profits. However, their cost-accounting systems are useless in the face of uncontrolled expansion. They are selling more, but rather than seeing their profits climb, they find themselves losing money. Anxious to maximize sales, Go-Gos award discounts to distributors, commissions to salesmen, and rebates to clients. But, because their elementary cost-accounting systems haven't kept pace with their growth, many find they don't know the real cost of goods sold. It's not unusual for companies at this stage to be selling their products at prices that don't even cover their costs. Obviously, the more they sell, the more they lose. If their sales grow rapidly and cash comes in bountifully, they may be so thrilled with what looks like overnight success that they become arrogant. No longer suffering the pains of Infancy, they perceive their climbing sales as proof of runaway success. They see themselves as the genius stars of rags-to-riches stories, and they undertake all manner of ventures. All too often, they have no business being involved in the ventures they choose.

If Infancy is management by crisis, Go-Go is crisis by management.

Parents of a two-year-old know they cannot let the toddler out of their sight. Children that age constantly get into trouble. Everything looks exciting to them, and they are ruled by a very short attention span. They open drawers and spread the contents throughout the house. What a mess. Following a toddler around, parents are always saying, "No! No! No!" Go-Go companies need the same kind of attention. In the transition from Infancy to Go-Go, a company's vision broadens from its narrow, nose-to-the-grindstone perspective to a wide-ranging panorama of endless possibilities. The Go-Go company has an insatiable appetite for quantifiable growth, and its one-and-only leader is not a good listener. Go-Go leaders do not listen because single-mindedness is what made them successful in Infancy. Back in the early days, people told them that what they aimed to do could not be done. It was too risky. They didn't heed those naysayers, and they have proven them wrong. Now that they are successful, they know for sure that they don't have to listen to anyone's advice. After all, they achieved their high-flyer status despite earlier recommendations and cautions.

That arrogance and sense of omnipotence can take very unusual dimensions. The more successful founders perceive themselves to be, the more acute is their sensation of omnipotence. One founder I know truly believed that he was invincible. He truly believed that Jesus himself was guiding him and that he therefore could not err.

Don't expect Go-Go leaders to attend meetings. They rarely do, but if they decide to come, they dominate the proceedings. Nobody else will have the opportunity to say anything of substance. The leaders demean, demolish, and personally attack anyone who dares to disagree with them. If people dare even to suggest that a Go-Go leader's idea is not so sound, he considers it a deliberately personal offense. So people sit, listen, suffer, and wonder, "How can we work with this monster?" Even the board of directors fears a confrontation.

Why do people bear such treatment? I have found that leaders of abnormal Go-Gos overpay their subordinates as if to bribe them to follow. Because they are paid so well, many such employees feel they have no alternative, and they endure the offensive behavior. Those who cannot tolerate it quit, and their anger burns with hatred.

Go-Go leaders buoyed by successful sales believe in their own genius, and they surround themselves with people who behave as if they do, too. I refer to such worshipful employees as *claqueurs*. *Claqueurs* is the French word that describes the people opera managers hire to come on opening night to start artificial applause. After the show, those paid clappers may make faces and sneer in disgust, but during the performance they applaud enthusiastically.

In Go-Go companies, meetings are show time. Subordinates show reverence and enthusiasm for their boss's ideas no matter how half-baked and dangerous they may be.[3] After the meeting, you see the staff congregating around coffee machines wondering how in the world they can avert the disastrous decisions they just applauded. Fortunately, more often than not, Go-Go leaders change their minds: Their ideas were not decisions—only ideas no one should implement. If people try to implement those wild ideas, their bosses may get angry because they have changed their minds. At the same time, everyone worries that the boss actually *wants* the idea implemented. The employees are in a bind. Should they or should they not do what they *think* they understand? They feel frustrated to the limits of their emotional endurance. They're damned if they do and damned if they don't.

Another aspect of that frustration arises from the entrepreneurial perception of time. Go-Go leaders' ability to estimate the time needed to accomplish tasks seems remarkably skewed. In their arrogance, they might announce that certain problems ought to be solved within an hour. Invariably their estimates are several hours short. The bigger their egos, the bigger this time bias. I, for instance, suffer from this same malady, and my coefficient of error is six. If I tell someone, "it will take an hour," it usually takes six hours. If I believe the task should be done in a month, it will take six months. And what I consider a delay feeds my managerial paranoia. "They must be fooling around. They don't work hard enough. They are sabotaging the effort," I say to myself.

To make matters worse, most entrepreneurial types who lead Go-Gos have real difficulty articulating their ideas clearly. One listens and wonders, "What in the world does he want me to do?" The few who understand and can interpret the ideas become the people who get business rolling. They become critically important insiders— the Go-Go's trusted confidants.

Alan Bond, who led the Australian sailing team to win the America's Cup, was one of his country's most successful entrepreneurs. He went bankrupt three times, and the last time he ended up in jail, owing billions of dollars to the banks. I've known Bond since his heyday, when nobody could get a minute of his time. He was Go-Going galore, buying and selling companies as if they were stacks of cards. His company *was* a stack of cards, and I told him so. I warned him that the time of reckoning would come. His company had no infrastructure, and there was no one to tell him that he was hyperventilating managerially. Believing himself invincible, he thought he could survive and escape any problem or trouble. Did he not go bankrupt twice before and survive it? These entrepreneurs behave like kids who want to test the limits of their power and the only way to find that there is a limit is to cross it. So they take more, harder, and bigger risks, challenging fate—and healthy logic.

Go-Go leaders plan on miracles. They do not just
rely on them.

It appears as if they plot miracles on their critical-path project-management charts. Should anyone dare to challenge them, they smile as if to say, "You can't understand, but if you just watch, you will see." Leaders of Go-Gos test their limits and challenge their fate. Alan Bond had his right-hand man, and he was the only person who understood what he said. When, however, Bond appointed that man to an executive position in one of his companies, he lost his "brakes." No one really understood what Bond wanted, and nobody dared to ask for clarification. And anyone who did understand dared not challenge Bond. After all, he was so very successful—a real genius in his own mind. Besides, they were fabulously well-paid. Why rock the boat? Bond, like so many other Go-Go leaders, believed his own press releases. But his success was a balloon, and a mere needle could make it all collapse.

Go-Go leaders do not pay attention to details. And we all know—or should know—the Arabic saying that the Devil is in the details. It takes only a "detail" to deflate a balloon full of gas.

Go-Gos have tremendous appetites for results and growth. Their leaders don't listen to criticism or warnings about difficulties of implementation, and they lack organizational structures that define who should do what.[4] Go-Gos can fall prey to a pathological condition: lack of accountability. With no accountability, nobody is responsible for results. Everyone claims inadequate information or authority to make the right decisions. Everyone is the victim of decisions other people made. Under such conditions, few decisions are final, and directions are always too vague for efficient implementation. I am describing a prescription for a disaster.

Inevitably, disaster will strike. The questions are: When will disaster strike, and what form will it take? Will it be a stockholders revolt? A suit from the Federal Trade Commission? A class action filed by customers who feel duped? A product liability case because there was inadequate quality control? When disaster strikes Go-Go companies, no one takes responsibility. No one feels accountable. Go-Go leaders are frustrated beyond belief. They feel people let them down. They feel betrayed. No one warned them of the tricky dangers ahead. Everyone just let them fall and watched them fall. The subordinates turn against each other. No one takes the blame. No one owned the decision or knew what exact part was his to carry out. So fingers point in all directions, and no one survives unscathed.[5]

The finger pointing and bickering don't start with the surfacing of problems or failures. Go-Go leaders subconsciously nurture mutual mistrust.[6] Because their aspirations for their companies exceed their accomplishments, Go-Go leaders harbor paranoia that their people aren't working hard enough and lack adequate commitment. They share those suspicions with their subordinates—one at a time. Picture, for example, a Go-Go leader: He tells Adrianne how bad and unsuitable John is, he tells John how betrayed he feels by Joel, and to Joel he confides that Adrianne is terribly unproductive and unreliable. The leader turns people against each other and all of them against himself. On the surface, the company seems to be doing fine. The sales curve is pointing to the sky, but in its heart, soul, and guts, something is very smelly in the Kingdom of the Go-Go.

When I lecture, I say that no company—absolutely no company—should let its sales skyrocket. I make a hand movement that starts low and rises exponentially pointing to the sky. "In this case," I say, "the company can go only one way." And the audience knows the answer. "Down!" everyone roars in a chorus.

I continue my lecture. "Let's say you have the foundation for a three-story building. But the neighborhood is flourishing, rents are rising, and you are doing so well, you decide to add a fourth, fifth, and then, a sixth floor. If you continue, eventually, inevitably, what is going to happen?" I ask. Everybody knows. The building will crack. Before you expand, you must reinforce the foundation. Think of a gold mine. If you only dig, dig, dig, the mine will collapse on you.

> *After you have been digging for a while, you must*
> *shore up the infrastructure.*

Go-Gos need continuous restructuring. They are like growing children who keep outgrowing their clothes. Pants that last week were dragging along the floor, this week are barely grazing the ankles. Leaders of Go-Gos attribute little importance to structure, managerial processes, or systems. They are preoccupied with the external world—sales, joint ventures, strategic alliances, sales, and more sales. Most Go-Go leaders get their kicks from their capability to beat the competition head on. Even when the leaders are women, the behavior of Go-Go leaders seems to be dominated by male testosterone.

Budgets, organizational structures, roles, responsibilities, and reward systems all require attention to detail, discipline, and self-restraint.[7] And those qualities are quite alien to an entrepreneur. I see them suffering when they sit in planning meetings. The step-by-step process of defining managerial detail causes them pain and discomfort. They crack their knuckles, squirm in their chairs, continually check the time, talk incessantly to their neighbors, write memos, try to leave the room, and fail to show up for the next session. They criticize me privately and publicly, asserting that the meetings are a waste of time. What they want to talk about is growth, ideas, and opportunities. They insist on making the meeting agendas to suit their own psychological needs rather than the organization's needs.

Go-Go leaders say they want help resolving personal issues, but, in fact, they want space to vent their managerial paranoia. They rage against others, accusing them of failing to perform. They rely on guilt to motivate, saying, "You could do better and more if only you would . . ." Rather than realizing that their system needs fixing and that their employees are as much victims of the nonproductive system as they are, they personalize the problems and attack their people.[8]

In Go-Go companies, physical space is scarce because the organization is growing so fast. They acquire new office space as it is needed or long after they've felt the squeeze. It's not unusual to find a Go-Go company scattered all over town—or all over the country.

The rapid growth the company experiences has organizational manifestations. In Infant organizations, you won't find organization charts, job descriptions, or real salary administration systems. They are like healthy families, and everybody does whatever needs to be done. When there is money and the founder is in a good mood, people might get salary increases, but don't expect performance appraisals. With everybody knowing what everybody else is doing, such formal appraisal systems are perceived to be unnecessary. That behavior works in Infant organizations. It is to be expected. For Go-Gos, however, it can be abnormal, and can become pathological.

Lack of Consistency and Focus

At the Go-Go stage of development, a company might have a broad array of incentive systems, and employees with diverse capabilities. Who does what and for how much remuneration is determined by a random patchwork of decisions. Lacking systems and established policies, the Go-Go hires employees at different times, under widely divergent agreements. Some are highly qualified, and some are not. The Go-Go organization has neither the time nor the focus to weed out incompetents.

Arrogance bred from success, a reactive sales orientation, and ambiguity about tasks and responsibilities shrink the attention span of most Go-Gos. Managers jump from task to task, trying to cover all bases simultaneously. Both the organization and its managers lack focus. If this lack of focus continues, the organization may go bankrupt. Survival depends on developing policies about what *not* to do, rather than on what *else* to do.

Company Organized around People

In Go-Gos, people share responsibilities, and tasks overlap. For example, the president of a Go-Go I knew well was the chief buyer, the top salesperson, and the designer. The salespeople also did some buying, and the accountant was the part-time office manager. If you ask for an organizational chart, they ask with a smile: "Which one? Last night's or this morning's?" If you ever do get an organization chart for a Go-Go company, it looks like a piece of paper a chicken has walked over: dotted lines, straight lines, and broken lines drawn in every direction. If you ask an employee, or even an executive, "To whom do you report?" you get a vague, confusing answer. "I mostly report to Sam, but sometimes I report to Lee. However, whenever there is a quality problem, I report to Jane, and come to think of it, to Al as well." And so on.

Go-Gos organize around people, not around tasks. Their growth is unplanned. They react to opportunities rather than plan, organize, or position themselves to exploit future opportunities they create. They don't control their environment.[9] Their environment controls them. They are driven by opportunities, not driving them.[10]

Behavior is reactive, not proactive, and as a result, people are assigned tasks based on their availability rather than their competence. I know, for instance, of an organization whose department of Canadian sales reported to engineering because the head of engineering had grown up in Canada. It's not unusual to find the staff of, say, Region A, reporting to Mr. Z, solely because Mr. Z happens to have some free time. I discovered a most extreme example of assignment-by-availability: The founder of one of my client companies assigned one of his employees temporary responsibility for a rather significant job. "Why you?" I asked the employee. "I think," he replied, "it's because I just happened to be riding the elevator at the same time."

My sister told me once that "there is nothing more permanent than continuous temporary." Imagine the fellow who got the assignment in the elevator. Years go by, and the temporary assignment is still his. He feels he owns it. Should the boss decide to reassign the responsibility, he'll have to give him something else in exchange. In other words, the structure is a patchwork of decisions made under duress, and expediency is the ruling factor. How can anyone really know who is supposed to do what? Under such conditions, whenever a question arises, to whom does everyone turn? Obviously, to the one-and-only.

While the one-and-only may, for a while, find his or her indispensability a reassuring comfort, eventually it will become overwhelming. Go-Go leaders feel they are under tremendous time pressure, and they cannot free themselves. The more they delegate, the greater the confusion, conflicts, and problems. Exasperated, they stop delegating, only to find they cannot go it alone. They desperately search for a savior, someone who will take over and finally free them from the mess. Of course, the first thing the saviors want to do is to put an end to all the turbulence. But what is the source of the turbulence? The Go-Go leaders themselves. Thus, as should be expected, the savior managers—the professionals—try to insulate and isolate the leaders from their companies, launching their companies into the next stage in the lifecycle.

Although I often use the term "founders" to designate company leaders, the word should not be understood literally. By the time companies reach the Go-Go stage, their original founders might be long gone. Nevertheless, the people who head Go-Go–stage companies usually behave as if they founded and own the companies they run.

A normal problem of Go-Gos is that everything is a priority.

As the companies grow up, they learn what not to do by making the inevitable mistakes. They engage in a trial-and-error process of learning, and when the Go-Gos make major mistakes—and lose market share, a major client, or money—they are thrown into the next phase of their lifecycle. A major crisis cures organizations of their arrogance. And the magnitude of the Go-Go's success and arrogance defines the size of the crisis that will induce the organization's management to recognize the need for rules and policies of business conduct. The development of rules and policies indicates emerging emphasis on an administrative subsystem and the transition to the next stage of development, Adolescence.[11] Failure to focus on administrative systems signals a pathology called the founder's trap.

Courtship organizations that lack sufficient commitment to pass the test of reality slip into a premature death called an Affair. What, after all, is an affair? Lots of enthusiasm with no real commitment. An Infant organization dies young if it doesn't receive adequate feedings—cash—or if the love and commitment of the founder die. Go-Go organizations that cannot develop their administrative systems and institutionalize their leadership, fall into the founder's trap.

What is the founder's trap? From Courtship through the Go-Go stages of the lifecycle, founders are their companies, and the companies are their founders. They are inseparable. When young companies need bank loans, their founders must pledge personal

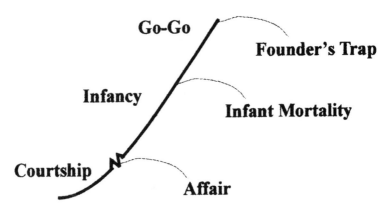

Figure 4-2: The Founder's Trap

The Founder's Trap

"I can't solve your problem. I am the problem."

assets. Banks perceive founder and company as a single entity. The banks rely on the driving force of the founders to get their loans repaid.

Founders are simultaneously their companies' biggest assets and biggest risks.

Companies outgrow the founders' capabilities to implant their personal leadership styles and philosophies. They can no longer act as one-person shows. That's when founders attempting to delegate authority and responsibility end up decentralizing and losing control. It usually does not work well. How does that happen?

A Go-Go will get into more trouble and lose more money the first week it ventures into real estate than it made all year in the shoe business. And the typical reaction to such calamities is to implement controls. Whenever those super entrepreneurs find themselves losing control, they respond by announcing, "We need to get organized. We need better controls around here."

The Go-Gos then create rules and policies, but who are the first to violate them? The one-and-only founders. In an alternate scenario, a founder might call management together and say, "As you all know, and have constantly reminded me for the past few months, this company is just too big for one person to call all the shots. I'm starting to delegate authority around here. You each have your own areas of responsibility and you're free to start making decisions as of today. However, ask me first before you make any big decisions. And don't make any decisions I wouldn't make."

They try to delegate authority. But rather than delegating, they end up decentralizing. Let me explain the difference.

Delegation involves transferring tasks down the organization hierarchy and creating a sense of commitment for carrying them out.[12]

Tasks can be to make decisions or to implement the decisions. When a task calls for implementing a decision that has already been made, the designated authority is only tactical in nature. That is delegation. When the task calls for initiating decisions that involve strategic change, that is decentralization.

A Go-Go organization cannot decentralize well. Workable decentralization requires a system of control. Decentralization provides a centrifugal force, which requires management to impose a centripetal force if it hopes to retain control.[13] Centripetal force is provided by policies that describe what the decentralized units can *and cannot* do. Those policies maintain unity in spite of decentralization. The administrative subsystem—rules and regulations—acts as the centripetal force. In Go-Gos, this administrative subsystem has yet to be fully developed, and the one-and-only usually disrupts its development by being the one least likely to adhere to it.

Founders who try to delegate without a system of controls unintentionally end up decentralizing. People begin to take initiative, and the founders feel threatened when the employees' judgments, values, needs, and preferences don't reflect their leaders' own judgments, values, needs, and preferences. Let us not forget that when they were in the Infant stage, the founders delegated nothing at all. The sudden jump from autocratic centralization to decentralization is justifiably frightening to the founders, and their subordinates don't believe that the founders will really do it. The founders fear they are losing control. So, in fact, founders are saying to their people, "You make only those decisions I would have made myself." When the subordinates fail, and that is inevitable, because only through trial and error can they learn what is expected of them, the founders recentralize authority. And the subordinates say, "We have been to this movie before!"

Once again, the founders find themselves with too much to do. They cannot embrace and control their companies so they turn back to delegation, which ends up as decentralization. The founders again feel a sense of betrayal and loss of control. The relationship between founders and their Go-Go companies is like a yo-yo. "You are in charge. No. I am in charge." With so much turbulence, people suffer pain and mental anguish, complaining that "Nothing is going to happen here until the old man—or woman—dies."

Some companies try to escape this mess by implementing matrix organizations, in which the leaders, who recognize their inability to manage everything, appoint groups of leaders to oversee certain markets or products and take responsibility for results. What

The Seagull Syndrome

"That's the last time I go on vacation."

they do not do is change the functional structure of their companies. That, they fear, would introduce too much political turmoil and might threaten their control. What they fear is what happens. Matrix managers have responsibility with little authority and end up frustrated and ineffective.[14] By postponing the pain of restructuring, the organization suffers years of prolonged anguish.

If you are a sailor or like to go boating, you probably do not like seagulls. When you see them coming, you know they're going to crap on your boat, and you do your best to chase them away. Leaders of Go-Gos frequently are seagulls to their companies. I know a CEO whose employees referred to his helicopter as "the silver seagull."

What is the Seagull syndrome?

What began in Infancy and Go-Go as a founder's loving embrace becomes a stranglehold that stifles the company's continued growth and development. But the founder is also frustrated. Measured in terms of sales, the company is successful: Climbing sales are proof that the product works. Incredible economic success gives founders the impression that they have really made it. Proud that they have made their marks on the economy, these founders want to extend their reach. They want to move beyond the day-to-day operation of their companies. They become enchanted and interested in community organizations, politics, health, travel, and other businesses that are not even remotely related to their previous successes. Simply bored and frustrated with the details of running complex organizations, they yearn for the excitement of Courtship and Infancy: That's when everything is new and fresh and so easy to do.

Looking for anything that will provide more meaningful outlets for their entrepreneurial energies, they get bored selling pizzas, or shoes, or whatever put their names in lights. Those whose companies have rewarded them with substantial fortunes might prematurely cash in on the fruits of their labor. They want to take advantage of the wealth to fulfill the dreams that used to be beyond their financial means. The chairman of Wells Fargo Bank told me that bankers watch out for the founders who take out loans for their businesses, experience some success, and start acting and dressing like different people. The bankers aren't surprised to see such types returning to the bank for a loan to buy a fancy car, a boat, or a plane. Finally, they come for financing for the most expensive luxury of all, their divorces.

Have you noted the complicated dynamic of the Go-Go stage? The founders want to escape day-to-day management, but they don't want to yield control. The founders' incremental distancing and the difficulties of delegation impose a remote-control embrace—the worst possible situation. The founders leave, but no one else has the right, the chutzpah, or the courage to make decisions. The Go-Go leaders believe that after they delegate authority, their subordinates will run the show. So they take off. But not forever or for a predictable period of time. When they do reappear, they return like seagulls. Everyone watches the sky, hoping the founders will not crap on them that day.

What happens when founders return to visit? Perhaps they hear about or notice changes that displease them. That's when all hell breaks loose. The founders always have better and newer ideas. The employees should have predicted, known, and followed them. In a matter of hours, the founders have recentralized power only to disappear once again. Nobody knows what to do or not to do, and everyone grows increasingly anxious. Trying to imagine what their founders would have wanted them to do is risky at best. Most founders are quite creative and, by the Go-Go stage, their arrogance defies second guessing.

The greatness of Go-Go leaders encompasses their ability to run their businesses by intuition. However, these geniuses are rarely capable of articulating their intuition or transferring it to others who can act in their stead. And their subordinates, incapable of action, let paralysis reign. And when the peripatetic leaders make their next appearance, the accusations and frustrations begin anew. They are upset that no one took action, no one dealt with the problems. Of course, when people have made decisions the founders question, heads roll. People begin to dread their founders' visits, adopting a fearful damned-if-you-do, damned-if-you-don't attitude.

Meanwhile, founders feel trapped by their creation. A frustrated founder told me a riddle that illustrates this point.

"When do you stop making love to a 200-pound gorilla?" he asked.

I didn't know.

"Whenever the gorilla wants to!" he said.

That good idea for a nice little company in Infancy got away from the founder during the Go-Go stage. What started out as a cute, little furry thing is now a huge ape that demands its founder's attention. And at this stage, the founder is unable, doesn't know how, and no longer wants to give those attentions.

> *Go-Go is a dreadful period of love–hate ambivalence. The employees might not love their leaders, but they fear and respect them.*

They characterize these leaders as "genius, crazy, eclectic but still genius; hard to work with but worthwhile if you can put up with the style." They want their founders to stay, but they wish they would change. And the founders are exhausted from their marathon races. They feel that the mountains they have been climbing don't offer the rewards they had expected. Granted they made money, but they are as fed up as the parents who complain that the child they've been raising has a mind of its own, refuses to listen, and is way too rebellious. Founders feel betrayed and unfulfilled. They want to leave and sulk, but they can't take off: There is no one to replace them, and if there is a capable replacement, the founders fear this new leader will hijack the company and steal their dreams. They tell the executives to change their behavior, and they are stuck in a stalemate. Everyone wants the other one to change. What they have to realize is that the entire organization must change. But they can't easily change it by themselves.

What is going on? It is highly influenced by who does the *integration*.

Who Integrates?

From Courtship throughout the Go-Go stage, founders are the integrative forces of their companies. They interpret market forces and synchronize sales with manufacturing, financing, and executive recruiting. Founders are the glue. In the advanced stages of Go-Go, that glue no longer holds everything together. There is not enough of it. It's not unusual, but it is a misguided solution for Go-Gos at this stage to try to find another person to act as the glue, to replace their founder. Founders hate the idea of being dispensable, and they will fight to retain their unique position. The organization needs to design a new depersonalized "glue" as part of the process of institutionalizing leadership. The Go-Go organization needs to move from absolute monarchy to a constitutional monarchy. If it fails, and it ends as a republic that guillotines its emperor, the founder will be fired, bought out, or replaced one way or another.

It is the difficult process of transferring the integration function that retards companies' abilities to institutionalize entrepreneurial functions.[15] That's what makes it so difficult to escape the founder's trap. And founders do nothing to facilitate this transition. They sow disintegration by turning one executive against the other. This disintegration is not done consciously, mind you. Founders don't decide to create dissension and internal conflict. On the contrary. Suffering from the internal conflict themselves, founders don't know its cause or what to do about it. Why, then, does everything they do seem intentionally designed to foment disintegration?

With no formal, well-oiled system of controls, Go-Go leaders rely on rumors and other ad hoc information. Compounding a situation that is already fraught with suspicion, most entrepreneurs have tremendous aspirations that, more often than not, exceed their achievements. They suffer from latent and mild paranoia. If you talk to Joe, you'll hear what's wrong with Bill. And when you talk to Bill, he'll tell you everything that's wrong with Lucy, and Lucy will tell you about Joe, and so forth. I was fascinated to discover that in situations like these, there is one person who is always in the penalty box: That person is responsible for the company's problems. But if that person gets fired, someone else will appear—as if he had been deliberately chosen—to fulfill the scapegoat role. The scapegoat can be a senior executive. The leader rejects him and privately accuses him of being responsible for the company's difficulties. Rather than fire him, the leader just makes his life miserable.

The solution then is to depersonalize the role of Integration. A single person should not do it anymore. It must be systematized, institutionalized in the governance function. So why doesn't the leader do that? "You can never see the picture if you are in it," someone once told me, and I realized that truth applies to me and my Institute, too. Despite my having "written the book" on the subject, I have suffered many of the diseases I describe here. I can do for my clients what I have a great difficulty doing for myself. In the abnormal situation when the leader cannot develop and implement the administrative subsystem and policies that institutionalize integration, an external force has to be involved, whether it is a consultant to whom the leader listens, or a necessary change in leadership.

If a company is caught in a founder's trap, it means that when the founder dies, the company might also die. A founder's trap can develop into a family trap if a family member takes over on the basis of ownership and bloodlines rather than competence and experience. In such situations, the company has failed to separate ownership from management. Management has not adequately depersonalized the leadership role; and rather than selecting a leader based on competence, management permits ownership to define leadership. This nepotistic behavior is poison to many companies. If the new leader is not competent, the competent managers will abandon the ship.

How many generations does it take to destroy a company caught in a family trap? I have posed that question in every country where I have lectured, and I always get the same answer: three. In Mexico, the folk saying is "Father—Merchant; Son—Playboy; Grandson—Beggar." In China, the saying is "From peasant shoes to peasant shoes in three generations." In the United States, the expression is, "From sleeveless to sleeveless in three generations."

> *One of capitalism's most important innovations was to separate ownership from professional management.*

For a company to preserve its hard-won gains, it must make the change from management-by-intuition and management-by-the-seat-of-the-pants—Go-Go management—to a more professional process. That should happen during Adolescence. Organizations that don't make that transition fall into the founder's or family trap.

A major crisis—caused by the mistakes of the arrogant Go-Go—is the catalytic event that introduces the transition to Adolescence. Go-Go companies, characterized by arrogance, uncontrollably fast growth, centralized decision-making, and a lack of systems, budgets, policies, and structure are primed for crisis.

I have cautioned CEOs of Go-Go companies. I've warned them that they were sitting on the makings of a crisis. All that was missing was the spark. Most CEOs ignore my warnings, pointing to what they perceive as their irrefutable success. "Do you realize that our sales have been growing 180 percent annually? We appeared at the top of *Inc.* magazine's list of the fastest growing small companies in the United States. Our stock price has climbed from $2 to $12 a share."

Then disaster strikes. The company sells a product of poor quality, and customers sue. Or maybe the company invests in a deal that "goes South" fast. A common textbook crisis is the result of planning-by-wishful-thinking. For arrogant founders, wishing is equivalent to reality. That lack of reason, and that ability to make dreams come true, to prove the doubters wrong, make Go-Gos viable endeavors; but when their companies are successful, their founders grow even bolder. They project exponential growth and spend money to prepare for that growth. Some of that money might cover such fixed costs as computers, office space, plants, and so on. What happens when the new dream doesn't come true?

What if the new markets aren't so welcoming as the first markets they penetrated? Cutting costs means admitting that the dream was not reasonable. It means accepting defeat, even if it is temporary. Unlike the earlier fights against the naysayers, the new difficulties are demonstrably real. Arrogant Go-Go founders nevertheless fight that reality and deny it. The more they fight, the more their companies lose. Only a major crisis can awaken the arrogant.

Problems of Go-Go

Normal	*Abnormal*
Self confidence	Arrogance
Eagerness	Lack of focus
High energy	Energy too thinly spread
Sales orientation	Sales and premature profit orientation
Seeking what else to do	No boundaries on what to do
Sales beyond the capability to deliver	Selling despite inability to deliver quality
Insufficient cost controls	No cost controls
Insufficiently disciplined staff meetings	No staff meetings
No consistent salary administration	Overpaid employees

Leader surrounded by claqueurs	Leader surrounded by fifth columnists (traitors in hiding)
Increasingly remote leadership	Seagull syndrome
Leadership's inflated expectations	Leadership's paranoia
Unclear communication	No communication
Hope for miracles	Reliance on miracles
Unclear responsibilities	Lack of accountability
Company subject to criticism	Company object of legal action
Internal disintegration	Diminishing mutual trust and respect
Cracking infrastructure	Collapsing infrastructure
Workable people-centric organizational structure	Unworkable people-centric organizational structure
Everything is a priority?	Everything IS a priority!!!!
Founder indispensable	Founder still indispensable, but beyond remedy

Notes

1. See G. Hamel and C.K. Prahalad, *Competing for the Future* (Boston: Harvard Business School Press, 1994), for a discussion of the proactive framework that is needed to compete in the global marketplace.

2. J. Collins and J. Porras, in their article, "Organizational Vision and Visionary Organizations," *California Management Review* 34 (1991): 30–52, have argued that visionary organizations create markets and clients, not simply respond to them.

3. See H. Hopft and J. Maddrell, "Can You Resist a Dream? Evangelical Metaphors and the Appropriation of Emotion," in D. Grant and C. Oswick, eds., *Metaphor and Organizations* (Thousand Oaks, CA: Sage, 1996). These authors note that charismatic leaders often use evangelical metaphors to mobilize emotional commitment in others.

4. See C. Morrill, *The Executive Way: Conflict Management in Corporations* (Chicago: University of Chicago Press, 1995). He argues that conflict in organizations is often related to the management's refusal to incorporate feedback into the business goals; thus, employees are left out of the loop and the quality of the decision-making suffers.

5. See B. Sheppard, R.J. Lewicki and J.W. Minton, *Organizational Justice: The Search for Fairness in the Workplace* (New York: Lexington

Books, 1992). They describe the problems that result when the organization engages in blaming activity.

6. See S. Moscovici and W. Doise, *Conflict and Consensus: A General Theory of Collective Decisions,* trns. W.D. Hall (Thousand Oaks, CA: Sage, 1994). They provide a detailed theory in the stages of consensus building in groups, as well as some interesting discussion about the relationship between organizational values and conflict.

7. See D. Krackhardt, "Constraints on the Interactive Organization as an Ideal Type," in C. Heckscher and A. Donellon, eds., *The Post-Bureaucratic Organization: New Perspectives on Organizational Change* (New York: Sage, 1994). Max Weber's ground-laying arguments on organizations and bureaucracies (1891–1922) are accessible in M. Weber, *Theory of Social and Economic Organization,* trns. A.M. Henderson and T. Parsons (New York: Oxford University Press, 1947). The suggestions are that the "Iron Law of Oligarchy" keeps power centralized, and this centralization actually reduces the responsiveness of the organization.

8. See C. Morrill, *The Executive Way: Conflict Management in Corporations,* for his discussion of organizational conflict as reflected in interpersonal conflicts.

9. See R. Hall, *Organizations: Structure and Process* (Englewood Cliffs, NJ: Prentice Hall, 1972; 1982), for a discussion of the factors that hinder organizational responsiveness.

10. See D. Katz, *The Social Psychology of Organizations* (New York: John Wiley and Sons, 1978), who suggests that organizations must attend to their meaning and meaning-making processes. This social psychological perspective on organizations suggests that business success is related to how organizations understand their own interaction with the environment.

11. See M. Weber, *Theory of Social and Economic Organization,* for the classic account of the features of the bureaucratic organization.

12. See K. Weick, *Sensemaking in Organizations: Small Structures with Large Consequences* (New York: Sage, 1995). He discusses the relationship between meaning-making and organizational commitment, arguing that the "sense" an organization makes of itself directly impacts it effectiveness.

13. See the discussion by M. Weber in *Theory of Social and Economic Organization* about the concept of "control" in organizations. See also C. Heckscher and A. Donellon's *The Post-Bureaucratic Organization: New Perspectives on Organizational Change* for a series of articles that critique Weber's notion of "control." This collection makes the overall point that relationships (in teams and other organic organizational forms) and interaction provide the basis for stability in organizations.

14. See G. Morgan, *Images of Organization* (Beverly Hills, CA: Sage, 1986), for an interesting examination of the problems associated with matrix organizations, particularly Chapter 2.

15. See J. Klein, "The Paradox of Quality Management: Commitment, Ownership and Control," in C. Heckscher and A. Donellon, eds., *The Post-Bureaucratic Organization: New Perspectives on Organizational Change*. While this author is not addressing the problems of entrepreneurs, she does address the question of how to institutionalize commitment throughout the organization.

CHAPTER FIVE

The Second Birth and the Coming of Age: Adolescence

During the Adolescent stage of the organizational lifecycle, companies are reborn. The transition from Courtship to Infancy is comparable to physical birth. In Adolescence it's an emotional rebirth: companies find life apart from their founder or from any management that behaves like a founder. In many ways, the company is like a teenager trying to establish independence from family—any family.

Rebirth is more painful and prolonged than the physical birth of Infancy. Conflict and inconsistency characterize the behavior of Adolescent organizations. They are recognizable by their

- Us-versus-them/old-timers-against-newcomers mentality
- Inconsistency in organizational goals
- Inconsistency in compensation and incentive systems

Those traits mean many unproductive meetings, and they can bring about the departure of entrepreneurial leadership and the demise of the organization. In Figure 5-1, the Z symbol on the curve between Go-Go and Adolescence pinpoints this transitional stage.

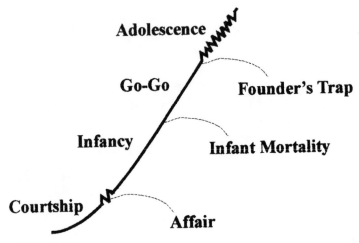

Figure 5-1: Adolescence

Why is the transition from Go-Go to Adolescence so difficult? There are three principal challenges:

- Delegation of authority
- Change of leadership
- Goal displacement

Delegation of Authority

The move to Adolescence requires delegation of authority. In a society, this move is analogous to the transition from an absolute monarchy to a constitutional monarchy, headed by a king who abides by a constitution. The founder must say, "I am willing to subject myself to the policies of the company rather than have the company be subject to my policies, which frequently change. I will be bound by the same policies that bind everyone else." It is rare that a king voluntarily yields his absolute power. To the best of my knowledge, only the King of Thailand—and maybe King Carlos of Spain—yielded absolute power without the pressure of a revolution. By and large, such changes are accompanied by revolutions. Revolution erupts not just because the king loves power and does not want to relinquish it, but also because the king has developed behavior based on circumstances that may no longer be relevant. He has trouble changing his behavior to fit the new environment.

In the Adizes Institute, I am subject to this phenomenon too. Being a doctor does not make one immune to illness. At the Institute, we spend a lot of time developing rules that I am often the first to break. Why? When there is a change in the circumstances upon which a policy was based, I find myself changing the policy then and there, rather than requesting that the person with that particular responsibility attend to the problem. My behavior is a remnant of Infancy, when I *had* to make on-the-spot decisions by myself. And I loved that sense of power and independence. Now, with the company in its Adolescence, when I seek the same thrill, it's no longer appropriate.

This desire to impose rules and policies without being subject to them has its price. When I violate policies, others follow my example. We end up with a set of policies that no one follows, causing the organization to behave unpredictably and emphasizing my sense of losing control.

You can't command your teenage daughter the way you did when she was a cute little baby. If you demand and insist too much, she will likely rebel, and you might lose her altogether.

Some leaders have the role of president, but they insist on acting as chief salesperson, bill collector, product innovator, and financier. They must move away from their Lone Ranger style of management. Specialization is required now that the business has outgrown the founder's individual capabilities. There are not enough hours in the day for anyone to manage the organization as a one-person show. The trick is to delegate authority without losing control.[1] It's not easy. Founders want to do it; they just don't know how, and they fear the potential repercussions.

During Infancy, founders don't and shouldn't delegate responsibility for major decisions. As a result, they become the major depository of critical information on company decision-making. This, however, is a double-edged sword. Employees probably don't have enough information to make decisions of the same quality as the founders, and that means the founders must take charge at crucial points. The longer founders hold on, the longer it takes others to learn how to make and implement their own good decisions. The lack of delegation creates an environment which prohibits further delegation.

From crisis to crisis, leaders of Adolescent organizations begin learning how to delegate. They give the troops chances to prove themselves. In the beginning of this process, they are as incompetent at delegating as their subordinates appear to be at making decisions.

With the first signs of a potential mistake, the leaders quickly recentralize authority. Such behavior is normal—up to a point. It becomes pathological when leaders continue to repeat the behavior, no matter how competent their people are: They are falling back into the founder's trap. In despair, founders often resolve to find professional managers who can lead them through the nightmare of decentralization. This step can happen either by hiring an individual or by selling the company to a more professional "parent." Let us focus on the difficulties that stem from bringing in a professional manager. I will discuss the difficulties associated with selling out in the section on acquisitions and takeovers.

Change in Leadership—From Entrepreneurship to Professional Management

Bringing in a professional manager changes the leadership of the company. [2] In this context, leadership implies a process of changing organizational culture—taking the company from one stage of the

"I think it's time we established new guidelines for corporate behavior."

lifecycle to the next. In reality, it means taking the organization from one set of problems to another. Leadership calls for resolving today's normal and desirable problems and preparing the company for the problems it will face tomorrow. The new manager must be a leader, not another gofer imported to carry out the founder's decisions. This new person is a chief executive officer, a chief operating officer, or an executive vice president, whose purpose is to take over from the founder.

She or he is there to get the gorilla off the founder's back and solve the problems of the Go-Go organization. The company must become more professional—less intuitive in its decision-making—opportunity-driving rather than opportunity-driven. This new leader should create systems, design compensation packages, redefine roles and responsibilities, and institutionalize a set of rules and policies. He will be saying "No! No! No!" to a company used to hearing only "Go! Go! Go!" from its founder.

What type of leaders do Adolescent companies need? Infant organizations need leaders oriented toward risk-taking and results—results-oriented doers willing to step forward and make commitments: "Here is my $10,000. Who else is in?" Go-Go companies have achieved some success with their original ideas and have started to explore new options. They need to get past their product-oriented myopia. In addition to their short-term orientation, they need a market orientation. The Go-Go leader's job description matches the profile of a typical business entrepreneur: creative and results-oriented. But Go-Gos run into problems as they approach Adolescence. That's when emphasis must switch to systems, policies, and administration. Adolescent companies need leaders with a totally different set of skills.

Many founders recognize that the needs of their companies have changed, and they realize that they lack the requisite skills and interest to continue to lead their companies. They try to satisfy the need by hiring professional managers from the outside. It doesn't take long to discover that the "hired guns" are not like them. The professionals come to work on time, and—heaven forbid—they leave on time. They sit in their offices all day long with their computers and paperwork. They don't talk much, but when they do, they usually say what *not* to do. They're not particularly open or friendly.

Gradually, it dawns on the founders how different the hired guns are from themselves: "This guy is not like me. If I had run the company like he does, we never would have gotten this far." Such logic starts a revolving-door syndrome. The hired managers get fired because they "don't fit in." That's when founders try a different kind of administrator, someone who "is like us and doesn't sit in his office all day."

That solution doesn't work either. Everyone may like the new administrator who is out selling now, but there seems to be no leadership. The new guy isn't getting the company organized, and, still, there are no systems in place. But the biggest problem is that the new leader is not controlling the founder. "We need someone stronger than that person," the people say. However, when a stronger person is brought in, it is too upsetting to the organization's culture. The founder feels threatened, and, once again, the revolving door is turning. The paradox is that the founder is looking for "someone like us," who will "do the things we do not do." Inconsistent demand, right?

The founders are looking for pilots who can fly submarines. What they must realize is that the leadership style required for Adolescence is different from that required in the earlier stages. For this critical transition, Adolescent companies don't need leaders like their founders; the new leaders need to complement the founders' style.

To ensure healthy transitions into Adolescence, founders must pass the baton to the administrators at precisely the right time.

Good management is not a marathon race.[3] It is a relay race.

When is the right time? The right time should be when the company is doing well, so there are no excessive pressures to go out and sell. The situation should not force the wrong style of leadership.

Are you puzzled? Are you asking, "If the revenues are fine and the company is doing well, why change the leadership?" It's time just because there is no pressure! If the transfer occurs when the company is facing a crisis, inwardly turned leadership is not popular.

It's difficult to pass the baton. At this stage of the lifecycle, the organization is disorganized, and, to an outsider, everything appears confused and confusing. The company's organization chart can't possibly fit on one piece of paper. Everyone and his brother report to the founder for one reason or another. The compensation system is a patchwork of special deals that have turned into policies through default. There is no management depth. Organizational behavior mirrors the founder's behavior, and the style is best compared to a guerrilla or partisan culture.

Employees are always talking about the old days, and they have their own rituals and pecking order. Seniority is often rewarded by founders desperate for stability. [4] Because there are no documented policies, the senior people serve as the organizational memory. If they leave, their departure throws everything into chaos until someone else figures out how to do their jobs. Their indispensability gives those senior people immense political power.

Furthermore, the founders—who remember that the senior people stuck with them through Infancy—value loyalty. The seniors and the founders carry the same scars. Founders listen to their old-timers.

Such is the environment that must now receive new managers charged with "professionalizing" operations. Their efforts to develop rules and policies are perceived as direct attacks on partisan seats of power. Long-time employees generally resist the newcomers' efforts. When a newcomer tries to grasp the levers of power, the real battle begins. The old power structure bypasses the new chain of command, going directly to the founder to complain about the new boss.

"He is ruining morale."

"She doesn't understand how this company works."

"He is going to destroy this company."

And the final blow: "He or she doesn't do it the way you do it."

Whom does the founder support? The new administrator? Probably not. So, the new person is forced to resort to hiring his own supporters to outflank the "old boys" in the organization. Sides are chosen and guerrilla tactics prevail. Antagonistic cliques create an us-versus-them culture. [5]

Some administrators try to establish new incentive systems that remove personal bias in favor of objective rewards based strictly on performance. Such systems arouse opposition from the old-timers, who risk losing their special deals. The new administrators may also want to restructure jobs and reassign responsibilities. That, of course, is attacked by the old-timers, who fear losing their power bases. New managers face opposition everywhere they turn.

In most companies, however, the biggest source of problems is the founder who hired the manager in the first place. It is the founder who supplies all the priorities for new projects and products;

and, as usual, those ideas are neither fully planned nor articulated. The new manager is requested to develop a budget, and goes to great lengths to prepare it. It's probably the first budget the organization has ever prepared on time, but the new activities the founder wants or has already started are not included. The founder changes his mind faster than the professional manager can change budgets. The founder is the first to violate the administrator's newly established policies and procedures.

The old-timers watch "the game." When the founder sets the example with the first violation, they assume the professional manager is a lame duck and that all rules are subject to violation. Guess who gets called on the carpet? Guess who has to explain why the new budgets, rules, and policies are not being followed? Of course it's the new manager. Such treatment is enough to cause the manager to develop a strong persecution complex, as well as intense dislike for the founder and his or her old buddies. The manager sees herself in a no-win situation and begins to wonder why she accepted the job in the first place. She feels impotent, exhausted, disliked, and completely unrecognized for her attempts to make a contribution to the organization.

In some companies, we see a reverse syndrome occurring when their entrepreneurial leaders realize they can no longer drive their companies from the back seat. Their professional managers tell them so. Their boards of directors tell them to get out and let the company be. Even some employees openly hint that a transfer of leadership is absolutely necessary.

So the founders abdicate. They truly pull away. But their companies, having been structured around their founders' preferences, lack task-based structures and institutionalized systems of governance. Because those companies have no systematic way to make decisions or make course corrections, their new managers find themselves with virtual blank checks. I have seen situations where the new management goes on shopping sprees: buying computers, hiring consultants, appointing administrators, and spending money, all in the name of controls and systems.

While those controls are necessary, revenues might not support such profligate spending. The professional managers are used to control—they aren't sellers—and they often spend the money to increase controls on companies with flagging sales. The founders feel the *real* pain now. They feel as if someone has hijacked their companies. They are damned if they get involved and return to back-seat driving, and they are damned if they sit on the sidelines watching their companies get ruined.

The pain of raising an organization in Adolescence is real and often prolonged.

Goal Displacement

A further complication in the transition of authority is that companies must undergo a displacement of goals.[6]

They must switch from a more-is-better goal to a better-is-more goal: from working harder to working smarter.

If you ask leaders of Go-Go companies how business is going, they typically answer, "Great! Sales are up 35 percent." If you ask about profits, they are less expansive. "Gee, I don't know. Ask accounting." The orientation of Go-Gos is toward more sales; they assume that higher sales mean more profit. They run their businesses as if the profit margin on sales were fixed. That attitude can get Go-Gos into trouble.

Many actually lose money when sales increase. When someone finally adds up all the direct and indirect costs of sales, it often turns out that the companies are losing money. Why did nobody know that? Typically, it is because Go-Gos have so many products, in so many markets, with so many special (and continuously changing) price deals that it is impossible to keep up with all the data. The accountants usually figure it out—about six months too late to make a difference.

Due to such turbulence, morale starts to decline, and good people leave or show signs that they might leave. Founders, desperate to keep the show together, try to buy employees' commitment and offer stock and/or profit sharing. Those moves create a new set of problems: political problems. Whereas in the past the employees had *tried* to control their founders' behavior, now, they believe they *should* control it. After all, now they own a piece of the action, and the founders are endangering *their* assets. The employees start to confront the founders.

Profit sharing presents additional problems. To create new incentive systems, organizations must develop clear responsibilities, authority structures, and information systems that evaluate individual performances. [7] Without those guidelines, profit sharing is like a windfall, and unless the windfall is very high, it neither creates higher commitment nor controls management turnover. It functions more like a bribe.

Although everyone wants the business to run smoothly, most people have negative responses to those organizational initiatives: "My department's fine. Go work on sales, that's where the problems are." But to make the transition, everyone must participate in the restructuring, and to be effective for the long run, the reorganization must be based on trust and respect.

For a transition to be effective, it must follow the correct sequence of events. It takes time to effect changes—lots of thinking time in the office, away from the firing line, where most of the action has been taking place. But leaders of Adolescent organizations don't want to spend time in the office. They are still really Go-Gos at heart. They want to get organized, while sustaining the same rate of growth. The problem is, they must relax the hectic pace of sales in order for systematization to take place. A typical Go-Go solution to this problem is, "Fine, we'll just get organized faster." So they buy computers to speed up the process, often calling it reengineering. But not having devoted time or energy to consideration of their organizational needs, they merely computerize their ignorance. Now they have the ability to make mistakes faster.

Furthermore, in the absence of a task-based structure that specifies responsibilities and authority for making decisions, the computer produces plenty of data and no useful information. Information is organized data upon which people can base decisions. In Adolescence, it is far from clear who actually makes decisions. So, although the computer works overtime, it's producing data, not information.

Many times, I've had to insist that my clients abort their computerization process or their reengineering project: They were designing processes without having aligned the structure. The process of reengineering and its computerization were actually unhealthy for their organizations. They froze their companies to certain structures that were dysfunctional. They were institutionalizing the wrong power structures. They were legitimizing what *was* rather than realigning components to achieve the future. Later, when the structure has to change, it's impossible. The computerization and process engineering has to be redone to reflect the new structure, and, because the organization needs to reengineer systems that have already undergone reengineering, the process becomes so financially and emotionally taxing that people avoid it. If attempted, it causes all hell to break loose. Everyone warns, "The computer systems and the business processes cannot handle it." Like a badly set broken arm, it needs to be broken again before it can be fixed properly. Who wants to endure that pain?

The end result of these three factors—delegation of authority, changes in leadership, and goal displacement—is conflict with a capital "C." This conflict has many dimensions. It includes the conflict between:

- old-timers and newcomers
- founders and professional managers
- founders and their companies
- corporate and individual goals

Normal vs. Pathological—The Divorce

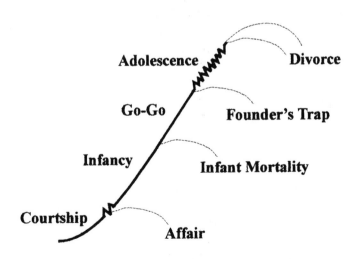

Figure 5-2: The Divorce

The conflicts manifest themselves in cliquish behavior. Management and employees gravitate into cliques—factions for and factions against any particular project, system, or individual.[8] The conflict and resultant pain causes personnel turnover, especially among entrepreneurial types.

"It's not fun anymore."

"We're not dealing with clients or with the products."

"We've forgotten why we're here. We're only fighting."

The energy that was dedicated solely to the market and promulgation of service, now turns almost totally inward. People waste energy on internal fights, regulating conflicts that are feeding, or being fed, by the rumor machine.

In companies that were established by a partnership or cofounders, the more creative, risk-taking partners may be perceived as threats to the efforts for stabilization. The more stable, better-organized partners, the administrators, resist their creative partners and fight to oust them.

In companies where the entrepreneurs retain control, they fire the administrator, once again starting the revolving door for administrators.

If an external board of directors has control, the professional manager or the administratively oriented leader and the board develop an alliance. When that happens, there is a good chance that the entrepreneurial founder will be squeezed out and the administrator will become chief executive officer.

An alliance with the administrator develops when the board realizes that the power struggle is not only between the administrator and the entrepreneurial leader. The conflict is also raging between the board and the entrepreneurial leader. As long as the entrepreneur was successful, the board didn't mind that, in reality, it had limited authority. Now that the entrepreneur's results are less impressive and the mistakes of the Go-Go leader are having a bad effect on the company, the board insists on having control. By the time the board has installed the administrator as chief executive officer or president, it has the authority it wants. And unlike the entrepreneurial leader, the new president is willing to accept that.

The most painful transition occurs when the leaders' partnership also involves family—spouses, parents, children, and other relatives.[9] When the lawyers are called in, close families break up, and people stop talking to each other. The Dart family owned Crown books. Two years before everything blew up, I warned Robert, the son who challenged the authoritarian father, that they would soon find themselves in a struggle for control.

The restaurant chain Carl's Junior provides another example. Carl Senior built the company from nothing, peopling the board of directors with his friends and cronies. They, he believed, would vote with him and for him no matter what. But, when his company entered the Go-Go stage, Carl Senior started to hyperventilate managerially. Success went to his head, and he went into new concept development and real estate development. He started borrowing money from the company as if it were his own. Granted, it was his—but not all of it. The board started to worry. It was liable and responsible for the company. So the buddies of yesterday became the enemies of today, and the board initiated a palace revolt to force their old pal out. I followed the newspaper accounts of the story, imagining the pain Carl Senior was experiencing. His own baby was turning against him.

It was all predictable. Nevertheless, did I predict it when it happened to me?

As the Institute was doing well, I got the idea—or should I call it the knee-jerk idea—of opening a first-class restaurant. Why? Why not? I had no problems. I was doing well, and I had the right experience: I had been a consultant to many restaurant chains. Why shouldn't I let my expertise serve my own organization? My wife also loved the idea. The location I had chosen had enough space to accommodate her dream: a gallery for contemporary art.

In reality, what did I know about restaurants? Nothing. I knew all about management of chains that employed ranks of experienced executives. Did I know how to control wine and liquor? Did I understand how to control pilferage? What did I know about service and synchronizing cooking with customer demand?

"So," you say, "it's obvious. Hire a manager."

That advice is easier given than taken. My wife developed a taste for the excitement of running a real-time feedback enterprise. And that requires creativity and sensitivity, both of which she has in abundance. But it also requires time—lots of time. What do you say to 8 A.M. to midnight? "Who needs that?" I wondered. But by that time, we were caught in the baby-versus-family conflict I described in the chapter on Infancy. Our dream was becoming a nightmare. We were saved by our real four-year-old baby at home. He's the one who put up the fight. He wanted to see more of his mother, and so the family won.

But when the family won, we were back to needing a professional manager. I knew what our restaurant needed: somebody who would treat it as if he owned it. We needed a cost-conscious police officer who could track pilferage, a psychologist who would know how to treat the enormous egos of the chefs, a theater director who could create the right atmosphere, a purchasing director who would watch that suppliers not overcharge us, and a public relations wizard who could handle the rich old ladies whose talk can ruin a restaurant's reputation. In other words, we needed a very capable person who would really care. Such people better be owners. In other words, for a restaurant like ours, we needed an owner-manager, not just a hired gun. And guess who I hired? A complementary team member, as this book prescribes? Surely not. (Do I read the books I write?) So I hired someone I was excited with, someone full of ideas and not at all control-oriented. As I should have expected, such a person had his own ideas, and synchronizing his with mine required time, time, time.

So there I was, dealing with menus and questions about lamb, fish, or chicken. You won't be surprised to learn that while I was spending so much time overseeing my demanding restaurant, I became a seagull to my own Institute! In my despair, I hired a professional manager for the Institute. He's a man I have known for years, and he is complementary to me in style. I trust him, but can I be sure that he will share my vision for the Adizes Institute? Stay tuned.

Conflict in the three dimensions I describe above is normal in the Adolescent organization. Pathology occurs when those who have formal and informal control of the company's decision-making process suffer a critical loss of mutual respect and trust. [10] The entrepreneurial people leave feeling they have many other ideas and opportunities to realize. Why, they ask, should they put up with the nonsense? They liked the company when it was small and flexible. When it became too inflexible or political, it stopped being fun. They get paid off and leave the company. Their exit can produce a pathological phenomenon.

Having lost the entrepreneurial component that gave it flexibility and the environmental awareness that provided its vision and driving force, the organization falls into premature aging. When the numbers people take over, the system becomes more efficient but loses effectiveness. Profits might go up, but sales after a while either go flat or fall. That, depending on which sales are eliminated, is not necessarily bad. *The Organization Man* is the behavioral model, and the motto is, "work with the system, and follow the rules."[11] I describe that condition as premature aging. Although the organization has enjoyed the momentum and entrepreneurial energy of Go-Go, it never achieves its full potential: It never entered Prime.

If, however, the company creates effective administrative systems and institutionalizes its leadership (later in the book, we will see how this should be done), the organization moves to the next stage of development, entering Prime.

Problems of Adolescence

Normal	*Abnormal*
Conflicts between partners or decision makers	Return to Go-Go and the founder's trap
Temporary loss of vision	Inconsistent goals
Founder's acceptance of organizational sovereignty	Founder's removal
Incentive systems rewarding wrong behavior	Bonuses for individual achievement while the organization is losing money
Yo-yo delegation of authority	Organizational paralysis during endless power shifts
Policies made but not adhered to	
Board of directors' attempt to exert controls	Rapid decline in mutual trust and respect
Love–hate relationship between the organization and its entrepreneurial leadership	Board's dismissal of the entrepreneurial leader
	Excessive internal politics
Difficulty changing leadership style	Unchanging, dysfunctional leadership style
Entrepreneurial role monopolized and personalized	Entrepreneur's refusal to delegate the role to a depersonalized role
Integration role monopolized	
Lack of controls	Divide-and-rule management
Lack of accountability	Imposition of excessive and expensive controls
Low morale	
Lack of profit-sharing scheme	Profit responsibility delegated without capability to manage it
Rising profits, flat sales	Excessive salaries to retain employees
	Premature introduction of a profit-sharing scheme
	Rising profits, falling sales

Notes

1. See R. Lund, A. Bishop, and A. Newman, *Designed to Work: Production Systems and People* (Englewood Cliffs, NJ: Prentice Hall, 1993), for a discussion of the features of work systems that are highly productive.

2. See H. Lansberg, et al., "The Succession Conspiracy," *Family Business Review* 1, 2 (1988): 119–144. The authors address the complexities of moving a family business toward professional management.

3. See P. Davis and D. Stern, "Adaption, Survival, and Growth in Family Businesses: An Integrated Systems Perspective," *Human Relations* 34, 4 (1980): 207–224 for a discussion of succession planning.

4. See H. Levinson, "Conflicts That Plague Family Businesses," *Harvard Business Review* 49 (1980): 90–98.

5. See J. Rothman, *Resolving Identity-Based Conflict in Nations, Organizations and Communities* (San Francisco: Jossey-Bass, 1997). He has described the pattern of "us" vs. "them" as a stage in the evolution of conflict. Specifically, he suggests that this formulation is core to the "antagonism" stage.

6. See G. Fairhurst and R. Wendt, "The Gap in Total Quality Management," *Communication Quarterly* 6 (1993): 441–451. These authors suggest that TQM, as a process, does not enable organizations to address issues of authority *that must be addressed as goals change.*

7. See D. Schwandt, "Learning as an Organization: A Journey into Chaos," in S. Chawla and J. Renesch, eds., *Learning Organizations: Developing Cultures for Tomorrow's Workplace* (Portland, OR: Productivity Press, 1995), for an interesting discussion of the relationship between performance evaluation and the learning organization; collaborative learning processes create new challenges for the design of performance evaluation processes.

8. See J. Bartunek and R. Reid (1992), "The Role of Conflict in a Second-order Change Attempt," in D. Kolb and J. Bartunek, eds., *Hidden Conflict in Organizations: Uncovering Behind the Scenes Disputes* (New York: Sage, 1996). These authors note that conflict reduces the ability of the organization to undergo second-order change.

9. See I. Boszormenyi-Nagy and G. Spark, *Invisible Loyalties: Reciprocity in Intergenerational Family Therapy* (New York: Harper & Row, 1973), for an explanation of the power of intrafamilial lines of loyalty.

10. See S. Moscovici and W. Doise, *Conflict and Consensus: A General Theory of Collective Decisions,* who note that although conflict can be constructive, left unaddressed, it can lead to the destruction of relationships.

11. W.H. Whyte, in *The Organization Man* (New York: Simon and Schuster, 1956), makes a related point.

CHAPTER SIX

Prime

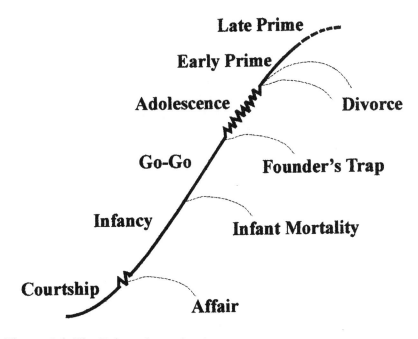

Figure 6-1: The Prime Organization

What is Prime? It is the optimal condition of the lifecycle, the achievement of a balance between self-control and flexibility.

In this book—unlike the first edition, in which I located Prime as a spot on the lifecycle curve—Prime covers a segment of that curve. Why? Flexibility and self-control are incompatible and they engage in a constant "struggle." There can be no stable equilibrium.[1] Sometimes the organization is more flexible than controllable, and sometimes it's not flexible enough. Don't hold your breath. Like happiness and other good things in life, Prime cannot be constant; if you do not keep up with it, you lose it.

Whether a company stays in Prime or slides away depends on what management does to maintain its Prime condition. A company cannot simply reach Prime, sit back, and rest. Does management promote activities that retard aging and sustain the vitality of Prime? When management becomes too flexible, making decisions on the fly, what corrective actions does it make?

Even if you are on the right road, you will eventually get run over if you just sit there.

ANONYMOUS

There are two parts to Prime: a still growing Prime, which I call Early Prime, and Late Prime, which I sometimes identify as the Twilight Zone. In reality the signs that indicate whether the organization is in Early or Late Prime might appear in both situations. Since no organization is in one spot on the lifecycle anyway, this confusion might not be critical. That is especially true for Prime because flexibility and self-control are in a continuous struggle, periodically exchanging dominance. This ambiguity imposes difficulties only in terms of how I present the material. Although in reality, the signs of Early and Late Prime are not mutually exclusive or discrete, I first present Early Prime, and my description of Late Prime follows at the end of the chapter.

Early Prime

These are the characteristics of organizations in Early Prime:

- Vision and values—"they walk their talk"
- Institutionalized governance process

- Controlled and nurtured creativity
- Coalesced goals
- Conscious focus and priorities
- Functional systems and organizational structure
- Predictable excellence
- Growth in both sales and profit margins
- Organizational fertility
- Intra- and inter-organizational integration and cohesion

Vision and Values

Open your arms to change, but do not let go of your values.

ANONYMOUS

A Prime organization is not subject to the shifting wishes of a single person. It is guided and led by a message—a vision of its reason for being. The people in the organization believe that what they are doing is important. They know who the stakeholders are and they recognize their needs. The vision might be to become the worldwide leader for a certain product line, serving a certain industry, while maintaining such values as social responsibility. One company we work with has hundreds of stores that focus on the low-income population. Its management put a lawyer in each store to offer free legal advice to those who couldn't afford to pay for legal protection. The goal was not to attract more sales. It was a true expression of the organization's intention to benefit the communities it serves. Sustainable growth is another value that guides behavior.

Organizational Prime has a military analogy. In times of war, soldiers know that their mission is to defend their homeland. They should know also how they are expected to handle captured enemy soldiers, and they have values that don't allow them to leave their own wounded or dead on the battlefield. They know the *what* and the *why* as well as the *how*.

Likewise, organizations in Prime are analogous to self-actualized people: They know who they are, who they are not, and what they want to do in the future.

They have a sense of purpose and a sense of what they will and will not do. They have boundaries that save energy because they won't even consider alternatives that violate those boundaries. They are focused, energized and predictable.

Companies that want to be recognized for the quality of their products have a senior executive in charge of quality assurance. But concern for quality is not reserved for their products alone. They work to preserve the values of their organizational cultures. While that is not less important than product quality, it is more difficult to protect and nourish. When an organization reaches Prime, it usually assigns someone to be responsible for monitoring and auditing its vision and values: Do we truly walk our talk? The person charged with that responsibility also works to develop community projects and involve his or her colleagues in those initiatives. Such activities reach far beyond giving money to the arts or to charity. They require giving time and human caring. Organizational values include integrity, honesty, and responsibility to our world.

"'Honesty is the best policy.' O.K.! Now, what's the *second-best* policy?"

As it advances through its lifecycle, a Prime organization continuously develops and nourishes its vision and values.

The vision and values of such companies galvanize their employees. There is a sense of mission in life that goes beyond just earning a living.

At this point, I want to interject a caveat:

Simply having vision and values does not make for a
Prime organization.

In my keynote speech to the Social Ventures Network in 1996, I warned those socially conscious organizations against getting carried away with values and culture, ignoring such realities as business practices. Those companies have more difficulty reaching Prime than the non-socially conscious: Their ideology sets the bar higher, building sometimes unachievable expectations among their employees. If the only "priests" of those values are the founders, their organizations are more easily caught in the founder's trap. Not only does the organization depend on these leaders for all entrepreneurial energy, it also needs them to keep the organization focused and energized with the values as well.

Thus, organizations need vision and values, which, while necessary, are not sufficient. They also need structure and processes that free the leaders of personalized decision-making.

Institutionalized Governance Process

To be in Prime, organizations must be free of decision-making that is dominated by an individual or a small group of powerful executives. They need institutionalized processes of governance: People must know and understand where and how decisions are made. Every Prime organization needs a "constitution" that defines the forums of governance.

Well-established organizations thrive with unwritten
but practiced constitutions.

They are comparable to the British system of government. There is no written constitution, but everyone honors the rules. Royal Dutch Shell ran that way for years. People knew who made decisions and how they were made; people knew which papers to submit to whom, by when, and how. And they could predict pretty accurately how long it would take before they would get the results of their queries. There was tradition and a well-rehearsed process. Because that process couldn't keep pace in our fast-changing global economy, the company had to change. Making such a move, which requires writing a new "constitution" and enforcing it, is as difficult as moving from one political system to another.

Organizations that lack a tradition have to write their constitutions. I have helped several organizations do that. A constitution must begin by explaining *why* the document exists. Then, it should define the decision-making forums, including a description of the membership of each one, its authority, and the requirements of each (unanimity, majority, chairman's approval, and so forth). Some constitutions even account for the possibility of appeal. And, so that it can adapt to changing conditions, every constitution should specify the precise procedure for amending it.

A constitution puts order to the ambiguities of the decision-making process. And, because a constitution usually affords veto power to the chief executive officer, it also assures leaders that decisions will not be beyond their control. Until the need to veto arises, leaders can monitor the open decision-making process. I should point out that in all the companies in which I have established constitutions, no chief executive has invoked the veto to override the decision-making body. Never. Because constitutions open the decision-making process, chief executives have ample opportunity to participate long before there is reason for a veto.

Constitutions also describe the appropriate way to run meetings, defining agendas and specifying requirements for distributing materials ahead of time. I believe that constitutions should state that nobody may make presentations in a decision-making forum. Everyone should have reviewed presentation materials before the decision-making meeting. This stricture helps avoid the wasteful practice of endlessly tedious overhead slides that bore everyone beyond numbness.

Controlled and Nurtured Creativity

Uncontrolled creativity squanders resources. Engineering dominates the organization, driving it to develop products the market does not necessarily cherish. In high-tech companies, the engineers may be so enamored of their ideas, that they generate more products than their companies can afford to sell. At the same time, if sales dominate a company, it becomes a "me-too" company. That's unacceptable for businesses in industries whose markets demand newness.

What now, then?

I look at organizations as power structures. If I want my power-boat to go in a certain direction, I have to engage its engines in a certain manner. If I want to go right, I have to decrease the power of the right engine while increasing the power of the left engine. The same holds for an organization. Describe to me the power structure of any organization, and I will tell you how it really makes decisions and how it behaves. To get the boat to turn to the left, the skipper must do more than simply scream, "Left! Left! Left!" and threaten pestilence to those who do not heed his orders. Nor can the skipper elicit action simply by preaching the value of going left. In order to go left, the skipper has to change the power structure.

In a high-tech company where the engineers call the shots, it's possible to achieve controlled, profitable innovation. But for that to happen, manufacturing and the financial controller should have commensurate power. The chief executive needs to align the structure of the process. In this case, the chief executive needs to align the new-product development process. The organization needs to define who has authority for every step: from inception of an idea through its release to full-scale production. I see the process, which includes even the possibility of aborting it, as an accumulation of appropriate "visas." As a product-development project progresses from one stage to the next, it passes through "gates" at which go/no-go decisions are made. The approval process is similar to the Japanese system of *ringi:* Implementation requires the signature of each affecting or affected constituency. Following that system, by the time a new product is ready to be shipped, everything has been done right and in sync with engineering.

To balance opposing forces—creativity and control, innovation and commercialization, market and technology as driving forces— we need the appropriate power structure that delineates respective authorities and the processes that integrate their engagements.

Coalesced Goals

I know an executive who keeps a plaque with this motto on his desk: *All our revenues come from our customers.* Prime organizations know why they exist. They focus on their customers and seek their satisfaction by doing what needs to be done. In aging organizations, the focus is on return on investment; in Adolescence, it is on how to win the internal political fight. The Adolescent's customers are on its radar screen, but they are waiting in the background for somebody to address their concerns—eventually. For companies in Prime, just as for Infants and Go-Gos, the customers are smack in the middle of the radar screen, but there is one major difference. The customer is not the exclusive focus of the company in Prime.

Infants focus on customers because they want approval of their efforts. They listen to their customers, catering to them to the point of self-destruction when powerful and experienced customers take advantage of their weakness. Go-Go companies are intensely focused on their customers. They are always looking for at least one more deal. They seek customers at almost any price. In that stage of colonialization, more means better, and for more, Go-Gos are willing to initiate wars.

In aging companies, customer focus is displayed on elaborate posters at the entrance to the corporate offices, and the posters boast the signatures of all the executives. And for many aging companies, that's where the customer focus ends.

In Prime, customer focus is real, but it's not exclusive. Prime companies can tell their clients what they *should* want. They don't subject themselves to whatever clients request. Moreover, they decide what the customer has no right to want. They say "no" if a customer's request violates such organizational goals as its values, growth strategy, or profit goals, or if it puts too much pressure on its human resources or inventories. A Prime company is knowledgeable about what it wants and what it doesn't want. It is disciplined enough to protect its complex multi-faceted basket of goals. It is responsive not only to financial issues, but to relationships as well. Employees and customers alike are treated with care.[2]

Focus and Priorities

In Courtship, the focus is on *why* to do; in Infancy, on *what* to do. In Go-Go, the focus is on *what else* to do, and, through painful experience, the organization in Adolescence learns *what not to do*. Companies in Prime know what *to do* and what *not to do*. Prime organizations know why (and why not), what (and what not), when (and when not), how (and how not) to do. They enjoy a certain composure and peace of mind when they make decisions. They are not like Infants. They never engage in shoot-first-ask-questions-later behavior. They don't engage in the Go-Go's helter-skelter minute-by-minute changes of direction. They don't suffer from the paralysis caused by the internal struggles of Adolescence. And the endless bureaucratic impotence of aging corporations doesn't plague them. They seem to have all the time in the world whenever they make decisions. They practice their trade *Beheshket u bebitha*, which in literal translation means: peacefully and confidently, as the Bible advises its believers.

Companies in Prime, like those in Go-Go, make money and grow. But they are not the same:

> *Go-Gos can tell you how and why they* made *money.*
> *Primes can tell you how and why they are* going *to*
> *make money.*

And they do.

The variance for better and for worse, between budget and actual performance, is always significant in Go-Gos—that is, if they have any budgets.

Companies in Prime have aggressive budgets, but the variance of actual over budget is within a predictable and tolerable range. A Prime organization has the vision and aggressiveness of a Go-Go, with the controllability, supported by the predictability of implementation, acquired during Adolescence.

Functional Systems and Organizational Structure

My emphasis here is on the word "functional." Systems that serve their purposes are functional and, therefore, effective. Not all systems in all organizations are always functional.

Adolescent companies run amok with too many systems and way too much paperwork. Some of these processes survive over time, beyond their functionality. Tactical decisions, with the passage of time, become policies by default: No one has challenged their validity. As conditions change, those processes prove superfluous. They don't serve the purposes they ought to serve or were designed to serve. Or they become dysfunctional, interfering with the desired process of decision making. In Prime, companies trim their processes, integrating them into functional systems. The organizational structure is correctly aligned: Mission is aligned with its authority and power structure as well as the information flow and reward systems.

Let's talk about reward systems. B.F. Skinner discovered and scientifically articulated what every mother has always known: If you want certain behavior, you must reward it. You cannot expect behavior A while rewarding behavior B. Basic! Right? But how many organizations actually have systems that reward the values they believe in and the vision they want to follow? Reward systems are often inflexible, and although organizations change their goals, values, and desired behavior, their reward systems can't keep pace with change. They end up with unaligned systems—mission, authority structure, information, and rewards—functioning at cross-purposes. A company in Prime is continuously realigning those subsystems.

Predictable Excellence

Companies in Prime have leadership, structure, and alignment of rewards reinforcing desired behavior. They are guided by visions that are not the ego trip of any one individual. Their plans and control systems monitor their performance and initiate timely corrections. They endeavor to satisfy their clients' needs.

With vision, values, structure, process, systems, and leadership that develop and maintain their location in Prime, why shouldn't these organizations enjoy predictably excellent results? Only events beyond their control can knock them off track. Even then, however, companies in Prime are better prepared to survive than competition that lacks managerial strength. When market forces take their toll, the less qualified competition will crumble, leaving the field open for organizations in Prime to grow stronger yet.

My friend and colleague, Peter Schutz, the former managing director of Porsche, the car company, tells a story about car racing. Most car companies that have won car races pray that the race commission will not change the rules. Because, to win under new conditions, requires additional work. After Porsche won a most prestigious race, Schutz, for his part, did hope for new race rules. "If the rules do not change, the mediocre companies eventually catch up," he explained.

If you are in Prime condition, change works to your advantage, and you outpace the weak competition.

Change is a challenge, and it is a challenge for everyone. For the weak, however, the challenge may be insurmountable.

Growth in Both Sales and Profits

The dream of Go-Go leaders is for growth in both sales and profits, but as they aim for more sales their profit margins plummet. In their frustration they become emphatic about sales growth, demanding increases in profits, too. At the Go-Go stage of the lifecycle, those goals are impossible to attain simultaneously. In order to be profitable, organizations have to be efficient, not just effective. "Efficiency" is not, however, in the vocabulary of entrepreneurs. They pay more attention to the revenue side than the cost side of the profit formula. It takes Adolescence to acquire an efficiency orientation and cost controls. Finally, in Prime, organizations can be both effective and efficient. They can increase both revenues and profit margins to their optimum level.

Organizational Fertility

To be in Prime means being organizationally fertile. Does that mean that they are introducing new products and entering new markets? That's what Go-Gos do. Companies in Prime do more than that. They create new companies—new business units that have their own products, their own production capabilities, and their own sales capability. The new units are whole entities able to stand on their own. Like a mature tree, fruits of a company in Prime contain the seeds of new saplings. These are not just new functions. These are new profit centers. If they do not have their own sales organization, for instance, they have the budget to pay for the services of a sales organization. They are responsible for profitability and have the managerial capability to achieve those profits. A Prime organization is a group of profit centers that share certain functions because of economies of scale or because of efficiencies of coordination or for maintaining a critical mass for creation. The Prime organization is an extended family of businesses, well-coordinated and disciplined with a common focus and system of values.

Intra- and Inter-organizational Integration and Cohesion

Prime companies are characterized by cultures of mutual trust and respect. There are conflicts, but they never deteriorate into personality clashes. [3] Conflicts are disagreements at worst and misunderstandings at best. People disagree without being disagreeable. Before making final decisions, there are discussions with those who will affect or be affected. Points of view are considered and taken into account, and there are no hard feelings if the recommendations are not heeded. All people really expect is that their opinions should be heard and be given respectful consideration. That's all.

That internal cohesion frees the organization to dedicate its energy to external cohesion. Prime organizations are well-integrated with their clients, suppliers, investors, and the community in general. They are admired for their services and practices. The high degree of customer loyalty is reflected in repeated sales. Employees enjoy working at these companies. Few leave willingly, and there are steady streams of people applying for positions.

Problems of Prime

Everyone should have problems if they are alive, right? But with so many virtues, what could be the typical problem of a Prime organization?

Most companies in Prime don't talk about being short of cash. That doesn't mean they have plenty of it. Cash crunches in Prime companies are expected and controlled events. They are sensations, not problems. The same applies to the workload in Prime companies. A Prime has no less to do than a Go-Go, but the work burden is anticipated, planned for, and controllable.

The complaint I most frequently hear in Prime companies concerns inadequate management training. In Prime, human factors come into play. I certainly don't mean to suggest that Infants, Go-Gos, and Adolescents have outstanding managerial capabilities. On the contrary, they have those problems in spades. But those youthful organizations are so preoccupied with other more pressing problems that management training doesn't surface to their organizational consciousness. It takes a back seat, and in many organizations it has no seat whatsoever.

What is going on? The Infant organization is product-focused; the Go-Go is sales-focused; Adolescent organizations focus on systems and administration. As they take care of those pressing needs, one by one, at each new stage, organizations grow and learn until, eventually, concerns about managerial depth surface in Prime.

The main challenge and the greatest problem of
Prime is staying in Prime.

In the analytical part of this book, I will address the question of what causes an organization to move out of Prime. What must be done to keep an organization in Prime or to rejuvenate it is discussed in the prescriptive part of the book.

How do we know that the Prime organization is losing its Prime condition? Vladimir Horowitz, one of the world's best-known pianists, once said: "If I do not practice a day, I notice the difference in my playing. If I do not practice a week, my wife notices the difference, and if I do not practice a month, the audience notices the difference."

There is a twilight zone where companies are still in Prime, but they seem to be slipping out of it. It is still light, but the sun has set.

If you trace the bell-shaped curve of the lifecycle, you will not find Prime at the zenith. As they say in the fruit business, "If it's green it's growing; if it's ripe it's rotting." If a Prime organization is at the top of the mountain, there is only one way to go—down. Prime does not mean that you have arrived, but that you are still growing, or to use the Vladimir Horowitz analogy, you are still practicing. It is a process, not a destination.

Why is the curve still rising? The curve depicts the vitality of the organization—its ability to achieve effective and efficient results in the short and the long run. In this case, short-run effectiveness, as measured by sales, is still rising and so is short-run efficiency, as measured by profitability. But long-run effectiveness and efficiency are declining. So while the curve is still rising, its propensity to go up is declining.

The increases in short-run effectiveness comes from the organizational momentum generated in Courtship, tested in Infancy, refueled in Go-Go, institutionalized and channeled in Adolescence, and fully-capitalized on in Early Prime. If Prime organizations don't refuel that momentum, if they lose enterpreneurship, if they keep capitalizing on the momentum rather than nourishing it, their rate of

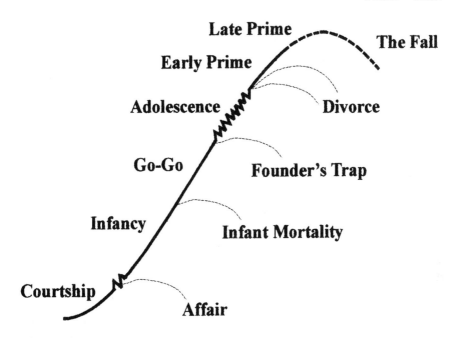

Figure 6-2: The Fall

growth will decline, and, eventually, organizational vitality will level off. That will be the end of growth and the beginning of decline.

The next chapter is dedicated to that subject. Here we should note that the earliest signs appear in Prime, when people least expect them. The first mild signs of decline appear in Late Prime, expressing themselves more fully during the Fall, and emerging quite emphatically during the aging stages of the lifecycle.

For humans, aging does not start with white hair. Even the middle-age spread of one's midsection is not the real start of aging. Aging starts in the mind, when one gets lazier and lazier about initiating and, then eventually, even responding to change. As one's state of mind changes, that change eventually expresses itself in the body and its functioning.

When organizations are getting out of Prime, they still perform as if they were still in Prime, but the drive to improve and therefore change is no longer there.

*It is time for us to realize that we are too great a
nation to limit ourselves to small dreams.*

*We are not, as some would have us believe, doomed
to an inevitable decline. I do not believe in a fate that
will fall on us no matter what we do.*

*I do believe in a fate that will fall on us if we
do nothing.*

RONALD REAGAN, INAUGURAL ADDRESS, JANUARY, 1981

Late Prime/Fall

It is very difficult to distinguish whether a company is still in Late
Prime or whether it is already in the Fall. The behavior is the same.
The difference is the frequency with which Prime characteristics
manifest themselves and how long those behaviors persist. For that
reason, I present Late Prime and the Fall as a single stage in the lifecycle.

A company in Late Prime/Fall is a company that has been feeling content—complacent, perhaps—for some time. It's still strong,
but it's starting to loose flexibility. It has used nearly all the developmental inertia it had amassed during its growing stages, and it's starting to lose its driving, generating force—the desire to change, to
create something new. The organization suffers from an attitude that
says, "If it ain't broke, don't fix it." The company is losing the spirit
of creativity, innovation, and enthusiasm for change that brought it
to Prime.

As flexibility declines, the organization mellows. Although it is
still results-oriented and well-organized, there is less contention than
in previous stages. More and more, people are adhering to precedence and relying on what has worked in the past. The company's
stable position in the marketplace has given it a sense of security that
may, in the long run, be unjustified. From time to time, creativity and
a sense of urgency emerge, but such eruptions are increasingly short-

lived. Orderliness prevails and, in order to avoid endangering past achievements, people opt for conservative approaches.

In contrast to earlier stages, people spend increasingly more time in the office, talking among themselves, reducing the time they spend with clients or on the line. In military organizations, you can see that phenomenon expressed in the ratio of fighting units to support units. In social service organizations, it is expressed in the number of social workers who are real case workers, treating families and children in the field—as opposed to the number of administrative social workers who are equally, or maybe even better-trained—in the office. On profit-and-loss statements of operations, it is expressed in the rise of the general and administrative expense as a percentage of revenues as opposed to the cost of operations as a percentage of revenues. On macro systems, it can be measured by the growing government expenditure as a percentage of the GNP.

Whereas during the growing stages, disagreements were expansive and vocal, now, people express their opinions with sheepish grins, as if to say, "It's not really *that* important." The sense of urgency is not there. People don't mind prolonged meetings. When they are asked to attend meetings, they no longer object or rage. Nobody screams, "Where the heck do I find time for another meeting?" The atmosphere is decidedly more formal. Later on, when the organization ages, people come to meetings because they want to protect their own turf rather than protect the company's interests. Meetings are where the politicking takes place.

In Late Prime/Fall ideas get a hearing, but there is little excitement for investigating new territory. Like a company in Early Prime, people still discuss long-term strategy, but short-term considerations increasingly creep into the decision-making process.

Moreover, the centers of power are shifting. The financial and the legal executives are gaining power, and measurements are taking the place of anything the new power base considers "conceptually soft thinking." Intuition and judgment play decreasing roles as facts, figures, and formulae rule the day.

The Late Prime/Fall organization hesitates to take risks. Sales continue to rise, but the revenues that are generated by new products that did not exist, say, three years ago, are declining. More often than not, new products are not really breakthroughs. They are merely product enrichments. The entrepreneurial spirit is dwindling. (The detailed manifestations of this behavior and the reasons for it will be discussed in the next chapters.)

If entrepreneurship remains dormant, eventually the company's ability to meet customers' changing needs will suffer.

The slide into Aristocracy, the next phase of the lifecycle, is subtle. The organization experiences no major transitional events as it did moving from one stage of growth to the next. From Prime on, movement along the lifecycle is a process of deterioration. When organizations grow, they reach transition points, bud, and flower. When, however, organizations age, there are no distinct points in the continuous process of incremental rotting. It is a process of decay.

Problems of Early Prime

Normal	*Abnormal*
Insufficient managerial depth	Insufficient decentralization

Problems of Late Prime/Fall

Normal	*Abnormal*
NONE! There are no normal problems of aging	Signs of disintegration
	Signs of decreased entrepreneurial activity
	Satisfaction with the results and the process
	Reliance on what has worked in the past
	Sense of security, no sense of urgency
	Order for the sake of order
	Increasing time spent in the office, behind the desk

Increase in overhead as percentage
of revenues

Power shifts to staff positions away
from line

Increased reliance on hard,
measurable data; decreased
attention to judgment

Hesitation to take risks

Loss of vision

The challenge of a Prime organization is to stay in Prime. If it does not do what it needs to do to stay in Prime, that failure will eventually become an abnormal and eventually a pathological problem.

Notes

1. See F. Capra, *The Web of Life: A New Understanding of Living Systems* (New York: Anchor Books, Doubleday, 1996). He describes the integrative processes that are essential to the life of systems (organizations) and the instability of equilibrium.

2. See Lynn Richard's dissertation, *The Heart of Knowledge: The Epistemology of Relationships* (Ph.D. Thesis—Santa Barbara, CA: The Fielding Institute, 1998), for a description of "relational knowledge" and its contribution to the growth and development of systems.

3. See S. Boardman and S. Horowitz, "Constructive Conflict Management: An Answer to Critical Social Problems," *Journal of Social Issues* 50, 1, (1994). In this volume, the positive aspects of conflict are addressed. Conflict is seen as both inevitable and also as an opportunity to deepen relationships and build trust.

CHAPTER SEVEN

The Signs of Aging

MOHANDAS K. GANDHI, on things that will destroy us:

Politics without principle,
Pleasure without conscience,
Wealth without work,
Knowledge without character,
Business without morality,
Science without humanity,
Worship without sacrifice.

If an organization is slipping out of Prime, the symptoms won't show up on its financial reports. Financial analyses and reports are analogous to blood or urine tests. By the time something shows up in those tests, it's already a problem and time to be looking for curative treatments. Like medical tests, financial statements discover disease when abnormal symptoms appear, and we can only hope that we have caught the problems before they have reached pathological status. We should do better than that. We want to discover the signs of deterioration when there is still the chance to do some preventative treatment.

*When people age, the first symptoms aren't apparent
in their actions or bodies. Aging starts in the mind
with changes in attitude and goals.*

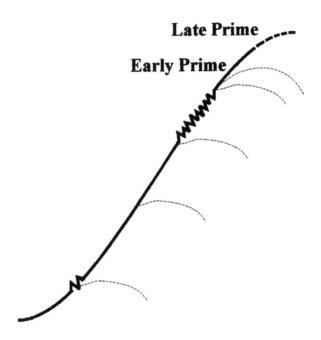

Late Prime

Early Prime

Figure 7-1: Degrees of Prime

Organizations age the same way. When an organization starts to
slip out of Prime, when it is at the advanced stages of Late Prime, the
first symptoms start appearing in its culture.

Prime is the intermediate stage between growing and aging. It
is the end of the beginning and the beginning of the end. There are
two ranges of Prime—rising Prime and waning Prime. There is no
single optimal point. Organizations should recognize the signs that
signal the waning stages of Prime. Awareness permits them to take
measures that will retard aging and rejuvenate them while they are
still in Prime. They need never leave Prime.

The following table compares the subtle differences between
growing and aging organizations.

Comparing Growing to Aging

Growing Companies	Aging Companies
1. Personal success stems from *taking* risk.	1. Personal success stems from *avoiding* risk.
2. Expectations exceed results.	2. Results exceed expectations.
3. The organization is cash poor.	3. The organization is cash rich.
4. The organization emphasizes function over form.	4. The organization emphasizes form over function.
5. People focus on *why* and *what* to do.	5. People focus on *how* to do and *who* did it.
6. People are kept for their contributions to the organization despite their personalities.	6. People are kept for their personalities despite their lack of contributions to the organization.
7. Everything is permitted, unless expressly forbidden.	7. Everything is forbidden, unless expressly permitted.
8. Problems are seen as opportunities.	8. Opportunities are seen as problems.
9. The marketing and sales departments have political power.	9. The accounting, finance, and legal departments have political power.
10. People on the line call the shots.	10. Corporate staff calls the shots.
11. Responsibility is not matched with authority.	11. Authority is not matched with responsibility.
12. Management drives the organization.	12. The organization drives management.
13. Management drives the momentum.	13. Management rides the inertia.
14. Change in leadership can lead to change in organizational behavior.	14. To change organizational behavior, it's necessary to change the system.
15. The organization needs consultants.	15. The organization needs "insultants."
16. The organization is sales-oriented.	16. The organization is profit-obsessed.
17. The organization exists to create value.	17. Political gamesmanship governs decision-making.

To discover whether an organization is aging, pay attention to those changes while they are still subtle. Later, once the organization has aged, the signs are not at all subtle.

In Late Prime, the signs of those changes occur one at a time, as intermittent events that don't concern anyone. They are rare, infrequent, and only mildly irritating, but they are signs nevertheless. It's time to do something, and I will introduce what needs to be done in a later chapter.[1] For now, let's juxtapose those changes as two extreme changes. By seeing how they differ as extremes it should be easier to notice them when they are much milder.

1. From Risk Taking to Risk Avoidance[2]

We are all in favor of progress, providing we can have it without change.

MORRIE BRICKMAN, KING FEATURES

During Infancy, the cost of risk appears quite small. There is little to lose. During Go-Go, founders, arrogant because of their companies' fast growth, simply disregard risk. Go-Go management grows accustomed to intermittent feast and famine. People aren't especially upset if some adventures yield poor results. They are confident that other unanticipated successes will compensate. Go-Go organizations are characterized by a high level of permissiveness. People ask and receive forgiveness for mistakes they have already made.

Prime organizations enjoy a climate of repetitive success. Management, which is self-controlled, perceives even bad results as successes because it could not have done better and the company has a realistic plan to overcome the situation. And that is what really counts. In Prime, management doesn't analyze failure strictly in terms of results. Had performance been as good as possible? The concern is with the process as well as the results. A failure—not having performed at peak—is unusual. Each failure gets analyzed, studied, and corrected.[3] People are aggressive but simultaneously cautious.

As the company grows, there is more to lose. The numbers become bigger, and the stakeholders more aggressive. The number of interested parties has also increased. Risk is becoming an issue. "You can't be hung for what you don't do," is an expression I once heard. Why take the risks? To succeed in a Bureaucracy, you are not expected to do something. People even joke about it.

"I don't know why they fired Joseph," a bureaucrat says. "He didn't do anything!"

Or, here is another one:

"What is your brother doing now? I heard he wanted that job with the government."

"Nothing," is the reply. "He got the job!"

Growing companies give. Aging companies take. When you are young you are expected to be idealistic and aspire to change the world. As we age we conserve energy and worry not how to change the world but how to survive it. Thus risk avoidance comes with aging, conserving energy, rather than risk taking, which can be afforded when energy is abundant.[4]

When things stop growing, they begin to die.

CHARLES GOW

Energy declines with aging because more and more goes to internal marketing—the struggle to keep the disintegrating pieces together. As energy goes inside, less is available for the outside, and, thus, there is less willingness to take risk.

When a company is in rising Prime, such caution is a desirable counter to the aggressiveness of late Go-Go. As an organization passes the point that marks the peak of Prime, it works to balance risk avoidance with risk taking. In waning Prime, risk avoidance overtakes risk taking.

With success, people become satisfied and content to depend on the momentum created in the past. Their attitude becomes, "if it ain't broke, don't fix it." Now that the organization has plenty to lose, people don't want to disturb the smooth sailing, and they begin to perceive the costs of risk as being too high.

As caution becomes a dominant pattern, and risk avoidance overtakes risk taking, a company's culture changes.

2. From Expectations Exceed Results to Results Exceed Expectations

During Infancy, management can tell you how well the company *did* in a year—only after that year has ended. Its people have difficulty predicting their future. Managerial behavior is now-oriented. Neither the past nor the future is immediately relevant. Management might have a dream about the distant future, but it is vague at best. Infant organizations react to immediate pressures, and their results are still meager. By definition, their expectations for the future exceed the current results. This phenomenon of expectations exceeding results continues into Go-Go, which in its arrogance, frequently expects the unachievable.

In the Go-Go organization, there is experimentation. Go-Gos over-stretch. Management attempts to budget and plan, but it won't really honor those budgets. Go-Gos are often still planning their budgets several months into the fiscal year. When they compare actual results with the budget, the variance can be quite significant. The deviations can be even staggering—as much as 200 to 300 percent above or below budget. Go-Gos are not under control, and their expectations are not reflections of results based on experience. Even when results are under budget, arrogant Go-Gos don't correct the budget. They believe that the results will catch up. Their plans seem to assume there will be miracles. When the state of Israel was established and its chances of survival were questionable, David Ben Gurion, the founding Prime Minister, was asked if he relied on miracles. He answered, "We do not rely, we *plan* on miracles." Go-Gos believe more than they think. They expect and aim for more and more. They are by and large unhappy with the results, no matter how good the results are. Their horizon moves as they advance.

During Adolescence, the organization begins to learn how to regulate itself. By Prime, it achieves control. A Prime organization can have the Go-Go's growth results, and it can predict and achieve those results. A Prime company can tell you its plans and accomplish them with only minor deviations.

In order to achieve repetitive predictability during Adolescence, organizations learn to formalize budget systems, reward achievement, and punish deviation. The Go-Go culture of quasi-anarchy welcomes the necessary discipline. But what is functional and desired at one stage of the lifecycle becomes increasingly dysfunctional and undesirable at later stages of the lifecycle.[5]

Because Infancy and Go-Go established that more is always better, Adolescent organizations don't afford equal treatment to deviations above and below budget. If actual sales exceed budget, people are rewarded—no matter how large the deviation. If sales fall below the expected, people are punished—no matter how small the deviation.

This unequal and often inequitable system of reward and punishment introduces order and predictability to the organization, exorcising it from daydreaming and making budgets based on wishful thinking. The organization has ambitions—remnants of its Go-Go culture—but its ambitions are gaining discipline as it comes of age.

What impacts behavior is not the process and purpose of budgeting, but, instead, the system of rewards.[6] If negative deviations get punished and positive get rewarded, it doesn't take much to predict what people will do. Everyone will focus on minimizing undesirable deviations from the budget, aiming to maximize the deviations that earn rewards.

One way to minimize undesirable deviations and maximize rewards is to reduce expectations. During the budget process, people set goals that they are sure they can exceed, or at least achieve. To account for any uncertainty, they aim low. When this behavior first starts, it functions to counterbalance the culture of Go-Go's wishful thinking. After Prime, however, such behavior is dysfunctional, causing organizational aging.

In Infant and Go-Go organizations, people get rewards for *what* they do, regardless of *how* they do it. No one has fully fixed the *how*, anyway. Budgets are rare. Bonuses are based on actual results, functioning much like sales commissions.

When companies base their reward systems on *how* people meet their goals, behavior changes. The reward system increasingly rewards the *how*, rather than the *what*.[7] There are rewards for how well people beat the budget. The lower the target, the better the chances of beating it and reaping the payoff. Eventually, the system rewards people who successfully lie about how much they cannot do.

To ensure that they never end up below budget, people aim low. As a matter of fact, subordinates at any level aim low because they know their superiors at any level will bargain to raise the target. A group dynamic of mutual deception develops. Superiors bargain to raise goals for the budget because they expect their subordinates to aim artificially low, and subordinates aim low because they know their superiors are going to raise the goals anyway. The budget that finally gains approval reflects neither the real capabilities of the organization nor the real opportunities of the marketplace. It merely reflects the trust or mistrust among the levels of the organizational hierarchy.

Consider the man who wanted to be sure his horse would win every race it ran. He entered the horse only in mule races. The horse did win—for awhile, until it started to behave like a mule.

*There is no long-term winning unless you're willing
to take the risk of short-term losing.*

There is now a new fad: benchmarking.[8] Organizations work to meet or exceed the best-known results of comparable organizations. Because a company focuses on an externally established standard, it bypasses the process of mutual deception. Still, I wonder about the long-term side effects. Although it is too early to know, I do have my suspicions. Would I point to the best student in my son's class and pressure my son to match that kid's grades, or else? Would I continuously compare my son to that kid and admonish my son for not being so good? I doubt that I will ever do that, but that is the process of benchmarking. What, I ask, is wrong with the old-fashioned, simple system of doing one's best and sharing the spoils? Maybe, because management is unsure about what "best" is, it has to look elsewhere for answers. Or, worse, maybe the managers don't trust each other so they have to negotiate to identify the limits by pushing back and forth.

Benchmarking is excellent as a vehicle for planning, but does it work for rewarding or punishing?

As the company becomes averse to risk, and results exceed expectations, it starts to accumulate cash.

3. From Cash Poor to Cash Rich

A company with expectations that exceed results is always hungry for more cash. Cash fuels growth. Organizations that want to grow always consume more cash than is readily available. Infants and Go-Gos are always short of cash.

In organizations where results exceed expectations, people spend less than they could or should, and cash starts to accumulate. In the advanced stages of aging, we find highly liquid companies with more cash than they can use. They don't have a plan for using it. Such a situation befuddles entrepreneurial Go-Gos, attracting them to attempt a takeover.

4. From Emphasis on Function to Emphasis on Form

The shift of emphasis—from function to form—is a transition that starts in Adolescence with a transition from "more is better" to "better is more." In Adolescence, organizations realize they can become more profitable by doing things right, rather than by doing more things. They realize they can generate profits by cutting things out rather than by adding things on.

Entrepreneurial types—and, by definition, founders of companies are entrepreneurial—make profits by increasing sales. Administrative types make profits by slashing expenses. The entrepreneurial type asks, "What else can we do?" The administrative type asks, "What less can we do?"

Administrative behavior and orientation are functional during Adolescence, when it is time to cool the hyperactivity of Go-Go. Adolescence is the time to trim extra leaves and branches so energy can be directed, rather than diffused. Attention, which has been dedicated to effectiveness as measured by revenues from customers, turns to efficiency. This sets the focus on form rather than function. Because form is almost nonexistent in the Go-Go organization (it is perceived as unnecessary), the marginal utility of any system—its form—developed during Adolescence is of great benefit.

In Prime, form and function achieve balance.[9] But the relationship of flexibility, function, and form (discipline) is not stable. Form overtakes function although the development of form has a decreasing marginal utility. It continues to grow nevertheless. Here, I believe, is how it happens.

Form grows because it feeds itself by itself. How?

Form implies rules of conduct to maximize control and predictability of behavior. Its purpose is to minimize, if not eliminate, deviations from the norm.[10] Since it is inconceivable to control absolutely *everything,* there are always some deviations; the organization, which is on a control binge, establishes new controls to eliminate those deviations. But that increase in controls creates more opportunities for newer deviations to emerge. The more controls we have, the more we identify deviations of increasingly minute character. Those deviations call for more stringent controls that will identify even more minute deviations, and so on, and so forth, until Kafka applauds.[11]

The organization's emphasis on form affects function. Why? Flexibility suffers when form increases, and in a changing environment, decreasing flexibility implies declining functionality. In the later stages of the lifecycle, only form remains. The tree has died; the stump is still there. People go through the ritual of rain dancing, acting as if it will bring the rain. People continue to go through the motions of budgeting, although they know the numbers are not at all realistic. They behave as if by worshipping the form, they will realize the function. And when that doesn't work, do they stop the rain dance? No. They dance even more furiously. They seem to assume that the reason it did not rain is that the form was insufficient—that they did not dance well enough. The same with Bureaucracy. The controls do not work, and, by definition, they cannot work perfectly because there are always uncontrollable deviations. What do the administrators do? They increase controls. If there is any function remaining, it hides underground—despite form. It is because there are no controls on control that form, for the sake of form keeps growing.

The Blob is continuing to grow. By the Blob I mean the educational bureaucracy, that part of the educational system which does not consist of students, does not consist of teachers, does not consist of principals. It consists of others, many doing a very fine job. But, do we need them all?... [I]f the number of students in a school district or in a state declines, the Blob still grows. The administrative bureaucracy gets bigger and bigger. And, I can tell you as someone who's in charge of administrative bureaucracy, when it gets bigger and bigger, it gets harder and harder to run, and accountability tends to get lost.

EDUCATION SECRETARY
WILLIAM BENNETT,
AT A FEB. 10, 1998 NEWS CONFERENCE, *WALL STREET JOURNAL*

Why does form overtake function? Why does it keep growing despite decreasing marginal utility? Because it is emotionally and psychologically easier to enforce form than to perform function. I use the words "enforce" and "perform" on purpose. To enforce means to repeat rituals. It does not require creative energy. It is not accompanied by anxiety, the byproduct of uncertainty, that is always present when we do something new. To perform a function, one must adapt to changing realities.[12] Change creates uncertainty. Uncertainty generates anxiety and demands psychological energy. It's very difficult and exhausting to learn something new. On the other hand, to enforce the already existent, repeating, "No, No, No," you need only stamina and the stubbornness not to give up.

Form is simple. There is no need to think. We have only to repeat what we are used to doing. Over time, form wins over function because it is emotionally less taxing.

As long as some degree of function exists, even illegitimately, form can survive. When no functionality is provided, when form is barren, there will be a breakdown and a rebirth of function, and a new Courtship will take place.

5. From Why and What to How, Who, and Why Now?

During Courtship, everyone talks about *why* things should be done. *What, how,* and *who* are only marginally interesting.

In Infancy, after the organization is born, one hears only *what* to do. *Why* gets hardly a mention; it is even bothersome to some people. "Do it now." The management-by-crisis motto, "Ready, Fire, Aim," probably emerged from the culture of an Infant organization. Everyone's focus is on the fires. First extinguish them, then we might worry about *how* to prevent them and *who* should prevent them.

Organizations eventually do pay the price of ignoring the *how* and the *who* factors. As they outgrow their capabilities, organizations become such messes that they can no longer ignore *how* and *who*. First *how* demands attention. Adolescent organizations spend their time addressing questions of *how*. They try to establish the *what not* to do and *why not* to do it by focusing, for a change, on the *how* it should be done. When they finally address the *who* factor, organizations are fully proactive. "Whom do we need to do the job?" And organizations really show maturity when they know, based on experience, *whom not* to appoint.

> *Organizations in Prime take time to find what*
> *they want, rather than being driven by expediency.*
> *They are opportunity-driving,*
> *not opportunity-driven.*

They know what they want because they know what they do not want. By the same token, they know whom they want because they know whom they do not want. This *who* orientation is pro-

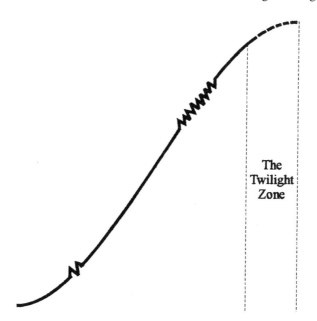

Figure 7-2: The Changing Focus

nounced in Prime organizations. They attend to human resource factors, staffing decisions, and getting the best people money can buy.

In aging organizations the *how* is pathological. Rather than concerning themselves with *how* to achieve *what* they set out to achieve and *why*, they pursue *how* for the sake of *how*. Period. It is a ritual.

For organizations that have aged considerably, the *who* factor becomes pathological. They are involved in witch hunts. Everyone is looking for *who did it*, rather than *whom will we need* to do it. Rather than looking at what an individual can offer their organizations, they look for the person's misdeeds. The *what* factor also becomes pathological. The organization is lost, and it asks desperately *what should we do* to survive. That is not the healthy, proactive, forward-looking, energetic *why*-driven *what* of Infancy. The *what to do* is based on fear, not faith.

Faith dominates growing cultures. Fear dominates aging cultures. In Prime there is a faith and a healthy dose of fear. Andrew Grove, chief executive officer of Intel, a company in Prime, paid homage to that condition in his 1996 book, *Only the Paranoid Survive.*[13]

In companies that die, the *why* factor has become pathological. Why should the organization exist? It has no right to.

6. From Contribution to Personality

The increasing emphasis on form at the expense of function affects personnel administration. In the growing stages, what really counts is what people produce or contribute. Even people who are real "skunks" are okay—as long as they make valuable contributions. As form takes over, the *how* becomes more important than the *what*. *How* people behave, talk, dress, and *whom* they know overshadow the importance of *what* they do for the organization. This behavior is especially prevalent in large organizations where interdependencies are so complex that—with the exception of sales and manufacturing—it's almost impossible to attribute a specific contribution to any single individual. The higher one is on the organizational echelon, the tougher it is to evaluate his or her personal contribution. In response, the organization focuses on the *how*, adopting the assumption that the *how* can predict and assure the existence of the desired *what*. When the *how* becomes dysfunctional—rather than producing desired results, it impedes them—there is no functional *what* or *how*. All that remains is a *who* orientation: *Who* did it? Whose fault is it?

Thus, while growing organizations hire and promote people because of their contributions and despite their personalities, aging organizations hire and promote because of personality and despite the lack of contribution.

In mature companies, particularly those with lax or nonexistent performance and review policies and procedures, advancement is achieved through seniority and connections rather than being based on qualifications or performance.

7. From Asking Forgiveness
to Asking Permission

*Turtle: I am lucky I am going slowly; I might be
going the wrong way.*

Because in young companies, form is weak and function dominates
("Did you do it? We don't care how."), what counts is results, results,
results. As long as the results are good, it's not difficult to slaughter
a few sacred cows. People who tried but failed to achieve good
results can ask for forgiveness. When form takes over, how one does
anything is far more important than the results. People get repri-
manded despite their extraordinary results because they didn't follow the correct procedures—the right form. As a result, nobody
dares to take chances. Everyone asks permission if there is any possibility of having to make even the slightest deviation from the norm.

In growing companies, meetings are devoted to criticizing *what*
someone already did. In aging companies, discussion centers on
whether something should be done at all. In growing companies,
executives might say, "No one said it shouldn't be done. Let's go for
it!" In an aging company they say, "No one said we can do it. Why are
we jumping the gun?"

More than 30 years ago, I wrote my doctoral dissertation on the
effect of decentralization on organizational behavior. My study of
industrial democracy in Yugoslavia focused on what happened when
the country distanced itself from the Russian model of central planning and moved to a market-oriented economy. Some 25 years later,
when the Berlin Wall fell, my topic became a hot subject. I noted that
when the country was under the Russian Central Planning System,
the prevailing attitude was, "If it is not explicitly permitted, assume
it is forbidden. Don't take risks." When Yugoslavia moved to free
itself from the Russian Central Planning System, allowing market
forces to regulate the economy, the climate changed. People had to
take risks if they wanted to thrive. The market economy required a
behavior that assumed, "If it is not explicitly forbidden, it is permitted. Let's try it."

It isn't easy to introduce changes into an organizational culture.[14] People are more comfortable assuming that something is forbidden rather than assuming it's permitted. Nobody can hang you for what you don't do, or as the Sephardic saying goes, "In a closed mouth, flies can't get in."

Consider the ensconced bureaucrat who indignantly complains, "I don't know why they fired Smith. He didn't do anything!" He seems to say that doing something is bad and doing nothing is the desired norm. Aging organizations expect inaction, and they reward it. Action makes waves and increases uncertainty. The following somewhat crude joke makes my point:

A person joins a bureaucratic organization. As part of his orientation, personnel directs him to report to an office where he will talk to some of the old timers about the company's motto. When he gets there, he opens the door and discovers a roomful of people submerged up to their lower lips in a swamp of fecal matter. Puzzled, he asks, "What's the company motto?" Straining his ears, he hears a slow, cautious whisper, "Doooooon't maaaaaaake waaaaaaves."

Those who make no waves, keep their mouths shut, and accept the status quo, are the people who win rewards and promotions, while those who try to initiate change are rejected because they make waves, and each wave reduces the comfort of others. Once when I was visiting a rather stodgy company, one of its livelier employees confided, somewhat bitterly, "Here, you can tell the innovators by the arrows in their backs."

Here's a parable from the early part of this century. Two shoe companies sent salesmen to Africa, instructing them to check out the market there. One informed his company, "There's no market here. Everyone is barefoot." The other wired headquarters, "Incredible market here. Everyone is barefoot." The first salesman worked for an aging company; the second represented a growing company.

The Talmud says: "For a believer, there are no questions. For the skeptic, there are no answers."

Growing companies have believers.
Aging companies have skeptics.

Growing companies create new needs. They have vision. Unless proven wrong, they assume they are right. Aging companies exploit proven needs. They are risk-averse and skeptical, and their attitude is "until it's proven right, assume it's wrong."

8. Are Those Problems or Opportunities?[15]

Entrepreneurial types see no problems, only opportunities. Every problem presents opportunities to do something else or something better. But, when entrepreneurs follow too many opportunities, they create problems. That's why Go-Go companies live in a situation of crisis-by-management, rather than management-by-crisis.

For administrative types who concentrate on how to implement new ideas, every opportunity is a problem. "How in the world are we going to make it work?" More often than not, they decide that if there are any problems of implementation, they are insurmountable.

From Adolescence onward, as administrators take over from the entrepreneurs, more and more opportunities are deemed problems, and those who introduce opportunities are perceived as trouble makers. Naturally, they end up with arrows in their backs. The company is stymied; it doesn't anticipate change, and, eventually, it fails even to react to change. The switch from opportunities to problems is accompanied by a change in the power centers of the organization.

9. From Marketing and Sales to Finance and Legal

The role of marketing and sales is to exploit opportunities, and in the growing stages of the lifecycle, those departments carry the flag. They have the power to determine what product, system, or idea will live or die. Line departments dominate, and in the growing stages, there is no real corporate staff function. In Prime, the role of administrative staff is to plan, control, and provide unifying centripetal forces. The center of power moves to the executive committee, which includes staff and line representation. As the organization moves into the aging stages, the center of power moves further into the staff—finance and legal—departments. Their role is to prevent the company from making mistakes. Their role is to say, "No!" And they do. Line departments keep losing power, and the system becomes increasingly centralized.

10. From Line to Staff

This change in authority and power—from line to corporate staff—means that those with no responsibility for results now have authority over those who do have that responsibility. Before, marketing and sales were responsible for producing results, and they had the authority to do so.

The switch in the power center has broad repercussions.

11. Responsibility vs. Authority

In young companies, authority is clear. Responsibility is not. In aging companies, the situation is reversed: Responsibility is clear. Authority is not. I'm sorry to tell you that this is not just a cute game of words.

In a growing company, there is so much to do that everyone pitches in. Responsibilities are fuzzy because everything is frequently changing. It's impossible to draw lines of responsibility. Still, everyone knows that "at the end of the day," the one-and-only has complete authority for and over everything.

Adolescent companies delineate responsibilities and depersonalize authority. Change decelerates after Prime, and responsibilities become increasingly clear. Authority becomes depersonalized and increasingly fuzzy as the organization ages. Aging companies are different from Go-Go or Infant companies where it is clear who has the answers—who has authority. Committees, procedures, and the like make it more and more difficult to identify authority. People are overcome by their sense of disempowerment. They are held responsible, but they can do little about their responsibilities.

In Prime, responsibility is clear and authority is not yet fuzzy. People work in the climate of a constitutional republic rather than an absolute monarchy.

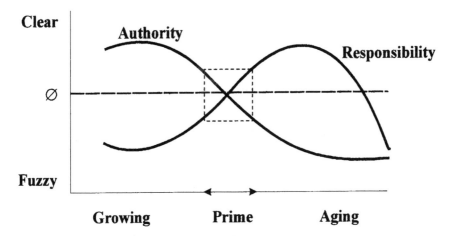

Figure 7-3: Authority and Responsibility[16]

After Prime, the finance and legal departments gain authority and power, and responsibility remains with sales and marketing. Authority is split from responsibility. Those with authority (staff) don't have responsibility, and those with responsibility (line) lack authority.

Authority without responsibility makes accountability fuzzy. The same holds true for responsibility without authority. Resentful of both aspects of the situation, people don't feel really accountable. Oddly enough, even chief executives of aging companies feel they lack the authority and power to initiate change. There are so many committees and forums for making decisions that many chief executives really cannot lead change. After Prime, fuzziness of authority slows decision-making and swift implementation, eventually leading to organizational paralysis. Organizational paralysis nourishes internal marketing, or infighting, and that diminishes the organization's capability to dedicate itself to effective and efficient competition in the market place.

When authority emigrates beyond the organization, as it does, for example, in governmental bureaucracies, the organization is on the critical list, dying of old age. It's unclear who can and, therefore, should act. If the organization neither takes preemptive action nor reacts, eventually it will become a political liability and die.

The repercussions of those changes affect the organization's sense of control.

12. Who Is Managing Whom?

One afternoon I was scheduled to make a presentation to a company's top management. The meeting was taking place at a famous retreat, and there were horses for rent. I decided to use the morning to ride up the hill and down the valley. It didn't take long for me to realize that the resort had been renting out this horse for many years. It knew the path by heart. It also knew how long an hour was without knowing how to read a watch. I kicked it to go up the hill. It moved two steps to the right and stopped, swishing its tail back and forth. "Perhaps it prefers the valley to the hill," I thought. Please note that I had already started to negotiate and compromise. So I pressed my heel against its side, signaling it to go left. It went two steps to the left and stopped. Its ears inclined forward, and I got the message. If I wanted to ride, I would have to behave myself and return to the path. Now, who was managing whom? I sat on the horse, looked left and right, and acted as if I was in control. But for the rest of the ride, I tried not to upset "the system."

Many businessmen, looking for a challenge, take on a leadership role in a governmental bureaucracy. In their vision, they see themselves galloping up and down the landscape, making a difference, leading a strategic change. Soon they recognize the power structure of the organization and start muddling through—no more than two steps to the right and two steps to the left. On the surface, they act as if they are in control, but underneath they carefully watch each step. They understand that the system is stronger than they are, and if they should disturb too many power centers simultaneously, they would be thrown out.

Think about what happens when political parties get power. When they are in the opposition, seeking power, they are busy making lots of promises. Maybe they even mean to keep them. Once they gain power, however, they find their promises are very difficult to keep because so many interest groups would be affected.[17] The governmental bureaucracy—professional public servants—have inertia working in their favor. They won't easily relinquish the vested interests they have established, reinforced, and sanctified over the years.

To gain power and implement change, politicians try to extend their reach by making more political appointments, feeding fuel to the us-versus-them syndrome. Public servants are used to changing riders. They know how to handle them and reign in their impulses. For their part, the politicians resort to offering broad smiles, making lots of promises, and doing only as much as they can.

By the time a company has aged, its administrative systems, policies, precedents, rules, and guidelines dominate behavior. No matter how hard management works to appear in control, the decisions and reward systems of the past are what determine the company's behavior. In a sense, the company itself, rather than any particular person, manages management. The skippers are at the helm, but the engines of their boats have frozen. For as long as anyone listens, they can shout "Left! Left!" or "Right! Right!" (depending on their political convictions), changing direction while making as few waves as possible. They watch the polls, trying to gauge what they can do without losing votes. A friend of mine, a corporate chief executive officer, accepted a major political appointment and moved to Washington. We spoke after he had resigned the position. "Do you know, Ichak, what you get for kicking an elephant in the ass?" he asked. "A sore foot!" he said with a sigh. I'm sorry to report that my own personal experience, working with a number of prime ministers and cabinet level officials, confirms his assessment.

Many people find it difficult to understand how a system could manage itself. Journalists, charged with informing the masses, are unable to explain how a system could be so messed up that it runs itself. So they pick a villain. Similarly, when organizations in the advanced stages of aging run into trouble, they go on witch hunts, finding people to hold responsible and ritualistically firing them. Perhaps they fire the people who had been assigned to oversee the situation. In that sense, attribution is not rootless. Nevertheless, the "responsible" people haven't had control since the company left Prime. Since then, the system has slowly but surely taken over.

Consider the United States. Its Go-Go stage lasted until 1929. As a result of the stock market crash, the government involved itself in "guiding" the economy. Keynesian economics legitimized government intervention; we were into Adolescence. In the 1950s, the country was approaching Prime. Now, the government, which was functional during the Adolescence stage and brought us to Prime, is the source of its current aging. The New Deal, which was a blessing when it was introduced, is today an Old Deal and a curse of entitlements and disempowerment.

We need a new economic theory: Not Milton Friedman or Friedrich A. Von Hayek, whose theories, I suggest, fit a Go-Go and not John Maynard Keynes whose theories fit the needs of a Go-Go-to-Adolescence transformation. We need an economic theory that retards decay, rather than promoting development.[18]

13. Momentum or Inertia

Growing companies need to sustain momentum. To keep a racehorse running well, one feeds it, exercises it, and keeps it healthy. A well-maintained horse needs no prodding. It will run and change direction as instructed. But if you want to make an old mule run and change directions on a dime, that's a different story. One needs to train a mule to race like a horse before one can take it to the races. Until it transforms itself into a racing horse, all you can do with a mule is keep it going: You have to capitalize on inertia.

In the aging stages of the lifecycle, managers try to capitalize on inertia. Rather than attempting to change direction, they try to find something good about going "wherever the organization is willing to go." Older organizations, because they lack flexibility, can't focus on effectiveness. In order to shine, management tries to maximize efficiency, worrying less about sales and more about cost reductions.

14. What to Do? Change Leadership or Change the System?

Managers of aging organizations typically—and mistakenly— believe that a change in leadership will rejuvenate the company. But, changing the rider won't make a mule into a racehorse. New leadership affects results only in the growing stages of the lifecycle. No doubt you've noticed that young children grimace, speak, walk, and even laugh like their closest caregivers. Later, they develop their own styles, and we parents wonder who they are emulating. Likewise, in its youthful stages up to Adolescence, a company's behavior reflects the style of its leader. In Adolescence, organizations emancipate themselves from their founding fathers and mothers. They develop their own identities with new constitutions to which their leaders subject themselves. The organization takes over. That development is fine and desirable because it brings the organization to Prime, where the importance of leadership balances the importance of a depersonalized constitution.

Later, however, the "system" takes over.[19] New leadership will help extricate organizations from the aging phases only if it changes the system, spending time, not racing the mule but converting it into a racehorse. (We will consider how to change organizational cultures in the analytical and prescriptive part of this book.[20])

In the early 1980s, I worked with the Bank of America. At the time, the media were campaigning for the ouster of the president and chief executive, Sam Armacost. They maintained that because he had not produced immediate results, he should be replaced. I urged further analysis. If you see an old truck standing in the road, what is your first instinct? Would you change drivers? Perhaps the driver is busy under the hood. Only if the driver is doing nothing and the truck is not moving, should you consider getting a different driver. But, if the driver is busy fixing the truck, even if it is not moving, why would you fire him? First check to see how his repairs are progressing. Let's look at the process. Don't make a decision based only on premature results.

Contemporary management theory is preoccupied with management by results and by objectives.[21] Such approaches are appropriate for the Go-Go stage. Public administration science and recently the humanistic school focus mainly on management by process.[22] Both are legitimate driving forces as long as they are in the right sequence: management for results, for objectives, by process.

Who leads whom?

The leaders of growing organizations animate the character of their organizations with their behavior. In aging organizations, culture determines the style of leadership.

The driving and driven forces exchange places. Leaders of growing companies determine their organizations' behavior. The culture of aging organizations dictates the behavior of their leaders. The situation mirrors an expression from the Bible, "P'nei ha'am ke p'nei ha kelev," which means, "The face of the people is like the face of the dog."

If you let your dog walk unleashed, it runs ahead of you and seems to be leading you. Right? But from time to time, it turns to look at your face so it can tell where you are heading. If you change direction, it will run to get ahead of you, but does that mean it's leading?

During the growing stages, people follow their leaders. As the organization ages, the flow of energy changes: Now, the leaders follow the people.

In the growing stages, changing the leadership changes organizational behavior; in aging we must change the behavior of the organization in order to change the leadership. Changing the leadership of an aging company without changing the system is like lifting your hand out of water. It doesn't make much difference to the ocean.

Unless he or she changes the system, a new leader won't make much difference to the system. As of 1998, when the United States was beyond Prime, already in the aging stages of the lifecycle, the president ought to have been spending his political "bank account" on efforts that would change the system rather than solve problems. That way, the next president would have enough power to deal with and solve the problems. A four-year term is too short to solve any of the complex problems that beset a country like United States. During the first year of their terms, presidents accumulate experience. By the third year, they are already thinking and preparing for reelection, and in the fourth year, they are busy running. In sum, a president nets about one year of the first four during which he can take the political risks necessary to deal with serious issues. The president has better chances of making a difference during a second term. In aging systems, however, witch hunts reduce the probability of reelection, no matter who is president.

When their companies are growing, leaders attract people with their message. In the aging phases, the people choose the leader who reflects what they want. The saying "people deserve the leadership they get" applies to organizations in the aging stages of the lifecycle.

Leadership in aging cultures is the consequence, not the cause, of organizational behavior. To appraise leaders of aging organizations, we must look beyond performance. We must also look to see whether the leadership is initiating cultural changes that, eventually, will bring about desirable results.[23] The systems—organizational structure, rewards, and information—all need to be changed. We must change the truck's mechanism, not only the direction it is taking. In aging organizations adjustments to product line, pricing, and advertising are only superficial treatments. Those are cosmetic changes that may bring temporary relief, but they don't address the roots of the problem: Why were there wrong products, wrong prices, and wrong promotions in the first place? One must treat causes, not symptoms. Who should do that?

15. Internal and External Consultants vs. Insultants

To deal with causes and not just symptoms means to deal with the organizational guts—authority and responsibility structures, information and reward systems. You have to expect pain when you meddle with an organization's power centers. You need to get neck-deep in company politics. Consultants give advice on what to do. They pride themselves on the length of their relationships with their clients; they cannot afford to be fired. As a result, they certainly won't look forward to disturbing corporate politics. To keep their accounts, they avoid causing pain.

Consultants who won't risk losing a client are the wrong remedy for an aging organization. The best they can do is to relieve some symptoms. An aging organization needs someone who will work to change the power structure. I call such people insultants: They are consultants who can afford to give pain and risk losing the account.

It is very difficult for internal agents of change to be insultants. They cannot step knee-deep into organizational politics and preserve any career life expectancy. Being too low on the totem pole, they will be rejected, that is, fired. Outside insultants are best suited to the job.

Such internal consultants as organizational-development specialists can institute change in growing organizations because in those companies people know that the pie is expanding. Turf wars are relatively mild, and the dangers of violating political power centers are not so severe. Furthermore, excitement about the company's successes compensate for the pain. In aging organizations, internal insultants will be rejected or be ineffective.

16. From Sales to Profit Orientation

At each stage of the lifecycle, organizational goals change. The goal of an Infant organization is obvious: Cash! The Infant needs to grow. It needs working capital—milk. The faster it grows, the more cash it needs. Infant companies often sell their products and services at a loss simply to generate cash. However, if they reach Go-Go, they have survived the cash crunch. What do those companies look for once they are in Go-Go? They seek growth, measured in sales and market penetration. Go-Go managers describe how well they are doing in terms of sales: "We sold 35 percent more than last year." In a Go-Go company, *more* usually applies to sales. In Adolescence, the company focuses on profits. That's when efficiency begins to have importance.

The transition from a focus on sales to a profit orientation is extremely difficult.[24] Both the bonus system and the hiring practices are geared to sales. During Infancy and Go-Go, organizations became addicted to sales. People's performance is pegged to how well they produce sales. Sales growth counts. When the organization begins looking for profits—seeking to work smarter, not harder—that behavior has to change. To change behavior, organizations need to alter their goals and reward systems. They must reconsider their hiring and training practices. And that is easier said than done.

Adolescent organizations must transform their consciousness, focusing their decisions on quality rather than quantity. When form begins to rival function, the two orientations engage in a difficult struggle.

Go-Gos ask me, "How can we have more sales and more profits?"

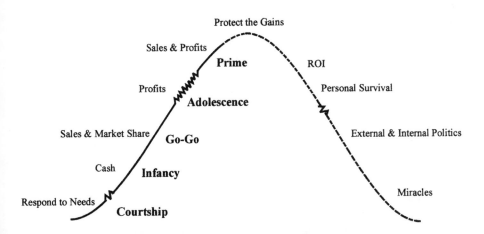

Figure 7-4: Goals Over the Lifecycle

I tell them, "You must first take time to get organized and systematized. Remember, as Bikram Choudury, a famous yogi, teaches, "The road to heaven passes through hell." To realize its dream, a Go-Go organization must first endure and survive the pain of Adolescence.

Because, in Prime companies, function and form and quantity and quality have equal weight, their organizational goals are both sales and profits. They *can* increase both sales and profits.

As companies leave Prime, profit goals gain more importance than sales goals.

This, then, illustrates the shifting importance of goals:

Growing stages: sales > profits

Prime stages: sales = profits

Aging stages: sales < profits

17. From Customers to Capital

In Courtship, there are several groups of stakeholders who will benefit from the establishment of the organization, but their interests are not yet taken into account. Only founders' self-interests count. From Infancy on, one by one, stakeholders' interests are expressed and addressed until, finally, when the company reaches Prime, all interests are fully integrated and balanced.[25] Since integration is not a steady state, as a company ages, one by one, the interest groups lose their power until only their "shadows" remain. That's what we know as politics.

For the Infant organization, cash reigns supreme. In Go-Go, the company is the founder's personal sandbox, and the customers are the kings. In Adolescence, the company along with its own managerial class becomes the client, and it starts to protect its own interests, frequently against the interests of owners and even customers. In Prime, the human factor emerges as a stakeholder and is coalesced and balanced with all other interests. The interests of top and middle management, capital, labor, and present and future customers are optimized.[26] As the ability to adapt to change declines in the aging stages, customers become less and less important. The personal goals of management also lose importance because, instead of being the driving forces, they are driven forces. In advanced age, the goal is personal survival, and people start to jump ship. In excessively bureaucratic organizations, political survival is the goal. That means outside interest groups dominate the decision-making process, and the interests of the parties comprising the organization are no longer relevant.

That process results in goal displacement: Deterministic and constraint goals exchange places.

18. From Cash to Politics

Deterministic goals are those goals we want to maximize; constraint goals are those conditions we don't want to violate. Serving the market was a deterministic goal in Infancy and Go-Go, while profit was a constraint goal. Dividends were viewed more as payments on a bond—the minimum that had to be paid to the owners in order to keep them from withdrawing financial support. Dividends were not the owners' goals. The owners were looking for stock appreciation, not fast yields. Their goal was to maximize sales while keeping profits at the minimum acceptable level.

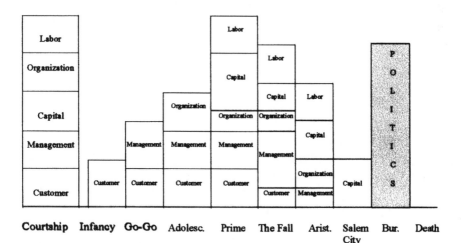

Figure 7-5: Interests Over the Lifecycle

In Adolescent organizations, when profits become a measure of significance and more sales do not necessarily produce more profits, sales are the constraint goal and profits the deterministic goal.

Goal displacement does not come easily. In Adolescence, although profits should be the primary goal, the sales orientation still dominates the culture. Companies become addicted to the sales orientation in Infancy and Go-Go. Back then, more was better. Thus in Adolescent companies, it's hard to know whether profit goals are deterministic or constraint goals. Managers oscillate between focusing on profits and pushing for sales. They want more of each. When, because of their location on the lifecycle, they cannot achieve those incompatible goals, they get annoyed and frustrated with each other.

Prime companies seek and achieve growth in both sales and profits, and for them, both goals are deterministic. The constraint goals—what they should not do—derive from their expansion strategies.

From Prime on, as organizations age, profitability tends to become the deterministic goal, while sales becomes the constraint goal. Instead of satisfying client needs, management learns to make money through interpretive accounting and by responding to the short-run expectations of the stock market. Because profits—measured in earnings per share—are the goal, the investment community takes over the client's position. In companies that are privately-held, the owners become the demanding, rather than the giving, factor. It is now the organization's turn to feed, rather than be fed.

This development sequence is a universal phenomenon. The growing stages are characterized by *giving*. Prime is a stage of *being*. And an aging company is absorbed in *taking*. As people age, they grow more and more egocentric—stingy, demanding, and complaining. What is happening? As the system ages, maintenance requires higher levels of energy just to keep functioning. As the system falls apart, it needs more and more energy to achieve internal cohesion.

As people see their end approaching, they become protective: They egocentrically hoard time, money, and anything else they can. Likewise, as organizations age, they take more and give less. They invest less in the future, milking the cash cow to squeeze out whatever is there.

As a company ages, its managers act as if it exists in the marketplace mainly to produce profits. They cut services—advertising, promotions, and research and development—in order to maximize those profits. In the process, they also eliminate the factors that stimulate flexibility and enterpreneurship.[27] Since the organizational climate encourages short-term profitability, those who promote that goal enhance their standing in the company's political power bank. There are fewer people fighting to have resources allocated for change that can promise only long-term results, and the cultural climate has no interest in long-term yields. People who activate change step on too many toes. The others label them insensitive and accuse them of not being team players. For their efforts they find themselves politically isolated and functionally insulated. Eventually, they stop trying, quit, or get fired.

With aging, the system shortens its horizon; it becomes short-term oriented.

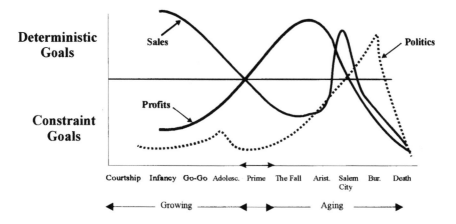

Figure 7-6: Deterministic vs. Constraint Goals Over the Lifecycle

When the organization ages, it is milking time. Owners rush to extract a return on their investment. They want the shortest payback they can get. As a result, they consume not just the fat, but the flesh as well. As they downsize, they often sacrifice what's left of the remaining vitality.

When the company reaches the advanced stage of aging, the stage I have named Salem City, the witch hunts start, and the goals change once again. Now everyone focuses on individual—not organizational—survival. People no longer strive for dividends, return on investment, or sales. They worry about who will survive and who will get fired. They are like senile, old men who no longer feel commitment even to their own wives. They are concerned only about their personal peace of mind and health. In aging organizations, politics devour most of the managerial energy.

In Bureaucracy, there is blissful silence. By that time, the organization is under a proctorship, and there is nothing to fight for. In order to survive or be promoted, one only need go through the motions. As long as people behave by the book, they have nothing to worry about. If you lie low, make no waves, and neither offend nor threaten—as long as you avoid confrontations—you might even become the chief administrator. Your primary goal is to be a political asset, not a liability.

Lifecycle Stage	Deterministic Goal	Constraint Goal
1. Infancy	1. Cash	1. Quality of the founder's personal life
2. Go-Go	2. Sales measured in market share and profits	2. None—if the founder can get away with it. He is testing the limits.
3. Adolescence		
4. Prime		
5. Fall	3. Profits	
6. Aristocracy	4. Profits and sales	3. Sales in dollars
7. Early Bureaucracy	5. Protection of the status quo	4. Strategic decisions
8. Bureaucracy	6. Return on investment	5. Not to make waves
	7. Personal survival	6. Sales in unit terms
	8. Political power	7. Political goals
		8. Political constraints

Let us now describe the manifestations of aging and what happens at every stage of an aging organization.

Notes

1. For a more extensive treatment, see I. Adizes, *The Pursuit of Prime* (Santa Monica: Knowledge Exchange, 1996).

2. See L. Marchall, S. Mobley, and G. Claver, "Why Smart Organizations Don't Learn," in S. Chawla and J. Renesch, *Learning Organizations: Developing Cultures for Tomorrow's Workplace* (Portland, OR: Productivity Press, 1995). These authors argue that risk management is related to organizational learning: specifically C. Argyris's notion of single- and double-loop learning provides a process for assessing risk, "Teaching Smart People How to Learn," *Harvard Business Review* 69, 3 (May-June, 1991): 99-109. Consistent with Argyris, the Adizes methodology provides a way for organizations to institutionalize double-loop learning, maintaining Prime.

3. This reflection is consistent with those practices advocated by D. Schön and M. Rein, *Frame Reflection: Toward the Resolution of Intractable Policy Controversies* (New York: Basic Books, 1994). In this book, these authors show how reflection not only on events, but the way events get framed, leads to conflict reduction and second-order change.

4. See D. Breunlin, "Oscillation Theory and Family Development," in C. Falicov, *Family Transitions: Continuity and Change Over the Life Cycle* (New York: Guilford Press, 1988): 133–158. He describes an "oscillation theory" which predicts the oppositional swings in systems over the aging process—whereas the young are risk-takers, the aged are risk-avoiders.

5. See B. Carter, M. McGoldrick, and G. Ferraro, *The Changing Family Life Cycle: A Framework for Therapy* (Boston: Allyn and Bacon, 1989), particularly their "Overview" chapter, pp. 3–28. They make the point very clearly that systems have transitions that are sequenced; tasks pertinent to one stage in the sequence may not be at all functional in another stage. While organizations are not families, the analogy of the "system" is useful here.

6. See A. Donellon and M. Scully, "Will the Post-Bureaucratic Organization Be a Post-Meritocratic Organization?" in C. Heckscher and A. Donellon, eds., *The Post-Bureaucratic Organization: New Perspectives on Organizational Change* (New York: Sage, 1994). In this article, the authors critique the reward system that is found in bureau-

cratic organizations, arguing that it limits team effectiveness. Instead, they advocate a post-meritocracy system that supports interdependence and focuses on skill development and more egalitarian salary structures. They also report data from a study by Donellon (1992), "The Meaning of Teamwork" (manuscript), that extrinsic rewards alone do not provide sufficient motivation for high performers; these people reported needing challenging work.

7. See J. Baron and K. Cook, "Process and Outcome: Perspectives on the Distribution of Rewards in Organizations," *Administrative Science Quarterly* 37 (1992): 220–240. They discuss the differences between reward systems that focus on outcomes and those that focus on processes.

8. See O. Mink, *The Behavioral Change Process* (New York: Harper & Row, 1970), and later writings by Oscar and Barbara Mink, for comments on the benchmarking process.

9. See G. Bateson, *Mind and Nature: A Necessary Unity* (New York: Dutton, 1979), for reference to this interdependence. Also see R. Donaldson's edited version of G. Bateson's work, *A Sacred Unity: Further Steps to an Ecology of Mind* (New York: HarperCollins, 1991).

10. This is equivalent to what P. Watzlawick, in *Pragmatics of Human Communication: A Study of Interactional Patterns, Pathologies and Paradoxes* (New York: Norton, 1967), referred to as "negative feedback," or information that was designed to reduce deviation. They also note that many systemic problems result from the use of negative feedback.

11. G. Bateson, in *Steps to an Ecology of Mind* (New York: Ballantine, 1972), has argued that attempts to correct systems by increasing control (as negative feedback) generate pathology.

12. See G. Bateson's, "The New Conceptual Frames for Behavioral Science," in R. Donaldson's *A Sacred Unity.* Here Bateson makes the argument that adaptation is a functional process requiring creative responses to "capricious" environments. He notes that this is an extremely complex process that constantly challenges form.

13. A. Grove, *Only the Paranoid Survive: How to Exploit the Crisis Points That Challenge Every Company and Career* (New York: Doubleday, 1996).

14. See G. Morgan, *Images of Organization* (Beverly Hills, CA: Sage, 1986), for an excellent review of the concept of organizational culture. He ends by noting that organizational cultures are tightly wound around organizational politics which make them very difficult to change. This view is in opposition to C. Hampden-Turner's view in *Creating Corporate Culture: From Discord to Harmony* (San Francisco: Addison-Wesley, 1990). This author has argued that it is possible to change organizational culture, and he offers a six-step procedure for fostering cultural change.

15. See also S. Birley and P. Westhead, "A Comparison of New Businesses Etablished by 'Novice' and 'Habitual' Founders in Great Britain," *International Small Business Journal* 12 (1993): 38–60. In both cases, these authors are examining the ways entrepreneurs interpret "opportunity."

16. See R. Dahrendorf, *Class and Class Conflict in Industrial Society* (Palo Alto: Stanford University Press, 1959). Using a Marxist framework, he argues that tension between management and line staff is inevitable over time in an organization; he notes that the split between authority and responsibility is a result of differences in function, i.e., staff have little control over output, yet they have authority to regulate; line have control over output but no authority to respond to changes in the local environment. This suggests that the struggle in aging organizations can also be understood as a struggle over power.

17. See J. Forester, *Planning in the Face of Power* (Berkeley: UC Press, 1989). This author makes the argument that public policy and planning is a process deeply impacted by power relations between stakeholder groups. From this perspective, effective public policy could only be enacted by facilitating an ongoing dialogue between disparate political and social groups.

18. A new theory of economics developed by Brian Authur of Stanford ("increasing returns" economics) draws on chaos theory. It assumes an unstable environment in which "them that has, gets." The move to prevent decay is typical of a Newtonian approach to economics, as if it would be a machine that would wind down. Instead, the new school calls for an "evolutionary" model. See M. Waldrop, *Complexity: The Emerging Science at the Edge of Order and Chaos* (New York: Touchstone Books, 1992).

19. H. Maturana, *Autopoiesis and Cognition: The Realization of the Living* (Boston: D. Reidel, 1980), has written extensively on the process of "autopoeisis," where systems self-regulate in order to maintain current states of equilibrium. See also F. Varela's *Principles of Biological Autonomy* (New York: Holland Press, 1979) and H. Maturana and F. Varela's *The Tree of Knowledge: The Biological Roots of Human Understanding* (Boston and London: Shambhala Press, 1987). However, Maturana notes that the responsiveness of the system to the environment is limited by the internal conditions, which are aimed at their own reproduction! While organizations are not biological systems, as social systems they also exhibit self-regulation or autopoestic processes, a perspective offered by H. von Foerster, *Principles of Self-Organization* (New York: Pergamon Press, 1962).

20. For more elaborate treatment, see I. Adizes, *Mastering Change: The Power of Mutual Trust and Respect in Personal Life, Family, Business and Society* (Los Angeles: Adizes Institute Publications, 1993).

21. An excellent example is J. Westphal, G. Ranjay, and S. Shortel, *The Institutionalization of Total Quality Management: The Emergence of Normative TQM Adoption and the Consequences for Organizational Legitimacy and Performance* (New York: Addison-Wesley, 1996).

22. For an excellent example of the more process-based approaches to management, see D. Boje and R. Dennehy, "Postmodern Management Principles: Just the Opposite of Modernist-Bureaucratic Principles," in *Proceedings of the International Academy of Business Principles* (Washington, DC: International Academcy of Business Disciplines, 1992): 442–448. Basically, the more humanistic approaches to management are following in the tradition of Mary Parker Follett (c. 1924), *Creative Experience* (New York: Peter Smith, 1951) and M. Follett, *Dynamic Administration: The Collected Papers* (New York: Harper and Brothers, 1942), who recognized the central role that relationships and identity play in organizational processes.

23. See L. Smirich and G. Morgan, "Leadership: The Management of Meaning," *Journal of Applied Behavioral Science* 18 (1982): 257–273. These authors provide a framework for understanding leaders as people who mobilize meaning across the organization, proactively building organizational culture in planned directions.

24. For an interesting discussion of profit orientation, see K. Palepu, "Diversification Strategy, Profit Performance, and the Entropy Measure," *Strategic Management Journal* 6 (1985): 239–255.

25. The integration of stakeholders; interests require communication practices that surface and address differences. See D. Bohm, *On Dialogue* (New York and London: Routledge, 1996), for a description of the dialogue process. The balancing of interests is an ongoing process that is never fully achieved, but it is not the outcome that matters; it is the process.

26. There is an emerging process called "team inquiry" that draws on the use of White's "reflecting team" to create organizational contexts for building relational knowledge. See S. Simon's doctoral dissertation, "Restoring the Organization Using Team Inquiry as a Participatory Action Research Tool to Co-Construct Alternative Approaches to Leadership Within a Sub-Division of a Multinational Manufacturing Corporation," (Santa Barbara, CA: The Fielding Institute, 1998). This process of "team inquiry" balances the interests of multiple parties in the organization and builds trust within and across groups.

27. See M. Peteraf, "The Cornerstones of Competitive Advantage: A Resource-based View," *Strategic Management Journal* 14 (1993): 179–192. This author argues that flexibility is central to ongoing success in competitive environments.

CHAPTER EIGHT
The Aging Organizations: Aristocracy

THE FAR SIDE By Gary Larson

Larson 11-25

"Through the hoop, Bob! Through the hoop!"

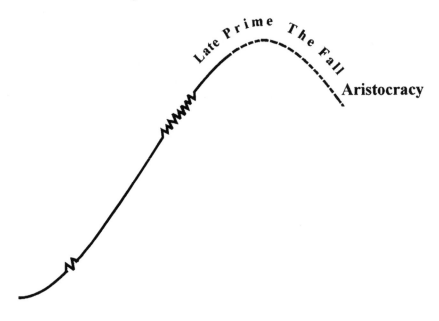

Figure 8-1: Aristocracy

As organizations approach the stage I call Aristocracy, interaction among the people who make up the organization grows increasingly important. People want less conflict, less change. The growing stages, by comparison, encouraged and nourished change even though change introduced conflict. The quality of interpersonal relations was of only minor significance.

To reduce conflict, a company in Aristocracy keeps change to a minimum. There are fewer disagreements and an important "old buddy" network emerges. The lack of conflict produces no noticeably dysfunctional results—yet.[1] The organization is reducing its velocity of change, and it will feel the results later. The organization is engaged in a process of steadily increasing the distance between itself and its clients, and the decline of entrepreneurial spirit leads it from Late Prime to the Fall and eventually to Aristocracy.

Aristocratic organizations characteristically:

- Have reduced their expectations for growth
- Have little interest in conquering new markets, technologies, and frontiers
- Focus on past achievements rather than future visions

- Are suspicious of change
- Reward those who do what they are told to do
- Are more interested in interpersonal relationships than in taking risks
- Spend money on control systems, benefits, and facilities
- Care more about how things are done than they care about what and why things are done
- Value formality in dress, address, and tradition
- Employ individuals who are concerned about the company's vitality, but the operating motto is "Don't make waves"
- Engender only negligible internal innovation; they buy other companies to acquire new products, markets, even entrepreneurship
- Are cash-rich takeover targets

An Aristocratic organization's steadily declining flexibility, which began in Prime, has a long-range effect. The capability to achieve and produce results is also declining. Because it has neglected to pursue long-term opportunities, the company's ability to respond to short-term needs suffers as well. The company produces results, but it cannot anticipate them. Its goals are, for the most part, short-term and low-risk. The organization has sown the seeds of mediocrity.

With less of a long-term view, a new style of organizational behavior emerges. The climate in an Aristocratic organization is relatively stale. What counts is not what people accomplish or do, but how they do it. As long as they lie low, making no waves, they survive and even earn promotions. Their accomplishments—or lack of accomplishments—are not significant factors.

Members of an Aristocratic organization are distinctive. Their behavior is remarkably different from those of other organizations on the lifecycle. Watch how they dress, where they meet, how they utilize space, how they address each other, how they communicate with each other, and how they handle conflict.

Dress Code

In an Infant company, if you can produce, you can wear your clothes inside out. No one will care as long as you get results. By the time the company has reached the Go-Go stage, its people start wearing suits and sport coats with ties, but there is no hard-and-fast dress code. Prime companies require their people to look professional. The suits they wear—with white or blue shirts—are neither too expensive nor too cheap, and the ties all have a certain look. There is a functional uniformity that communicates a premeditated image. By the time the organization is an Aristocracy, only the uniformity remains. It is not necessarily functional to present a desired image. The dress code is there for the sake of uniformity. Management is dressed as if going to a wedding or a funeral. The conservative uniformity of everyone's dress reflects the conservative uniformity of everyone's thinking. Form dominates function in the organizational climate and expresses itself in the furniture, dress code, memos, and the space people utilize.

Meeting Rooms

Where do members of Infant organizations meet? They don't have time for meetings, so there is no formal meeting place. Meetings occur in taxis on the way to airports, in restaurants during meals, in corridors, and in elevators. Go-Go staff members, if they meet at all, do so in the founder's office: at the center of power. Working breakfasts, lunches, and dinners are part and parcel of the Go-Go way of life. Because, by and large, the founder makes all decisions, discussion is abbreviated. People wander from topic to topic, and it is often difficult to understand how the discussion led to a decision.

Adolescence involves many power shifts, and there are many meetings. Instead of being on the road, people are in meetings, deciding responsibilities, rules, policies, information needs, and reward systems. In abnormal Adolescence, the real meetings take place outside the official meetings—in hallways or at people's homes in the middle of the night. The rumor mill reigns over those unofficial meetings.[2] The formal meetings are dull, filled with tension and restrained anger. Behavior is cliquish. Everyone is watching everyone else. Who is talking with whom? Who is having lunch with whom?

By the time a company reaches Prime, it has a highly official meeting room where the executive committee works. The meeting room is furnished for utility more than comfort: sturdy chairs and tables, good lighting, large easels, and white boards with colored markers.

When an Aristocracy plans and designs its boardroom, the results are strikingly different. In a typical conference room, you would almost certainly find a huge, highly polished, dark wood table surrounded by matching plush chairs. The carpet is thick. The lighting is dim, and the windows are heavily draped. From the paneled walls, a larger-than-life portrait of the unsmiling founder looms over the room, as if warning everyone to remember his or her place. Of course, not all Aristocracies keep portraits of their founders on their boardroom walls. Many hang pictures of all their past presidents or very classical pieces of art.

The roar of silence is overwhelming. When participants walk into one of those conference rooms, the dim lights, the uniformly dark suits, and the somber portrait make them feel uncomfortably out of place. How can they possibly tell the corporate leadership, "Hey, guys, we're losing market share." I once worked with a very large bank. Its boardroom was on the most prestigious floor. Its doors were not doors but honest-to-goodness gates: They were two stories high and made to look like the tablets of the Ten Commandments Moses received from God on Mount Sinai. There were no doorknobs. An electronic eye signaled the doors to open whenever someone approached. As I walked toward the bank's boardroom, I had the weird sensation that the gates of heaven were opening for me. A long, long mahogany table, big enough to accommodate as many as thirty people, dominated the room. Each participant sat in a deeply cushioned chair, facing a microphone. The room was dark because heavy drapes shut out the rest of the world. I definitely felt intimidated.

Industrial psychologists point out that space, lights, and color have impact on workers' behavior. Executives are not beyond such influences. The formal boardroom decor orders everyone who enters, "Don't make waves!"

Use of Space

An Infant organization has no space. Everyone shares tables, typewriters, and telephones, and every member of the shoestring operation is very cost-conscious. The personnel of a typical Go-Go company are spread all over town or the country. The sales department is on Main Street, accounting is several miles away in another building, and the headquarters is in another town. Why? The Go-Go is an opportunity-driven company. It does not plan, it reacts. When sales take off, it reacts, renting additional space and hiring new staff. As the Go-Go matures and proceeds to Adolescence, that collection of scattered space acts as a catalyzing influence that fuels the gossip machinery.

The company consolidates its space when it reaches Prime, moving to a location that can accommodate all related operations. The people are proud of the efficient ways they utilize their space. The office space is well-planned, and facilities support the functions for which they were designed. Companies in Prime don't indulge in excessive opulence, luxury, or showmanship.

By the time an organization reaches Aristocracy, however, form has overtaken function. Its empty corridor alone could adequately serve the needs of several Infant companies. The rent for the president's suite—with its private bathroom, dining room, and secretary's office—is probably higher than the rent the company paid for all its facilities back when it was a Go-Go. It's not unusual for a company in Aristocracy to drop a cool million dollars on its president's office, furniture, and decor. One such presidential suite boasted the most lavish bathroom I have seen in my entire life.

How They Address Each Other

The personnel of Infant and Go-Go organizations customarily address one another by their first names. The names people use for one another in an Adolescent company are not fit for print. When an organization reaches Prime, its people use both first and last names. By the time the organization has reached Aristocracy, people at meetings address each other almost exclusively by last name. They become very formal. It's Mr. Smith and Ms. Jones. They may be Bob and Mary inside their offices, but in those formal meeting rooms, the address is formal. In certain countries, formality is accentuated by elaborate military, educational, and social titles: In German cultures it is: Colonel Shwartzer (retired), or Dr. Alexburg (although his Ph.D. is in medieval literature and is completely irrelevant to his position in the company). In Mexico it is Don Alexandro, or

"Senior Vice-President buffington reporting, sir. Requests permission to advance and be recognized."

Licensiado or Inginiero Gonzales. In Italy, people who have completed an undergraduate course of study get addressed with the honorific, "doctor," and in Brazil, simply being an executive earns one that title.

Communication

Discussion during the Courtship stage is characteristically vague. People talk about their thoughts and feelings. They are repetitive; they contradict themselves; they are easily annoyed; and it takes little to insult their sensitivities. In a sharp departure from the romantic meandering people enjoyed during Courtship, Infancy demands that talk be short, straightforward, and occasionally offensive in its brutal honesty. Action speaks for itself, and action speaks louder than words. "Get it done now!!!" is the motto of an Infant organization.

The communications in a Go-Go company are a continuous source of confusion. People make demands whether or not there is somebody who can respond to them. Staff members are expected to do the best they can, but no matter what they do, it's invariably less than what the aggressively arrogant founders expect. Four-letter words are the standard of expression. In Adolescence, paranoia reigns, and everyone is engaged in endless interpretations and reinterpretations of who said what and why.

What a relief it is to work in a company enjoying its Prime. Communication is clear. Everyone knows what, why, when, how, and who. The work is demanding, but achievable. People consider their words. Speaking in deliberate and measured tones, they seem to be weighing the importance of what they say. By the time the company has slipped into Aristocracy, the mode of delivery is the essence—the medium is the message. People speak slowly, but that has nothing to do with the content. Managers overuse visual aids and written communications. During meetings, people hedge, using endless strings of double negatives and qualifiers. "It seems that, under certain circumstances it may be assumed, however, on the other hand, and not necessarily so, we might conclude that…" One leaves such a meeting wondering what really happened. The transcript of meeting proceedings reads like a maze of hints, insinuations, and veiled innuendo. Only the initiated really know what is going on. Problems in Aristocracy are handled the way the Victorians handled sex: Everyone knows it's going on, but nobody will talk about it.

A joke I used to hear in communist countries applies to aging companies: A person comes to a medical center and asks for an eye–ear doctor. "There is no such thing," the nurse says. "There is either an ear-nose-and-throat doctor or an eye doctor. Why do you need one?" she asks. And he answers, "I hear one thing and see something totally different."

If, privately, you ask someone to explain what went on in the meeting, he might tell you, "We're losing our market share." Why don't people come right out and say that? They would have in an Infant or a Go-Go company. They won't because the company's problem has not yet reached an acute condition, and everyone knows how dangerous it is to make waves.[3] So people *hope* that the company will weather the storm. They believe that if the company does survive its current difficulties, it will not be due to any action the company takes. Survival depends, they think, on events beyond their control. "Maybe the government will change the laws." Or, "the competition cannot continue to expand this way. They will certainly experience growth pains." A company in Aristocracy doesn't depend on its own efforts and wits to change situations. Enchanted with its past, it is paralyzed to deal with the future. There is one other reason for the apparent paralysis or the slow-motion approach to problems that require change: The power center is weak.

Weak Decision-Making Bodies

Working with the highest levels of government, I have often been disappointed to find Aristocratic behavior where I had expected control. At the lower levels of government, I am not surprised to see bureaucratic behavior, but I was sure I'd be meeting with the centers of power when I met with prime ministers or presidents. But I, like the employees of an Aristocratic company, was wrong. Employees believe that the president of their company is all-powerful. I expected that from prime ministers. But, like the children's story says, the emperor has no clothes! Leaders of Aristocratic organizations— whether they are governments or corporations—act as if they can do a lot. In reality, however, they can do little quickly. There are so many committees that need to agree and decide. And there are many, many interest centers that need to be coalesced and appeased. It's no wonder that any decision involving change is slow in coming if it comes at all. The leaders of Aristocratic companies do only what politics allow them to do, and as their companies continue to age, that inability to act gets much worse. Those leaders can do nothing that tests the limits of their power. And nobody forces action until problems escalate to crisis levels, and all the parties needed for a decision share the heat.

We can understand this phenomenon with business organizations once we discuss how organizations deal with conflict and cash.

Conflict and Crisis Handling

The way members of an Aristocracy deal as a group with conflict is another factor that distinguishes this stage. Vittorio de Sica illustrated the situation in his 1971 feature film, *The Garden of the Finzi-*

Continis.[4] His film examines the behavior of an aristocratic Italian-Jewish family just prior to World War II. When the Italian Fascists started to persecute Jews, the Finzi-Continis refused to believe that anything serious could happen to them. "We've been here for a long time," they said. "We are one of the most distinguished families in Italy." So they continued to play tennis behind the high walls of their estate, and they ate in their chandeliered dining rooms, continuing business as usual. While individually, each member of the family was terrified, as a group, life went on as always. Enchanted with their past, they were paralyzed to deal with their future. The group dynamics overpowered individual fears.[5]

The Aristocratic corporation behaves similarly. Hidden in their own beautifully opulent high-rises, squandering space as though it costs nothing, the managers are individually worried about the company and its future. In formal meetings, however, none of them would think of assertively voicing apprehensions. When a consultant faces managers collectively and points to competitive threats, they are prone to reply, "Don't worry, we've been here long enough. They need us. We have a name, tradition, and know-how." But individually, the managers agree with the consultant. The situation is bad, and someone (usually someone else) should do something. In one organization, managers explicitly said, "We don't like to compete. We'd rather serve." They doom themselves to repeat tomorrow what they did yesterday.

A sclerotic person gets treatment for his ills. A sclerotic organization is impressed with its state of health.

VLADIMIR BULATOVIC

The Aristocratic company denies the current reality. While it is losing market share and is increasingly incapable of competing with products or marketing skills, its members maintain their business-as-usual attitude. They feel obliged to maintain the company's track record, matching its historical performance. "We must distribute dividends. We cannot afford to disappoint the widows and orphans who have invested in us." So they distribute X dollars per share every year, and X becomes an increasingly larger share of their profits.

I worked with a company that declared dividends amounting to 93 percent of the year's earnings, even though its product was becoming obsolete and the company had no new products in development. This was organizational suicide. I asked, "How come?" The answer was typically Aristocratic. "We plan top-down, teleologically and structurally. It works like this: Top management decides how much return it should give shareholders. From that, managers determine how much profit the company needs to show, and how much profit each unit has to contribute, its sales goals, and the acceptable level of expenses."

Please note: The process they described had nothing to do with what was happening in the marketplace. Such behavior is self-centered, arrogant, aristocratic, and detached, and it can happen only when companies think they can operate as if they exist in a vacuum. In reality, because the units could not meet the sales targets, the profit goals were also unattainable. Nevertheless, top management felt

"And though in 1979, as in previous years, your company had to contend with spiralling labor costs, exorbitant interest rates, and unconscionable government interference, management was able once more, through a combination of deceptive marketing practices, false advertising, and price fixing, to show a profit which, in all modesty, can only be called excessive."

obliged to meet its annual commitment to distribute dividends at a certain level.

Aristocracies, by and large, attempt to increase profits by raising revenues rather than by cutting costs. And they raise revenues, not by increasing unit sales, but by raising prices. Raising prices in the face of declining market share is as dangerous as throwing gasoline onto a fire. It only accelerates the company's slide into the next stage of aging—Salem City.[6] And, as you might guess, in Salem City witch hunts are commonplace.

From time to time, Aristocratic cultures do cut expenses, but they do that only if they have no alternative. What's more, they eliminate only the most trivial expenditures. In a moment of rage, a frustrated executive once told me, "They are trying to clean up a whorehouse by kicking out the piano player!" But that was ten years ago. Nowadays, downsizing is how companies cut expenses. At the time that I was writing the first edition of this book, only companies in their death throes would resort to downsizing. In the last ten years, however, companies have downsized prior to having crises manifested in their financials. Companies appear to be more proactive and less patient than they had been in the past.

Mergers and Acquisitions

Aristocratic organizations are more than cash-rich. They are cash-heavy. If you compute the Dun & Bradstreet ratios of Aristocratic and Prime organizations, the Aristocratic ratios are higher. Aristocracies are conservative and liquid. Their internal units make few demands for investments. The prevailing sense of organization-wide complacency overpowers aggressive aspirations of any individuals. People rarely propose a risk-taking endeavor. The Aristocratic organization uses its cash to acquire growth, externally.

When they go shopping for acquisitions that will fuel their growth, what do Aristocracies buy? Not Infants. "They're too young and risky!" Not Adolescents. "They're too problematic!" Not Primes. "They're too expensive!" Normal Aristocracies buy Go-Go companies. Go-Gos and their new technologies in growing markets are very attractive to Aristocracies, and the Go-Gos, tired of trying to get organized and having to grow using their own resources, are receptive to offers. They figure an Aristocracy can make everything easier because it is bigger, richer, and more organized.

What really happens? Every time the new acquisition wants to make a move, it has to submit a budget and a business plan to the board. Because it always takes the board of an Aristocratic company time to do anything right, by the time it approves the action, the Go-Go—accustomed to moving quickly—finds that it's already too late. The opportunity has evaporated. It doesn't take long for key managers of the Go-Go to take off, leaving a shell of a company behind. A Go-Go's biggest asset is its entrepreneurs, and when the Aristocracy appoints one of its own administrators to run the Go-Go, even the remnant of entrepreneurial spirit might be lost.

However, Aristocracies are not always the acquirers. Being cash-heavy, they are themselves attractive takeover targets. And what kind of company will want to acquire an Aristocracy? A Go-Go organization. In their eagerness to grow, and with arrogance as to their capabilities, Go-Gos have limitless appetites.

In either case, it's difficult to make a good marriage. When the Aristocratic organization buys a Go-Go, the latter suffocates. What made the Go-Go exciting and vigorous was its flexibility—its high-speed decision-making. Go-Gos are apt to make most decisions intuitively, and they have little respect or patience for ritual. The Aristocratic climate couldn't be more different. The ritual is rigorous: It requires budgets in a certain form, by a certain time, and with certain details. Go-Gos find all that stifling.

When a Go-Go acquires an Aristocratic organization, it is like a small snake that swallowed a very large gopher. Digestion takes a very long time. The Go-Go is overwhelmed by the problems of the Aristocratic organization, and the leadership discovers that milking cash out of the Aristocratic company will not move it back to Prime. What remains is only a bankrupt Aristocracy. The vigorous Go-Go management introduces sudden and forceful waves of change that may paralyze the Aristocrats with fear, making a workable merger even more difficult. Furthermore, while it is trying to digest its latest prey, the Go-Go may sacrifice its own growth momentum and orientation for several years. If the Aristocracy is very old, and the Go-Go company cannot easily solve the problems inherent in old age, the Aristocratic organization gradually consumes the Go-Go executive's time, putting both companies in jeopardy.

If a cash-heavy Aristocracy cannot acquire a Go-Go, it may merge with another Aristocracy, compounding its problems.[7] Recent studies of conglomerates show that by and large, the anticipated synergies do not occur. I don't find that at all surprising. Mergers always introduce culture clashes, and only the best trained and talented manager is prepared for and able to handle them.

The Silence Before the Storm

The product lines of companies in the advanced stages of Aristocracy are out of date. The clients know it; the sales people know it; and even the chief executive knows it. Still, nobody does much about it. People file their complaints. Management holds endlessly nonproductive meetings. In short, everyone is waiting for someone else to do something. In an effort to save their necks, many people leave the organization. Those who, lacking attractive opportunities, cannot leave, accuse the deserters of disloyalty.

A sense of doom pervades the organization. The company tries to lift morale by awarding gold medals for obscure achievements or by holding seminars in resort hotels where most of the time is spent vacationing, not working. Many Aristocracies react to the overpowering sense of impending calamity by building expensively elaborate and unnecessary new buildings. Managers spend on form as if it affects the content. We see similar behavior in some failing marriages. Some couples try to repair their relationship by making new commitments, such as having a child or building a new house. They confuse cause and effect, input with output. A baby or a new house should be expressions of commitment. A couple cannot expect that building a new house or having a child will create commitment. Such acts should satisfy functional needs rather than follow form. Form cannot cause function. It must follow function.

What causes the Finzi-Contini syndrome? Why do people hint about the problems, expecting and waiting for someone else to do something about them? Everyone knows what is happening. Privately, people analyze their problems with remarkable acuity. So why doesn't management provide leadership and act? My theory explains that behavior focuses on what I call "the present value of a conflict." We know that the value of a dollar received a year or ten years from now is not equal to a dollar received today. We calculate the present value of a stream of income over time. The same might hold true for the cost of a declining market share or a future problem. A problem in the future is not so costly as the same problem facing us today. The anticipated, dreaded future might never occur.

This old story illustrates my point. Many years ago, a Sultan's officers threw two thieves into jail, and their executions were immediately scheduled. One of the thieves sent the Sultan a message, saying that if he were given three years, he could teach the Sultan's favorite horse to speak. "How can you promise that?" the other thief asked him. "You can't teach a horse to speak!"

"You never know," the first responded. "In three years, the Sultan might die, the horse might die, or maybe the horse will speak!"

Like the scheming thief, Aristocratic organizations are playing for time. Yes, they are losing market share, but right now, with their resources, that's a minor factor. In the future, they say, who knows? The government might change, government policies might change, the competition could go broke, or customers might change their taste in goods. Maybe they will survive or even flourish. Note: They do not rely on their own efforts to survive. They count on the environment's turning in their favor. Some time ago, a senior banker told me a joke about a country I'll call Calico. It easily applies to every country, corporation, or individual human being.

Waiting for . . . (?)

"As we all know," the banker said, "Calico has deep economic problems. There are two possible solutions to these problems. One is rational. The other is a miracle. The rational solution is that Saint So-and-So will come down from heaven and save Calico." I interrupted him. "If that's the rational solution, what could the miracle possibly be?" He continued, "It will be a miracle if the Calician people get off their butts and start working really hard."

By the standards of that joke, Aristocracies have rational solutions to all their serious problems.

Compare it with another joke that applies to Go-Go companies: A guy comes to his friend's store and says, "I was so sorry to hear that you had a fire in your store." And the store owner leans toward him and whispers, "Shhh . . . It's tomorrow."

Go-Gos take charge of their lives. Aristocracies want
the environment to become favorable.

Why, rather than taking action, do Aristocracies rely on external factors? The problems of the future are not yet pressing. The company is liquid and profitable. Taking action now means making waves and becoming embroiled in a political fight. And the individual who has the temerity to make waves has to pay the price of causing an uproar today—not three years in the future. The political costs of making waves today is higher than the present value of solving future problems.

With the concomitant decreasing sense of control, people allude to problems, hoping that someone else will do something. That's what consultants are for. The organization hires them to say what it doesn't dare admit itself. Management lets someone else "take the chestnuts out of the fire." And how do the executives react to the consultants' reports? They read them, but they take no action until Salem City—the next stage of aging—sets in. During that stage, the erstwhile future problems become current problems, and immediate action is no longer optional. By that time, however, the Sultan's horse still refuses to talk. It is kicking, and kicking hard. Market share is shrinking; cash flow is negative; and good people are streaming away. All the vital signs of an organization are screaming, "Emergency!"

Desperate over continually declining market share, revenues, and profits, the Aristocratic organization enters Salem City. This is not a gradual transition. It is quick and forceful. The Aristocracy has been covering its losses through acquisitions and by raising prices. As the prices go up, the number of units sold goes down. When management first raises prices, revenues climb, but eventually, the demand curve becomes inelastic. Now, the increase in price reduces quantity sold to the point that total revenue is now lower than before the price was raised. The organization has expended all the goodwill it had so painstakingly started building from its Infancy. The price increases—artificial facelifts—stop working because they are not the real way to increase revenues. The real thing is satisfaction of client needs—providing real value.

The day of reckoning arrives: The company cannot raise prices another penny, and acquisitions are no longer possible. The truth surfaces rapidly. Then the niceties are gone. Knives are drawn, and the fight for individual—not organizational—survival begins. Caution! You are entering Salem City.

Notes

1. There is considerable research that suggests that conflict is a generative process—the process of addressing differences leads to increased trust and organizational learning. See D. Sandole and H. Van der Merwe, eds., *Conflict Resolution Theory and Practice: Integration and Application* (New York: Manchester University Press, 1993). There are several articles in this volume that address the constructive nature of conflict. See also D. Schön and M. Rein, *Frame Reflection: Toward the Resolution of Intractable Policy Controversies* (New York: Basic Books, 1994). From the perspective of these writings, the absence of managed conflict is symptomatic in an organization.

2. There is some literature to suggest that informal channels of communication (gossip) are useful for organizations, in that they promote innovation. See C. Conrad, *Strategic Organizational Communication: Culture, Situations, and Adaption* (New York: Holt, Rinehart, Winston, 1985; 1990), particularly Chapter 7, "The Personal-interpersonal Dimension of Organizational Communication: Foundations and Assumptions," pp. 55–186. However, research also suggests that organizational gossip can have a destructive effect on its culture, if this informal channel replaces the formal lines of communication. Kreps writes, "The less the formal organization is used to provide relevant information to organizational members, the more they depend on the grapevine for information, and the more powerful the grapevine becomes." [G. Kreps, *Organizational Communication* (New York: Longman Press, 1990): 201.]

3. See M. Witten, "Narrative and the Culture of Obedience at the Workplace," in D. Mumby, ed., *Narrative and Social Control: Critical Perspectives* (New York: Sage, 1993). In this article, she describes how

a culture of obedience which silences dissension is created and maintained.

4. A. Cohn and G. Lucari, prods., *The Garden of the Finzi-Continis,* written by G. Zavattani, V. Bonicelli and V. Pirro, based on a novel by G. Bassani (Warner Brothers: 1971).

5. This process of "groupthink" has been described in the literature as detrimental to effective decision-making. See I. Janis, *Victims of Groupthink: A Psychological Study of Foreign-Policy Decisions and Fiascoes* (Boston: Houghton Mifflin, 1967).

6. I chose in this edition the name "Salem City," borrowing from Arthur Miller's 1956 play *The Crucible,* which depicts a witch hunt where innocent women were victimized by the collective in Salem; see also, A. Huxley, *The Devils of Loudun* (London: Chatto & Windus, 1952), who analyzes the psychology behind a similar event in France during the same years, in a period when modern bureaucracy is beginning to take shape. Huxley shows the connections between the collective hysteria and the functions of bureaucracy.

7. See the very interesting account of such a merger in C. Hampden-Turner, *Creating Corporate Culture: From Discord to Harmony* (New Jersey: Addison-Wesley, 1990), particularly "The Year of Ideas," Chapter 6, pp. 125–138.

CHAPTER NINE

The Final Decay: Salem City, Bureaucracy, and Death

Salem City

Companies in Salem City exhibit the following characteristic behavior:

- People focus on *who* caused the problems, rather than on *what* to do about them. Problems get personalized.
- Rather than dealing with the organization's problems, people are involved in interpersonal conflicts, backstabbing, and in discrediting each other.
- Paranoia freezes the organization.
- Internal turf wars absorb everyone, and nobody has time to deal with the needs of external customers.

The Witch Hunt

If an Aristocracy prolongs its complacency with the status quo, its artificial repairs—unjustifiable price hikes, for example—eventually have negative effects. Demand becomes inelastic, revenues decline, and market share steadily contracts. Watching in horror, management's mutual admiration society dissolves. The good-old-buddy days of the Aristocracy are gone, and the witch hunt begins.

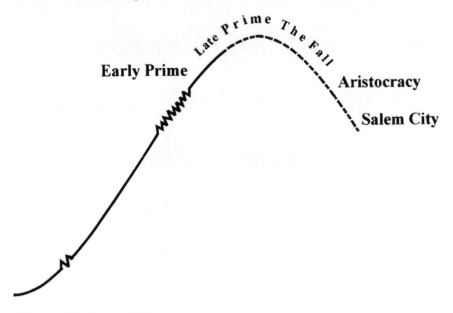

Figure 9-1: Salem City

Everyone is busy trying to find out who caused the disaster. With blades drawn, it's backstabbing time in the boardroom. Like primitive tribes afflicted by extended drought or famine, there's a rush to appease the gods. The organization needs a sacrifice: the fairest maiden, the finest warrior, the cream of the crop. Whom does it sacrifice? Management sacrifices its most valuable and scarcest treasure—the last vestiges of creativity. The company fires the head of marketing, explaining, "We're in the wrong market with the wrong products." The corporate strategist and the engineering chief are the next to find themselves out on the street. Management dismisses them, saying, "Our strategy does not work. Our products, technology, and advertising are obsolete."

The people who get fired as if they were causing the problems don't feel they are responsible for the company's situation. The marketing head has often said that the company ought to change its direction. The strategist has most likely developed an ulcer worrying about the lack of organizational direction. Privately, they complained, urged, begged, and threatened, but it was like pushing wet spaghetti up a hill. Those who seek to reform their Aristocratic organizations from within, do so at the risk of their careers. The organization ends up forcing them out whether or not their efforts were effective. Eventually, the creative employees—those the organization needs most for survival—leave, become useless and discouraged, or get fired.

One factor distinguishes the Aristocratic organization from Salem City: managerial paranoia. In the Aristocratic organization, silence precedes the storm. People smile. They are friendly, handling one another with kid gloves. In Salem City, when the bad results are inescapable and undeniable, managers start fighting each other. No gloves. Bare knuckles. They initiate a ritual of human sacrifice. Someone must take the blame. Someone must be the sacrificial lamb. Annually or even every few quarters, someone takes the blame for the company's bad condition and gets fired.

There is a joke that one hears in companies in trouble. A new chief executive is hired to replace the head of a troubled company. In transferring the task, the exiting executive tells his replacement that in the drawer are three numbered envelopes. Should the new chief encounter a major problem, he should open one envelope at a time. The incoming executive remembers the advice, and, not long after, the first crisis did arrive. The new chief executive opened the first envelope. It said, "Blame everything on one of your vice presi-

"Ms. Ryan, send me in a scapegoat."

dents." Soon, the second disaster struck. He opened the second envelope. It said: "Blame this on another vice president or the unions." Not much later, the third crisis arose, and he opened the last envelope. The instructions started, "Get three envelopes..." Because nobody really knows who will be the next sacrificial lamb, everyone is enveloped in paranoia—even the chief executive officer, who is scared of his board.[1] Everyone watches everyone else with suspicion. Cover-your-ass strategy dominates behavior.

The poisonous atmosphere encourages the circulation of outrageously far-fetched rumors. If, for instance, the sales manager announces a discount, the other executives don't interpret it in rational terms by referring to competitive conditions. Instead, they attribute the move to the sales manager's Machiavellian strategy to discredit the marketing department and expose the incompetence of the marketing vice president.

The paranoia accentuates and accelerates the decline. Managers fight each other, spending most of their time building cliques and coalitions that are constantly changing. They expend their creative energies in a fight for personal survival. Individual security, they know, depends on eliminating and discrediting internal "competition." Organizational performance continues its relentless decline, and the paranoia intensifies. Talented people, objects of fear and distrust, either get fired or leave. This cycle of vicious behavior continues until the company ends up bankrupt or becomes a full-fledged Bureaucracy, subsidized by the government.

Bureaucracy: The Clinically Sustained Life

Subsidization or nationalization can extend the company's life. Although it should be dead, the company is kept alive artificially, introducing a third Z, connoting birth, on its lifecycle curve. The first Z appeared after Courtship: The organization was born by taking risk. The second Z occurred after Go-Go, when, emancipated from founding parents and entering Adolescence, the company is born a second time. This third Z is a new birth: The company should have died, but with an artificial life-support system, it is getting a continuance on its life.

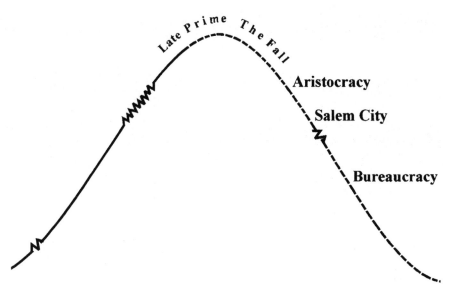

Figure 9-2: Bureaucracy

What kinds of people remain in such a protective environment? Administrators! Entrepreneurs come and go; administrators accumulate. Since the administrators have only to administer, the company is a full-blown Bureaucracy, focusing only on rules and policies. It shows no interest in improving results by satisfying customer needs.

In the Bureaucratic stage, companies are incapable of generating sufficient resources on their own. They justify their existence by the simple fact that they are of interest to another entity willing to support it: the politicians. The organization requires artificial life-support systems to fend off death. Where does it come from? Political decision.

What is the Bureaucratic organization like? What is the artificial support system like?

The Bureaucratic organization:

- has many systems, but they serve little functional purpose;
- disassociates from its environment, focusing on itself;
- has no sense of control; and

- forces its customers to develop elaborate approaches in order to bypass or break through system roadblocks.

A manager told me this joke about a man who went to Paris, wanting to find the best jewelry store in town. He asked his friend for advice. The friend told him, "Go to Rue La Michele, 25. I've heard that is the best place." So the fellow agreed and headed out for Rue La Michele, 25, where he was greeted at the door by a valet dressed in a red uniform with golden epaulets and shiny buttons. The valet tipped his hat and asked, "May I help you, sir?"

"I'd like to buy some jewelry."

"Left door," the red-uniformed valet instructed.

He entered the left door, and another valet, this one dressed in blue, asked, "Are you looking for men's or ladies' jewelry?"

"Ladies'," he replied, and he was ushered down the right corridor where yet another valet, dressed in purple, asked if he preferred gold or silver.

"Gold," he answered.

"Take the corridor to your right, please." Subsequently, he encountered three other valets who asked him his preference on several other things, and pointed him from one to the other in the proper direction. Finally, the last valet asked if he wanted diamonds or rubies.

"Rubies."

"Left door, please." He opened the door and found himself in the street. Frustrated, he went back to his hotel and sought his friend.

"How was it?" the friend asked.

"I didn't get to buy anything, but, boy, do they have a system!"

Bureaucratic organizations accomplish very little of any value. They are like broken records, endlessly repeating the same phrases. Ask a question, and the answer will most likely be, "Wait." Or, "Someone will inform you soon." There is rarely a real or a prompt answer. Bureaucratic managers are among the nicest people you'll ever meet. In public, they couldn't be more agreeable, but they do little if anything, and usually little ever happens. With no inclination to change and no teamwork, everyone's day is filled with systems, forms, procedures, and rules.

One of Bureaucracy's most distinctive characteristics
is its worship of the written word.

The response to a client's request or even another executive's suggestion is almost always, "Write me a memo." But writing to a Bureaucratic organization is usually a waste of time, paper, and stamps. Everything ends up getting filed. When it was nearly too late, one of my clients discovered that his company had filed a letter in which the writer had threatened to sue unless his complaint was expedited. A clerk had stamped the letter "received on" and filed it. Asked why the letter had gone unanswered, the file clerk explained that it lacked certain required information.

Bureaucratic companies are disintegrated. Nobody in the Bureaucracy knows everything that should be done. Everyone has a small piece of the necessary information, and it's up to the client to put it all together. New employees don't know salary policies; salespeople don't know marketing strategy; marketing people don't know the strategic plan; finance doesn't know what sales to anticipate; production has no idea how well products are selling; and the customer doesn't know where to get effective attention. The customer service department often consists of a switchboard operator whose job it is to listen, record complaints, and answer them with a standard, routine letter: "We regret any inconvenience, but we will do our best to . . ." Mostly they respond to clients' efforts for satisfaction by demanding yet another document. Bureaucracies do not ask in advance for everything they will require. Rather than show its entire hand, a Bureaucratic organization shows only one card at a time.

Disassociation

People of a certain age remember their youth as if it were yesterday, but they easily forget what they ate for breakfast. Bureaucratic organizations are similar. People know all the rules, but they can't remember why they exist. If you ask why they do things in a certain way, managers in a Bureaucracy will likely tell you, "I don't know why," or more commonly, "Because it's a corporate policy."

Bureaucracy runs on ritual, not reason.

Like an older person who avoids disruption and cannot endure the grandchildren for more than a few hours, Bureaucracies resent outside interruptions so much that they aggressively create obstructions to outside interference. Customers are considered distractions. They work to isolate themselves from the environment, connecting to the external world through very narrow channels. Perhaps they allow only one incoming telephone line or they keep their customer service departments open for only a few hours a day. They keep people standing in lines, only to tell them where they must next report.

Lack of Sense of Control

What causes that disassociation? Why are Bureaucracies incapable of action? Executives feel they cannot do or accomplish much, but they know they must perform rituals as if they were accomplishing something. In order to make things happen, one needs the cooperation of others, a near impossibility in a Bureaucracy. A single executive cannot mobilize people across organizational lines. Rituals must substitute for action. Meetings take place. Minutes are taken. Papers get filed. There is plenty of voting, and debates rage but one sees little, if any, action.

Bypass System

To get results from such an organization, a client must do the legwork. It seems as if the organization's nervous system has broken down. The left hand does not know what the right hand is doing. One department rejects what another one requests. The client is puzzled, frustrated, and lost.

How do older people function when their organs, one by one, stop working efficiently? Their families put them in a protective environment—a hospital—where the experts connect them to machines that bypass the ineffective organs. Similarly, businesses that need to work with a Bureaucracy usually have special departments, fully staffed to provide bypass systems. Such departments go by different names. Some organizations forthrightly call them their government-relations offices. In others, they are disguised as public relations. When these departments become experts on the inner workings of a particular government agency, they divide responsibilities. Mr. A works with undersecretary Y; Ms. B works with bureau director Z. Because it is highly likely that Y and Z will not always agree or know how to work together, A and B decide what they want, and they help Y and Z reach the "right" decisions.

Following a lecture I gave in India, a company president came up to me and said, "You Americans talk about marketing strategies. That is irrelevant to us. What is crucial to our success is understanding the government's inner workings. Government policies on licensing, pricing, import quotas, and labor relations can make or break us. To know how to manipulate government rulings and regulations is far more important to our success than even the most successful marketing strategy. If a company can make the government machinery work in its favor, it gains the critical competitive edge. Those who have to develop know-how about the government and its working relationships, have to develop connections. Because that is so difficult, they are competitively disadvantaged. Government bureaucracy is my best ally. It is my best barrier against competition—better than any market positioning that you are talking about."

The health of full-fledged Bureaucracies is very delicate. Although they appear to be dangerous monsters, it may be relatively easy to destroy them. Many are rotten to the core, teetering on the brink of bankruptcy. Any sudden change could ruin them. Bureaucracies forced to reorganize quickly do not often survive the effort. A new computer may throw a Bureaucratic system into a spin. Since they get their financial resources from politicians, they survive as long as they are political assets. When they become political liabilities, and the funds are withdrawn, they collapse promptly.

Because bureaucracies rely on laws that provide them with a monopoly on services and allocation of funds generated by taxation, heads of bureaucracies spend more time in halls of government and with politicians than they spend on the line, where customers are served.[2] They have to watch the source of their funds, and that is not customer satisfaction. They depend on the satisfaction of politicians. What annoys politicians the most is negative press. So, heads of bureaucracies are careful to assure that there is no negative press about their agencies. Ask people in a bureaucratic organization, "Who is your client?" The answers: a state or federal agency that either supervises its performance or allocates its budget; the newspapers; other media; the unions; or other Bureaucracies on which it depends for data. Lost on an endless list of stakeholders are the real customers who need to be served.

When the law changes, when the monopoly is lost, when the share of taxes stop coming in, when the Bureaucracy is privatized, the organization confronts a crisis with lights flashing and sirens wailing.

Bureaucracies have no client orientation or sensitivity to client needs. They lack cost accounting or other information about cost-value relationships. There are no performance appraisals based on results achieved in the marketplace. There are no sales efforts because in a monopoly, there was no need to sell. There is no marketing research, no service, and no product development. There is nothing that resembles business structure or culture. It is as if someone took a manufacturing plant—a part of a business organization—and overnight established it as a stand-alone business organization that should survive in a competitive environment: It has no sales, no marketing, no economic analysis—nothing to enable it to make or implement decisions of a competitive nature.

I have consulted in privatization efforts in Eastern Europe and in the commercialization of a privatized company in Mexico. Such efforts are akin to taking a burn victim through intensive care and multiple skin grafts. A single treatment won't help. Such efforts require successive treatments, each creating and nurturing another missing entrepreneurial piece. It is not enough to train managers in accounting so that they know what profits are all about. It isn't enough to develop a stock market so that they understand how equity grows. Nor is it enough to train them in marketing theory and practice. To deliver business-based decisions, privatized bureaucracies need to develop entrepreneurial capabilities, anchored in a business-like structure.

Bureaucratic organizations—if they are allowed to operate isolated from the external environment—may survive a protracted coma. Monopolies and government agencies—quarantined from competitive pressure—endure indefinitely. Because, for example, no one dares eliminate an agency that provides employment, some Bureaucratic agencies live very expensive, artificially prolonged lives, evading real death for years.

Years ago, in Brazil, Mexico, and Israel, I encountered an interesting phenomenon. People would report to their government offices every morning, drape their coats over their chairs, and make their desks look busy. Then they would take off for their moonlighting jobs. In the evening, they returned and gathered their things as if they had just finished working, and at the end of every month, they came by to collect their checks.

How can that happen? Where is management? Management might be doing the same thing. That can happen when government's purpose is not to function for the marketplace, but to provide employment and a payroll. The political bribe is financed either by taxes or by the government, which prints the money that feeds the bureaucracies and keeps them alive.

Death

Organizational death is defined as lack of resources to reward members of the organization for working. The organization is dead when no one is willing to show up at work: There is no reason to. Death occurs when no one remains committed to the organization. If there is no viable political commitment to support a languishing industry or a company, death can occur before bureaucratization. When polit-

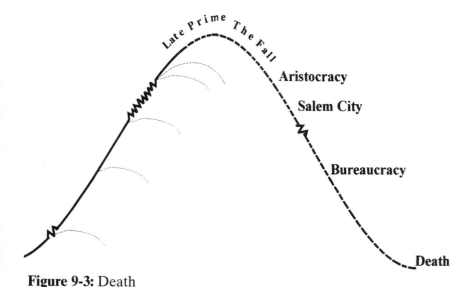

Figure 9-3: Death

"Look, I'm dying. Gotta go."

ical interests keep it alive, a Bureaucracy's death can be prolonged indefinitely. If it had to depend on its disgruntled clients, the Bureaucracy would be long gone.

How to Decide Where a Company Is on the Lifecycle Curve

You are as young as your faith, as old as your doubt; as young as your confidence, as old as your fear; as young as your hope, as old as your despair.

DOUGLAS MACARTHUR

Years ago, a friend of mine invited me to measure the age of my heart. I thought that sounded strange. My body and my heart were born at the same time. Wouldn't they be the same age? I learned something new. My friend had a computerized exercise bicycle. He attached a small device to my fingertip, explaining that it would measure my heartbeat. Then he punched my chronological age into the computer. After I had pedaled strenuously for about 20 minutes, the computer informed me how old my heart was.

That's when I realized that all the parts of our bodies do not age at a single rate. Even if I had been born 40 years earlier, my heart could have been older or younger than the hearts of other 40-year-old people. Similarly, some units that comprise organizations age faster than others. An accounting department, for example, can progress from Infancy to Aristocracy in 24 hours, while healthy marketing departments seem to remain in a perpetual Go-Go stage.

As you read about the various stages of the lifecycle, you will find yourself trying to associate them with your own organization and other organizations you know. Don't try to place an organization at a single stage in the lifecycle. Different units of each organization can be at different places. Where the organization is overall is analogous to where a person is behaviorally with respect to his or her age. We have to generalize. We have to examine how each organization as a whole behaves *most* of the time.

You will find there is a distribution within a distribution. For instance, if an organization is in healthy Adolescence, it sometimes exhibits the characteristics of a Go-Go and sometimes those of a

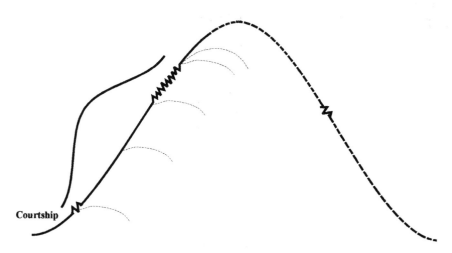

Figure 9-4: Location on the Lifecycle

Prime. Most of the time, however, most of its behavior is that of an Adolescent. That is normal.

What complicates the diagnosis of where an organization is on the lifecycle is that in times of stress, organizations retreat behaviorally to the previous stage of the lifecycle. When an organization, in its collective consciousness, feels confident in itself, it evidences signs of the next phase. This phenomenon, however, helps me analyze whether the organization is advancing or retreating in its development. In the abnormal stages, organizations evidence no signs of moving in desirable directions on the lifecycle. Companies seem to be stuck. When they try to get unstuck, they regress to the previous stage. It is as if they confuse forward with reverse. They retreat to behavior they recognize—behavior that feels comfortable to them. That is usually behavior that, in the past, was successful. It got them to where they are now. They are chronically preoccupied with problems of the present, or worse, of the previous stage. In pathological situations, there is no forward movement whatsoever. The situation is only deteriorating.

The behavior of a healthy organization is normally distributed along the bell-shaped curve of the lifecycle. Some of the time, it behaves as if it were in its previous position in the lifecycle, and some of its behavior reflects the next position. Most behavior, however, is

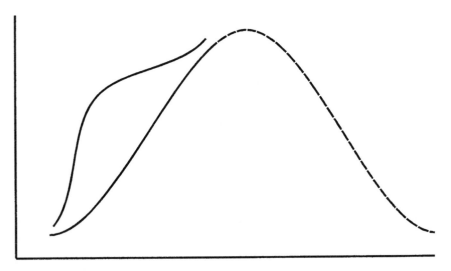

Figure 9-5: Unhealthy Lifecycle

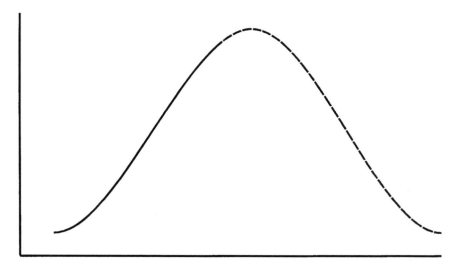

Figure 9-6: Healthy Lifecycle of One Organization

a manifestation of its main position on the curve. If it is healthy, the standard deviation in its behavior is small.

Careful. A Prime could be confused with an unhealthy organization because a Prime organization comprises parts in different stages of the lifecycle. It has some parts that are in Courtship; it has Infant units as well as Go-Gos that get financed by Aristocratic units, and so forth. (See the therapeutic parts of this book for further elaboration.)

An unhealthy lifecycle doesn't have units on different stages. It has the same unit behaving differently at different times: At one point, it acts like Go-Go; and under duress it reverts to Infancy and sometimes it freezes into, would you believe, Bureaucracy. It seems to be suffering from a multiple-personality disorder. A healthy Prime, on the other hand, is an extended family, and its many members act in appropriately different ways but in concert. (See Chapter 17: Treating Organizations on the Typical Path.)

In diagnosing organizations, there is another important point to understand. The abnormal stages of growing organizations resemble the abnormal stages of aging. For example, there is Aristocracy in the founder's or family trap. That complicates the diagnosis. In such cases one sees a mixture of the two behaviors. In the Aristocracy of a family trap, one will see all the signs of Aristocracy as well as the

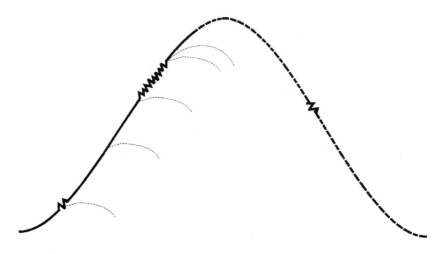

Figure 9-7: Abnormal Locations

signs of the founder's trap. It will be a slow-moving, unresponsive organization, dominated by a family member who behaves like a founder when the real founder has been dead for years. Although its power structure looks like a Go-Go, it behaves like an Aristocracy.

This ends the descriptive part of this book. So that we will understand how to bring an organization to Prime—by balanced growth in its growing stages or by revitalizing it if it has started to age—we now proceed to analyze why organizations behave the way they do.

Notes

1. See J. Westphal and J. Zajac, et al., "Who Shall Govern? CEO/Board Power, Demographic Similarity and New Director Selection," *Administrative Science Quarterly* 40 (1995): 60–83, for a discussion of the complex power dynamics of CEOs and Boards.

2. For a discussion of the complexities of this political process, see E.F. Dukes and F. Dukes, *Resolving Public Conflict: Transforming Community and Governance* (New York: Manchester University Press, 1996). Professor Dukes describe the difficulty that government has in responding to public disputes.

PART TWO

Analyzing
Organizational Behavior

CHAPTER TEN

Tools for Analysis

Now, let's analyze the behavior of organizations on the lifecycle. We'll consider what causes organizations to develop and subsequently to age, what causes flexibility and self-control, and why organizations have the problems described in Part One.

I will present a postulate to explain organizational behavior. I will not prove the postulate beyond demonstrating that it explains what happens in organizations and that its conclusions allow me to introduce organizational changes that foster Prime performance. Like electricity, my postulate is a phenomenon we don't understand. Nevertheless, we know how to use it.

I postulate that all living systems—and every organization is a living system—seek to be effective and efficient in the short and the long run.[1] It is as if they know what they are doing. It is as if conscious forces guide organizations. Human leaders play their roles, but they neither write the script nor can they control it.[2] The players can speed the plot by turning the pages faster; they can even skip pages if they can find the shortcuts. There are reasons why things happen in our bodies, why planets move in their orbits, and why the sun rises and sets. There are reasons for everything. If we don't know the reason for something, we shouldn't make the mistake of thinking that there is none. It means only that we do not understand it yet.

In organizations, what causes behavior is the system's drive for effectiveness and efficiency in the short and the long run. An organization is in Prime when it is both effective and efficient in the short and long run. Organizations seem to drive to Prime, and management, if performed correctly, is the process that facilitates getting there. If, however, management is performed badly, it inhibits, retards, and even blocks this innate tendency to progress to Prime. I once heard that children are born capable of perfection.[3] We the parents can either help the process of its realization or mess it up. We need to know how and when to get out of the way. Similarly, our bodies want to develop and be healthy. They tell us what they want, and each of us could be healthier if only we listened and followed the instructions our bodies give us. The same seems to apply to organizations.

Don't, for one minute, think that I am saying that there is no place for leadership or that we humans are mere puppets in a show we had nothing to do with writing. Not at all. Knowledge of medical science allows us to help or undermine the medical "reasons" for a healthy body. The same holds true for organizations. The role of management is to provide leadership and keep the organization in the healthy part of the lifecycle, preventing or treating abnormal or pathological problems along the way. The role of leadership is to lead the organization to its Prime and sustain it there. For that reason, leaders and those who have chosen the consulting profession need to understand what makes an organization healthy and what makes it sick. They must understand why organizations move along the lifecycle and why they develop normal, abnormal, or pathological problems. They have to know not only how to diagnose problems but also how and when to solve them.

In this section, I present the theory that I have been developing now for over thirty years to explain organizational behavior and to provide the tools for changing that behavior. Those are the tools for directing organizational culture away from abnormal problems, getting the organization on the typical path, moving it toward Prime, and sustaining its position there. As you will see in subsequent chapters, this theory has been tested to produce predictable results by the practitioners of the methodology in over fifteen countries.

Once we understand the movement on the typical path, we will discuss how to get to and advance on the optimal path. (See Chapter 18.)

The Origins

Some thirty years ago, I discovered that for an organization to be effective and efficient in both the short and long run, four managerial roles must be performed. I made that discovery in the course of preparing my doctoral dissertation. I was studying the Yugoslav system of self-management.[4] To Western minds and experience, that system seemed alien. Nobody owned capital. Capital was the heritage of society. The Yugoslavs called it social ownership. That doesn't mean government ownership. The ownership of capital was analogous to the ownership of air. The entire society had access to capital but was not allowed to deplete it. Thus, organizational profits before depreciation had—at the very least—to equal depreciation. Rather than salaries, people received allowances based on a system similar to surplus sharing among the partners of a law firm. Employees elected representatives to the workers council, and the council interviewed candidates for the job of managing director. All the candidates presented plans of what, if elected, they intended to do for and with the company. The elected managing director's term was four years long, but managing directors were subject to impeachment if they acted illegally, say, acting without the authorization of the workers council. Sound familiar?

Yugoslavs applied political democracy to their industrial and non-industrial organizations, and they called that system industrial democracy. The system's weakness was that it discouraged—actually destroyed—the entrepreneurial spirit. Entrepreneurs are individualistic, and few enterprises were able to find managing directors who knew how to take risks under these circumstances.

For all practical purposes, the entrepreneurial spirit was legally prohibited. The system mandated group entrepreneurship or bust. And bust it went. The goal was to create a New Human, whose motivations, according to Karl Marx, would be very different from those of "Old Humans" plagued with exclusive materialistic motivations.[5]

Anyway, the situation proved lucky for me. I was like that British doctor who found himself on a ship with no available sources of vitamin C. When he saw that the sailors, long deprived of vitamin C, suffered from scurvy, the doctor recognized the connection between vitamin deficiency and a predictable disease. Observing organizational behavior in Yugoslavia, I discovered that if a certain role of management, say, entrepreneurship, is suppressed, organizations develop certain predictable managerial "diseases." My book *How to Solve the Mismanagement Crisis*[6] describes the styles of mismanagement that develop when one or more roles are deficient in an organization. The point is that I discovered a diagnostic and therapeutic methodology. Because I could see the relationship between each role and specific kinds of organizational behavior, I was able to identify which role deficiency causes which managerial "diseases."

Input	*Output*	
Management Role	*Makes the organization:*	*Time range*
Purposeful	effective	short run
Administrative	efficient	short run
Entrepreneurial	effective	long run
Integrative	efficient	long run

Using the above model I learned to analyze and diagnose organizational problems. Noting that a company was slow to react to change, I suspected deficiency of the **E**, entrepreneurial, role. On the other hand, I suspected inadequacies in the **A**, administrative, role if a company routinely delivered late, lacked cost controls, or failed to document its engineering approval processes properly. I then discovered that if it were possible for me to "inject" the missing roles, the organization would become effective and efficient in the short run and the long run. And we did so, for instance, taking one company from twelve million dollars in revenues to seven hundred million dollars in revenues without any dilution in ownership. (Today the company's revenues are 1.5 billion dollars.)

Because no organization is "born" in Prime, each one has to develop those roles. As organizations develop the management roles one by one, they follow the typical lifecycle curve, experiencing the problems associated with deficiencies in one or more of those roles. When an organization gets "stuck" and is incapable of developing a particular management role, it experiences abnormal problems. If the development delay is prolonged, the organization's lack of that management role may threaten its ability to survive.

Since organizations develop the four management roles in a predictable sequence, the problems are also predictable, and so is the therapy.

The Four Management Roles

Let us now investigate with some depth what those roles are. Those four necessary roles explain the development of organizational cultures, and in particular, the *why, when,* and *how* of change in the lifecycle.

The P Role

Leadership's first function is the **P** role, which makes the organization effective in the short run. The **P** stands for the organization's **P**urposeful **P**erformance. What is the **P**urpose that must be **P**erformed? Is it profit?

Imagine five people are walking down a narrow path along the top of a mountain. The path is so narrow, they must walk single file. To their right, there is a deep canyon, and to their left, there is a steep incline. They have been walking for hours, singing, joking, laughing, whistling, and talking. In the eyes of an organizational behaviorist, anthropologist, psychologist or social psychologist, the five people are interacting as an organization.

From a management point of view, although we can see that the five have formed a socially interactive organization, we recognize no managerial process until the group encounters a rock so large that it blocks passage and none of the five can move it alone. At that moment, the managerial process begins. Someone needs to plan, organize, motivate, and control (or correct) actions that will allow the group to move the rock. That someone does not necessarily have to be an individual. It can be a team making those decisions. Nevertheless, decisions have to be made that will move the rock: There are processes that need to be performed for a goal to be identified and achieved.

The managerial process exists when there is a task to be performed, a task that requires interdependence among people.

If a single person could lift the rock, there would be no managerial component to the group's organization. If the same five people were walking along the path with a purpose—say, rock climbing or spelunking—that required interdependence, the management process would have started even before they encountered the rock. What if the group simply went to have fun with no explicit plan? So long as there is a purpose, the group needs a managerial process. It needs to articulate, operationalize, and re-articulate that purpose as needs develop. Unless the purpose is to have no purpose, purposes are not realized by themselves. (Come to think of it, it takes effort not to have a purpose too. In Zen Buddhism, they say, it takes a tremendous effort not to think!)

The first role of management is to define or enable a definition of organizational purpose. What is the function for which the organization exists?

Every organization must have a reason to exist. That reason, that "rock," is the focus of interdependency among people.

Whenever I work with an organization I ask the top managers, "Why are you together? What does accounting have to do with marketing, or personnel with research and development? What's the purpose of your organization's existence?" I'm amazed how frequently they tell me that the purpose of their organization is to make profits. That's the wrong answer. I gave this same answer in interpreting the **P** role in *How to Solve the Mismanagement Crisis.*[7]

Economic theory teaches us that the purpose of economic entities—of commerce—is profit. Who dares to argue? However, many organizations are so preoccupied with profits that they go bankrupt. Why? If a company focuses on profits, shouldn't it generate profits? No. That reasoning confuses input with output.

Profit is like love, health, and happiness. If you focus on happiness and say "I must be happy today," you may become quite miserable. If you say "I must be healthy," you may become a hypochondriac. And to say "There must be love" can create a great deal of hate. What you must ask yourself is *what* makes you happy, healthy, or feel that you are in love. That should be your focus. Focus on the inputs in the direction of the output. If you focus on the output and ignore the input, you create expectations that might not be realizable.

If you were playing tennis, the scoreboard would be the profits. Who can play successfully if his eyes are always on the scoreboard? You should ignore the board and *play the best you can.* Follow the ball, and hit it across the net to the opponent's court. Organizations that focus on earnings per share and profit margins, rather than the input and throughput that produce the profit, might be going bankrupt, not in spite of, but because of all their focus on profit. They are failing to keep their eyes on the ball.

If you hit the ball effectively—repeatedly and efficiently (for which the other three roles are also necessary)—you will win the tennis game. Winning means you will be profitable. What then is the purpose of a business organization? What is the "rock" it must move? What is the "ball" it must watch? What **P**urpose should the organization **P**erform?

Let's think about the very earliest stages of Courtship, when founders are dreaming about starting their organizations. What do they see in the future? Profits? That's possible, but that's not what gets them out of bed in the morning. They see opportunities to make profits. Note my choice of words: *opportunities to make profits.* Profit is an output; opportunity is the input. We have to focus on the input if we want the output to occur. We have to hit the ball, exploit the opportunity, and treat every volley as a first volley.

What are the opportunities that founders notice? They perceive unsatisfied needs in the marketplace, needs that they believe they can truly satisfy.

From a managerial point of view, the distinction between profit and nonprofit organizations is no longer valid. Both organizations have clients and both organizations, to be effective, must satisfy clients' needs. The end results for the two are different: economic profit for one and political survival for the other. But in both cases, input management must have the same focus: to **P**erform a service, and to satisfy the needs of the clients for which the organization exists. That is, both must aim to add value.

Every organization—whether it's a unit within a larger organization or the large organization itself—has clients for which it exists. There is no organization and no management without clients. The clients of the sales organization are called customers, and the accounting department and the personnel department have only clients, not customers. Their clients are within the organization.

By definition, each organization has a reason to be: to satisfy clients' needs that cannot be satisfied by an individual.

If an organization does not focus on its clients' needs, it behaves like a cancer: It exists and consumes resources, but it serves no client functions. It serves only itself.

When a manager makes a decision, he must first ask himself what the **P** role is. Who are his organization's clients? What are their needs? Which needs can, and will, the organization satisfy? That is the **P**urpose of the organization he manages. This applies not just to top management, but to managers at every level.

If the organization performs the **P** function, it will be effective because it satisfies the needs for which it exists. We measure effectiveness in terms of repetitive demands for the organization's services. In business, that is called brand loyalty. Do the clients come back for more? If they don't come back for more of the same service or product, it means their needs are not being satisfied, and the organization is not effective.

Profit, as I have stated, is the indicator of how well the organization performs all four management roles. That is, it indicates how effective and efficient the organization is in the short and the long run.

Organizational effectiveness indicates performance of the purpose for which the organization was created. A pen is effective if it writes. What if the pen doesn't write but you can use it to scratch your head? If it was designed for head scratching, it would not be called "pen," it would have been called "head scratcher." How about a chair? It is a chair if you can sit on it. Why don't you call it a cow? You should, if you can milk it. "I can sit on a cow, so why don't I call it a chair?" a student once asked me. "Because a cow has not been created for sitting."

I am postulating again that everything, absolutely everything, is created with a purpose. The light is for illumination; the heater is to provide heat; and so forth. The same is true for us as people. Some of us are created to write. We nevertheless spend our lives scratching our heads. When you do that for which you have been created, you feel fulfilled. When I present my material in lectures that last six hours, even after a long flight from home through several time zones, I feel rejuvenated. I end up with more energy than when I started. But if you want me to do bookkeeping, I'll beg you to shoot me first!

I have no doubt that my accountant would ask for the firing squad if he had to present a lecture.

But not only chairs, cows, and people like me and you have a purpose. Organizations also have purposes. They should follow their calling and stop scratching their heads if they were designed to write. Just as I can't do bookkeeping, some organizations cannot and should not conduct basic research. They know how to commercialize technology. They cannot develop it. Some companies are excellent retailers, but do not ask them to create high fashion. Even if they hired creative designers, the designers would never survive the penny pinching that prevails in the retailing culture with its bone-thin margins.

In today's business lingo, people talk about core competencies. *Organizations should stick to them, but core competencies are not just know-how and equipment. They include the organizational culture as well.*

Years ago I studied performing arts organizations. (I established the first Master's program in the world in Management of the Arts at UCLA in 1969). In the process of my research, I visited the Minneapolis Symphony, which is now the Minnesota Orchestra. At the time, Stanislaw Skrowaczewski was the artistic director and conductor. The symphony's board of directors was debating whether or not to inaugurate a summer season of pops-in-the-park, similar to the Boston Symphony's Boston Pops. Skrowaczewski was adamantly opposed. "You cannot," he said, "take a musician who plays Paganini during the winter season, ask him to play Sousa in the summer, and at the end of the summer tell him to play a Mendelssohn concerto." In my business language, he was saying, "You cannot produce a Rolls-Royce and a Yugo using the same labor force." Yugo producers don't have Rolls-Royce's compulsive dedication to quality. That takes years to develop and make an integral part of the culture. Two product lines are fine. Boston offers two distinct product lines, and there are two orchestras: one plays pops and the other is the symphony orchestra. The concert master and other leading musicians play chamber music during the summer, while the others play pops-in-the-park.

In other words, every organization must decide who it is and what it does. It cannot be whatever makes money at that minute. You should not try to milk a chair even if the price of milk is sky-rocketing.

How does an organization identify its **P** role?

Rabbi Hillel, in the Wisdom of the Fathers, asks, "If I am not for myself, who is for me? And when I am for myself, what am I?" As I have said, everything has a purpose, and that is to serve others. The lamp is here to shine light so I can type. The food I just ate is to nourish me. The bed across the room is for me to rest and sleep upon. Nothing in life exists for itself. Anything that serves only itself is like cancer which serves no function but death. Some people are cancerous. Existing for no one but themselves, they are exclusive takers. They take more from the land, water, and people than they leave behind. They destroy social value. They are socially cancerous. *Sustainable* growth is not an empty slogan.

To be functional, that is, effective, an organization must, from the outset, define for whom it exists, who are its clients, and which of their needs will the organization satisfy. No organization can or should be everything for everyone. Segment your market. Next, go and do it. That means: **P**rovide the desired needs of your clients; **P**roduce the results to which you are committed; **P**erform as expected.

That is the **P** role that, if **P**erformed, causes organizations to produce the results for which they exist.

The A Role

How about efficiency in the short run?

To be efficient in the short run, management must systematize, program, and organize. It must see to it that the right things happen at the right time, with the right intensity, in the right sequence. That means **A**dministration. For that, management needs to think linearly, logically, and with attention to details. Proper **A**dministration prevents an organization from reinventing the wheel every time it needs to wheel something around.

The **P** and **A** roles can create effectiveness and efficiency in the short run. With only those two management roles, the organization will be profitable in the short run.

The E Role

Imagination is more important than knowledge.

ALBERT EINSTEIN

What do we need for long-term effectiveness?

Again, let's consider the tennis example. Hitting the ball over the net into the opponent's end is the **P** role. The volley was effective. We **P**erformed the **P**urpose for which we hit the ball. In training to play tennis, practicing and perfecting motion to utilize minimum energy for maximum impact, we provide for the **A** role, making our game efficient.

But winning a volley is not winning the game. To win a game you must do more than win a single volley.

You must perform two additional functions in order to be effective and efficient in the long run. The first of those is the **E** role.

To win a tennis game, efficiently getting the ball over the net one time is just a start. To hit the next ball, you must be prepared, anticipating where the next ball will go and positioning yourself to respond. You must be thinking strategically. Should you run to the net? Should you move back to the center of the court? To be effective in the long run, you must anticipate that long-run event and get ready to respond to it when it arrives. That requires two factors: creativity and risk taking.

Long-term effectiveness calls for us to predict the future. Where is the next ball going to come to? What is the next generation of needs? To answer those questions requires creativity to predict what did not happen yet. But that is not all. We position ourselves on the court according to where we anticipate the ball will come, but the ball might land far from where we were awaiting it. Taking position on the court entails taking risk.

The ability to plan what to do today in anticipation of tomorrow requires creativity and the capability to take risk.

The role that visualizes future changing needs, and proactively positions the organization for that future, I call the **E**ntrepreneurial role. If it is performed right, the organization will be effective in the long run. It will be prepared to meet future needs. **E**ntrepreneuring is like planning—deciding not what to do tomorrow but what to do today in light of what we expect and want to happen tomorrow.

You must be creative to anticipate the future. You must imagine what it will look like so you can prepare for it. What does that mean?

Creative people can see through the fog of the present. Peering through fog, we have only limited information, and the validity of our information is subject to continuous change. We see bits of scenery, and as the fog moves, that scenery disappears, and the information changes. Creative people use those bits of information like pieces of a jigsaw puzzle. They fill in the missing pieces by imagining a complete picture.

Creativity alone, I repeat, is not sufficient. In order to act on that future, one must take risks.

What prevents a tennis player from getting to the place where he or she believes the next ball will come? Perhaps the ball is moving fast, and the player is out of shape and too slow. Or it might be that he doesn't want to risk moving until he knows *exactly* where the ball will land. He waits for the ball to land, and only when he knows where the ball is—once there is certainty—he advances toward the ball. Obviously it is already too late.

Some managers behave that way. They say, "We don't yet know how the market will behave. Let's wait for the picture to clear."

In a rapidly changing environment, if management behaves so cautiously, failing to match the speed of change, the organization will be only reactive. The role of **E**ntrepreneuring is not to *adapt* to the changing environment. Adapting implies reactive, not proactive behavior. We must anticipate, projecting the future and acting on it now. Make no mistake about this.

We cannot afford the luxury of waiting
to see the future before we decide what to do
in the present.

The **E** role makes an organization effective in the long run by making it proactive. We will be able to hit—**P**—the next ball and have a successful volley if we predict the future and take the risk in preparing for it.

*The **I** Role*

What about long-term efficiency?

Let's examine this role in detail. I believe that it goes some way to explaining the temporary dominance of Japan's management style over Western management style. It also explains why the Japanese are gradually losing that competitive advantage and why West Germany's economic performance excelled until the unification. Also, and not incidentally, it explains why organizations age and how to get to Prime with a shortcut. Read carefully.

There are examples of organizations managed by a single person who excels in the **P**erforming service role, the **A**dministration role, *and* the **E**ntrepreneurial role. Such **PAE** managers make decisions that focus on the needs of customers, and their organizations are highly effective—**P**. They are efficiency-oriented, and they run a tight ship. They waste no resources (a function of **A**). Furthermore, they are highly **E**ntrepreneurial, projecting the new needs of the marketplace. And they take anticipatory action to satisfy those future needs.

What happens when such managers—rare birds, indeed—die or leave their organizations? By and large, the organizations suffer serious difficulties and, in some cases, they die.

In order for an organization to achieve long-term survival, it must be independent of any individuals who comprise it. The Catholic Church, for example, has existed for 2,000 years and it might continue for another 200,000 years, independent of who is the Pope. That has happened because it is an organized religion.

If we excised religion from the Catholic Church, it would be subject to the same survival challenges that confront any other organization. This suggests that to achieve long-term survival, an organization needs a culture of values that unites it in a transcendental way that far exceeds the power of any single individual. What organizations need is vision (purpose of existence), values, philosophies, rituals, patterns of behavior, and beliefs that unite people beyond the immediacy of the functions they perform.

The **I**ntegrating role develops a culture of interdependency and affinity, nurturing a unique corporate culture.

To Integrate means to change an organization's consciousness from mechanistic to organic.

Let us explain each and every word in the definition of Integration.

First, you must understand that to Integrate means *to take action,* to do something, to act. It is not passive. You have to change, not wait to be changed. If you wait and do nothing, the system disintegrates by itself. Buy the best car money can buy, and never drive it. Do not do anything to it. Over time you will not be able to use it. It will fall apart. The same is true of your garden. The best gardens, unless maintained, disintegrate over time.

Because of entropy, all systems fall apart over time. To Integrate, one must continuously work to counter entropy.

To change means to do something today, so tomorrow will be different from yesterday. Integration does not happen on its own. We must act to make it occur. The manager who performs the I role must be actively engaged.

Organization is difficult to explain. Frequently, in the course of a lecture, I might ask someone how large his organization is and how many people work for it. Usually, the person answers after checking the organization chart or the salary list; but neither is the right place to look.

For a manager to know how many organizational members she needs to Integrate, she should look at the rock from our earlier example. What needs must her organization satisfy? And the next question is, whom does she need to move the rock? There is a task interdependency that she must manage. The questions I am asking are, "Who are the people whose interdependency you must manage, and how do you reward them correctly so they are motivated to move the rock?" Some of those people you pay with salaries, others with commissions, and perhaps you pay some by taking them to dinner and massaging their egos. How you pay is irrelevant so long as it is ethical. What is relevant is that you know what your rock is, whom you need to move the rock, and how you should provide the rewards that move the people to move the rock.

An inexperienced manager might mistakenly claim that he cannot accomplish a certain job because the people he requires to work on it do not report to him exclusively. There is no manager—in my experience with hundreds of organizations and thousands of managers—who has all the requisite people reporting directly to him. The president of Bank of America, Sam Armacost, supported this point when he said, "You don't need to own a highway in order to drive on it. You just need to have a token to get on it."

Good managers first identify their rocks—their responsibilities or tasks—by identifying their organization's clients. The next question they answer is, "Whom do I need to complete this task?" The third question is, "What rewards do I give those people in order for them to help carry out the task?" Some will be paid in salary. Some will be "paid" in another way.

Managers are as good as their ability to analyze the Purpose of their organizations as well as the needs and wants of the people who will accomplish the purpose.

Deficient managers move only pebbles, not rocks. They focus only on those tasks the people who work directly for them can do.

A good way to rate managers is to total the number of IOUs they possess in the bank of commitments. The more people who owe them commitments, the more they have to cash in when they need to move their own rocks. Support your colleagues. See how and where you can be helpful. Help them move their rocks. Build your bank account. The day will come when you will need their help.

Good managers recognize interdependency across organizational lines. They do their best to support and cooperate with others, and people support them in return. In short, a good manager is a team player.

Organizational membership depends on the task at hand. It usually includes more than those people who report directly to the manager or who are salaried. I consulted to an insurance company that used independent agents to sell its policies. Because those agents also represented products of the insurance company's competitors, the company harbored animosity towards them, referring to them as "they" rather than "we." People made disparaging and derogatory remarks about them. I asked management whether the company needed the independent agents to get the job done. Management responded that they were absolutely necessary. If that's the case, I said, even though they are not on the salary roster, and they don't report to you, they are members of your organization, and you need to manage, direct, and motivate them. You need to integrate them into the whole of your organization. You will treat them differently from your salaried people, using different approaches to motivate, direct, and control their actions, but you must manage them because you need them.

Companies that expand by franchising need to confront the same issue. Too often the franchiser and the franchisee are separated by a Grand Canyon rift, and franchisees end up bringing suit against their franchisers. Are the franchisees members of the organization? By my definition, they absolutely must be. Whether or not they are salaried employees, they are part of the organization because they share the rock.

This is an enormous issue with hidden dimensions. Whenever I consult with an organization that franchises, I ask that leaders of the franchisees meet with us so that we can solve the problems together. Invariably, franchisers demur. Management refuses to invite to the decision-making forum exactly those parties with whom it has problems.

Let's take one more step now.

Do a company's workers share the rock? Do you as the leader of the organization need their support, enthusiasm, and passion to move the rock?

The answer is obvious, but it's not that easy to take appropriate action. Management has a real difficulty bringing unions into meetings where they can solve problems together. In some cases, that reticence might be justifiable. Perhaps your workers are represented by a union that encompasses the entire industry, and the union leaders worry about a totally different rock—the union and their political standing in it. Since you and they do not share the same rock, their self-interest will interfere with the process of lifting your rock. They will want a solution that will lift their rock, and that might undermine your capability to secure their cooperation to lift your rock. But if that is not the case, why not have your workers share your problems and help solve them?

Here is another case. Are volunteers of nonprofit organizations members of those organizations? Can you manage them as if they were salaried employees? Better not. Do they need to be led and managed? Sure! How? Ask them why they have volunteered. Find out what their needs are, and ask yourself how you can satisfy those needs in ways that help lift your rock.[8]

Mechanistic vs. Organic Consciousness

Now that the words "to change" and "organizational" have been clarified, let us turn to the word *consciousness*. What does it mean?

Every organization has personality, behavioral patterns, and style. Once we know an organization, its behavior is predictable. For example, we know that Bureaucratic organizations lose files, take a long time to respond to queries, and even after long delays, respond inadequately. To Integrate means to change an organization's mechanistic consciousness, behavior, culture, and system of beliefs, making them organic.

What is *mechanistic consciousness*? Look at a chair that has four legs. You identify it as a chair because you can sit on it. If you could not sit on it, it would not be a chair. We define an object by what it does.

A hammer is a tool if it is used to pound nails. If someone uses the hammer to harm another person, it is not a tool; it is a weapon. If it hangs on the wall as folk art, then it is not a hammer; it's a decorative object.

What happens to a chair if one of its legs breaks? It stops functioning as a chair; nobody can sit on it. For the chair to perform, someone from the *outside* must repair it.

Why doesn't one of the other legs move to the center of the chair and create a stool so that the chair can resume functioning as a chair? The obvious answer is that in an inanimate object or a machine, there is no internal interdependency among parts. A multibillion dollar spaceship fails to function because of a few dollars' worth of deficient O-rings. If it is to function, it requires external intervention to repair any breakage or weaknesses. That is the nature of the mechanistic consciousness. It lacks internal interdependency of parts to perform the function of the total unit.

In organizations, mechanistic consciousness is recognized as parochialism, tunnel vision, or silo mentality. Each unit acts by itself and for itself—not as a part of the total system. To get the system to perform as a whole, someone *from outside the system* must manage the interdependence of those parts.

Some companies' disintegration is such that customers and suppliers are considered outsiders. Others perceive even their employees as outsiders. Certain organizations view their presidents as outsiders.

Let's contrast an organic consciousness with a mechanistic consciousness. Look at your hand. We use our hands to write, point, and hold things. What happens if I break a finger? Will my hand still function? Sure. Other fingers compensate for the injured one. I could lose three fingers and still have a hand—not so good as before, but better than no hand at all. The hand continues to perform. Why? What makes a hand? Five interdependent fingers, each of which "thinks" like a hand.

If I lost my hand and replaced it with a prosthetic claw, I would need physiotherapy to learn how the parts of the claw work together. When I teach the parts of the claw to behave like a hand, I am performing the **I** role, creating interdependency among the components for a common purpose. That is *organic consciousness.*[9]

Here is an analogy. Three people are laying bricks. A man walking by stops and asks the first laborer what he is doing. "I'm laying bricks," he says. The pedestrian then turns to the next worker and asks him the same question. He answers, "I am building a wall." When the third worker is asked the question, he responds, "We are building a place to worship God."

The third man understands the interdependence and the purpose of that interdependence. When the components of a system recognize their interdependency and the purpose of that interdependency—nobody is indispensable—the organization is efficient in the long run.

That internal sense of belonging, of interdependence,
I call Integration. And it is integration that makes an
organization efficient.

A well-integrated organization needs no extra resources in reserve for when there is a default. To fulfill their common purpose, the components support one another as needed, and no one is indispensable.

Such interdependence does not require physical proximity or connection. If you broke your finger, your eyes might fill with tears. What is going on? "Well, we belong to one another," the finger and the eyes might answer if they could talk. "We are one. Its pain is my pain." A skeptic might object and say that their interdependence is purely a physical nervous connection. To that, I would ask, "If the finger that broke was not yours but your own little son's finger, wouldn't you feel pain?" You don't need to be connected physically to rejoice or feel the pain of something or someone you believe is part of you.

Input (Role)	*Throughput*	*Output*
Provide the desired needs	Functional	Effective in the short run
Administer	Systematized	Efficient in the short run
Entrepreneur	Proactive	Effective in the long run
Integrate	Organic	Efficient in the long run

Testing Your Understanding

I give this exam to my classes to make sure everyone understands each of the four management roles. Here's a familiar situation:

Some time ago, when my sons were three and four years old, I was in the living room, reading the Sunday newspaper. The boys had been playing quietly in their room for a while, but suddenly, they started to fight.

"Daddy," wailed one, "it's mine!"

And the other screeched, "No, it's Miiiiine!"

"Daaaaddddyyyyyy!"

Here is my first question. If the boys were calling me to resolve their dispute, is their relationship organic, by my definition, or is it mechanistic?

Their relationship is mechanistic. They cannot resolve the issue by themselves. They need outside intervention to solve whatever is not functioning between them. I went into their room. At that time, when I still had energy to make and enforce such rules, all toys were shared. There was no such thing as "mine" or "his." I expected them to share. On that particular Sunday, both boys wanted to play with the xylophone, and the urge to play with it hit each of them at precisely the same moment.

"It is mine!"

"No," the other countered, "I touched it first."

"Daddy, tell him he has to give it to me!"

You know the scene. What would be the **P** solution? How would you solve the problem using the **P** role, the **P** "vitamin"?

Here is the response I get most frequently when I ask that question: "Take the xylophone away from both of them!"

That is a solution, but be careful. Who is the client in that solution? The parent. I want peace and quiet. So I satisfy my needs. The kids still want to kill each other, and I am taking away their pretense.

I see this so often. It happened to me in Italy. When I had a problem, I asked for help. Everyone answered, "No problema." Apparently, that's Italian for, "It's not my problem." Some managers, even though they aren't Italian, take the same approach to problem solving. When colleagues or subordinates approach them with problems, the managers solve their own problems: They get out of the firing line. But the people who asked them for help are no better off.

Next solution: "How about buying the boys a second xylophone?"

That's a good solution if your underlying assumption is correct. Are the kids fighting because they really want to play music on a xylophone? If they really want to play music on Sunday morning, and each must play only a xylophone, I should go out and buy another xylophone. That would be a **P** solution because the clients' needs have to be satisfied. But do you believe that my kids really wanted to play music that Sunday morning? Maybe they were fighting because they wanted to make noise. In that case, I should get some pots and pans from the kitchen, and one could bang on the pots while the other bangs on the xylophone.

From the *Wall Street Journal*. Permission, Cartoon Features Syndicate.

Perhaps noise wasn't their need either. Maybe they fought simply because of sibling rivalry, testing their relative positions of dominance. If I don't let them fight over the xylophone, they will fight about the pots and pans. They need to fight over something. In that case, I should let them have it their way and tell them, "Listen, boys, don't call me unless there is blood flowing!"

To find a **P** solution, you need first to identify the client and, then, using a process of trial and error, try to identify the need. The client can be internal or it can be external, in which case it is called a customer. You will know you have identified the need correctly when your client is content. Don't paternalize or maternalize the client. None of us really understands why we do the things we do—especially the first time around. How many people can really explain why they bought the car they bought? They can give a reason, but can they prove scientifically that that is the true reason? Consumer behavior theories can't explain consumer behavior because nobody can explain human behavior. We postulate, we believe, and we test our hypotheses to see what works. Even when a hypothesis works, we have no scientific explanation for why it works.

Clients have a need and they believe it can be satisfied by a certain product or service. But unless the product or service is a routine repetitive purchase, they don't know whether that product or service will satisfy their need for sure. As a manager, you have to test your solution—what you believe is the clients' need. Offer A. Do they buy it repeatedly? If not, try product B. If they like B, they should come back for more. You need to keep trying until they routinely return for more. That's when you know you have identified a real need.

Brand loyalty—repeat purchasing—is your proof that you are satisfying a need whether or not you can specify or define that need. And really, what is important is not to know for sure what the need is. The important thing is to satisfy a need—whatever we believe it to be—as proven by the fact that people keep buying our solution.

To know whether a family works as a family, ask whether the spouses come home because they want to be together or because they have no choice. If family members stay away from home, there is always a reason.

What about the **A** solution?

To apply an **A** solution, you must look for routine, repetition, law, and order. You have to go by the book, applying the family's standards. Perhaps the rules say that the toy goes to the child who touched it first, had it first, or had it the shortest. Perhaps the rules require the younger always to yield to the older, or the older always to yield to the younger. Or maybe they are supposed to flip a coin. If you apply an **A** solution, the children's immediate needs are ignored. The **A** solution focuses on the needs of the family unit, which abides by consistent standards: *The same rule must be applied when the same conditions exist.* You apply order and the appropriate rule, and then you enforce it. Under such circumstances, the children are not the clients. The family unit is the client. To sustain the efficiency of your parental—managerial—energy, you must apply the same solution to similar future situations. What about the kids' needs? What if their need is to beat up each other in order to see who is really the "boss"? If they have to play alone, and one at a time each gets time to play the xylophone, most probably they will forget the xylophone and start to fight over a ball or something else.

How about the **E** solution?

"Cut the xylophone into two pieces and let each play by himself!"

This creative solution is really a variation of the **P** solution: You are still trying to satisfy what you believe is the need the xylophone represents. You believe the boys are aching to make music or noise.

An **E** solution is not just any creative solution. The **E** solution—a proactive response to the problem—projects another, more powerful need that might redirect the children's energy away from their immediate need, whatever it is. **E** solutions might be to suggest watching television, playing soccer, or—one I find is a consistent winner—going to the movies. The kids focus on a new need, one that is different from the need that caused the conflict.

The **I** solution is the most difficult to identify. If you apply an **I** solution, you do want to move away from dependency on external intervention. You want to avoid having your children come to you to resolve all their differences. If they continually come to you to resolve their conflicts, it should be clear to you that your children share no organic consciousness. It is mechanistic.

Someone from the class will usually suggest that I should "teach them how to play together."

That is not a purely **I** solution. That solution assumes dependency on external intervention: The parent has to provide resolution. It is as if the parent is fixing the broken chair.

Alternatively, someone might say, "Give each boy one of the sticks, and let them play the xylophone together." That solution, like the last one, depends on me to impose order.

A truly **I** solution requires the children solve their problems by themselves. As their parent, my role, like that of any manager is, as Ralph Ablon, CEO of Ogden says, "to create an environment in which the most desirable will most probably happen."

So, invoking an **I** solution, what did I do? First, I admonished them, explaining that, "I am not here to solve all your problems. What would you do if I were not home?" In the future, I wondered, when they grow up and I am not around anymore, are they going to go to lawyers to solve their disputes? As a punishment, I took the xylophone away from them, and I sent them to the bathroom, where, I told them, they had to stay until they came up with the solution.

Of course, their first reaction was to protest quite loudly. They wanted a solution from an outsider. Outside refereeing is easier than having to find their own solution, but an outsider's solution will be good only temporarily. The children need to deal not only with the xylophone, but also with their relationship. Our goal in the **I** role is to make our children, like members of any organization, interdependent rather than dependent on external intervention.

If I went with the boys to their room and moderated their search for a solution, or if I asked them to agree on toy-sharing rules, which I would enforce, how would that be defined in **PAEI** terms? What if I made them make their own rules and insisted that they enforce those rules themselves? Would that work? Why or why not?

So how did the boys do in the bathroom? How long do you think it took them to find a solution and get out? I could picture the two of them in that bathroom looking at each other, one saying to the other, "Oh, man!" Obviously, they found a solution in no time.

What if they had come out of the bathroom and said, "We have a solution! We're going to burn the house down!" I would have sent them back until they had a solution I could accept. That is, they had to come up with a solution that resembled mine. They had to develop my outlook. They had to develop a family-wide perspective.

Next time your vice presidents start to compete among themselves for budgets, don't step in and solve their problem. Sure, you know the correct solution, but don't tell it to them. Send them to the "bathroom," and instruct them to stay there until they solve their problem in a way that takes into account the organizational perspective.

The Incompatibility of the Roles

Here's a new question. If instead of taking the xylophone away from the children, I had let them keep it as they worked on their assignment to find a solution. How long would it take to find a solution under those circumstances? A little longer, right?

You have just discovered that the four roles are incompatible. It is more difficult to **P** and **I** than it is to **P** alone and **I** alone.

Organizations in which all four management functions— Performance, Administration, Entrepreneurship, and Integration— are performed will be effective, efficient, proactive, and organic. They will be effective and efficient in the short and the long run. The roles, however, are interdependent and undermine each other, making the goals very, very hard, practically impossible, to achieve simultaneously.

P-I Incompatibility

Here's a familiar scenario. Your company holds a meeting. There is time pressure. It's important to make a quick decision. There is **P** pressure. You still try to be open-minded and receptive to everyone's opinions. You have **I** aspirations. How easy is this meeting for you?

P-E Incompatibility

P and **E** are also incompatible. How often do you say, "I have so much to do, I can't think clearly." What you are really saying is that you are so busy doing that, you have no time to change. Likewise, people in bad marriages keep themselves very busy so they have no time to think about changes they need to make in their lives. What if they try to fix everything up by taking a vacation? When they come back, they'll be ready to file for divorce. Why this timing? After a glorious vacation that was supposed to fix everything? They want a divorce because during the vacation they had time to think.

As we have seen, **P**erformance has impact on **E**ntrepreneurship, and the reverse can also be true. **E**ntrepreneurship has impact on **P**erformance. People in production might say to the corporate planners and to the people in engineering, "If you guys don't stop changing your minds, we will never get anything done."

*To get action, we must freeze planning. We have to
decide when to stop changing, so action can start.*

If there is too much change, we can accomplish little. Countries
overwhelmed by too much change are paralyzed. To stop inflation in
Brazil during the 1980s, the government was continually introducing
new laws and economic policies. All those changes produced so much
uncertainty that long-term business investments came to a near stand-
still. **E** threatened **P**. The more erratically the government fought
inflation, the more it fueled it. To get supply, you need stability. The
higher the inflation, however, the more frantic and crisis-oriented the
politicians became, enacting laws and introducing policies to demonstrate action which undermined the steady supply of goods. During a
period of high inflation, Argentina changed its treasury minister
almost annually, inciting rather than restraining inflation.

P-A Incompatibility

To win a tennis game you have to hit the ball into the opponent's
court. This makes your volley effective. Simply hitting the ball into
your opponent's court any way you can is analogous to providing the
P role. It makes your game effective. Can it be inefficient? Sure! You
manage to hit the ball, but your body is a cartoon of contortions.

How do you become efficient? When you train to play tennis,
you program your body to move and hit the ball right. By training to
use your hands and body correctly, you learn how to be efficient, to
have maximum hitting power with minimum energy. That is applying
the **A** role.

Can you be efficient and not effective? To be efficient and not
effective means to make all the right moves without hitting the ball
because the ball is somewhere else. Imagine a player who becomes
extremely efficient at hitting the ball a certain way. Rather than moving to where the ball is going to be, he stands in his favored spot,
complaining that the ball wasn't sent to him where he stood positioned to hit it most efficiently.

Bureaucracies behave that way. Bureaucracies go through the
motions, making every move by the book. They are perfect. The
needs of their customers, however, are somewhere else. Bureaucracies love doing things right, but they fail to do the right things. Their

systems are so efficient that they stop being effective. The customers and their changing needs mess up Bureaucracies' efficiency. The bureaucratic managers would rather be efficient and ineffective than effective and inefficient. They prefer to be precisely wrong than approximately right.

A-I Incompatibility

A and **I** are also interdependent. **A** focuses on the *how,* while **I** focuses on the *who* and with *whom*. Both are how-oriented, but **A** is a mechanistic *how*, and **I** is an organic *how*. Here's an example of their incompatibility. Where is crime higher: in large, highly industrialized cities or in small villages where almost everyone knows everyone else? Crime is more prevalent in large cities where people feel a sense of alienation. They lack feelings of belonging and interdependency. There is an **I** deficiency: Crime is a manifestation of economic, social, emotional, and political disIntegration.

The typical law-and-order response to crime is an **A** solution to an **I** problem. The more we rely on **A** solutions, the greater the **I** problem becomes. **A** is a substitute for **I** in the same way that **I** can substitute for **A**. The legal environment grows increasingly intense as people, relying less on social values to govern interdependencies, sue each other and attempt to resolve their disputes in court. The more **A**, the more disIntegration. And disintegration calls for more **A** which calls for more and more **A**.

The United States has the world's highest per capita rate of incarceration. As change accelerates, disintegration intensifies, and we become more likely to deal with crime in the mechanistic ways of **A**. That is the favored approach of most elected legislators. They are lawyers by training, and they believe laws can solve problems. **A** means are effective ways to arrest crime, but only an **I** solution can really solve the problem of crime in socio-economic terms, like community councils, neighborhood watch, and community pride, or "taking care of your own."

People are more likely to provide **A** solutions to **I** problems because **A** solutions require us only to enforce rules. They don't demand that we think about the spirit of the solution and how to reinforce intricate interdependencies. **A** is the more efficient *how* in the short run; **I** takes much more time. But, its effects are more enduring. **I** is the long-term *how*.

The more we rely on the short-term how, *the greater the long-term* how *problems that eventually emerge.*

What country is strong on **I** and has a competitive advantage because of it? How about Japan? Its main strength was **I**. It was called Corporate Japan. Business and government cooperated; labor and management were in a love embrace. In Japan, there is a strong sense of interdependency, affinity, and loyalty between corporations and their employees.[10] Its **I** is so high that **I** has the debilitating effect of **A**. And, Japanese **A** is very strong, too. Nowhere have I seen cleaner taxi cabs. The drivers wear white gloves. Japanese acceptance and adherence to rules and rituals is legendary. And the people are also extremely diligent and hard working, making **P** high. Being culturally **PAI** made them very successful in the short run, but I have been thinking for some time of the fall of Japanese hegemony in the long run because of its lack of **E**. Japan is deficient in individualistic **E**. Japan's educational system teaches people to learn to know, not to learn to learn and create freely.[11] Among individuals, **E** is weak.

Which country is growing in **A** and declining in **I**? The United States of America. How can the United States beat Japan's advantage?

The United States should export **A**, and import **I**. How? I jokingly suggest that the United States should send professors of business administration to teach the Japanese the traditional management theory: span of control, unity of command, the exclusive rights of management versus labor, elitist managerial decision-making, and a management practice based on adversary relations. All those concepts increase **A** and threaten **I**. Next the United States should learn Japan's participatory systems and the mutual cooperation and long-term loyalty that characterizes Japanese management practice. That, in fact, is what has been happening. The Japanese admire and emulate the United States. Many Japanese executives have complained to me about the inefficiencies of the Japanese participatory system, saying how much they admire the management teachings of the Harvard Business School.[12]

And what did the Americans learn from the Japanese? They learned to **I** the Japanese way of participatory management. That exchange can make the United States stronger and Japan weaker.

There is a difference between **A** and **I**. **I** can cause both short- and long-term efficiency while **A** is functional in the short run only. As environments change, if **A** remains for the long-term, it becomes dysfunctional. **I** is flexible and adaptable. **A** is neither.

Can a company be efficient in the short run, using **I** alone, without **A**? Yes. That, in fact, is what happens in partisan or guerrilla forces. They have no manuals like those of established military hierarchies. Instead, the people honor a set of values that serve as the rules of conduct. Likewise, Asian business dynasties manage their extended family businesses not with **A**, but with **I**. Peter Drucker predicts that in the next century Asian business clans will dominate the world.[13] I do not think he's right. Families do fall apart without **A**, and in those clans, **E** is individualized. They can suffer the family trap. Multinational corporations, on the other hand, can learn to **I** without losing the **A** and the **E**. I base my predictions on work I have done in Japan, Malaysia, Indonesia, and Singapore.

A and **I** serve the same organizational function: They are the glue that provides for interdependency. The difference between them is that **A** is documented; **I** does not have to be. **A** is not co-opted behaviorally, it is enforced by external forces. **I** will not exist unless the participants identify with it and make it their value system. **I**, therefore, is regulated and enforced by those who share it.

In an **AI** situation, the organization accepts the manual. Chester Barnard called that "authority by acceptance." The legislated rules reflect social mores and are enforced by the people as well as the authorities.

E-I Incompatibility

The **E** and the **I** roles are also incompatible. The **E** role of creativity and risk taking, usually attributed to an individual, can be hampered by the sense of affinity, belonging, and group pressure that characterize the **I** role. Some creative **E** individuals find the **I** process stifling. On the other hand, individual creativity—which is a deviation from the norm—can threaten the sense of affinity and unity that the **I** role produces. Religious organizations like cults, for instance, start out with strong **I**, but they quickly become **A** systems because the **I** dominance discourages **E**, which is perceived as aberrant behavior. Integration goes and should go with any other **PAE** role.

Integration makes organizations organic, rather than mechanistic. Although Integration can exist by itself, that is as undesirable as **P**roducing, **A**dministering, or **E**ntrepreneuring alone. Integration alone has no purpose to focus it. **P** alone is like a spinning top, turning and turning without purpose, without a purpose just keeping busy. **E** alone means lots of creative ideas and plenty of noise but no action, direction, or continuous purpose.

To provide efficiency, **I** needs a common purpose. The purpose can be tactical, short-term in nature: **PI**, like the hand example above. In wartime, people work together with long-term strategic purposes: **EI**. Combining with **A**, **I** can smooth implementation: **AI** enhances organizational efficiency.[14]

Let us summarize. For organizations to be effective and efficient in the short and long run, they need the four **PAEI** roles to be performed. Those roles need to be developed or applied in the organization. However, those roles are incompatible. Thus, their development and integration into the organization happens in a sequence. If the sequence is the optimal one, the organization follows the optimal path. Most, however, follow the typical path, for reasons to be explained in subsequent chapters. Some get stymied and cannot advance to develop the new role. Those are the organizations with pathological problems.

Let us first address the typical path most organizations take.

Notes

1. See the research on autopoiesis processes, particularly H. Maturana and F. Varela's *Autopoiesis and Cognition* (1980), and *The Tree of Knowledge: The Biological Roots of Human Understanding* (1987). See also the discussion of self-regulation that is circulating in the complexity literature, particularly F. Capra's *The Web of Life: A New Understanding of Living Systems* (New York: Doubleday Anchor, 1996), esp. Chapter 5, "Models of Self-organization." This line of research has shown that systems reproduce themselves, selecting for their own survival; that is, evolution occurs with directionality.

G. Bateson has called this process "orthogenesis" and notes that this process is the "outward and visible sign of interactive process" [G. Bateson, "From Anthropology to Epistemology," in R. Donaldson, ed., *Sacred Unity: Further Steps to an Ecology of Mind* (New York: Harper, 1991)]. He was referring to the interaction between the component parts of the system, and its environment. So the directional "choices" that a system makes as it self-regulates are a function of the local and specific conditions which provide the information for the "choice."

2. One of the central mistakes of organizational theory has been the embedded assumptions about intention and rational "choice" that are attributed to organizational processes. See the critique of this positivist paradigm in D. Polkinghorne, *Narrative Knowing and the Human Sciences,* SUNY Series in the Philosophy of the Social Sciences (Albany: State University of New York Press, 1988), as well as J. Hassard, "Exploring the Terrain of Modernism and Postmodernism in Organizational Theory," in D. Boje (ed.) et al., *Postmodern Management and Organization Theory* (New York: Sage, 1996): 45–60.

3. See J. Hillman, *The Soul's Code: In Search of Character and Calling* (New York: Warner, 1997), which posits that each one of us has the capacity to realize our potential, just as an acorn will inevitably grow into an oak tree. Problems, he argues, are a function of the inability to unfold ourselves into our potential; it follows that if we have a context to support "unfolding," health and self-actualization follow.

4. I. Adizes, *Industrial Democracy: Yugoslav Style* (New York: The Free Press, 1971).

5. See discussion of the issues in M. Djilas, *The New Class: An Analysis of the Communist System* (San Diego: Harcourt Brace Jovanovich, 1983 [first U.S. publication, 1953]).

6. I. Adizes, *How to Solve the Mismanagement Crisis* (Bel Air, CA: Adizes Institute Publications, 1980 [first printing, New York: Dow Jones Irwin, 1978]).

7. I. Adizes, *How to Solve the Mismanagement Crisis.*

8. I. Adizes, "Seattle Opera Association," in *Business Policy: Strategy Formation and Management Action,* ed. by W. Glueck, 2nd edition (New York: McGraw Hill, 1976): 610–634.

9. See R. Penrose, *Shadows of the Mind: A Search for the Missing Science of Consciousness* (Oxford: Oxford University Press, 1994). This book seeks to describe human consciousness by examining the limits of computer intelligence. Also see the classic, A. Young's *The Reflexive Universe: Evolution of Consciousness* (New York: Delacorte Press, 1976). Young makes explicit the connection between reflexivity and consciousness. And finally, see A. Scott, *Stairway to the Mind: The Controversial New Science of Consciousness* (New York: Springer-Verlag, 1996), for a complete review of the area of consciousness studies. All of these books, as well as several excellent academic programs devoted to this topic, suggest that consciousness is a concept increasingly central to our understanding of mind and society.

10. See K. Ohmae, *The Mind of the Strategist: The Art of Japanese Business* (New York: McGraw Hill, 1982). He provides a thorough description of the relationship between the culture and the productivity of Japanese business.

11. For instance, see *USA Today*, March 10, 1998, page 13A.

12. Even while the Japanese were beginning to develop their sophisticated management and production models (TQM, JIT, Kaizen, and so on), the HBS was beginning to publish works on leadership and the organic company which would become the hallmark of 1990's thinking; for example, see E.C. Brusk's *Human Relations for Management: New Perspectives (1956)*. Other typical titles in leadership, team management, production development, banking, etc.: A.M. Kantrow, *Survival Strategies for American Business* (1982); E. Collins, ed., *The Executive Dilemma: Handling People Problems at Work* (1985); R. Howard, ed., *The Learning Imperative: Managing People for Continuous Innovation* (1993); F. Bartolomé, *The Articulate Executive* (1986), and others.

13. See P. Drucker, *Management: Tasks, Responsibilities, Practices* (New York: McGraw Hill, 1973).

14. See R. Axelrod, *The Evolution of Cooperation* (New York: Basic Books, 1984), for an excellent theoretical discussion of the nature of cooperation. His work is resonant to the current postmodern perspective on participation in organizations. See also R. Pascale and A. Athos, *The Art of Japanese Management* (New York: Simon & Schuster, 1981), for a description of the differences between Japanese and American management.

CHAPTER ELEVEN

Predicting the Lifecycle: A Metaphorical Dance

In Part One of this book, I described the individual stages of the organizational lifecycle. Are there reasons why an organization moves from one stage of the lifecycle to another? Using the tools I described in Chapter 10, this chapter explains why organizations develop and deteriorate as they do.

If the four managerial roles—**P**, **A**, **E**, and **I**—are mutually incompatible and threaten each other, can it be possible for an organization to emerge, at birth, with all four roles simultaneously developed and balanced? The answer is no. Those roles have to develop in a certain sequence synchronizing their development as they go.

At any point in time—because one or more of the four roles is missing, dormant, or not fully developed—every organization manifests problems that stem from not having the role fully developed and from the difficulties of having to synchronize the incompatible roles.

But an organization's lifecycle may follow either the typical or the optimal path. Those paths are differentiated by the sequence in which the roles develop and how they are integrated.

Let us first understand the typical path, which we have already described. Once we understand how the development and interplay of **P**, **A**, **E**, and **I** roles explain organizational behavior, we will discover how it is possible to accelerate and improve the development and interplay of the four roles, creating an optimal path.

Organizations need to perform all four roles in order to be effective and efficient in the short and long run. Since the four roles are incompatible, they develop in a certain predetermined sequence, seeking the route of least resistance, and striving to synchronize along the way. Organizations learn new roles and institutionalize them through the problem-solving process. After all, problems are caused by the absence or lack of development of one or more of the management roles and by the difficulties of synchronizing those roles. In the course of solving a particular problem, an organization develops and institutionalizes a new role in its consciousness.

When an organization fails to develop a role or to resolve incompatibility of existing roles, it will find that it is "stuck." It continually replays the manifestations of that shortcoming. Although the lack of a role or the difficulty of integrating it may manifest itself as what might appear to be numerous different problems, those problems will all be of a similar nature. The organization acts like a broken record, and its problems are no longer normal. In such cases, organizations usually regress to a former role. Unable to proceed forward, they retreat to the familiar. If there are significant changes in the environment, lacking certain roles will cause the problems of an organization to become pathological, threatening its very existence.

For example, companies in Go-Go are missing the **A** and **I** roles. For companies on the typical path, such a deficiency is normal. Later, however, if it becomes clear that the founders—who hire and fire an endless succession of chief operating officers—fail to develop **A** and **I**, the problem takes on the abnormal dimensions I call the founder's trap. Investors usually recognize the vulnerability of organizations dependent on a single person, electing not to risk capital in such shaky situations. If it becomes impossible to raise funds to finance necessary expansion, the founder's trap can prove to be a pathological problem.

In order to facilitate therapeutic interventions, it's crucial to understand the process of change, how the roles develop and integrate, and the normal—as opposed to abnormal or pathological—problems that develop in the process of that change

Why does the lifecycle follow a typical sequence? Because each of the roles emerges and later submerges, giving way to and balancing with the next role in a predetermined sequence. Since the roles develop in a predetermined sequence, the problems created by the incompatibility of the roles are predictable, and we have the power to anticipate those problems. Because we have a diagnostic and therapeutic theory that allows us to associate deficiencies of specific roles with specific problems, we can cultivate as yet underdeveloped roles and thus remove or prevent the problems from emerging.

It is during the growing stages of the lifecycle that organizations need to develop the four **PAEI** roles and integrate them. Organizations in the aging stages must prevent the roles from decaying. Organizations that keep the roles strong and in balance can remain in Prime.

Organizations need to develop each role, integrate each with those already developed, and operate using all of them. But every organization has an energy allocation problem: At any point in time, each system has a fixed amount of energy. We know that from physics. Energy can grow over time in a system that is dynamic and symbiotically interacting with its environment. At any point in time, however, in a static situation, the energy is fixed. How, then, do systems allocate that energy? How do they do it most efficiently? The energy is used for developing a role, for synchronizing incompatible roles and for practicing a role that is already developed.

The Dance: The Sequence of PAEI Role Development on the Typical Path

Imagine a very unusual square dance: There is no one calling the steps. Each of the four dancers has to develop its own dance and represent a different culture from around the world. Imagine Mexican, Thai, Balkan, and African dancers. The dancers have accepted the following assignment: By the end of the dance, they must develop their individual dances that represent their cultures, and they must integrate those individual dances so the four of them can dance the same dance together.

If you know anything about folk dancing, you know that these dancers face a formidable challenge. If you are not familiar with the variants of international folk dancing, imagine giving the same assignment to four dancers, each one with different training: classical ballet, modern jazz, folk, and Prussian marching.

In our case, the four dancers are **P**, **A**, **E**, and **I**.

P   *A*
E   *I*

How should the dancers proceed? In what order should they dance, and why should there be an order?

Who Is First?

In the first edition of this book, I stated that **E** is the first managerial role to develop. This is what we learn when we study economic theory (Joseph Alois Schumpeter)[1] and even psychology (David McClelland):[2] Entrepreneurial spirit fuels economic growth.

On the typical path, the **E** dancer goes to the center of the square dance and dances alone. Because neither he nor any of the others arrived with a well-developed dance, then and there, in the center of the square, he develops a dance that represents his culture. What is his dance about? It is about long-term effectiveness, and it is represented by the word *why*, which is synonymous with *what for*. **E** gives purpose to the dance. The other three dancers watch intently. The configuration of the dance at this point is **paEi**: **E** is dancing, while **p**, **a**, and **i** watch from their spaces, mimicking **E**'s movements. That's why I note **p**, **a**, and **i** in lowercase letters. That was the Courtship dance. If the **p**, **a**, and **i** don't watch and participate on some level, they won't be able to join later. We would have an Affair, **00E0**, instead of a Courtship, **paEi**.

Who Is Second?

Once **E** is comfortable and has developed the routine, who should join in? There are three candidates:

P represents	short-term		effectiveness.
A represents	short-term		efficiency.
I represents		long-term	efficiency.

Since

E represents		long-term	effectiveness,

who would **E** find to be the most compatible partner?

Let's first identify the most difficult partner and remove it from consideration. Because **E** is long-term effectiveness, **E**'s first partner must represent either the dimension of long term or of effectiveness. The most alien of the three would be a partner representing short term and efficiency. Such a partner has nothing in common with **E**. **A**, therefore, is beyond consideration. If, at this stage, **A** insists on dancing with **E**, it would ruin the dance. The two would interfere with each other, getting their legs so entangled that **E** would quit. That is exactly what happens in societies where government's intervention in business is too intense or in aging companies dominated by **A**.

Years ago, when I was a student, I read an article in *Fortune* magazine. The article, "The High-Flying that Might-Have-Been," stated that if all the companies, like TRW, Litton, and LTV, which had been established by Hughes Aircraft veterans, had been created *within* Hughes, Hughes would have been bigger than General Motors.[3] But Hughes's **E**ntrepreneurs found it impossible to deal with Hughes's restrictive **A** atmosphere, and they left to start their own companies. When the spin-offs become as restrictive and suffocating as the company from which their founders escaped, subsequent entrepreneurs feel encouraged to leave and start their own spin-offs.

At this early stage of the dance, therefore, it's premature to allow **A** to join in.

The remaining candidates are **P** and **I**. What seems more like long-term effectiveness? Long-term efficiency, **I**, or short-term effectiveness, **P**?

Here, it's important to consider the local culture. In Western society, where the work ethic is so strong, **P** is the obvious candidate. By work ethic, I do not refer only to the Protestant ethic Max Weber described in his *Protestant Ethic and the Spirit of Capitalism.*[4] The work ethic, I believe, applies to all societies that are subject to the rigors of winter weather. People in cooler climates had to plan ahead, producing and saving for the cold weather, while year-round abundance allowed people in tropical lands to live a day-to-day subsistence life.[5]

In cultures ruled by the work ethic, short-term effectiveness, **P** is more likely capable of translating long-term effectiveness, **E**, into the short term. **P** is closer to **E**: Both deal with effectiveness. This closeness is also reflected in language: **P** stands for *what,* and as I stated above, **E** stands for *why,* which is synonymous with *what for* in every language group I checked: Latinate, Semitic, and Slavic. Following the same thread, we see that *what* is the short-term *what for,* and *why (what for)* is the long-term *what.*

Because **P** and **E** differ only in their time-span orientation, we have **E** move out of the center, giving **P**—**E**'s short-term cousin—a chance to learn and develop his own dance before the two try dancing together. The other dancers watch from the edges, perhaps imitating **P**'s steps. That **Paei** dance mirrors the Infant stage of the life-cycle.

What happens, however, if, while **P** is dancing, **E** gets bored and leaves, taking **A** and **I** with him? In that **P000** dance, **P** dances alone, gets tired, and retires. The dance is over: Infant mortality sets in. If, however, **E** remains, watching intently and making comments that **P** takes into account, by the time **P** feels confident, what happens? Well, rather than have the third dancer learn to dance alone, it makes sense for the two who already know their steps to work on learning how to dance together. Remember the fixed limited energy? First, all the energy went into developing a role. Now that the **E** and **P** roles have developed, less energy is needed. The saved energy goes now to synchronize them and operate their dance. It's the same energy, with a different purpose. And this is what happens. **P** and **E** move to the center. They try to synchronize their individual dances into a new dance of long- and short-term effectiveness. Because the two share a common heritage of effectiveness, it's not too difficult to integrate their dances. With the other two at the edges, imitating the dancers' steps, that **PaEi** dance looks like Go-Go.

So far the two dancers have been practicing only one genre of dancing—effectiveness. Function—effectiveness—has been doing well, while form-efficiency—has had no chance to do anything yet. **A** and **I**, so far only observers, are getting nervous as the dance gets more and more furious—all function, no form. **P** and **E** are having fun as **E** continuously feeds new steps to **P**. **A**—so completely different from those two—fears joining their dance. Like wild horses trampling an inexperienced rider, **P** and **E** could destroy **A**.

After a while, **P** and **E** get used to dancing together. Energy is saved because no energy is necessary to synchronize their dances; they are dancing together. It's time for a third dancer to join them.

Who Is Third?

Who will be the third dancer? **A** or **I**? The typical path prefers short run over the long run. That is the typical path of the Western society as opposed to Eastern cultures. **A** joins the dance, but, like **P** and **E**, does **A** first try it alone? No. That won't work. If **A**, working alone, develops a different dance, it's unlikely that **A** could integrate it with the dance **P** and **E** do so well together. The solution? One of those two has to dance with **A**, integrating **A**'s contributions. Meanwhile, the other one should leave the center, watch, and wait.

Just as dancing with the experienced **P** and **E** would overwhelm, overpower, and destroy the tentative new dancer, **A**, a newcomer **A**dministrator who joins a **PaEi** organization finds himself powerless to deal with the founder and his or her entourage. In a Go-Go culture, a succession of **A**s has a terrible time getting in and surviving. If **A** never succeeds in dancing with **P** and **E**, if he fails to achieve his assignment to develop the **A** role, eventually, the **PE** dancers either get exhausted and quit or, because they kick up so much dust, someone stops them, and the dance is over. Why do they get exhausted? Energy is fixed and is used for operating the dance. **E** without boundaries set by **A** and **I** might bring so many new steps in rapid succession that **P** simply gets overwhelmed. **P** often ends up on his knees and stops dancing altogether because he cannot learn the new steps fast enough to keep up. By the time **P** learns the newest step, **E** is into something new. So **P** finds it better to stop and wait. That was the **P0E0** dance: the founder's or family trap.

In our square dance, then, either **E** or **P** has to sit down while the other one dances with **A**. Who should dance, and who should step to the side?

On the typical path, **E** usually refuses to sit and take a back seat. He was the first to dance and he's most interested in dancing by himself. Only reluctantly does he agree to dance with anyone else. True, he dances with **P**, but **P** is a close cousin. Will he leave the floor to the "enemy," to **A**? Not on your life. He recognizes that he needs **A**, but he passionately hates and despises it. So, with no enthusiasm at all, he finally invites **A** to dance, but he keeps **P** there, too. The two of them drag **A** all over the floor, until kicked, stepped on, and bruised black, red, and blue, **A** quits and goes not to the sidelines to sulk, but home. Another **A** joins only to suffer the same experience.

E starts to get annoyed. **P** desperately wants **A** to control the wild **E** that has been absolutely exhausting him. He wants **A** to join because **A** is also close to **P**. **A** is short-term efficiency, and **P** is short-term effectiveness. **P** does not feel so threatened by **A** as does **E**. As a matter of fact, **P** seems to be talking to **A** behind **E**'s back, trying to convince **A** to join and promising all kinds of alliances against **E**. **P** is anxious for order so he can use operational energy rather than developmental energy. **E** is losing his or her confidence because **P** is complaining loud and strong about **E**'s driving the dance in multiple directions. **P** is not cooperating and **E** is all over **P**, accusing him of not being productive, not being a responsive dancer, and so forth.

E and **P** start to resent one another. **E** is irritated that **P** is slow to respond to his new steps, and **P** objects to **E**'s furious pace. In their mutual rage, the two occasionally tread on bystanders' toes. They want **A** but they don't integrate it into their dance.

Reader, please observe: I am giving you a hint about what will happen. If **E** is controlling the dance, and, as yet, there is no **I**, **E** will fire a determined **A** and look for an **A** who has learned not to undermine **E**. In that case, the poor new **A** becomes a speck on **E**'s foot, dancing with **E** in any way **E** wants. **A** fails to perform the **A** dance at all. He is a shadow of who he was while he was at the corner of the dance floor. Does **E** respect him now that **A** is so compliant? No way! **E** treats him like a surplus ballast, ignores him, and criticizes his ineffectiveness in public or behind his back. **A** will be unable to join the dance, and he becomes either a **0**—deadwood—or he quits.

There is still no **A** in the dance.

Here's another possible scenario. **A** joins and tries to slow the dance so he can participate. To do that he needs to control the driving force—obviously **E**—of the **PE** dance. **A**, aiming to undermine **E**, tries to get him out of the dance. The two begin to fight. Nobody is dancing now although their kick boxing might look like a dance to someone. Meanwhile, **P** is lost and cannot dance: **E** is pulling him in one direction, trying to show him new steps, and **A** is ordering him to stick to the dance **A** has planned. Bewildered, **P** sits down. Dissent among the dancers has ruined the dance, and eventually it is over. The dance has gone bankrupt.

Another scenario is that **A** does succeed in eliminating **E**, assisted by **P** who, exhausted, also wants **E** out. Now **P** and **A** dance together. It is a good dance—short-term effectiveness and efficiency—that both enjoy, but it's so highly regimented that it starts to look more like a march than a dance. The energy is used for **P** and **A**, but without **E** there is no new energy coming in, no new steps, and no new outlook. The dance repeats itself to the point of being old hat and obsolete. The audience leaves, and, with no one watching, the dancers, who miss the clapping that gave them the energy to continue, stop the dance altogether.

Stepping on Each Other's Toes

That dance describes the pain of Adolescence. What happens in Adolescence depends on who wins the struggle between **E** and **A**. Who will kick out whom? If, as described above, **E** repeatedly forces **A** to leave, the organization suffers the founder's trap, but if **A** kicks **E** out, the organization suffers from premature aging.

If **A** manages to get **E** out of the dance, **E** leaves and goes home sulking. What happens to the dance when **E** departs? Energy for dancing starts to decline because **E**'s interaction with the internal and/or the external environment—coming up with new ideas, new purposes—is the source of energy. **E** provides long-term effectiveness, and with **E**'s disappearance, the dancers no longer know why they are dancing. They cannot dance just for the sake of dancing. Their dance needs purpose. Granted, purpose changes, but the dancers need a reason for dancing. At first their purpose may be simply to win applause; then, they may want to perform in a festival; and later on they may be hoping to make a movie of their dancing. **E** is the factor that imparts the ever-evolving long-term goal. If it should disappear, when the dancers achieve their stated purpose, which is no longer evolving, they go home. They have no more reason to dance.[6] The dance dies. To have the dance continue indefinitely, **E** must be dancing all the time. If one **E** gets tired, another member of the **E** tribe should join to keep the dance going.

E, then, must always be dancing or ready to join. Is there a problem with that? When **A** squeezes **E** out and has control over the **P** dancer, a new **E** will find it difficult to join. The last thing **A** wants is someone to mess up his orderly dance. **I** might join so long as it abides by **A**'s rules. Without **E** everyone eventually runs out of energy, and one by one, dancers start to leave.

Energy serves three necessary purposes: to develop new dancers or roles, to synchronize the dancers who need to learn to dance together, and to support the actual dancing. When energy declines, role development is the first purpose to be deprived of adequate energy. **P** pulls out first: He misses having **E** to give him new steps. He dances all right, but after a while his dance starts to look like a march. Now that **P** has left, what energy remains is reserved for operations. Only **A** remains, dancing alone until it runs out of energy, freezes in a motion, and remains like a sculpture. That is premature aging and death. The organization dies, never having reached Prime.

As you can see, it is very difficult to make the transition from short- and long-term function, **PE**, to short-term efficiency, **A**. How, then, should organizations accomplish that transition? What is healthy, albeit painful? And what is abnormal and potentially pathological?

The Healthy Dance on the Typical Path

In the earlier edition of this book, I said **E** should stay and dance with **A**, and **P** should take a rest. I knew, when I instructed organizations to do that, I was asking them to do something very difficult and painful. I didn't know better. I thought that if an organization allowed **E** to decline, it would age prematurely. It does lose energy. But I was prisoner to the concept that **E** is indispensable. I was caught up in the near sanctity of the entrepreneurial spirit. Today, with more experience and a better understanding of the four roles, I am more courageous about challenging established concepts. Today, after several years, I see I was wrong. I forced **P** to retreat and boosted **E** by emphasizing vision and strategy. From where did we get the energy to synchronize the arch-enemies, **A** and **E**? I made **P** step to the sidelines and developed **A** by cutting **P**. My clients resisted and fought, but I insisted. And I was wrong!

What was wrong with my earlier assumptions? Let's consider. Who should retreat, **P** or **E**? The role that is closer in character to **A** should stay.

P represents	short-term		effectiveness.
A represents	short-term		efficiency.
E represents		long term	effectiveness.
I represents		long-term	efficiency.

If **A** is short-term efficiency, which other role is most like **A**? **E**—long-term effectiveness—is neither short term nor efficiency-oriented. **E** should leave the dance and wait on the back bench. **P**, like **A**, is oriented to the short term. True, effectiveness and efficiency are different, but let short-term efficiency integrate with short-term effectiveness first, allowing for the development of a system with short-term effectiveness and efficiency.[7] Later, we can try for the long-run orientation. Doesn't that make sense?

"Now, before we get busy with any new ideas, is the time to make old ideas work," Stuart Resnick, chairman of Franklin Mint, told me. He and other companies objected to my advice that their companies should keep **EA**, that is, that they should continue to develop their vision and strategy for expansion while systematizing their organizations. They insisted that they should focus on **PA**. And they were right. That is what should and does happen in successful companies on the typical path. Some venture capital companies make a living of doing that. They look for companies that are in the founder's trap, buy them out, appoint a **PA** to organize and systematize them, and take them public, making a good profit.

Adding I to Reach Prime

What is the difference between this **PA** version of the dance and the **PA** of premature aging, which I described above as highly undesirable? The difference is **E**'s state of mind and sense of control. In premature aging, **E** is kicked out, goes home, or tries to start another dance somewhere else. In the above healthy transition, **E** voluntarily and without losing control takes a back seat for a short time, giving the **P** and the **A** time to get to know each other. It takes self-discipline and, most important, it requires **I**. Now, reader, I am giving you another powerful hint: **I** is crucial. If there is no **I**, **E** and **A** fight and destroy each other. If there is **I**, self-discipline, and an understanding of the process, **E** can, for a short time, take a back seat and return later, rejuvenated and ready to help the organization reinvent itself.

Once **P** and **A** can dance well together, **P** should rest, giving his old partner **E** a chance to dance with **A**. Dancing with the somewhat similar **P** has prepared **A** for **E**, and the challenge is not too overwhelming.

That is the healthy dance on the typical path. The difference between normal and abnormal is the degree of mutual trust and respect **E** and **A** have for each other. And mutual respect is a function of **I**. If one kicks the other out, that event is abnormal and can be pathological. They need to give each other space, in the right sequence, and with the right timing.

What comes next? **P**, **A**, and **E** know how to dance together in pairs. Now is the time for all three to dance together. **P** rejoins, and we have a **PAE** dance.

To be sure we did not lose the sequence of the healthy dance on the typical path so far, here it is:

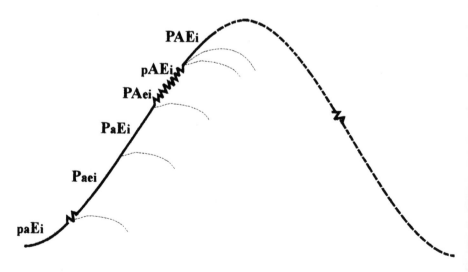

Figure 11-1: The Sequence of the Typical Path

Isn't it time for **I** to join? It sure is the last minute. It's almost too late. It should have joined no later than Adolescence when it was needed desperately to negotiate the fight for life and death between **E** and **A**. The earlier **I** joins, the better. This, reader, is my third hint to you. **I** joins with little difficulty because **I** can dance with anyone. **I** is a true polyglot able to speak any language, or I should say, dance any dance.

Do we have a **PAEI** dance? Are we there now? Have we reached the promised land—Prime? Yes. But you must take care of the land, irrigating, fertilizing, and cultivating it. Even the promised land can become a desert through negligence and inaction. It is clear, however, that the **PAEI** dance does achieve its assignment: The four do manage to dance together. But their dance will gradually come to an end.

Because it is very difficult to add **I** at the late stage where **P, A,** and **E** are dancing but not comfortably with each other, **I** will be vulnerable. Without **I, E** declines. **E** does not thrive in a threatening, aggressive environment. **E** needs nurturing. This is an interesting point. While **E** needs an Integrated environment, it sows disintegration. While **E**s hate people being aggressive with them, they are nevertheless aggressive with others. With low **I** or unstable **I, E** starts to retreat. When **E** goes down, the organization moves to late Prime and then to a stage of the lifecycle I call the Fall: **PAeI**.

The Fall

How does that happen? **E** is surrounded by form: **A** and **I**. And **P**, which is being driven by **E**, isn't helping **E**; it is driven by **E**. Unless **E** gets additional sustenance by shaking the overwhelming embrace of **AI**, the dance will look too much like the Depression-era marathon dance nightmare portrayed in the movie *They Shoot Horses, Don't They?*[8] **E** gets exhausted and pulls out. In Chapter 14, I explain the reasons for **E**'s decline, the causes of aging. The life span of Prime depends on how fast **A** takes over and starts shackling **E**'s feet and how fast the environment changes. Does the audience issue relentless demands for new dances?

When **E** goes down, which role should fall back? Reductions in long-term effectiveness affect short-term effectiveness. **P** is the closest to **E**. **E** drives **P**, and if **E** retires or leaves altogether, **P** will eventually have to leave, too. The Talmud teaches us, "If you don't know where you're going, any road will take you there." So when we lose our long-term goals, we lose the drive to run. **P** feels lonely. Surrounded by form and the lonely representative of function, **P** is ready to pull out. Time to go. What remains is a **pAeI** dance—mostly form, little function. That is the Aristocratic stage of the lifecycle.

With **E** and **P** down, function keeps falling, the organization's relationship with its environment disintegrates. External **I** has gone down. The competitive marketplace does not let that crime go unpunished. The company starts to lose market share. Eventually, the disintegration becomes pathological because the ability to survive is on the line. Internal disintegration follows, internal **I** goes down, and the witch hunts start: Who did it? Who can we blame? That is the Salem City stage of the lifecycle, and, when **I** disappears altogether, only a stump of **0A00** remains. The tree is gone. There are no leaves. Only the dead stump—memories of a tree that was once there. That is Bureaucracy. Because the organization serves no one,

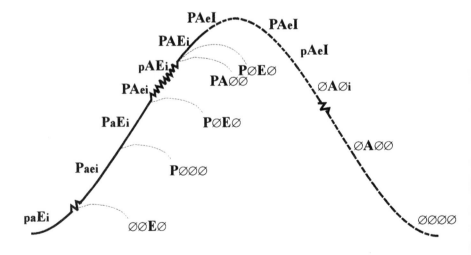

Figure 11-2: The Lifecycle of Organizations

when even **A**, the remaining stump, is eventually cut, the organization dies: **0000**.

Now that we have shown how the four managerial roles relate to one another on a metaphorical level, in Chapter 12, we will see how they manifest themselves behaviorally in the different stages of the lifecycle.

Notes

1. See J. Schumpeter, *Business Cycles: A Theoretical, Historical and Statistical Analysis of the Capitalist Process* (New York: McGraw Hill, 1939), for the development of managerial roles, especially entrepreneurship.

2. See for development of managerial roles, especially need and motivation, D. McClelland, *Motivating Economic Achievement* (New York: The Free Press, 1969) and *The Achieving Society* (Princeton, NJ: Van Nostrand, 1961).

3. Refer to G. Bylinsky, "The High-Flying That Might-Have-Been," *Fortune* 77, 15 (1968): 100-103.

4. Consider M. Weber, *The Protestant Ethic and the Spirit of Capitalism* (London: Unwin, 1930). The more accessible version was published in 1958 in New York by Charles Scribners.

5. See J. Diamond, *Guns, Germs, and Steel: The Fates of Human Societies* (New York: Norton, 1997).

6. This point is made by D. Bell in *The End of Ideology: On the Exhaustion of Political Ideas in the Fifties,* rev. ed. (New York: The Free Press, 1963).

7. George J. Stigler offered mathematical proof suggesting how short-term efficiency can be detrimental to long-term effectiveness with his formulations in price theory on how short-term and long-term variable and fixed costs curves behave. See G.J. Stigler, *Theory of Price* (New York: Macmillan, 1966).

8. I. Winkler, R. Chartoff, and S. Pollack, prods., *They Shoot Horses, Don't They?,* written by R.E. Thompson, based on a novel by H. McCoy (Palomar Productions, 1969).

CHAPTER TWELVE

PAEI and the Lifecycle: Stage by Stage

Now let us see how the dance manifests itself in the lifecycle of organizations.

Courtship—paEi

During Courtship, would-be founders develop commitment that will ultimately give birth to operating organizations. These founders identify needs and build commitment to respond to those needs. On the typical path, then, Entrepreneuring is the most important role. It provides for proactive behavior; it identifies future needs in the present; and it generates willingness to undertake risk in order to satisfy the needs. Building commitment is manifested by excitement, passion, or *falling in love* with an idea.

Organizations are born when commitment is tested, and they die when there is no commitment to functionality: when we don't know why we are doing whatever we are doing.

We can gauge an organization's vitality by the number of people in the organization who are committed to it and its functionality.

Since all four **PAEI** roles are necessary for an organization to be in Prime, there must be ingredients of each at conception.

The **P**erforming, **A**dministering, and **I**ntegrating roles provide reality-testing for the **E**ntrepreneuring role during Courtship. The difference between normal and abnormal Courtship is the presence or lack of the other three roles. A normal Courtship is **paEi**; an abnormal Courtship is **00E0**: The **P**, **A**, and **I** are missing. The organization experiences no reality-testing of the commitment. Reality-testing considers *what* we are going to do—**P**; *how* we are going to do it—**A**; and *who* is going to do it, *how,* and *with whom*—**I**.

A Courtship with no reality-testing is an affair. When confronted with a real test of commitment, the Courtship will dissolve. Thus, all four roles must exist, at least latently, in Courtship.

Why do **P**erforming, **A**dministering, and **I**ntegrating provide reality-testing of **E**ntrepreneuring? **P**erforming, **A**dministering, and **I**ntegrating are incompatible with **E**ntrepreneuring. So *small* doses of **P**, **A**, and **I** are the reality-testing challenges to **E**ntrepreneuring.

The composition of a business plan serves as Courtship's reality test. It is as if each of the questions is a small injection of **P**, **A**, and **I**. The founder must answer the *what, how,* and *who* questions because the incompatibility of those roles could demolish the **E** idea. Although each dose of **P, A, I** testing has to be mild enough not to destroy **E**, it must nevertheless be adequate to provide an indication of what is ahead. Without that, at the first sign of a *what, how,* or *who* difficulty, commitment will evaporate, and rather than a healthy Courtship, the organization is left with only an affair. Those small injections of **P, A, I** act like an inoculation to develop resistance and immunity to disease. They test to see whether all those roles are there, awaiting future development.

What if there were no test of the commitment to **E**ntrepreneuring during the Courtship phase? Later, in Infancy, the organization will come face-to-face with big **P**erformance demands, and if it lacks adequate commitment, the organization might dissolve.

In simpler terms, the transition from romantic dreaming to actual doing is not easy. When an organization is conceived, it must simulate the reality that will confront it in the immediate future and throughout its lifecycle. It must determine whether the organization can survive the simulation before real challenges confront it. The seeds of future subsystems must exist at conception.

A healthy Courtship is thus paEi while an affair is 00E0.

Infancy—Paei

The **P**roducing role develops in Infancy: The focus is on *what now?* To allow **P** enough energy to develop, **E** goes dormant. "I want no more ideas. Give me results—now!"

A healthy Infancy is characterized by **Paei**. An organization cannot survive Infancy as **P000** or, in the case of repetitive innovation, with no focus on results, **paEi**.

During a normal Infancy, the dominance of **P** and the relative weakness of **A**, **E**, and **I** allow for obsessive devotion to quantifiable results at the expense of the process. In this reactive environment, the lack of patience is regarded as normal. But, if it is not controlled later on, that impatience sows the seeds of destruction.

When commitment is tested against reality and risk is undertaken, organizations are born, and **P**erforming takes precedence. Administering and Integrating remain suppressed as they were during Courtship. However, the increase in **P**erfoming decreases Entrepreneuring. Why?

What propels founders? It is their commitment to the crying need they believe they are destined to fulfill. When their organizations finally open for business and they have assumed risk, the founders plunge in with gusto. It is a do-do-do time. Founders must protect their dreams.

Infant organizations must perform the function for which they were established. If they don't deliver, they quickly die. Furthermore, the risk undertaken during Infancy must be covered by action. Hard work delivers on the commitment for which risk was undertaken.

P is the functional orientation. This functional orientation exists with all infant systems, including human infants. During the first months of life, babies focus exclusively on functional needs—eating, sleeping, and being warm and dry. Likewise, Infant organizations focus on **P**. They must have cash—liquidity—in order to survive.

In Infant organizations, **A**dministering, **E**ntrepreneuring, and Integration are low, **Paei**. **P** dances alone, and **a**, **e**, and **i** watch. The **P**erforming role is dominant, and that is normal. An Infant organization managed by a Lone Ranger, who doesn't delegate and works like a one-man band, is perfectly normal. That's what the Infant requires. Think of the mother of a newborn infant. She is always feeding, rocking, and changing her baby. She wouldn't behave differently and, say, try to teach her baby Latin. She knows that her baby needs to have its functional needs satisfied first. Likewise, during Infancy, founders need to tend first and above all to the functional needs of their newborns.

Go-Go—PaEi

The **P**erforming role eventually reaches the threshold of stabilization. The supplier list is stable, and cash flow is secure because clients have started to repeat their orders. With **P** fully developed, **E**ntrepreneuring can increase. Why? In Courtship, **E**ntrepreneuring was high and a vision emerged. **E**ntrepreneuring fell during Infancy while the organization devoted its energies to testing the viability of that vision. **P**erforming had to be high. Once the organization passes that test, energy is available to support the vision, which once again propels the organization with full force: **E**ntrepreneuring goes back up.

At the end of Infancy, with both **P** and **E** roles strong and healthy in the organizational memory, the organization can expend energy to unite **P** and **E** and deal with their incompatibility. The **P** and the **E** roles need to operate together. Go-Go time is a **PaEi** culture. If the culture is characterized by **P0E0**, with neither minimal **A** nor threshold **I**, both of which need to develop next, the organization will be caught in the founder's trap. The organization needs all four roles, some seemingly dormant but nevertheless there all the time. On the typical path, companies develop one role at the time, absorbing and integrating each into the organizational behavior.

This sequence is important to note. During Courtship, **E** is up first. In Infancy, **P**erforming goes up and **E**ntrepreneuring goes down. During Go-Go, both **P** and **E** stabilize together before the third role can grow: Both the *what* and the *what for* stabilize before the *how* role can be developed.

If the **E**ntrepreneuring role cannot develop because the organization remains in a perpetual **P**erforming orientation, a pathological Infancy occurs. The Infant never emerges from its functional orientation. It is preoccupied with food, sleep, and wetness even though many years have passed.

An organization that can't get past the trials of Infancy—negative cash flow, an unstable client base, a continuous fight for survival—is developing abnormally. Eventually it will die because the energy required for development is higher than the energy necessary for maintenance.

Organizations embark on the Go-Go stage when **P**erforming and **E**ntrepreneuring are at high levels. Those high levels of **P** and **E** explain its behavior. A Go-Go is *what-* and *why*-oriented. It is results-oriented for the short and long run. There are dreams, like during Courtship, but the organization is trying to realize them instantly, as it did in Infancy. That's why the transition from Infancy to Go-Go is a transition from management-by-crisis to crisis-by-management.

A Go-Go company expands rapidly in many different directions, intuitively and quite flexibly. In a very short time, it might find that it has overcommitted its resources. It might run out of cash, not because the situation calls for it, but because management wants to do too much. The organization has little control. The difference between the budgets and actual performance is high. Policies, if there are any, are violated, and the power is highly concentrated with the founder.

In Go-Go, the **A**dministrative role is low. Its lack of development explains the lack of systemization, the lack of order, the lack of an organization chart, and the lack of clearly defined tasks and specialization. The organization is structured around people rather than around the tasks to be performed. In the Go-Go stage, the organization adapts to accommodate the people rather than the people having to adapt to fill the needs of the organization.

An organization finds itself caught in abnormal Go-Go if **A** cannot develop. **A** must develop next. The short-range *how* must precede long-range *how* before the **I**ntegrating role can develop. The need for **A** is less apparent if **I** derives from the social culture in which the organization exists. That is the situation in the Far East where entrepreneurial families can build huge trading companies with little **A**. They have abundant **I**.

The lack of planning processes causes Go-Gos to lose control, and the lack of patience—a trait left over from Infancy—combined with typical Go-Go arrogance lead to a lack of tolerance. That, in turn, causes a lack of mutual respect, which has the power to destroy an Adolescent organization: It won't allow **I** to join the dance, but without **I**, the **A-E** fight is dysfunctional.

Adolescence—PAei or pAEi

A crisis that demands the **A**dministering role prompts the transition from Go-Go to Adolescence. On the typical path, **A** emerges when the organization experiences pain. A crisis in Go-Go triggers the development of **A**dministration. The higher the Go-Go's arrogance, the bigger the crisis necessary to trigger the transition to Adolescence. The organization needs stabilization, order, and to set priorities. That means that the Go-Go's time for deciding what *else* to do is over. Now it's time to decide what *not* to do. The organization turns its focus away from the *what* and *when,* directing its attention to the *how.* If the organization doesn't allow that to happen, it falls into the founder's trap or the family trap, abnormal situations which could, over time, spell its pathological demise.

The A-E Struggle

Many organizations that try to progress on their own dynamics lose **E** because the growth in **A**dministration threatens **E**ntrepreneurship. **A** and **E** are opposite roles, and they are in conflict. That conflict might take the following form: To put his company in order, a founder might hire a chief financial officer or vice president of administration. The new person performs the **A**dministrative role. He may feel hostility toward the founder, who performs the **E**ntrepreneurial role. The **E** founder continuously changes direction, bringing new opportunities into the company. For an **E**ntrepreneur, every problem is an opportunity. But, for an **A**dministrator, every opportunity is a problem. The **A**dministrative person is focusing on *how* to do it and on the repercussions of doing it. What appears to be an opportunity for **E** is usually a problem for **A**.

Eventually, the **A**dministrative type starts to see the founder as the company's problem. The founder won't allow the system to stabilize. At that point, an alliance might develop between the chief administrative officer and the board of directors, which also seeks

Administrative stability. They form their alliance at the expense of the founder, whom they perceive as uncontrollable. If their alliance is fruitful, they might squeeze the founder out of his own company. If he is not fired, he might find that with no support and enthusiasm for his leadership, the atmosphere has become unpalatable. He might well decide to start all over again with a new company. I believe that's what happened to Apple Computer's founder Steve Jobs. The earlier departure of Jobs's partner, Steve Wozniak, the creative engineer, was the harbinger of an **E**ntrepreneurial exodus.

The struggle between **E**ntrepreneurship and **A**dministration is even more acute in partnerships. The founding partnership is usually a complementary team, a **PE** and an **AI**. During the advanced stages of Go-Go, the **PE**, who took the risk and brought opportunities to the company, is usually the driving force. In Adolescence, however, the **AI** rejects the opportunities **PE** wants to follow as being too expansive. So, the **AI** partner begins to resist the plans of the **PE** partner. "One more idea," **A** says, "and I'm going to break out in a rash." And **E** is thinking, "How did I get involved with such an inactive, placid, risk-averse partner? I built this company despite him, and now he is becoming a barrier to future growth."

When an **E** founder has neither a majority of the stock nor control of the board, by and large, the **A**dministrative type wins the struggle. Why? For one thing, entrepreneurs believe they can always put down roots somewhere else. Furthermore, they don't like the reality of running a highly complex organization. They prefer *building* to *running* their businesses. They hate detail. Entrepreneuring is incompatible with **A**dministrating. Entrepreneurs prefer the wide-brush approach to problem solving, but wide-brush solutions at this stage of the lifecycle are not functional. The side effects of such solutions for a company that is already operating are more threatening than the original problem.

Founders start dreaming about the good old days when their companies were small, flexible, and responsive. Now that their babies are too big to handle, they think that leaving and once again starting and leading something small and exciting seems very attractive. For their part, however, **A**dministrative types have no place to go, and besides, they like to manage systematically. They try to buy out the **E**ntrepreneurs. The boards, or those in power, generally side with the **A**dministrative types. They recognize the need for order, and they know that unpredictable Entrepreneurship won't provide that. So the alliance of **A** with the board squeezes **E** out.

We see that this phenomenon affects not only founders. As systems and controls are introduced, as "no" is heard more frequently than "yes," other entrepreneurial types also start leaving. There is an exodus of **E**s and an influx of **A**s. I call this phenomenon premature aging. The company got old before it reached Prime.

After Go-Go, **PaEi**, organizations need to develop **A**.

Which of the two roles, **P** or **E**, should be temporarily dormant, giving **A** the chance to develop?

Who should yield?

In the first edition of this book, my answer to that question was **P**. Now, ten more years of experience have taught me that I was wrong. **PA**, which I used to consider premature aging, is the right combination. **EA** is so prone to conflict that a dormant **I** can be destroyed. If, as I recommended in the previous edition, **P** declines, the enormous struggle between **A** and **E** prolongs the pain of Adolescence. A decline in **P** would cause too much trauma to an organization that still has memories of its Infancy, when **P** was king. **E** must rest for a while. It has been driving the company long enough. Also, if you reconsider the "dance," you'll recall that **P** dances more efficiently with **A** while **E** rests.

In a healthy transition there should be some temporary respite for **E**, but **E** should not lose control or disappear altogether. Instead, **E** should use its authority to enable **P** and **A** to develop. For healthy growth, the **PA** interval should be short. Then the **E** role must come back to create the **PAEi** culture of the organization, which is Prime.

Organizations in which **E** insists on dominating and refuses to cool off for a while, find they are continuously innovating and never finishing anything. A **PE** culture can be so strong that it repeatedly rejects any attempts to grow **A**. What starts as an abnormal problem will become pathological. The company gets sued for violating regulations; product quality deteriorates below acceptable standards; product shipments are so late that customers no longer accept them. Eventually, the organization goes bankrupt.

The founder's trap returns by virtue of the failure to institutionalize the *what* and *why*: The company has not developed Administration or Integration of the Performing and Entrepreneuring functions. Without the **A** and the **I** roles, the organization cannot function as a system. Instead, it centers on a single individual who makes decisions as he or she sees fit, refusing to allow a system that narrows the choices. The organization depends completely on the person leading it, causing the **E** role as well as the **I** role to become monopolized.

Institutionalization of **P**erforming and **E**ntrepreneuring allows decentralization of those functions without loss of control. For an organization to move into Prime, institutionalization must occur. There must be rules and policies, **A**, and/or sound values, **I**. And the founder must be subject to them. Only then can the organization emerge as a system independent of the founder who established it.

Administration gains authority at the expense of either **P**erforming or **E**ntrepreneuring, which are already developed. The energy the new **A** role requires for its development must come from somewhere. If it comes at the expense of **E**ntrepreneuring, development will be normal. If it comes at the expense of **P**erforming, the company will follow a pathological progression.

Self-discipline

Adolescence is a time of testing and screening. Some organizations advance and flourish, and others flounder. Success is the prize for those with self-discipline.

The entire sequence starts with **E**. Then **P** rises, and **E** falls. Then both **P** and **E** are up. The sequence is smooth, as if dictated by the dynamics of organizational growth. The founder just follows the cues. During Adolescence, however, founders face a choice. Will management take over or be taken over by events? Does management lead or does it follow?

Over the years, I have noted that in any endeavor—the arts, sports, business, even crime—champions are made not just because they have talent. Talent is, of course, a prerequisite for excelling, but talent alone is a waste, producing no lasting impact. To really succeed, one needs self-discipline to control urges and short-term temptations.

The greater the talent, the greater is the need
for self-discipline.

According to Jewish tradition: "Who is the hero? The one who can conquer his urges."

Self-discipline without talent is barren. Talent without self-discipline is a torrent of sparks that won't catch fire. For controlled burning, one needs a controlled spark. In Adolescence, the need for organizational self-discipline emerges.

Up until Adolescence, talent to sense the needs of the market is enough to manage an Infant or Go-Go. In Adolescence, discipline emerges. Will it match talent? If it does not, the organization will wander. If the rise in discipline destroys the talent, the switch has been too sudden, and the organization will become stuck.

Adolescent organizations must make conscious decisions to do less of one thing so they can spend more time doing something else. Their people must spend less time dreaming new dreams and more time in meetings and getting organized to deliver the current dreams.

This is not so simple and obvious as it might appear. I have worked with many company founders who refuse to get organized. One of them said to me, "Please, please don't put me in a box." He was referring to the organization chart. Discipline is alien to them. They succeeded, innovated, and were entrepreneurial by breaking boundaries and resisting discipline. Getting **E**s to accept discipline is the beginning of therapy for organizational transitions.

To allocate resources in order to accomplish *fewer* things *better* requires self-discipline. In the past, investing in *more—not better—* produced the desired results. An **E** needs the self-discipline to step back. That significant change in behavior does not occur naturally as it did when the organization moved from Infancy to Go-Go. For a successful Adolescence, organizations need to wean themselves from **E**. Will founders, who are strongly **E**-oriented, allow that? If not, the gaping jaws of the founder's trap may be inescapable.

The Significance of I

I have observed that organizations with the **I**ntegrating role present have an easier time making the switch from **E** to **A**. The higher the Integration, the easier it is for **A**dministering to emerge. This is explained by the fact that **I**—the long-term *how*—aids **A**—the short-term *how*. Those roles support each other.

Where did the Integration function come from? I could derive from the larger culture, within which the organization develops, or from the values of the people who comprise and lead the organization. Japanese culture, for example, provides I to its organizations. The organization does not have to develop it. That means that it's easier for a Japanese company to get to Prime than it is for an Israeli or Greek company that must develop I in an intensely Entrepreneurial environment with little Integration. Using the **PAEI** roles for analysis and prediction, it is also easy to see that the Japanese, weak on **E**, can age organizationally faster than an Israeli or Greek company. (If you can find a Japanese company led by Israelis, I suggest you buy the stock in a hurry.)

The role of Adizes therapy is to move organizations from Go-Go to Adolescence—from entrepreneurial management to professional management—developing the Administrative system through Integration, which frequently has to be nourished and protected.

Prior to Adolescence, the leader as an individual—most often the founder—performs the I role. Everyone reports to the founder, and everyone waits for his or her decisions in times of conflict. That has to change in Adolescence, which calls for systematization of the decision-making process and professionalization of management. The I function needs to be institutionalized before **E** can be decentralized. Let me explain what that means.

Up to Adolescence, external integration is achieved by the leader, often the founder, of the organization. Then the organization runs up against the problems of Go-Go, and the company experiences external disintegration. It hyperventilates and misses some markets or goals. It aims for too much, but it gets less than anticipated. Internal integration becomes an issue especially when the **A** is brought in or when the **A**, reacting to the crisis **E** has brought about, starts to assert itself. Who achieves the Integration now? The organization has grown large and complex, and Integration—internal integration—is not the forte of most founders. The organization needs to develop a system of governance. It needs to hold executive meetings of a known and established membership, following rules of conduct that govern decision-making and dissemination of those decisions. People need to know what is expected of them, where to go for help with decisions they are not authorized to make, and how to get those decisions made. There need to be organizational processes that are not dependent on the availability and the mood of the leader.

The **I** function needs to be transferred from the individual to the organization. Also, instead of being **I**ntegrated around **E**, which is great for excitement but not very helpful for follow-up on decisions, the organization needs to be **I**ntegrated through the **A**dministrative function. It needs the nuts and bolts of, for example, manuals for inventory control, policies on collection, and procedures for hiring and firing. "The devil is in the details," the Arabs say, and if the details are not ironed out, the devil will pay more than one visit.

I have observed American companies that are socially concerned and dedicated to the protection of the environment. Such socially conscious organizations rely on **EI** excitement—vision and values—to guide them to success. If those companies succeed and grow, **EI** is, however, not enough to make them successful for the long haul. There is excitement and passion, but their lack of attention to such details as supply management and budgetary control has a negative impact on morale and the commitment of people. Their passion for the vision eventually fades. Organizations need all the four roles. These days, **E** and **I** are in vogue. But watch out. Without **A**, **I** will suffer and eventually bring about the decline of **E**.

Goals

The general culture of a company is never the problem of a single individual: It's a problem of the system.[1] When a system is built on expediency rather than on tasks and organizational needs, function rules. The organization neglects form until dysfunction reigns.

Prior to Adolescence, function is everything. Form is less important. Integration and Administration are at low levels, while Performance and Entrepreneurship are high. The organization is structured around people, and its organization chart looks like the drawing of a kindergartner, with lines going in all directions. Eventually, the organization grows too big and too complicated to manage. The interdependencies look like a Gordian knot, and the more you pull on it, the more difficult it is to untangle. Change is the company's source of success, but now change presents more problems than opportunities.

When structure is built around people, functional accountability grows increasingly convoluted. *Controllable* change is difficult to achieve. Form must evolve to structure the function. The driving and driven forces exchange places. Until Adolescence, the organization is compromised to fulfill its participants' needs. In Adolescence, the organization becomes the *driving* force and people are compromised to fulfill the organization's needs.

In Adolescence the organization turns its attention inward. The deterministic and constraint goals change places. Deterministic goals are those we aim to achieve. Constraint goals are conditions we want to maintain. Our goal is not to violate those conditions.

Sales growth is the deterministic goal of Go-Go, and as a result of the efficiency of implementation, the constraint goal is profit.

During Adolescence, the organization experiences goal displacement. Profit, the outcome of efficiency, becomes the deterministic goal, while sales growth becomes the constraint goal. "We want maximum profits, and *no less* than X percent annual sales growth," replaces, "We want *at least* X percent annual sales growth, with no less than Y percent profit margin on sales."

Profits during the Go-Go stage are happenstance rather than predetermined. A Go-Go can explain why it *was* profitable, but it cannot explain why it *will be* profitable. And even though a Go-Go can explain why it was profitable, it cannot provide assurance that it can repeat that performance. It does not have enough control to make what's desired actually happen.

If the organization survives early Adolescence, avoiding pathological behavior, Entrepreneuring will emerge again in late Adolescence. Because the organization has simultaneously been institutionalizing **A**, when **E** emerges at this stage, rather than being individualistic, it will be an organizational effort. The organization can recreate itself, developing a more professional vision. The new vision, no longer just the dreams of an eager founder, has the foundations of a plan and strategy. Now is the time to trim the young tree, funneling the energy in positive and fruitful directions. Companies that manage to accomplish that enter the beginning of Prime. **P**, **A**, and **E** are strong. And **I**, which was absolutely indispensable for making the transition, has developed as well.

Up to Go-Go, the Integration role is fulfilled by founders, externally and internally. That gives them a monopoly on the Entrepreneurial role. **E** needs to be emancipated from personally individualized performance. To institutionalize **E**, **I** must first be depersonalized. External **I** calls for matching company capabilities to market opportunities. The company has to develop strategy that is supported by management. Then the company will need internal **I** to implement a new structure that reflects that strategy.

Early Prime—PAEi

When systems are in place, a function of **A**dministration, organizations are high-growth and high-profit in orientation, and they can afford to be. Let's review the transition.

In Infancy, the goal is cash because Infant organizations are function-oriented, and to function, Infants need cash—liquidity. The typical complaint of Infant companies is "We are undercapitalized." They grow faster than their ability to secure liquidity for future growth.

The goals of the Go-Go stage are sales and market share. Go-Gos assume that more sales mean more cash and profits and that the profit margin is stable. Only a crisis alerts Go-Go organizations to their declining margins. To achieve more sales they sacrifice profits by increasing the cost of sales. At a certain point, more is not better. More is worse.

In the course of reviewing the costs and expenditures of my clients, I have demonstrated to at least one of those clients that by the time the company had paid sales commissions and customer discounts on its skyrocketing sales, and had subtracted the cost of capital to finance those sales, there were no profits left for the company. As a matter of fact, the company was losing money. It's not unusual to find companies in the advanced stages of Go-Go awarding sales bonuses while they are losing money. What is occurring is called *suboptimalization*. Sales are not producing more profits, and if the company orients all rewards toward sales, profits likely suffer.

Why would a company reward individuals while it is going broke? Because it doesn't *know* that it's going broke. That happens in Go-Gos because most Go-Gos lack good cost-accounting systems and adequate information systems. They rely on a patchwork of organizational structures, reward systems, and information flows.

Go-Gos are opportunity-driven rather than opportunity-driving. This trait is a remnant of Infancy when organizations are so hungry they grab any opportunity that will stretch survival. Such opportunities present themselves one after another during the Go-Go stage. Remembering Infancy, Go-Gos are loathe to pass on any opportunity. They let opportunities drive the organization. It takes maturity, a sense of security, and self-confidence to pass up an opportunity. Without control systems, organizations become addicted to results. They reward those who exploit opportunities, whether or not those ventures undermine the whole. To judge opportunities sensibly, organizations need information, budgeting systems, and control systems. During Adolescence, organizations do develop those systems, and by the time they reach Prime, they are opportunity-driving rather than opportunity-driven.

In Prime, organizations know what to do and what not to do. They know when to pass up an opportunity and why to pass on it. Prime organizations possess talent and discipline, vision and self-control. They focus on both quantity and quality. Form and function are balanced, and they can grow profitably.

Getting to Prime is difficult. Staying in Prime is even more difficult. When a Prime organization starts losing its Entrepreneurship, the organization begins to leave Prime. Why is the loss of **E** a cause for aging? **E** provides flexibility; it is the proactive force that introduces change. An organization is dead when it can no longer react to its environment. It stops being proactive when it loses Entrepreneurship. Later, because of that loss, it loses the ability to react as well. It loses **P**erformance when it stops satisfying client needs, and unless there is external subsidization, the organization becomes dysfunctional and dies. Incidentally, Robert Solow won the 1987 Nobel Prize in Economics for his 1956 work demonstrating that a nation's success is a consequence of its technological developments and not a function of the size of its labor force or the richness of its physical resources. Technological developments are a function of **E**.

How organizations behave after Prime and after the Fall may be attributed to a decline in **E**. The difference between **A**dministrators and **E**ntrepreneurs is that for an **E**ntrepreneur, everything is permitted unless specifically forbidden. For an **A**dministrator, everything is forbidden unless it is specifically permitted.

It's easier to be an **A**dministrator than to be an **E**ntrepreneur: It's less risky and less demanding. People who are only used to following and sticking to the rules have trouble being creative and taking risks. Their past experience with the reward system works against

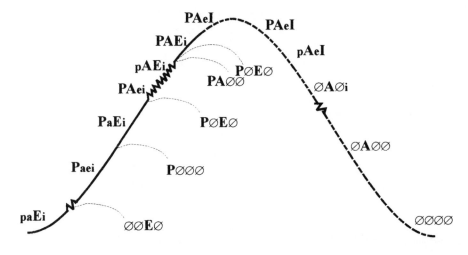

Figure 12-1: Organizational Lifecycle

creativity. Organizations need to introduce new reward systems, developing a different style and culture.

Bureaucratic behavior is like a lobster trap. It's very easy going in and very difficult getting out. Centralizing decisions is easy. Decentralizing is hard.

A drawing of the lifecycle shows that Prime is not at the top of the bell curve. Prime is on the way to the top. Why? In Prime, there is still **Entrepreneurship**—a source of flexibility that provides for organizational vitality as expressed in **PAEI** terms. Why do organizations move toward the pinnacle of the curve?

The bell curve expresses organizational vitality, and I define vitality as an organization's ability to be effective and efficient in the short and the long run. Organizational vitality does continue to rise, but it rises at a decreasing rate: The organization is losing its **E**. When it is green, it is growing. When it is ripe, it is rotten.

Prime is not a point in time. It is a process. Moving toward a certain point is better than being there. In human terms, it's not important what a person is; what's important is who he *was* and what he *will be*. What a person *is*, is transitory. We should focus on the process and not on the result. The process predicts the results.

When **A** develops and **E** returns, the three roles—**P**, **A**, and **E**—need to learn to act together synchronically. That is the challenge of

Prime. To succeed, the organization needs to develop **I**—in a big way. To bring **E** back, it needs to recreate itself, redefine its business, and define a potent, new unifying vision. To assure the development of **I**, the organization should not leave that process of creation to outside consultants alone. The organization ought to work with a facilitator, but the **I** role, which until that point had been provided by the founder or the **E**ntrepreneurial leader or had been subsumed by the **A** role, needs to be institutionalized throughout the organization. **I** needs to be organizational rather than individualistic. Likewise, new organizational **E** should not be individualistic. The process of leadership for **I**ntegrating the whole organization (**paEI**) should produce organizational **E**ntrepreneurship and the **paEI** culture of Prime.

An organization is in Prime when it is both effective and efficient for the short and long run. Emphasis, however, is on the long run. Since no organization can be equally positioned for the short and the long run, Prime is oriented more to the long-run **EI** than the short-run **pa**. And because effectiveness and efficiency are also in conflict, Prime is a condition in which the process, the form, **I**, is as important as the function, **E**.

Prime is not a location but an area on the lifecycle because the conflicts between long run and short run and between effectiveness and efficiency are such that Prime needs continuous monitoring and adjustment. Prime is not a stable condition.

How does an organization age? In the first edition of this book, I stated that aging was the result of the loss of **E**. **E** is what gives an organization its start, and its loss brings about organizational demise.

The Fall—PAei

During the Fall stage, **E**ntrepreneurship decreases. As **E** decreases, Integration—people orientation—increases.

Integration is an elusive term, and it needs clarification. First, there is the people orientation, and that is what I mean when I talk about the **I** role. Rather than an orientation to any single individual, it is an orientation to the human element, to people in their interactions. **I** focuses on the decision-making style. Second, there is the integration of interests. That integration is not included in my definition of the **I** role. It pertains to coalesced authority, power, and influence, a concept we will discuss and explore in Chapter 13. The third type of integration refers to the organization's relationship with the external environment within which it operates. Fourth, there is internal integration, which integrates people, interests, and systems into a cohesive unity. There is even a fifth integration that integrates the external and the internal into a totality.

This subject of Integration remains elusive and an ongoing subject of inquiry. I have been laboring over it for more than 30 years. Here, let it suffice to say that, in the Fall stage of the lifecycle, the first type of integration—people orientation—increases at the expense of making change, Entrepreneurship.

Why?

I believe the internally oriented **I** increases as the organization loses interest in the external world and turns inward. External **I**, integrating with the market, has importance in a materialistic society, which aims to achieve materialistic goals. You see people undergoing the same process. As we age, our career, money, and possessions take lower priorities. Family—immediate and extended—gain increasing importance. But that is true for the typical path. Those that integrate externally for a spiritual purpose do not lose **E**. On the typical path, the organization, having lost its external drive, turns inward to the people component. **I** goes up as **E** goes down. In Chapter 14, we address the question of why **E** declines.

As I explained earlier, Integration can be high in the growing stages of the lifecycle, and we will see later in our discussion of the optimal path that **I** *should* be high during those growing stages. Such behavior, however, is not common. For an Entrepreneur, what counts? The success of the organization as validated by sales, the acceptance of the product or service by the market for which it was created. The people element takes the lowest priority. If the founder focuses on the people element, it is only as a means to an end. Only after the external passion, commitment, and the obsession with ambition subsides can organizations turn to other aims. Thus, interest in people is low in growing companies. It is considered a luxury the organization should not afford.

Let me explain this further. It is not that founders don't care for people. On the contrary. I have observed, especially in less developed countries, tremendous attention to the people element in startups. But it happens for a business reason, not humanistic: founders have no professional managerial know-how that helps them control their organizations. Instead, they rely on loyalty and true friendship to get things done. Without **A** they must depend on **I**. They hire family members or members of the tribe. Affiliation plays a significant role because founders have no other means to motivate and control. Such attention to people is not for the sake of the people. The founders nourish the people for the sake of the interests of their organizations. In contrast, companies in the Fall stage have a people orientation for the sake of the people—a goal in itself, even though it might be hurting the interests of the organization.

Consider different educational approaches. Do you want your kids to feel good even though they remain ignorant, or do you want them to endure the pain of learning? During the 1990s, education in California earned a reputation for encouraging self-esteem at the expense of learning. Children don't fail even if they haven't learned. As a result, in 1998, California's kids felt very good about themselves, but in terms of their scholastic achievement, they ranked 49th among the 50 states. The question, then, is: Are you results- or process-oriented? At the Fall stage, the answer is clearly in favor of process, and in this case, we are referring to the process of people interaction.

Why E̲ Declines First

Why is **E**nterpreneurship the first factor to decline when an organization leaves Prime? Why not **A**dministration or **P**erformance?

Why **E** and not **A**? Administration has the highest survival rate. It is very difficult for **A** to join an organization, but once there, it's just as difficult to get rid of it. In Hebrew there is an expression, "Friends go and come. Enemies accumulate." Rephrasing it, I would say, "Entrepreneurs come and go, bureaucrats accumulate." Administration will not decrease on its own. It tumbles down when **P** is no longer there and **A** serves nothing. That's when it is no longer functional. Then new **E** surges, which gives meaning to a new **P** and, consequently, to a new **A**. So who goes down first, **E** or **P**? **E** precedes **P**. **E** drives **P**. **E** is the long-run effectiveness; **P** is the short-run effectiveness. The long-run effectiveness has to decrease in importance before it expresses itself in the decline of the short-run effectiveness.

Now, let's consider how the transition from Prime, **PAEi**, to Fall, **PAeI**, occurs. It's not the increasing **I**ntegration that drives

Entrepreneurship's decline. On the contrary, **E**'s decline allows **I** to grow. But why is the decline in **E** expressed in an increase of **I**? Why isn't it expressed in the increase of **P** or **A**?

I increases as **E** declines because the organization is successful and in its full vitality: Its fight for survival is not acute. It can afford the luxuries of turning inward and paying attention to interdependencies among people and to the values that dominate behavior. When that occurs during the early stages of the lifecycle, as discussed earlier, it is not an indigenous cultural development. It either piggybacks on the extant social culture within which the organization operates, or it is nourished by a very people-oriented founder. The latter is rare because it requires excellence in three roles, **PEI**, and, as a company builder, the founder cannot sacrifice any **P** or **E**.

Aristocracy—pAeI

Based on our discussion of the interdependency between **P**erformance and **E**ntrepreneurship, it should be apparent that if **E** is low for long enough, **P** will eventually decline. And that brings companies into Aristocracy. The code for Aristocracy, **pAeI**, indicates short- and long-term focus on *how,* rather than on the short- and long-term *what* and *why.*

The decline in **P**erformance implies declining attention to function and a growing emphasis on form. That's why in Aristocratic organizations, rituals take on extreme importance. How people perform is more important than what they accomplish. How people dress, speak, relate to one another, obey organizational rituals, and heed unspoken values far outweigh the results they produce. Aristocratic organizations can afford not being function-oriented. They simply capitalize on their past successes and rest on their laurels. A comparison of the balance sheets of Aristocratic organizations and Prime organizations reveals that Aristocratic organizations are more liquid because they assume less risk. They are more numbers- and security-oriented than Prime organizations are.

Once, as I sat in an executive committee meeting of an Aristocratic organization, the financial officer reported, "We have $300 million in cash." Then, completely without guile, he asked, "Does anybody have any suggestions for what to do with it?"

It's not unusual for a company at that stage of the lifecycle to have $300 million in cash. You might be surprised to read that not a single member of the committee ventured to recommend uses for those millions. I have interviewed members of other Aristocratic organizations, and they confirm that this is not an extraordinary situation. Top management waits for instructions. Nobody is willing to make a suggestion, especially if doing so entails assuming risk.

Aristocratic organizations are characterized by an atmosphere of calm before the storm. People do not offend or cross each other. Everyone seems to be thinking that if he lies low for long enough, he might become the president. Let someone else reach into the fire and retrieve the chestnuts.

Salem City—OAOi and Bureaucracy—OAOO

Organizational inaction in a changing world must have its repercussions. Clients do not come back. They find other ways to satisfy their needs. And because the Aristocracy was continually raising its prices, its product is not only competitively obsolete, it is also overpriced. Sales volume falls, market share shrinks, and cash flow slows down.

As liquidity dries, organizational alarm signals start screaming: Emergency! Urgently, the organization struggles to revive **P**. It cuts prices to encourage sales, but without cutting overhead, it sells at a loss. Cutting overhead quickly is likely to slice away not only fat but also flesh. To reduce expenditures, the company fires people and discontinues activities, but more than likely, it is reducing its capability to deliver **P**. The company is damned no matter what it does *in a hurry*.

When the organization's people can get no results outside, they turn inward and attack each other. As the **P**erformance level sinks beyond resuscitation, **I**ntegration falls. What dominates organizations in such dire straits? **A**dministration. And it looms over everything like a monstrous shadow.

The situation is bad, and people need explanations, solutions, and hope. How do they explain the situation? The problem, they maintain, is with the leadership. The company would revive, they say, with new, energetic leadership. They look for a person to lead the organization out of its predicament.

During the growing stages, people develop faith in the idea that new leadership can alter behavior in ways that cure problems. Under those earlier conditions, new leadership can make significant differences. Looking back, management of the Aristocracy asks, if that worked then, why wouldn't it help now? Changing leadership is easy and expedient. It's much easier to fire the president and hire a new one than it is to change organizational responsibilities, structure, information systems, and reward systems. Naturally, organizations do what is easy and expedient instead of tackling difficult and overwhelming tasks. Instead of doing what needs to be done, they do what can be done. They find easy answers and solutions: They engage in witch hunts. The first to go are those to whom the organization attributes the difficulties. And because the company's problems are the result of its having failed to adapt to change (its products are obsolete), the ones it sacrifices on the altar of organizational ignorance are those whose responsibility it was to provide organizational Entrepreneurship. The people in marketing, strategic planning, research and development, and engineering take the fall.

People are prone to confuse cause and effect. In the growing stages, new leadership can change organizational behavior, but that medicine won't work on companies in the aging stages of the lifecycle. The Administrative system, which was functional in Adolescence, stymies the organization now. Form is now stronger than function. Form has so expanded its reach that it suffocates function. To liberate function from form, the organizational system—as it is reflected in the structure of accountability, information flows, and rewards—has to change.

Aging is caused by declining Entrepreneurship. In Salem City, E does not just decline, it is ejected. The As expel and imprison the Es, accelerating the destruction of the organization. In the countries of the former Union of Soviet Socialist Republics, entrepreneurship was synonymous with market speculation, and entrepreneurs were called *spekulants*. If anyone called you a *spekulant,* you would spend a lot of time looking over your shoulder.

Death—0000

Death is close when **E** disappears. **E** imparts organizational life and its disappearance is the organization's death. An organization is born when commitment is tested. An organization is dead when no one remains committed to it.

With **A**dministration ruling exclusively, form rules for the sake of form, as if form were itself the function. The company insists on organizational rituals with no understanding of their purpose or functionality. There is rain dancing although everyone, including the Shaman, knows it won't bring the rain. People remain for security. They cannot be judged on performance. There is no pressure to compete or undertake risk.

The organization can survive as long as there is external support. After all, clients will pay for services they don't get only if the law forces them. With limited or no functionality, organizations are not effective in the short or the long run, and they virtually die. Business organizations go bankrupt unless emergency measures are undertaken to revive them.

Some organizations—if their political importance forces external powers to take responsibility for their survival—are kept alive by artificial means. We have seen governments nationalize or subsidize organizations despite their failure to satisfy the needs for which they exist. In such situations, the organization stays alive in order to satisfy such political needs as providing employment at any cost.

Such organizations are cancers, usurping energy. Resources that could support emerging Infant and growing Go-Go organizations are channeled to maintain nonfunctional Bureaucracies. Death occurs when the external subsidies are discontinued. What appear to be all-powerful, difficult-to-challenge Bureaucracies are nothing more than empty, dead shells. Without external financial support, they crumble for lack of internal support or reason to exist.

Death occurs when external support stops. Bureaucracies cannot justify their existence by functionality. At that point, it is evident that **A** is pure form that yields no functionality: A new **E**, a new Courtship, emerges.

As one organization dies, if there is encouragement, another cause rises from its ashes. Without encouragement, the larger system will be affected, and the entire society will suffer a slow economic decline.

Having discussed problems and why they emerge and exist, in the next chapter, we turn our attention to discussing what management can do to address and solve its problems.

Note

1. See R. Stacey, *Managing the Unknowable: Strategic Boundaries Between Order and Chaos in Organizations* (San Francisco: Jossey-Bass, 1992): 142. He notes, "Culture is a set of beliefs or assumptions that a group of people share concerning how to see things, how to interpret events, what it is valid to question, what answers are acceptable, how to behave toward others, and how to do things. The culture of a group develops as they associate with each other. The most important parts of it are unconscious and cannot be imposed from the outside, even by top management."

CHAPTER THIRTEEN

Predicting the Capability to Solve Problems

Perceptions of Problems

We have analyzed why and how organizations develop and age; why they have their predictable problems; and how to differentiate normal from abnormal and abnormal from pathological problems. Now let's consider organizations' ability to control and solve their problems.

The more an organization perceives it is empowered to solve its problems, the younger it is.

Once it starts perceiving itself as impotent, it starts to age. It's old when it perceives itself as powerless, as if destiny had taken charge.

First, for therapeutic purposes, we need to define what constitutes a problem. A problem need not be a fact: It can be the perception of a fact.

I consider any phenomenon to be a problem—whether it is a fact or a perceived fact—if those subject to it find it undesirable and/or unexpected.[1] Something undesirable is obviously a problem, especially if it is unexpected. Any unexpected event is a problem if, like negative cash flow, it could and should have been predicted. What about an unexpected situation that is desirable? That, too, is a problem even though most people consider it luck. I say it is a problem because such so-called "luck" makes the organization complacent. It has deep-seated problems—inadequate planning, forecasting, and assessment of the environment—that, as yet, the organization has had no reason to recognize. Recognition will be inevitable, however, when that ignorance causes undesirable, unexpected results.

To whom do such problems belong? Occasionally, those who can control a particular problem and, therefore, have the capability to solve it, are the people who have the least interest in its solution. At the same time, those who suffer from the problem can neither control it nor change it. So, whose problem is it? To find the answer, let us reverse the logic.

A problem is an undesirable and/or unexpected result or process you can control or affect. Don't worry about the rain: There's nothing you can do about that. What you should worry about is how to prepare for inclement weather: where to find an umbrella now that it is raining, or how to repair your leaking roof. Whatever is controllable *and* undesirable and/or unexpected is a problem for you because you can and should do something about it.

A bank, for example, should not be troubled by the unpredictability of interest rates. Fluctuating interest rates pose problems only for banks with no strategy to deal with that unpredictability. You must focus on what you can and should do and forget academic discussions about the sources and causes of problems. It's nice to understand the origin of a challenging situation, but that knowledge in itself does not lead to change. You have to define the problem in terms you can deal with, i.e., you can do something about it.

Whether a problem is a problem or just an unpleasant fact depends, therefore, on whether you perceive you can control it. Take chronic migraines, for example. In my opinion, migraines are not problems if there is nothing you can do about them: Medical science is at a loss. No matter how unpleasant they are, they are not a problem unless you can do something about them. You have to live with your migraines. Thus the problem, until medical science advances on this score, is not the migraines. Your problem is to figure out how to live with them.

Let's focus on controllability of problems.

To carry out decisions that solve problems, managers need certain energy. Authority, Power, and Influence are the sources of that energy.

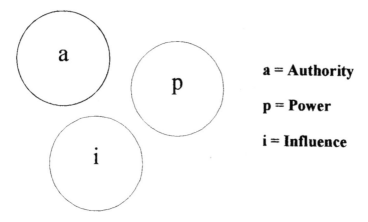

a = **Authority**

p = **Power**

i = **Influence**

Figure 13-1: Sources of Managerial Energy

Authority

I define authority as the right to make a decision, to say yes *and* no to change. That right is formal and inherent in a person's job, independent of his or her connections or education.

My definition, the right to say yes *and* no to change, is deliberate. If I had defined authority as the right to say yes *or* no to change, my meaning might be interpreted as the right to say yes without the right to say no (very rare) or the right to say no without the right to say yes (much more common).

What is the origin of the bifurcation of yes from no?[2]

From Infancy to Adolescence, the founder—the one-and-only—retains all decision-making authority. The founder can say both yes and no. When companies outgrow their founders' capability to manage, founders start to delegate authority. By start, I mean that they don't delegate complete authority—only the authority to say no. Founders prefer to retain the right to say yes. Over time, the numbers and layers of no-sayers grows, while the authority to say yes resides in a distant corner of organizational hierarchy. When people are authorized to say no, and, rarely, yes, their organization grows increasingly bureaucratic, losing its ability to react to changes in the environment. New needs arise in *what, how, when,* and *who.* Organizations need to address those needs by changing the way they do things. It's terribly difficult to proceed when the very few who are authorized to say yes are hierarchically remote. Those authorized to say no are many, and they are everywhere. Problems and their solutions are filtered by so many no-sayers that they rarely reach the attention of a yes-sayer. Effective consultants understand this syndrome. They demand access to the top person because that's the only way to get a yes.

Authority to say yes is necessary, but not sufficient. In many countries, authority and a dollar won't buy you a cup of coffee.

Power

Along with authority, power is the second source of managerial energy for implementing decisions.

I define power as the *capability* to punish or reward. The accomplishment of some organizational tasks requires the cooperation of more than one individual: Lifting the rock requires a working interdependency. If the person or people whose cooperation is needed to implement a decision stand in the way of progress by withholding their cooperation, that person or those people have power. How much power a person has depends on how much we need that person's cooperation, and how much of a monopoly he or she has over what we need.

Influence

Influence is the third source of energy for implementing decisions and carrying out tasks. Influence is a person's *capability* to cause people to act without having to invoke authority or power. Influence usually derives from information that convinces people to act as desired. When people independently recognize the validity of the decision to be implemented, they have been influenced. The effects of influence are entirely voluntary; neither coercion nor fear forces people to act.

Authorance and CAPI

The circles of authority, power, and influence overlap to form different combinations of the three sources of energy: Authorized power, *ap,* is the legal right to punish and reward. Indirect power, *ip,* is what occurs when the directing person believes he is influencing but the focal person perceives power. Perhaps a supervisor tries to convince an employee that a new methodology will work, and the employee, who is not at all convinced that the new approach is correct, acts only because he does not believe that he can exercise his own independent judgment. He acts because he is frightened or worried about the repercussions of refusing to comply. Professional management literature refers to the third combination, influencing authority, *ia,* as authority by acceptance or professional authority.[3] In such situations people accept and co-opt the decision of those to whom they report.

At the heart of those three circles is CAPI: Coalesced Authority, Power, and Influence. All the possible combinations are called *authorance:* authority plus power plus authorized power plus indirect power plus influence plus influencing authority plus CAPI (see Figure 13-2).

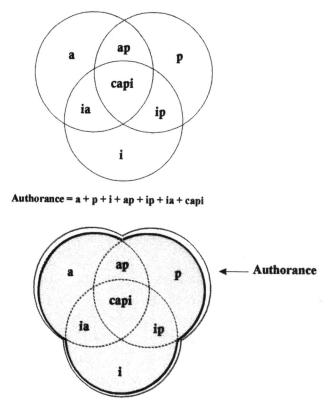

Figure 13-2: CAPI and Authorance

Let us see how this model works in reality.

Consider a mother who is trying to persuade her child to eat spinach. She uses several different components of *authorance*. In the beginning, she might say, "Eat it, it's good for you. Popeye eats spinach, and you can see how strong he is. You will be like Popeye." She is using the influence component of her *authorance*. If the child still refuses to eat, she might allude to the father who will soon be home. That use of indirect power may cause the child to eat the spinach. If, however, he still refuses to eat, the mother might get angry and punish him. If, according to the value standards of the family, the punishment is acceptable, she is invoking authorized power. If not, she is using power without authority. Perhaps the child still refuses to eat. At that point, the mother might make the classic management mistake. She may resort to pleading. "Why don't you listen to your mother? Why don't you ever do what I tell you to do?" She is using the last resort of her *authorance,* which is authority. That is tactically wrong. Once she invokes her authority, there is nothing left for an encore. It is even funny when she says, "Why don't you listen to me? Am I not your mother?" Is this news to the child that she is his mother? What is she trying to say? The impact is no better when a superior pulls rank on an employee: "Do it! I am your boss!" Is the employee surprised to find out that you are the boss? Does he need reminding? You know you are in trouble if you find yourself offering reminders you shouldn't have to make: Try, for instance, reminding a friend that he owes you money!

What the mother might use with better effect is *influencing authority*. She, herself, could eat spinach in front of the child, serving as a behavioral model. There's a chance that the child might emulate her.

The mother has CAPI when she suggests, "How about eating some spinach," and the child immediately eats it because he believes it is good for him, he worries about the repercussions of not eating it, and he respects his mother's suggestions.

While a single individual might not have total CAPI over his task, a group of people might jointly have the required CAPI. In order to assemble CAPI, a manager must create an environment of common interest for the various interest groups that comprise CAPI.

In an organization where CAPI is divided among people, authority usually lies with management. The board of directors has authorized management to make decisions. Most often, power lies with subordinates who may or may not cooperate. And the technocrats—professionals with decision-making know-how—have influence.

The interests of those three groups can conflict. Those in authority might focus on growth, market share, sales, profits, return on investment, or dividends. Those with power—the employees—might want more security at work, better working conditions, or higher salaries. And for their part, the technocrats might focus on larger research budgets, getting the best equipment, and finding the most precise solutions.

In the short run, the interests of those groups are incompatible, and the conflicts they engender could paralyze the efficient implementation of decisions. A win-win climate and commonality of interests are necessary to resolve the conflict, but such utopian visions are not operationally possible at any point in time, continuously, or forever. At any point in time, there is a win-lose climate. Conflict over diverse interests is normal. Consider your personal life. You want to see a stage production, and your partner insists on going to a movie. You want to listen to classical music, and the kids insist on rock 'n roll. Life is a conflict of interests all the time, at any point in time.

So, what to do?

To obtain an operationally win-win climate in the short run, the people who together comprise an organization's CAPI must develop mutual trust and a vision of a win-win future, which is a process of building **I**. They must believe that they will benefit from the long-term win-win, even if there is a win-lose in the short run. Unless the various constituencies develop mutual trust, the short-run conflict of interest will dominate behavior and impede the efficiency of implementation.

One can predict the effectiveness of a decision's implementation by gauging how much CAPI any individual has over the decision. When one individual does not alone possess all the necessary CAPI, we should analyze how much mutual trust and win-win vision there is among all the people it will take to implement the decision—the people who jointly have CAPI.

Predicting Who Has Control

To recap, *authorance* comprises all the energy management uses to cause behavior to occur. It is the combination of three basic elements: authority (the legal right to make the decision), power (the capability to withhold desired and expected cooperation), and influence (the capability to cause self-directed behavior through know-how). Combinations of those elements include authorized power, indirect power, influencing authority, and CAPI: coalesced authority, power, and influence, or control.

The following section describes the changing behavior of the different elements of control, over the course of the lifecycle.

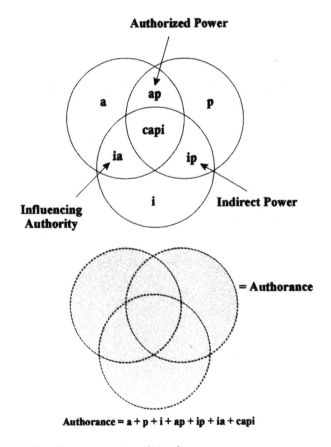

Authorance = a + p + i + ap + ip + ia + capi

Figure 13-3: The Components of Authorance

Authority over the Lifecycle

During Courtship, the question of authority never even arises. It's virtually irrelevant. Before marriage, during the falling-in-love period, no authority issues arise because the couple faces no real tasks. Courtship takes place in a make-believe world: Each person is careful to do nothing that might scare the other one away. It is a period of sharing.

When Courtship is over, and an organization is born, there are tasks to be carried out and there is risk. Time evaporates. We need to act NOW! Decisions must be made NOW!

The "now" imperative means that, due to the pressure of time, only one person can have the authority to make decisions. Naturally, that actual authority is concentrated in the founder—the person who is the most committed. That is the one person who has sacrificed most, measured in time, sweat, and sleepless nights. That is why leadership in Infant organizations is autocratic. In an equal partnership, the partners have to spend a great deal of time together, deciding how to split responsibilities. Usually, one of the partners, the **E**, emerges more dominant than the other.

In Go-Go, one person completely monopolizes authority. All the titles—chief operating officer, chief financial officer, chief executive officer, founder, president, chairman of the board—belong to one person. The organization—even if it is a partnership or a public company—becomes a one-person show. "I've created a monster here," said a partner in one of my client organizations about the equal partner who emerged as the leader. The founder communicates less and less with his followers, and, because the company is growing rapidly, arrogance accompanies his success. No one challenges the monopolized authority—yet. Nobody dares. There's no arguing with success.

In his arrogance, the founder feels his company's growth is his own doing. He thinks it is his talented leadership, good judgment, precision timing, and well-developed relationships with clients that make the company a success. "He believes his own press releases," one executive remarked. Arrogance makes him use his authority more and more and his influence less and less. The board of directors does not challenge him: A Go-Go's board is often comprised of the founder's cronies or family members. Everyone is making money.

"Leave him alone; if we knew better, we would be in his place" and "We need him more than he needs us" are typical reactions of Go-Go board members and executives. The executive committee does whatever the founder says. There is still no participatory system in effect.

Then things start to go wrong. The company starts coming apart at the seams, and people begin to question the founder's authority. The first to raise the flag of revolution against the founder, president, or chairman is Administration: either the person who has been hired or appointed to organize things, or the person with the finance portfolio.

A struggle for authority erupts between the Entrepreneurial types and the Administrative types, and the board watches from the sidelines. If the Entrepreneur gains final authority, the Administrator is fired, and the arrival of a new A initiates another cycle of authority struggles. If E does not gain final control, the board develops an axis with A, usurps authority, and squeezes the E out. In Prime, when E is institutionalized, the executive committee comes to life, and the board takes full authority; it delegates some authority to the executive committee. The governance function is well-delineated. The limits of authority of the executive committee, the board, and each executive are specified. Authority is delegated and decentralized commensurate with responsibilities.

The difference between the pre- and post-Adolescent stages is that authority is personalized during Infancy and Go-Go, while in Prime and successive lifecycle stages, authority is institutionalized and systematized. After Prime, that institutionalization and depersonalization grow to the point that eventually, no one person feels he has authority in real terms.

That transition requires further explanation.

Authority vs. Responsibility

Management textbooks say that authority must equal responsibility, and vice versa. At first glance, that makes sense: How can anyone be held responsible for things over which he has no authority? Why should anyone have authority without commensurate responsibility? Makes sense, right? Wrong! It took me fifteen years to figure out why the textbooks are wrong.

As I worked with client companies, I kept hearing the same complaints. People objected that they lacked the authority necessary to carry out their responsibilities. After a few years and several dozen companies, I started wondering why I never encountered a manager who told me that his authority equaled his responsibility. Is it possible that the theory cannot exist in reality? I persisted. I looked and looked, but I could find nobody who would say, "Yes, I have all the authority I need for my responsibilities." Now, I am convinced that that condition can exist only in an organization that is dead. Why?

Whenever there is change, levels of both responsibility and authority rise and fall. By definition, therefore, at any point in time, in any particular realm, authority may exceed responsibility, while in a different realm, at a different point in time, responsibility may exceed authority. Responsibility will equal authority perfectly and over time, only if nothing changes. And that means the organization is dead. Being alive means having to live with uncertainty, with ambiguity. Do we have the authority or not? Do we have the responsibility or not? The higher the rate of change, the higher the ambiguity.[4] Thus in a young organization, let us say 60 percent of authority and responsibility is given, and 40 percent is taken. In aging companies, 80 percent or 90 percent is given, and only 20 percent or 10 percent is taken. When 100 percent is given, and none is taken, the organization is a Bureaucracy and it will meet its end when outside authorities discover that it's more of a liability than an asset.

Let's consider how organizations handle uncertainty.

Is it possible to define responsibility *exactly,* leaving *absolutely* no question as to what must or must not be done, how we should or should not proceed, when we ought or ought not take steps, and who should or should not perform? Obviously, because there is always change, it is impossible. One cannot predict *everything* in advance and decide *everything* in advance. For each responsibility, an individual can be certain about the extremes: Up to this point is certainly my responsibility and beyond that point is certainly beyond my responsibility. But between those two points is a vast area of uncertainty.

How should people deal with uncertainty? Let's consider a tennis analogy. When people play doubles, the players always aim their balls to land between their two opponents. With a bad team, the area of uncertainty belongs to neither of the two: Each one waits for his partner to make the play. On a good team, the area of uncertainty belongs to both players: They both move toward the ball, and one of them takes the shot.

However, it's not efficient for both players to go for the ball. To improve their efficiency, should they draw a line that indicates exactly who is responsible for particular areas of the court? People can't play that way. They would have to wait for the ball to land before either of them could react. Obviously, once the ball lands, any response would be too late.

How does a Bureaucracy handle change and the ensuing uncertainties?

When the tennis players discover that neither of them has been covering a section of the court and that it would be inefficient for both of them to try simultaneously to respond to that need, they bring in a new person to handle that middle area. Nice idea, but what happens next? With the addition of the third player, now instead of one, there are two areas of uncertainty for which no one claims responsibility. They recruit two more people to handle the new areas of uncertainty, and that, of course, creates even more areas of uncertainty.

Eventually, there are so many people on the court that no one is watching the ball. They are watching and stepping on each other's toes. They start to wage war over turf. Everyone expends energy protecting his turf, and nobody is hitting the ball.

The big question becomes: Who is responsible for what? Some players, trying to avoid involvement in the turf wars, retreat to the areas most clearly identified as their own. Others who are conscientious attempt to cover areas that are unattended and end up in someone else's territory. Others accuse them of empire building, forcing them to retreat. Meanwhile, balls are coming over the net, and no one dares to lift a racket for fear of hitting someone else. So the balls fly by, and only the Bureaucrat, who gets hit by a ball right between the eyes, reacts.

As the turf wars rage, perceived authority, followed by perceived responsibilities, decline. Someone who has an overview of the court must take charge, watching for holes, directing the game, and calling the shots. That is how authority becomes centralized. People want to be told what to do. They would rather be precisely wrong, than approximately right. To give Bureaucrats the benefit of the doubt, such behavior might stem from the nature of governmental requirements. Bureaucracies are under constant scrutiny for waste and improper judgment. Naturally, **A**dministrators believe it's more prudent to do the *wrong things right* than to do the *right things wrong*.

The alternative—*continuously* doing the right things right—is reserved for saints; the alternative of doing the wrong things continuously wrong is reserved for schlemiels. Neither population is a resource for managerial talent.

Doing things right attracts **A**dministrative types who are risk-averse and prefer form over substance. **A** personalities feel at home with Bureaucratic behavior.

Bureaucracies endeavor to minimize uncertainty, but by doing so, they decrease flexibility. Attempting to minimize uncertainty, people try to define responsibility clearly. To make responsibility clearer when there is change, responsibility and authority must decrease to match the decreasing area of certainty. Systems become increasingly centralized as both responsibility and authority rise to the top. Mundanely small problems flow all the way to the chief **A**dministrator. Overwhelmed with mounting decisions and responsibilities, the chief leaves real problems unattended. That is the process of dying.

More and more, people feel they have no authority or responsibility. They feel their authority is commensurate with their responsibility only when they have neither. That is the situation in a full-blown Bureaucracy. The organization no longer responds to environmental change. Responsibility stops changing, and so does authority. The organization is dead. We are fully in control when we are dead. To be alive means to lack control over parts of our lives. Experienced managers understand that some things they can control, some they can't, and, in many areas, they do not know whether or not they have control.

God, give us grace to accept with serenity the things
that cannot be changed, courage to change the things
which should be changed, and the wisdom to
distinguish the one from the other.

REINHOLD NIEBUHR, "THE SERENITY PRAYER"

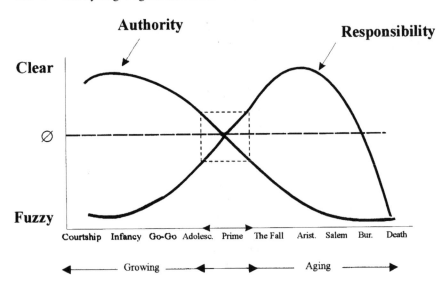

Figure 13-4: Authority and Responsibility over the Lifecycle

It's normal to have either more responsibility than authority or more authority than responsibility. Because both responsibility and authority change as conditions change, they cannot be equal.

Prior to Adolescence, authority is personalized. During Adolescence, it becomes depersonalized and institutionalized into the system. During Prime, authority is both institutionalized and personalized. After that point, people who have responsibility lose authority, and effectiveness declines. People in Bureaucracies find that their authority to make changes is almost nil. That's why we find very happy people in Bureaucracies. With no authority and uncertainty, there is little risk as long as everyone just goes by the book. Bureaucrats are very different from the unhappy people of advanced Go-Go and Adolescence, during which organizational uncertainty is at its highest.

The Behavior of Power in the Lifecycle

In Courtship, power is meaningful: The founder is trying to build commitment. By definition, people whose cooperation is crucial to the founder have power. By making regrettable promises, the founder tries to enlist the support of such people. That is how people whose value to the enterprise is only marginal end up owning large pieces of the action.

In Infancy, founders maintain a tight grip on their companies. They don't want to risk losing control. And those who do lose control in this early stage are like mother wolves who reject their cubs once humans have touched them. Founders' commitment evaporates, and they allow their organizations to die in Infancy.

Following the birth of a company, power moves from the people necessary to get things started to the people necessary to keep the company going. This is a very interesting transition. Loyalties change. During Courtship, the people who had power were outside the company. They were spouses, family members, bankers, and friends. Once the company is born, the company builders, who labor day and night, have the power. Founders' secretaries are quite powerful. They provide the **A** role to the founder's **PE** role. Good executive secretaries are worth their weight in gold. They are the people who, by delaying the implementation of bad decisions, keep the founders out of trouble. Founders rely on the opinions and the judgment of these so-called secretaries. The secretaries keep their founders informed about what is going on. They are the political gauges, explaining to the founders what is and is not politically acceptable. It's not surprising that many founders divorce their spouses in order to marry their secretaries or, in the case of artists, their business managers.

In start-up companies, titles don't matter; the role a person plays is what counts.

Sales managers and buyers in retail-distribution chains also play powerful roles in the earliest stages. The accountant is weak, and marketing hardly exists. Those roles are weak because Entrepreneurship is centralized in the founder who makes all the marketing and financial decisions. In small companies, there is no human resources or personnel department, either. Even if the company is large, personnel is of far less concern than sales, upon which survival depends.

In Adolescence, power and authority are diffuse and difficult to pinpoint. Authority and power move from the founder to the financial people and from externally-oriented to internally-oriented people. From Infancy to Adolescence, authority and power are coalesced. Authorized power is centralized in the founder, the one-and-only. During Adolescence, authority and power get bifurcated. The founder has the authority, but the financial person gets the power. Later, power and authority start moving together or they get "divorced," but for the organization to attain Prime, the two must coalesce.

In a healthy transition, the founder and the professional manager share such titles as chairman of the board, chief executive officer, president, and chief operating officer. The founder might be the chairman, chief executive officer, and president, while the professional hired gun takes the role of chief operating officer. In other cases, the founder might become the chairman, and the hired gun becomes chief executive officer, president, and chief operating officer. Sometimes a third person takes the operations role. With all those configurations, authority and power coalesce, allowing the organization to develop into Prime.

After Prime, authority and power separate, and as the organization slides into Aristocracy, power moves down the hierarchy and authority moves up. The organization becomes increasingly centralized. The more systemically centralized the organization, the greater the vertical disparity between authority and power. More and more, people claim to have authority without power, and others exercise power while claiming they lack authority.

Authorized power can also split. An antagonistic labor union, authorized to act for employees, could, for example, use its authorized power to fight management.

In Salem City, turf wars rage, and the lines of authorized power grow fuzzy. Responsibilities shrink, and authority adapts in size.

Peace and quiet reign when authority and power are separated for good. There is authority with no power and power with no authority. The peace and quiet is really a reflection of everyone's paralysis. Unions rely on management. Management relies on Washington. In Washington, the White House depends on Congress, and Congress is dependent on internal politics. Authority and power are so diffuse that it's nearly impossible to effect change.

Over the years, I have seen numerous examples of that phenomenon. A post office in Hawaii needed a machine to lift sacks of mail from its outside loading dock. The postmaster submitted the required request for approval. After waiting for months for Washington's reply, the local postmaster was astonished to be told that his requisition had been denied. Why? In their wisdom, the bureaucrats noted that the machine in question wasn't built to survive the snow outside post office buildings.

The Los Angeles Department of Social Services provides another example of dysfunctional, centralized authority. That department has thousands of employees and a $1.5 billion budget to spend on welfare. The director, however, has only $5,000 of discretionary funds at his disposal. Furthermore, a task as simple as moving a computer from one department to another requires approval from a person so high in the city's hierarchy, that the staff just doesn't bother trying.

In 1973, I was trying to diagnose how to rejuvenate Sweden's governmental machinery. I asked the principals of the various ministries to describe a problem they were unable to solve because they lacked appropriate authority. They described the difficulties involved in transferring a person from one ministry to another.

Say the ministry of foreign affairs needs a new person, and there are too many people employed in the ministry of agriculture. The principal manager—the chief administrator reporting directly to the minister of the cabinet, a political appointee—cannot make the transfer. Why? To find the answer to that question, we must look back in history. Some 200 years ago, in a move to limit the king's authority and power, each ministry was organized as an almost autonomous organization. The cabinet is the center in common, and the prime minister is only *primus inter pares,* first among equals. The prime minister has no authority over other members of the cabinet. To further complicate matters, each ministry has its own labor union, and the union has something to say on the subject of transferring people.

I found it would take the CAPI of 120 highly-ranked officials to change that law. That is paralysis. Is it any surprise that governments grow with no apparent growth in effectiveness?

The Behavior of Influence in the Lifecycle

In Courtship, influence is important. There is no real authority, and power derives from withholding cooperation. In Infancy, authority takes over, power switches to the inside people, and influence disappears. There is no time for talk; It is time to act! Influence takes time, and there is a shortage of that precious commodity. In Infant organizations, then, changes are accomplished without influence, using authorized power in a dictatorial way.

During Go-Go, influence returns, but it is integrated with authority and power. CAPI is concentrated in the founder. Success makes people accept anything.

When organizations experience failure and advance to Adolescence, under the best circumstances, influence moves to the technocrats, or worse, it disappears altogether.

In Prime, CAPI resides with the executive committee where management has both authorized power and influence. The company is systematically successful.

From the Fall phase on, the importance of influence grows as authority declines because it is being centralized. The centralization of authority signals its decline among people in the organization's lower echelons, and it doesn't take them long to discover that to accomplish anything, they need to use influence. Because that influence is, however, coupled with power, indirect power is the result. People behave nicely, but the object of such influence responds appropriately not because he is convinced, but because he fears the repercussions. The consequence of such changes is "politics." There are lots of rumors, veiled accusations, and cover-your-ass strategies. Everyone scrambles to secure a high-level guardian, mentor, coach, or—using a strategy that can prove legally treacherous—a lover.

With the next big breakdown—loss of market share and negative cash flow leading to Salem City—authority is empty, influence is gone, and power is the only remaining source of energy. This is war; There is no time for talk. To survive, all tools or weapons are considered legitimate.

CAPI over the Lifecycle

CAPI measures controllability, strength, and the predictability of organizational behavior.

The location and behavior of CAPI varies with an organization's position in the lifecycle. In Courtship, it doesn't matter who has CAPI; We are in love. That is why during Courtship, people are relatively promiscuous with control. Founders give stock to people who are excited about their ideas and willing to support the new organization. Founders are buying support for their dreams. They awaken to a day of reckoning when they discover that their promiscuous give-away programs have endangered their survival as leaders. That usually happens during Adolescence.

Once organizations are born, CAPI is consolidated and, most often, vested in the founders. If they have influence, which plays only a minor role at this stage of the lifecycle, founders' authorized power is sufficient to achieve implementation of solutions. But with authorized power alone, founders may later find that lack in influence is cause for a crisis. When organizations move into Go-Go, the more successful they are, the more arrogant their founders become, and the more power they use. The more power they use, the less they listen to others and the more detached they become. The more they behave that way, the bigger their mistakes that trigger Adolescence.

As Lord Acton wrote more than a century ago, "Power tends to corrupt, and absolute power corrupts absolutely." The more power founders have, the more they use. Nobody dares to challenge their decisions. Eventually, they make major mistakes that endanger their organizations and their own power.

In Adolescence, CAPI is erratic. There is a power struggle between professional managers and the founders, between the boards of directors and the families, and between the organizations and their founders.

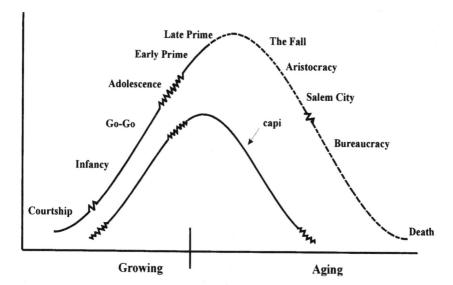

Figure 13-5: CAPI over the Lifecycle

If an organization survives Adolescence, CAPI stabilizes in the governance system and in the executive committee, establishing certain *modi operandi* among the board, executive committee, founder, stockholder, and professional managers.

CAPI's decline begins after Aristocracy because of conflicts of interest among stockholders, management, labor, and technocrats. Individual CAPI is almost nil in Salem City unless a caretaker is appointed. In Bureaucracy the right hand does not know what the left hand is doing. To accomplish anything, numerous committees form. They subvert each other, and there are intramural wars. When even individual committees cannot achieve CAPI, the organization is brain dead.

In the next chapter, which details the causes of aging, we discuss how and why CAPI and control break down.

Notes

1. See P. Watzlawick, J.H. Weakland, and R. Fisch, *Change: Principles of Problem Formation and Problem Resolution* (New York: Norton Books, 1974), which offers a similar definition of "problem."

2. This bifurcation operates similarly to those described by I. Prigogine and I. Stengers in their research on second-order change in biological systems. They noted that small variations may, over time, lead to bifurcations that, in turn, produce qualitative shifts in the system. See esp. *Order Out of Chaos: Man's New Dialogue with Nature* (New York: Bantam Books, 1984).

3. See the many writings of Chester Barnard, for example, *Organization and Management: Selected Papers* (Cambridge, MA: HBS Press, 1956); *Elementary Conditions of Business Morals* (Berkeley Committee on Weinstein Lectures: UCB Press, 1958); *The Functions of the Executive* (Cambridge, MA: HBS Press, 1968); *Philosophy for Managers: Selected Papers* (Tokyo: Bushido Press, 1986).

4. In M. Kossman and S. Bullrich's article entitled "Systematic Chaos: Self-Organizing Systems and the Process of Change," in F. Masterpasqua and P. Perna, eds., *The Psychological Meaning of Chaos: Translating Theory into Practice* (Washington, DC: APA, 1997), these authors note that change increased entropy in the system by introducing more ambiguity.

CHAPTER FOURTEEN

The Causes of Organizational Aging

What causes aging is a decrease in flexibility and an increase in controllability. As controllability increases and flexibility decreases, the organization increasingly loses touch with its environment; the environment changes faster than the organization's ability to adapt.[1] That disintegration with the external environment causes internal disintegration as well. CAPI breaks down because each interest group reacts to those changes differently and starts pulling in its own direction. Breakdown in CAPI decreases the organization's ability to act and react to changes. The organization ages.

Flexibility and control are functions of **Entrepreneurship** and CAPI. High **E** and high CAPI make organizations flexible and predictable. Low **E** and low CAPI make organizations inflexible and brittle.

What affects Entrepreneurship and CAPI?

The Behavior of Entrepreneurship throughout the Typical Lifecycle

Of the four **PAEI** roles, **E**ntrepreneurship is the most critical for changing culture on the typical path. It precedes and determines the **P**erformance function because it is the long-term component of **P**. **A**dministration should also be derived from the task that must be

Performed. In other words, *how* we do anything must be geared to *what* we want to do, and that, in turn, derives from the *why* we do anything.

Who does it with whom and *how*—the organic *how,* the Integration role—on the typical path is derived the same way the mechanistic *how* is derived—I like **A** is derived from **P** and thus from **E**.

Let's examine Entrepreneurship's critical impact on organizational behavior.

E is the locomotive force of an organization. When commitment—**E**—is born, the organization is conceived. When commitment evaporates, even though some parts of the organization still function, the organization seems to be brain dead.

To understand the lifecycle curve on its typical path, we therefore focus on the **E** role. It is a vital sign, and it must be monitored.

Figure 14-1 traces **E**'s behavior on the curve.

First, we should note that during Courtship, **E** is very high. There is a lot of noise, passion, excitement, willingness to take risks, creativity, imagination, and fascination with endless possibilities. This behavior, because it propels the organization into the future, is functional. With no love affair, passion, or excitement, the first challenge could dissolve the commitment necessary for the birth of an organization. The idea might be abandoned.

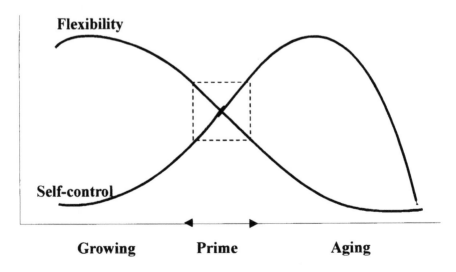

Figure 14-1: Flexibility and Controllability over the Lifecycle

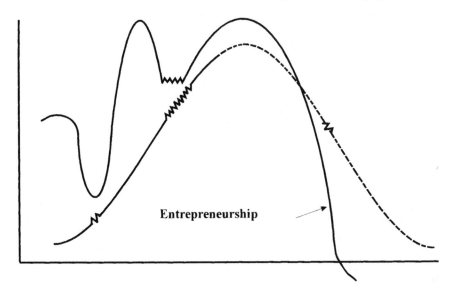

Figure 14-2: Entrepreneurship over the Lifecycle

It should be noted, however, that excitement remains high so long as there is no risk. When risk is born, **E** declines rapidly. There is no time to think and no time to create. It's time to get things done.

This transition introduces a measure of disenchantment. People begin to ask what happened. "Since we got this organization started, we no longer have the time to imagine, to get excited, to get together. Everyone is just working, day in, day out."

The need to work continuously is normal: The organization must cover its risk and work to satisfy its commitments to itself and to the marketplace. It is time to deliver.

If **E** stays dormant for too long, the organization might die. Management needs a vision to maintain its interest, to keep its commitment alive, and to ride out the difficulties of Infancy—continuous back-breaking work. If management does not get back to the dream, if it can't define what it is trying to achieve, then the Infant organization is nothing but a source of hard work, and enthusiasm eventually burns out.

It is mandatory to sustain **E**, at least latently. Eventually, the organization will be freed from cash pressures and the ongoing need to satisfy immediate demands from clients, suppliers, and bankers. Then, when people again have time to think, the dream can resurface in the organizational consciousness. When people are again dreaming, the organization moves into its Go-Go culture. At that stage, **E** rises, and there is time to try new things. It has already proven that it can survive the difficulties of Infancy.

What happens next? As the organization starts to grow, making bigger mistakes, it discovers the need for **A**. When the **A** role—the technocracy, bureaucratization, systematization, and institutionalization of the organization—rises, the structure of who does what, when, and how affects the Entrepreneurial spirit. No longer *channeling* energy, the Entrepreneurial spirit is *channeled by* **A**. People feel the constraints of all the new rules, processes, and forms governing who decides what, with whom, and how.

The **E** curve from Go-Go through Adolescence is erratic. It zigzags up and down. The founder and the organization engage in a tug-of-war. Founders want both to maintain control and to reduce their involvement. They want to have their cake and eat it, too. They want central controls and decentralization. Why can't Go-Gos have it all? Because they have yet to develop **A**.

Delegation is the transfer of **P** down. Decentralization is the transfer of **E** down. Founders want to delegate, to transfer **P** down, but they resent the limits **A** imposes. **P** without the boundaries of **A** can easily have the effect of **E**. The founders end up decentralizing, losing control, rather than delegating. When they realize they have lost control, they stop delegating and recentralize.

They say, "I want to decentralize. I want to institutionalize leadership so it won't be necessary for everyone to come to me every time. However," they continue, "don't you dare make decisions before you check with me." Alternatively, they say, "Make any decisions you want, as long as you are sure you're making the decision I would have made, if you had asked me." The organization is locked in a Catch-22 because it is very difficult to predict the decisions the founder would have made: He changes his mind too frequently.

You cannot decentralize unless you first have systems of control. Without **A**, delegation ends as decentralization, and decentralization becomes abdication.

In Adolescent organizations, the struggle between **A** and **E** is a struggle for systematization, order, and efficiency, on one hand; and growth, continuous change, and market penetration, on the other hand. It is a struggle between quantity and quality, flexibility and predictability, function and form. **A** provides for form, predictability, and quality; while **E** provides for quantity, flexibility, and functionality. The authority structure of Adolescent organizations manifests those struggles. The founders want to restructure their organizations, to attain systematization and order. At the same time, they want to dominate and control such critical activities as finance, marketing, and product development.

Moving discretionary powers from founders to their organizations, and systematizing and professionalizing decision-making, intensifies the struggle between **E** and **A**. Founders might say they are decentralizing and delegating, but people in the organizations can't be sure that the founders mean what they say.

If two partners represent the **A** and **E** roles, the conflict can be strong enough to make them split. In such cases, the **A** personality usually remains, and the **E** personality departs, leaving the organization's entrepreneurial spirit highly threatened.

What should happen in such cases is that **E** should temporarily step aside, allowing for **PA** systematization. Then, in late Adolescence, **E** should reappear, institutionalized instead of personalized. And that brings us to Prime. (Warning: This is a complicated maneuver: For more information, I refer the reader to Chapter 17 on treating organizations, and to my books, *The Pursuit of Prime* and *Mastering Change.*[2])

The institutionalization of **E** permits the organization to make entrepreneurial decisions in a professional way. The organization assembles relevant information, discusses it as it relates to policies, guidelines, and strategies, and makes decisions independent of any single individual and his or her idiosyncrasies.

What happens after Prime? **E** declines for reasons I will describe in this and the next chapter. During the Salem City era, when there is no **E** left, people start looking out for themselves. If there is any **E**ntrepreneurial spirit, it's applied not for the benefit of the organization but for the benefit of the individuals, even at the expense of the organization. During this period, the organization eliminates any traces of **E**, firing the **E** types. That is why I show the **E** curve going below the zero line.

Factors Affecting Entrepreneurship in the Lifecycle

What causes changes to **E** at the various stages of the lifecycle curve? Why do those changes occur? I have spent some thirty years working with organizations of all sizes, in a variety of technologies and cultures. Rejuvenating declining **E** at the aging stages and institutionalizing it at the growing stages, I have observed that several factors have dramatic effects on organizational **E**. If we understand those factors, we can take specific steps to deal with potential problems before they become pathological and endanger the organization itself.

The **E** spirit, both in individuals and in organizations, is a function of the disparity between desired and expected consciousness. As long as people desire more or better than what they expect, they are young. The day a person looks at the future and says, "I like and accept what I expect," accepting the expected as desired, that is the day one begins to age, when there is no inducement to change.

How young or old anyone is depends on how much change he or she is willing to cause or endure.

$$\text{Entrepreneurship} = \text{function of} \left(\frac{\text{desired}}{\text{expected}} \right)$$

In these thirty years, I have found that four factors affect the disparity between desired and expected, and, consequently, they affect the consciousness of Entrepreneurship. I know that those factors are valid, because by treating them, my associates and I have successfully rejuvenated aging organizations. Their time to market with new products improved dramatically; their market share increased; and the percentage of their revenues generated from new services, products, or markets increased dramatically too.

The four factors are:

1. Mental age of the leadership   ⎫
2. Functionality of leadership style ⎬ people factors
                                    ⎭

3. Perceived relative market share ⎱
4. Functionality of organizational structure ⎰ organizational factors

Those four internal factors are within the direct control of the company. There are, of course, also such external factors as culture, technology, market conditions, and political climate that strongly influence Entrepreneurship and CAPI. Those external factors can cause an organization to accelerate its aging or—in the case of market deregulation—even to jump stages. Since this book is oriented to leaders of change, we will consider only those four factors, which are or should be controllable by the organization.

1. Mental Age of Leadership

The first factor is the mental age of those who are the decision-makers—the people who control the organization and comprise CAPI. They are not necessarily owners. Often, the management controls the organization—not the owners who are scattered and badly represented on the board.

What is mental age? In one's own mind, it is the disparity between desired and expected. Mental age is not necessarily related to chronological age. Some individuals are young at 50, and others are old at 25. Do they accept the expected as desired or do they desire something different from the expected? The difference is expressed not only in quantity. Perhaps they don't want more quantity—just more quality. But they must want more *something*—quality or quantity. People who want nothing are aging. They accept things as they are, or, even worse, as they are going to be.

What about older people? They want something more. They want their youth back. That brings us to the point of controllability. It is not enough to want more and/or better. You must believe that you can achieve it with your own efforts. Otherwise it is only wishful thinking. Those who can do more and better but have no wish to do anything different are young in body and old in spirit.

When the mental age of the people controlling an organization is such that they accept the expected as the desired, the organization starts to age. The mental age of the organization is, in such cases, a function of the mental age of the leadership. The organization ages behaviorally because there is no drive and no impetus for change, which originates, as expected, at the center of control.

2. Functionality of Leadership Style

What do I mean by the functionality of leadership style?

As the organization proceeds along its lifecycle, it needs different styles of leadership. What kind of leadership is desirable? If an organization needs a certain consciousness, which functional type of leadership can provide that consciousness? Leadership implies a dynamic process that can take an organization from one level of consciousness to the next, from one stage of the lifecycle curve to the next. In other words, a leader is someone who can take a company from one set of problems to the next, resolving the problems of yesterday, while preparing the company for the problems of tomorrow.

Moses, for example, took the Hebrews from the problems of Egypt to the problems of Canaan. Leadership doesn't mean taking a system from a stage where there are problems to a stage where there are no problems. It means progressing to the next level—the next generation—of problems. In this way, organizations grow. You are as big as the problems you confront.

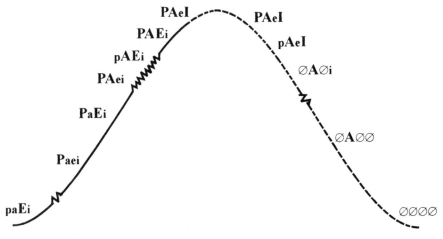

Figure 14-3: Organizational Styles over the Lifecycle

There is an interdependency between followers and leaders. In the growing stages, the leadership style affects organizational culture. The leadership is the driving force. In the aging stages, the organization is the driving force, and the organizational culture determines who will emerge as the leader. The saying "people deserve the leaders they get" applies to aging organizations.

Before we proceed with the desired leadership styles, let us learn how to use the **PAEI** model to codify styles in general.

Management Styles and the Nature of Conflict

Since the **PAEI** roles are incompatible, it is rare that any individual can fulfill and excel at all four roles simultaneously.

When at least one role is not being performed at all, I term that a mismanagement style. If the roles are performed to the threshold of necessary performance, I call that a managerial style, with its normal, human deficiencies.[3]

Mismanagement Styles: I am deliberately presenting extreme cases of mismanagement. It is easier to identify mismanagement styles than management styles. The difference between the two is a question of degree only.

In the extreme case of **P000**, the leader has the **P** quality to the exclusion of all the other roles. Such leaders are Lone Rangers, focusing on the task at hand, but unable to administer and lacking the vision or willingness to take risk consciously. They are not entrepreneurial, and they lack sensitivity to people, values, and group dynamics. They are doers, and that's it. They earn managerial positions because they are diligent, dedicated, hardworking, and loyal. They are productive despite their lack of **A**dministrative, **E**ntrepreneurial, and **I**ntegrative capabilities.

How about their style? They work very hard. Their timetable is neither FIFO (First in, First Out) nor LIFO (Last in, First Out). It is FISH—First in, Still Here. Their desks are a mess. They manage by crisis. There is no delegation, no training, no long- or short-range planning, and their subordinates are gofers. Lone Rangers react, they don't anticipate. They focus almost exclusively on *what now,* not on *how, when,* or even *why.*

How about the **0A00** style? I call such leaders Bureaucrats. They arrive and leave on time, regardless of what needs to be done.

Their desks are clean, and their papers are in neat piles. Subordinates learn that what is important is not their accomplishments, but how they do their work. What the subordinates do is not important so long as they arrive and leave on time. Bureaucrats manage by the book. While Lone Rangers never hold staff meetings (they have no time), a Bureaucrat is always having meetings. The way they run the meetings, however, remind us of Captain Queeg from *The Caine Mutiny*.[4] Their focus is not on the war, but on who stole the strawberries. Bureaucrats run very well-controlled disasters; their companies go broke—right on time.

And the **00E0** style? I label such individuals, Arsonists. When do they come to work? Who knows? When do they leave? Who knows? But the subordinates know they must be there before the boss and not leave until after the boss goes. Since no one knows when Arsonists come and go, their people are on call 24 hours a day, 365 days a year.

Do they hold staff meetings? Yes, but no one knows when. Is there an agenda? There is none that anyone knows about in advance or that even the Arsonist respects. Do they expect their subordinates to be prepared anyway? You bet! So people come to a meeting with their whole office in a mental suitcase. They have no idea what will be discussed or for what they will be attacked. Who does all the talking? The Arsonists. What do the subordinates do? They roll their eyes ("here we go again . . .") and hope their bosses will forget what they say they want. After all, they change their minds so frequently, nobody can keep track of final decisions. "It's too late for you to disagree with me. I already changed my mind," is a common retort to subordinates' questions. Subordinates just wait around for the dust to settle so something can be done. The more Arsonists try to activate their people, the less those subordinates do.

I call the **000I**s the Super Followers. They don't lead; they super-follow. Before everyone else, they sense shifts in the power winds, and they know how the undercurrents are changing. They then position themselves as leaders of the new current. To test the changing political climate, Super Followers send up trial balloons, "I have a suggestion to make, but I don't know if I agree with it." Or, "I suggest we declare dividends, but I don't feel too strongly about it." In Mexico, they call this slippery type *pez enjavonado*, soaped fish. You can't grab hold of them. Their subordinates serve as informers, telling them what's going on. These mismanagers hold many meetings, but who is talking? Everyone else. They listen, keeping their cards very close to their vest. Subordinates have a hard time concluding what direction they should take. While they are waiting for clear instructions, the Super Followers are sniffing the air, attempting to discover what it is the subordinates will agree to.

What organizations need is **PAEI**-style leadership: people who are task-oriented, dedicated, hardworking, organized, efficient, thorough, conservative, creative risk-takers with a global view; and sensitive, people-oriented team builders.

The problem is that there are not too many people like us left around! It is such a rare breed, you can't count on finding them. Such **PAEI** people exist only in textbooks, and that's what is wrong with the whole management or leadership theory. It's based on the perception that such people exist and other people can be trained to be like them.

We are all mismanagers to different degrees because none of us are perfect.

To achieve leadership of organizations that are productive, systematized, proactive, effective, and efficient in the short and the long run, we need complementary teams.

One such complementary team is the **PaEi–pAeI** team. Such teams run Mom-and-Pop stores—even when the store is a multibillion dollar enterprise.

Professor John Kotter of Harvard Business School made a name for himself by drawing a distinction between managers and leaders.[5] I have coded the two roles according to the differences he describes: Managers are **Paei** people, and leaders are **paEI** people. While I accept the distinction he draws between managers and leaders, I disagree with his conclusion that we need more leaders and fewer managers. We need both!

Because managers and leaders have different styles, there will be conflict. Let's address that inescapable reality.

Conflict is a necessary and indispensable ingredient of good teamwork.

The Nature of Conflict: Zen writings remind us that "if everyone is thinking alike, no one is thinking too hard." People who do not like conflict should not be leaders or managers. As Harry Truman used to say, "If you can't stand the heat, get out of the kitchen." The considerable short-term discomfort is necessary for long-term success.

Why?

Try the following exercise. Stand very steadily on both legs with your hands clasped in front of you. You feel comfortable and in control, don't you? If it's comfortable, this must be the normal state. Right? Wrong! If you stay this way for long, you'll certainly die. You can't leave to eat, go to the bathroom, or sleep, and the need to perform any of those actions requires change.

Now try another posture. Stand on one leg, extend the other in the air as if in mid-step, stretch one hand forward and one hand back. Because you are out of balance, you'll find it difficult to stand this way for long. To maintain "balance" requires minute but continuous adjustments. Balance is not a state, but a process

That position seems neither comfortable nor normal, does it? No, but it is a desirable posture because you are between points. You are coming from getting food and going to do something else. What seems comfortable in the short run is very uncomfortable for the long run, and what seems uncomfortable for the short run is comfortable for the long run.

Lack of conflict is very comfortable in the short run, but, in the long run, it leads to death. Conflict is uncomfortable in the short run, but it can be constructive in the long run, depending on what we do with that conflict. Conflict can be a source of either growth or frustration. The first is constructive; the second is destructive.[6]

What distinguishes functional from dysfunctional conflict? We can look to personal experience for an illustrative example.

Most couples divorce for the same reason they married in the first place. They marry because of their complementary styles. The two people were attracted to one another because of their differences, but if they cannot work out those differences, destructive conflict can lead to divorce. But conflict can also mean growth; it can strengthen a marriage. We move closer to one another after a fight. We bond because of our disagreements and conflicts, not in spite of them.

What makes the difference? Why should the same conflicts be destructive in one marriage and in another, constructive and love-enhancing?

Conflict is functional and constructive when it is handled with mutual trust and respect.

Let us define our terms. "Functional" means that the conflict, when resolved, produces desired changes. If the friction we cause by moving our soles against carpet is the result of the steps that took us to the refrigerator for an ice cream treat, that friction was functional. If, on the other hand, our feet rub uncontrollably against the carpet giving us a sore, that friction served nothing: It is not functional.

Mutual respect implies each party's acknowledgment of the legitimacy of the other's divergent position.[7] Mutual trust exists when there is a perception of common interests.[8]

When there is mutual trust and respect, we are willing to learn from one another. Such learning is the occasion of personal and marital growth.[9] With no mutual respect and trust, conflict is all pain and no gain.

There is both abnormal and normal conflict. Normal conflict impels organizations to develop the strength they need in order to function. Abnormal conflict leads the organization, the individual, or the system to repeat itself, to replicate, rather than proceed forward. It does not promote evolution or change. Abnormal conflict does not allow the organization to explore differences and perspectives; in normal conflicts, organizations explore differences that emerge as problematic. This exploration leads to change and growth, to life.

Now that we have clarified the issue of styles and the need for their complementarity, let us return to the question of leadership.

Leadership Styles

During the growing stages, the leadership style should reflect the next organizational style on the lifecycle. The leader's style is a model for the organization's next stage. That's why the person is a leader and not a follower. That is why a leader often outpaces the people she leads. Modeling the next stage of the lifecycle provides functional leadership only in the growing stages.

In the aging stages, unless the leader models earlier stages, the leadership accentuates the organization's decline, making therapeutic rejuvenation even more difficult. Leaders of aging companies have to swim against the current, and those of a growing company have only to swim faster than the rest of their organization.

Perhaps that explains why leaders of growing organizations have no sympathy for functional leaders of aging organizations. They can't understand what is taking so long and why everyone is so cautious. They don't understand that swimming against the stream is politically more difficult than having to swim faster with the current. In an aging organization, leadership must make painful choices and still survive politically. In the growing stages, the decisions are less painful and, except during Adolescence, the leaders are less vulnerable politically.

Leadership Styles over the Lifecycle: What kind of leadership is needed for Courtship, for conception? The answer is **E**. Right? Only partially right. As will become clearer later in the book, a minimal amount of **I** is necessary for the **E**ntrepreneur to be aware—conscious—of needs. That consciousness is what triggers ideas for new ventures and solutions. And the difference between the typical path and the optimal path is a function of an organization's level of **I**. The other **PA** roles must meet the threshold levels as well. Otherwise the organization will run into difficulties at a later stage when their time comes to be developed. On the typical path, then, leadership into a healthy Courtship calls for a **paEi** style.

Consider now what it means to lead organizations into Infancy and assume risk. Which leadership style is functional at that stage? How about leadership that emphasizes administration or **A**? That won't work at all, will it? An **A** constantly says, "No, no, no." Nothing would happen; the organization would never be born although it was conceived. We would have an organizational miscarriage.

What kind of leadership—**P**erformance, **A**dministration, **E**ntrepreneurship or **I**ntegration—can stimulate an organization to be born, coalesce, take risk, and make things happen?

It has to be a **P** person. Such a person is the one who says, "I'm putting in the first $5,000, and I'm taking the risk first. Let's go. Let's do it. I'm ready." This is a doer, because for the organization to be born, it takes a real commitment in action—not just words and dreams. It takes someone who sets a tone of *doing,* providing a behavioral model for an action-oriented organization.

A leader who is only dreaming does not give birth. A doer who has no dreams does not conceive. Thus for a healthy start up, if it is led by one individual, the organization needs a leader who can both dream and do, a **Paei.**

What happens when, as in a revolution, there is a complementary leadership team of dreamer-doers? There are the ideologues—the intelligentsia, the educated well-meaning theoreticians—and following them are the peasants, the down-to-earth guerrilla fighters who speak less and do more. When the revolution succeeds, and the new country takes form and is born, what happens to many of those ideologues? They are shoved aside, put in prison, or executed. If they were lucky enough to die natural deaths right after the success of the revolution, they remain pictures on the wall. The action-oriented, hard-nosed doers take over. Doing, not talking, is what makes it possible for an organization to survive Infancy. The style for Infancy is, then, **Paei.**

What is next? Go-Go. A new vision and new possibilities are called for. If the doers do not develop that vision, the system remains small and undernourished. The new vision helps companies to expedite their emergence from Infancy. So to get to Go-Go from Infancy we need **E** again, and the style is **paEi.** If there is no complementary

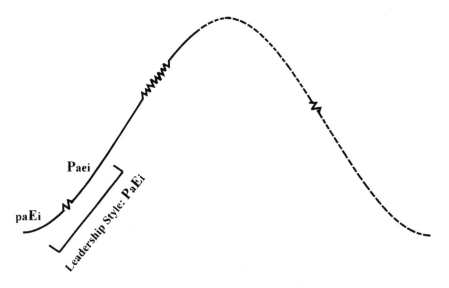

Figure 14-4: Leadership Styles for Courtship and Infancy

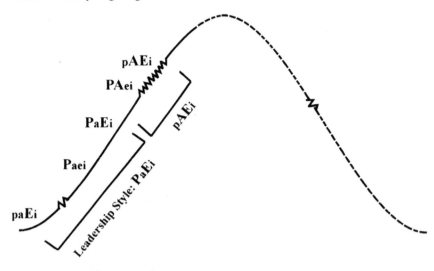

Figure 14-5: Leadership Styles for Go-Go and Adolescence

team, taking the organization from Courtship to Go-Go, the **PaEi** style meets the bill.

The **PaEi** is the most common style of founders on the typical path. These founders are Arsonist and Firefighter all at once. They start their own fires, and they are the ones who then rush to get the flames under control and start another one before the first one is fully extinguished.

By creating difficulties and then managing them, they force their companies to grow by leaps and bounds. These founders are hard-working dreamers. They thrive in an atmosphere of crisis-by-management.

In the Adolescent stage, organizations must be organized, systematized, and stabilized. At this point, quality is more important than quantity. What is the desirable leadership? A bias toward Administration is called for. Characteristically, companies at this stage experience difficult leadership transitions. The transition from Go-Go to Adolescence requires a switch from **PaEi** leadership style to a **pAEi** style. That spells trouble. First, an **A** style is altogether different from a **PE** style. **A** is slow, thorough, analytical, and risk-averse. Details matter. **PE** is fast, and has no interest in details or risk taking. The two leadership styles are incompatible. **E**s want their subordinates to be on the job when they get there and to stay even after the **E**s themselves have left. But, because nobody knows when the bosses arrive or leave, their subordinates behave erratically. The **E** types expect their subordinates to be on call at all times.

The **A** style is completely different. **A**s arrive at work on time and leave on time. That makes **E** types feel cheated. They consider the **A**s insufficiently loyal to the company, they think that the **A** types don't try hard enough. The **E** types shoot from the hip; an **A** likes to think things over. **E** decides first and thinks later. **A** thinks, and then decides. **A** types feel as if they must always follow the **E**s with a shovel to clean up the mess. The **E** types, for their part, resent being kept away from the sandbox, where they can do as they please.

A and **E** are bound to clash. Under an Arsonist **00E0**, **A**, alone, might end up as deadwood (**0000**), and although **A** might survive personally, that would be at the company's expense. As deadwood, **A** cannot fulfill the role the organization needs.

Entering Adolescence, the organization needs to become **PAei**. Thus, it calls for **PAei** leadership. But we must be careful. If the organization is a **PA00**, it will reject and eject the **PaEi** leaderof Go-Go, and the **PAei** leader will cause premature aging. Once the **PAei** stage in the lifecycle is completed, the organization calls for the **E** role back, and this calls for a **pAEi** style of leadership.

What is needed to link **E** and **A** is new leadership of the **AE** type, a **pAEi**, not just an **0A00**. Most good consultants are **AE**s. The organization can solve its leadership problem by hiring a consultant to guide the design of the organization chart, the budgeting system, and the manuals. Later, it should hire that person as a chief operating officer in the **A**dministrative role.

Introducing changes from an outside person has several advantages. First, it enables the founder to observe whether the outsider might be the right person. It is a test under live fire. The two of them watch one another to see whether they are compatible in spite of having different styles. If there is no ongoing mutual trust and respect, they are the wrong combination. What's more, it's easier to lead a cultural change from the outside than from the inside. You can test that easily enough. Try teaching your own tomboy child how to play piano.

There is no need to change leadership if the current leader can change his or her style from **PaEi** to **pAEi**. I found that ability is not so rare as it might seem. It depends on the magnitude of their **I**. The bigger their **I**, the more flexible their style of leadership.

It's difficult to manage an organization during its transition from Infancy to Adolescence because the leadership must either change its style, or the leadership itself must be changed. Managing an enterprise is not a marathon race; it is a relay race, and when individual leadership cannot change styles in response to changing conditions, the leadership role must move from one person to another.

This transition of leadership is universal. Take raising children. Parents are a complementary team. A male child grows attached to his mother for a few years, later he grows attached to his father, and later still, he seeks friendship away from the parents. Children seek the model, the leadership they need to grow in a balanced way. It is difficult for a single parent to raise a child. Children need both the yin and the yang energies.

After Adolescence, when the organization is moving into Prime, the leadership style of those managing it should emphasize **I**. Why?

In Prime cultures, the **P**, **A**, and **E** roles are performed by executives other than the leader. The role of leadership during Prime is to hire the right people, to integrate the desirable conflicts that emerge in a correctly structured organization, and to give direction. The structure is good, and the right people are in the right jobs. **P** and

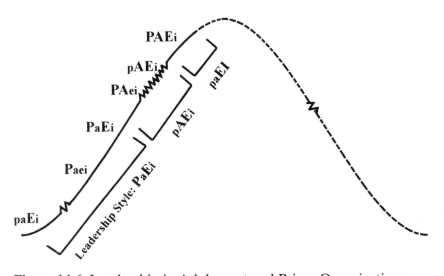

Figure 14-6: Leadership in Adolescent and Prime Organizations

A are delegated, as is **E**, which is now institutionalized. Now the organization needs a leader who can integrate it all—a leader who emphasizes the **I** role.

At any point in the lifecycle, the necessary styles of leadership are the styles that will guide the organization from its current stage into the next. During Courtship, the organizational culture requires leadership that dreams, **paEi**, and when it gives organizational birth, leadership that acts: It must be **Paei**. To move into Go-Go, organizations need **E** again—**PaEi**, and when the organization moves into Adolescence it needs **A** to cool Go-Go tendencies and prevent the organization from overloading itself. The functional style of Adolescence is **pAEi**. Getting into Prime now requires **I**, and staying in Prime requires **E**. The desired functional style for Prime should be **paEI**.

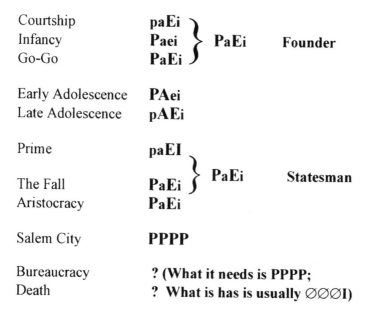

Courtship	**paEi**		
Infancy	**Paei**	**PaEi**	**Founder**
Go-Go	**PaEi**		
Early Adolescence	**PAei**		
Late Adolescence	**pAEi**		
Prime	**paEI**		
The Fall	**PaEi**	**PaEi**	**Statesman**
Aristocracy	**PaEi**		
Salem City	**PPPP**		
Bureaucracy	**? (What it needs is PPPP;**		
Death	**? What is has is usually ⊘⊘⊘I)**		

Figure 14-7: Lifecycle of the Organization and the Styles of Leadership

The leaders of the Fall organizations need to retard organizational aging. Now they need to start working against the current, swimming upstream. They need not only **E**, but **P**, as well. Soon, in Aristocracy, **P** will start to decline. An organization in Aristocracy must go back to concentrate on the basics—hard-nosed decisions, blocking and tackling—right away. Because organizations lose **P** during Aristocracy, the functional style that retards deterioration is **PaEi**.

The **PaEi** style, which is necessary for both the Fall and Aristocracy, is different from the **PaEi** style of a start-up. Aristocracy requires professional managers with the style of an Entrepreneur—professional soldiers, not guerrilla leaders. They must be able to make decisions and have vision for their large organizations. This is a significant distinction. Often organizations that are losing flexibility merge with or acquire Go-Gos with the explicit goal of acquiring Go-Go leadership. It doesn't take long for Aristocratic companies to discover that Go-Go leadership lacks the political maturity to deal with the internal politics that plague their aging organizations.

An Aristocracy needs to identify what business it is in and the value it has for its clients. It must get close to its clients, paying more attention to the *why* and *what* than it pays to the *how*. It must derive

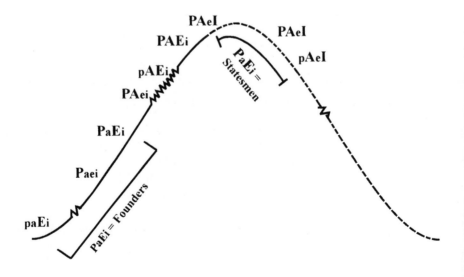

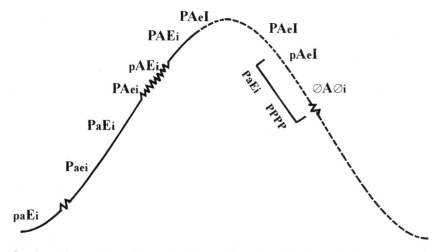

the *how* from the *why* and *what*, rather than letting the *how* dictate the *why* and *what*. That is a **PaEi** style.

Figure 14-8: Founders vs. Statesmen

Figure 14-9: Leadership in Aristocracy and Salem City

Many organizations in Salem City—failing organizations owned by government or those being nationalized—make the following mistake. Rather than appoint a **P** to lead the organization out of its difficulties, the government appoints an **A**dministrator or an **I**ntegrator. Why? From a political point of view, the purpose of nationalization was not to increase unemployment but to save employment. Leadership's explicit instructions are to save jobs—not the company. What happens? Instead of rejuvenating the organization, the **A** and **I** now create a bigger Bureaucracy, and that accelerates the decline of the company. In situations where the organization is big enough, it can accelerate even the decline of the country.

This, then, is the principle: Leadership style should, at every growing stage of the lifecycle, reflect the style of the organization in the stage from which it is departing and the culture and style of the stage to which it is moving. The reader should recall that the organizational culture determines the required leadership style during the growing stages. It is the style that leads the organization to the next stage of the lifecycle. After Prime, however, the desired leadership is not what the organization's culture will become. It is just the opposite. The appropriate leadership style is the one that will retard that development, or, I might say, retard the decay.

In the growing stages, the leader projects— behaviorally models—the style for the organization. . . . In the aging states, the organization selects leaders who reflect its culture.

During periods of growth, people have faith, and leaders can lead, knowing that the people will follow faithfully. To reverse aging on the other hand, means to request sacrifices, to induce pain. The organization experiences fear, not faith. The decaying organization chooses leaders who reinforce its culture, not necessarily making sacrifices. It seems as if this process is built into a mutually consistent, dynamic system: It enables growth and then enables death. For a growing company, leadership can come from within. For aging organizations, leadership should come from the outside. If leaders do rise through the ranks, defying the culture that raised them, they, like Mikhail Gorbachev and Frederick de Klerk, pay with their careers.

But how does leadership style affect organizational aging?

It depends on whether the leadership style is functional, serving the needs of the organization and advancing it to the next stage in its growth or retarding its decay.

Start-ups, from Courtship to Adolescence, require **PaEi** leaders who are aggressive dreamers-doers. Once leaders are successful, however, they become entrenched in their positions, and they remain long after they have stopped fulfilling the needs of the organization. **PaEi** refuses to make way for **paEI**, and **paEI** leaders, once entrenched, either refuse to yield to the next necessary leadership style, or are unable to change styles. An organization can, therefore, age if leadership is not transferred functionally at the right point in time on the organizational lifecycle. To change leadership itself or its style, there must be a clear need—real pressure from the organization. If we review the description of the organizational lifecycle, we can see that there is no pressure to change leadership in Prime, the Fall, or Aristocracy. In Prime, everything is fine. In the Fall, the problems are only latent. In Aristocracy, the company is liquid with good balance-sheet ratios, and the Finzi-Contini syndrome prevents people from expressing dissatisfaction with complacency. During this calm before the storm, there is no pressure to change leadership. So, A leadership that is functional and necessary to lead the organization through Adolescence, later becomes dysfunctional when it no longer offers what the organization needs and the conditions aren't politically ripe to force a change. The style of leadership and the needs of the organization are not in sync.

In the aging stages of the lifecycle, what retards rejuvenation is that the chosen leader is the one who reinforces the culture, not one who changes it. This leader surely wants to avoid making waves. They might topple the boat. In the aging stages sacrifices have to be made, and the organization needs a leader who does not watch the polls. Here we need a statesman—not a politician—to worry about the next generation, not the next election.

3. Perceived Relative Market Share

The perceived relative market share is the next factor that can affect Entrepreneurship. A company's market share is the percentage it reaches of all possible clients whose needs it could satisfy. In business language, it is the company's share of total sales of similar products that satisfy the same need. What, then, does *perceived* mean in this context?

A company's market share can be 100 percent or 0.001 percent with the same revenues. The definition of market share depends on the denominator—the reference market.

A company can claim any market share, depending on how it defines its market.

A company can have 100 percent market share by defining its market as only those people who buy its products. It can easily be the largest, biggest, best in the world at something. Its leaders need only identify where it excels uniquely. For instance, one of my clients is the largest, privately-owned, computerized, multi-media alarm company in the world. If you narrow your definition enough, you can be the leader of whatever you are doing. My point is that whatever market share companies believe they have, it is only a *perceived* market share.

Relative market share refers to a company's share of the market as compared with its largest competitor. Now let us assume a company has a perceived relative market share of a multiple of two. That means that it has 35 percent of the market, and its next largest competitor has about 17 percent. Will knowing that make the company competitive or complacent?

Being the largest, biggest, or best at anything is like being a champion in sports. One needs a challenging competitor to stay in shape. When a company's leadership believes it no longer has to compete in order to satisfy the perceived needs of its clients, that is, it believes its clients are a captive audience with no alternatives, the entrepreneurial spirit and the desire and propensity to adapt to a changing environment suffer. The company expects its customers to adapt to its needs, rather than having to adapt to the customers' changing needs. Organizations arrive at that stage when they believe they have the majority of their marketplace. The decision-makers think, "This is it! We've made it! We are there!" That is an attitude that can irreparably damage the creativity of organizations. They have forgotten that once they are at the top of a mountain, there is only one way to go: down.

Being a champion can make a company complacent. To stay in condition and at the top, there must always be a strong challenger. Market dominance is a goal that should be savored for no longer than one night of celebration. The organization needs to seek new visions, redefining its market. That new definition introduces new competitors into the picture. Horizons must move as organizations move, or people's eyes will focus lower and lower until they see only the tops of their toes. That's when they stop moving altogether.

4. Functionality of Organizational Structure

The fourth factor that impacts aging is organizational structure. In recent years, specifically the 1990s, structure has been seen as a concept that has become "politically incorrect." Today, open systems, open architecture, noncentered enterprises, vision, values, and cultures are the preferred alternatives. Many people consider structure to be synonymous with bureaucracy.

I disagree completely with the current theory and practice of "modern management." In fact, I disagree so strongly that I am dedicating the next chapter to a discussion of this factor.

Notes

1. The Bernal experiments showed that as structure increases, information (defined by Bateson, *Mind and Nature* [1979] as "news of difference") decreases. Ultimately these experiments showed the inverse relationship between structure (control) and information (flexibility).

2. See I. Adizes, *The Pursuit of Prime* (Santa Monica: Knowledge Exchange, 1996), and *Mastering Change: The Power of Mutual Trust and Respect in Personal Life, Family, Business and Society* (Los Angeles: Adizes Institute Publications, 1993).

3. I. Adizes, in *How to Solve the Mismanagement Crisis* (Bel Air, CA: Adizes Institute Publications, 1980 [first printing, New York: Dow Jones Irwin, 1978]), provides a detailed description and analysis of management and mismanagement styles.

4. S. Kramer, Prod. (1954), *The Caine Mutiny,* written by E. Dmytrik from the novel by H. Wouk (Columbia Studios, 1954).

5. Professor John Kotter of Harvard Business School draws a distinction between managers and leaders. See J. Kotter, *A Force for Change: How Leadership Differs from Management* (New York: The Free Press, 1990).

6. See the special issue of *Journal of Social Issues* 50 (I, 1994), devoted to constructive conflict management.

7. Sara Cobb has done research on conflict and shows that agreements themselves do not end conflict; conflicts end when both parties legitimize the other, within their own stories. She has described this process of "legitimization" as a narrative process whereby each party provides the other a positive position in their own story. Conflict, she shows, is directly related to the presence of delegitimizing stories. See S. Cobb, "Empowerment and Mediation: A Narrative Perspective,"

The Negotiation Journal 9, 3 (1993): 245-261; and her 1994 "A Narrative Perspective on Mediation: Toward the Materializing of Story Telling," in J. Folger and T. Jones, eds., *New Directions in Communications Research and Perspective* (Newbury Park, CA: Sage Press, 1994): 48–66.

8. See I. Adizes, *Mastering Change: The Power of Mutual Trust and Respect in Personal Life, Family Life, Business and Society* (Bel Air, CA: Adizes Institute Publications, 1992).

9. This notion is at the core of mediation and other forms of conflict resolution practice. See R. Bush and J. Folger, eds., *The Promise of Mediation: Responding to Conflict through Empowerment and Recognition* (San Francisco: Jossey-Bass, 1994).

CHAPTER FIFTEEN

Structural Causes of Aging

Structure, to my mind, encompasses three subsystems: The structure of responsibilities, the structure of authority, and the structure of rewards. They are interrelated and have to be aligned. You cannot expect success when people have high responsibilities, insufficient authority to fulfill those responsibilities, and unacceptable rewards. People need to know what is expected, feel that they can accomplish it, and have a personal reason for doing it.

In this chapter, I take one section of the puzzle, the structure of responsibility and authority, and discuss its impact on aging. The alignment of responsibility, authority, and rewards is a complex subject.[1]

The Functionality of Organizational Structure

The functionality of organizational structure is the fourth factor that affects an organization's entrepreneurship. Often an organization's structure inhibits the entrepreneurial spirit. Consider the example of a bare-bones company, organized functionally. In order to demonstrate how structure impacts behavior, I am presenting a simplified example.

Notice that the departments on this chart are on legs of different lengths. The differences reflect the orientations of the departments. Those with long legs have a long-term orientation; those with short legs have a short-term orientation.

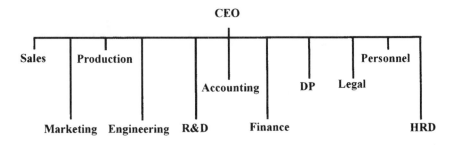

Figure 15-1: Typical Functional Organization Chart

The four **PAEI** roles of management describe the basic orientation of each of the departments.

What should the orientation of a typical sales department be in **PAEI** terms? Sales are closely oriented toward satisfying customer needs, thus Performance, the **P** role. Satisfying those needs efficiently is a function of **A**dministration. A sales department, aiming to satisfy client needs efficiently, should have the **PAei** style. Such a department has sales scheduling, quotas, and sales training.

Marketing is also oriented toward customer needs, **P**erformance, but that orientation is within the context of developing creative solutions to satisfy tomorrow's needs, or **E**ntrepreneurship. Marketing should have a **PaEi** orientation.

The accounting department is a story in itself. Obviously **A** should be its primary function, but **E** is also necessary. Why not **PA**? The **PA** style calls for the organization to provide effective service efficiently. That is the function of sales, not accounting. **AI**, a system of accounting that will be politically correct, is not right either.

Still, why **AE**? The **A** does not need explaining, but why **E**? The following joke helps make my point.

A small company was looking for an accountant. The three candidates who applied were asked, "How much is two plus two?" The first candidate had just passed the CPA exam. Like most people with no real-world experience, he answered instantly and without doubt: "Four! No question! Four!"

The second candidate had worked for many years at one of the world's largest auditing firms. With some hesitation, he said, "I'll have to check with the home office first."

The third candidate was a graduate of the University of Hard Knocks. He was street-wise. Through half-closed eyes, he looked at the interviewer and asked, "What do you have in mind? Are you selling or are you buying?"

The third fellow got the job, and rightly so. For accounting to be an information system rather than a data system, accounting must understand management's goals. It should be **A** or **E**, able to provide control of the company's direction. "Are we going into or getting out of the New York market?" Every question requires different information. In many companies, accounting is bookkeeping. Management gets data but no information. That happens when the management team doesn't include accounting in its discussions. The accountants are neither the driving nor the driven force. They just produce reports on what has happened, not what is or will be happening. And that reminds me of another story.

Two people are in a balloon flying over the countryside. Clouds form, and after some time, the balloonists realize that they are lost. Flying around, they finally see an opening among the clouds. They begin their descent, and when they see a man standing on the ground under them, they shout, "Hello! Can you tell us where we are?" And the guy yells back at the top of his lungs, "In a balloon!" Frustrated, one balloonist says to the other, "That guy down there must be an accountant."

"How do you know?" his partner asks.

"Because he gave us accurate, precise information—totally useless!"

The desirable **pAEi** orientation should also apply to organizations' legal and information technology departments. Each of those departments, in order to perform its function adequately, must first ask, "What do you have in mind?" Testing to see whether your legal people do ask that question is a good way to determine whether the organization has a lawyer, or a highly paid legal secretary.

Here is how it can go. Ask your lawyer to review a newly written contract and let you know whether you should sign it. If he says, "Fine, I'll call you in the morning," you should fire him. Anyone with legal training can check the legality of a contract. It takes only memory to know the rulings, precedents, and laws. What your organization needs is not a lawyer who tells you *why not* but one who tells you *how yes* to accomplish your goals.

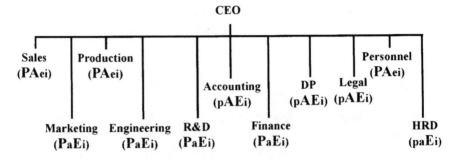

Figure 15-2: PAEI Orientation of Typical Departments

A lawyer worth keeping would have pushed the contract aside and asked, "Before I read it, tell me what you have in mind. What are you trying to achieve?" You can have confidence that that lawyer will check, not only the legalities of the contract, but whether and how it will achieve your goals.

The same rule applies to computer people. If they agree to tell you which computer or system to buy before they have reviewed the ways your organization aims to use it now and in the future, then they are only salesmen of computerized typewriters and calculators. They cannot be trusted to set up your company's information technology systems.

Where Is the Conflict?

In the above functional structure, how well do the various departments of most companies get along? The following list details the departments that have—and should have—considerable disagreement and conflict:

- Sales versus marketing
- Production versus research and development, and engineering
- Accounting, legal, and information technology versus everyone
- Personnel versus human resources development

A mistake most analysts make is to attribute conflict to the individual personalities involved.

If conflict is not the result of personality problems, why, then, do those units have trouble getting along? What is the nature of their conflict?

Sales accuses Marketing of not understanding the realities of the market. The sales people perceive themselves as working hard to implement a pricing-and-product strategy, and as soon as it is working, the fat cats from corporate marketing headquarters come along and change it. Marketing, on the other hand, accuses sales people of resisting change and dragging their feet. "Salesmen, you know, aren't that smart. If they were, would they be on the road all day?"

Production and Engineering are also at odds. Engineering always wants to change the technology, to update it. What do production people say? "Come back next year." They do not want anyone messing up their production schedule. Their performance is measured by productivity and manufacturing costs. The changes might work in the long run but they sure make a mess and retard their goals in the short run.

And Engineering is upset, too. "There is resistance to change from these small-brain production people. They have their eyes set on their own belly buttons. Heck, if we didn't push, they would still be working with spinning wheels."

Often the organization neglects the structural issues and tries to resolve the conflict by changing the personnel. The company might send someone from Sales to head Marketing, or someone from Production to head Engineering, so that "those guys up there will know the realities we face before they make their decisions."

Of course, those solutions won't work. If the sales person maintains his sales **PA** orientation when he is supposed to be directing the marketing effort, the company loses **E**. Likewise, it's no solution to put a production person in engineering. If, on the other hand, those people are able to change their orientation from **PA** to **PE**, their erstwhile colleagues will accuse them of being traitors.

Another mistake is to attribute such conflict to problems of style rather than structure, to assert that people are just not team players. So people cry out, "We need a team player." Out goes one player and in comes another. What happens? If the new marketing guy is aware of his predecessor's marching orders, "be a team player," he may try to fit in. Then he won't be able to exercise pressure for change, as he should. Who sets the tone now? Sales.

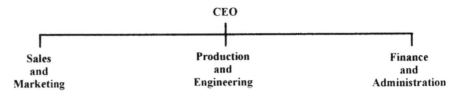

Figure 15-3: The Streamlined Organization

And, you might see the same scenario playing itself out in Engineering, but, in that case, the Production department is the driving force. The organization has team players but as the **PA** orientation dominates, the **E** orientation is lost. Engineering ends up doing maintenance.

The most common solution to such conflicts is to unite the warring departments and produce a streamlined organization.

What's wrong with this structure? Sales is **P**-oriented, short-term, and results-oriented. Marketing should be **E**-oriented, long-range, entrepreneurial, viewing, and analyzing. When Sales and Marketing merge, which orientation will dominate? The **P** or the **E**? The short- or the long-term orientation? The answer is obvious: the short-term, sales orientation will win. Marketing ends up doing statistical analyses of sales and preparing sales support material, and calling those activities marketing. They are not leading change as they should. And how could they? Their bonuses, orientation, the group they belong to, and the pressure they experience all focus on short-term selling, not long-term market development.

Similarly, when production and process engineering merge, they call the department, the Manufacturing department. Nevertheless, process or industrial engineering staff is probably doing maintenance, oiling and repairing production's machinery. **E** is dominated by **P**, and the short run is driving the long run, rather than the other way around. It's clear that hardly any **E** remains.

The so-called Human Resources division has a similar problem. It encompasses both the **EI** functions, the true human resources role of developing new capabilities, and the **PA** role of human resources administration. In the administrative role they fire, displace, and perform salary administration, and they oversee personnel evaluations, selection, and labor negotiations. It is **A**dministration for **P**erformance, and **P**roductivity. The **EI**, the true human resources development, and the **PA** role of administration, are in conflict. And as expected, **PA** wins. The department personnel, although trained in **I** and aspiring to provide **I** for the corporation, is by and large in the **A** business. They do management's dirty laundry, the evaluations and firings. It is not strange then that labor, by and large, does not perceive the Human Resources Development department as being in the human resources development business. Labor considers human resources to be management's long arm. So, when human resources presents its ideas for job enlargement, job enrichment, or participative management, how does labor react? "Aha! This is a new trick to make us work harder for less money. No, thank you."

The people in the Human Resources department are frustrated. The staff *wants* to develop people. They *want* to be humanistic and motivated. But they are accused of being manipulative. They are viewed with suspicion. "Those guys smile a lot; but they're wishy-washy soaped fish. You can't catch them. They'll wriggle right out of your hand. They are useless (or dangerous)."

Putting an **EI** like Human Resources Development (HRD) under Personnel will kill its **EI** function. It will be subordinated to personnel's **PA** function. HRD people end up at the bottom of the totem pole, ensuring that the coffee is warm and the refreshments have arrived for training sessions. They lose their **EI** functionality.

And now let's look at a real sacred cow of so-called modern management: the chief financial officer. It's a mistake to combine finance and accounting. Finance should cover investment analysis, treasury function, management of resources, investor relations, and use of funds. Its focus is on the future. Its style should be **Ep**. Accounting's province is the controller's function: accounts receivable, accounts payable, and general ledger bookkeeping. It focuses on the past. It should be **Ae**. By putting the two together, a company creates a very dangerous situation—a delayed reaction syndrome. The company skips a heartbeat, suffering arrhythmia. Let me explain.

Accounting's role is to be a pain. It should be and frequently is precisely wrong instead of being approximately right. Accounting returns a request because a signature is in the wrong place, and that's the way it should be. The accountants are the guardians of law and order, and the company needs that to maintain systemic control. As a consequence, accounting people are not widely popular, are they?

People accuse them of being bureaucratic, unresponsive, closed-mouthed, and closed-brained.

Now, consider a scenario in which a certain product line is doing poorly. The executive committee analyzes the problem in its meeting. Will the head of Marketing suggest dropping the line? Probably not. It was Marketing's idea in the first place. Instead, the marketing people will ask for a higher advertising budget. They will try to increase the budget of the marketing mix, making promises in order to keep the product alive a little bit longer.

Will the sales people try to kill the product? Not yet. Their incentive systems are based on sales quotas. They will suggest lowering the price. They will attribute the problem to lack of collateral marketing, prices being too high, and the incentive being insufficient.

How about Production? No vocal objection from this department either. Production's incentive system includes this product line. The production people might say that things would be better with another piece of machinery. "If only we had that machine, we could improve the product's quality, and it would sell beautifully."

Personnel has no interest in killing the product either. Its death might mean reductions in labor force.

Clearly, every department views the corporate problem through its own interests. Each solution is derived from its local orientation.

Who, besides the CEO, is not interested solely in market share, sales, or production, unless it produces profits? It should be the vice president of finance, who should be looking at return on investment. Period. If the internal cost of capital invested in this product line is higher than its return, the finance person should say, "Let's do something else."

If accounting and finance are in one division, the finance vice president's attempts to kill a weak product line might be misinterpreted. "Those accountants always say 'no' to everything, so what else is new? Big deal. If we let bean counters manage this company, we will be dead in no time!"

Several months or even years will pass before it's no longer in the interest of Marketing, Production, or Engineering to keep that product line alive. By then, the company will be in trouble, and now everyone wants to do something about the situation. When an axis develops, the CEO can easily act. I realize that I am being, perhaps, overly dramatic, but in my experience, after Adolescence, no CEO acts completely alone and without consulting his top subordinates. What they advise the CEO is colored by their interests, and their interests stem from the organization's structure.

If I see an organization chart with VP for Marketing and Sales (and true to the orientation, it is always called: Sales and Marketing, not Marketing and Sales), VP Production and Engineering (or the mistake IBM made in 1997: R&D and Production together); VP Personnel and Human Resources Development, Finance, Accounting, Legal and IT, all under one VP for Finance and Administration who is also the CFO, people will complain that the organization is stymied, slow to react to market forces, and lacks a really strategic outlook. So, the organization hires someone to be a strategic planner.

Figure 15-4 shows how that looks.

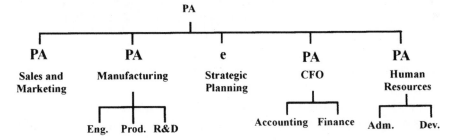

Figure 15-4: The Net Impact on "E" in the Streamlined Structure

You cannot make a submarine fly by appointing a very qualified pilot to look through the periscope.

Structure Causes Strategy

Please note:

Structure causes strategy, rather than strategy causing structure.

That disagrees with the famous treatise of Alfred B. Chandler.[2] In my view, Chandler was right that strategy *should* determine structure, but in reality, my experience is that present structure determines present strategy.[3] Existent structure has embedded interests, and when the time comes to make a strategic decision about change, guess what. People vote with an eye on their self-interests. And if the structure consolidates short-term interests, guess what, again. How do they vote?

Structure causes behavior; structure causes strategy. If one wants to change behavior, one must first change the structure. It's useless to develop a strategy for getting a submarine to fly. If you want it to fly, you must change the submarine to an airplane before you set a strategy for changing its performance. No new strategy can be implemented before a new structure is in place.

Let me illustrate what I mean with a story from my own adolescence.

Just after I finished high school, I was part of an Israeli high school delegation to France. We traveled overnight by train, from Biarritz to Paris. As teenagers will do, all twenty of us tried to sleep in one compartment that could accommodate eight people at best. It took almost two hours and plenty of cooperation before each of us was able to find room for feet, arms, and head. Some tried sleeping on the floor. Some were sitting on others' laps. One head was behind somebody else's shoulder. The sleeping arrangement was structured around people.

Just as we finally fell asleep, somebody announced that he needed to go to the bathroom. Incredible commotion. He could go only if he upset the entire group. One had to move a leg; that one had to move a hand; this one had to move his body; another screamed, "Don't step on my toes."

When an organization is structured around people and not around a task, it may well be easier to wet your pants than to cause widespread commotion. And for that reason, in organizations structured around people, change can be very difficult. There is a saying that, in such organizations, you can recognize innovators by the arrows in their backs. To make a change requires so many buy-ins, approvals, and arrangements that the innovator simply gives up before even starting. Eventually, not only one person is wet. A lot of people are feeling damp, and someone will say, "This organization stinks!"

What should the new structure be? For that we need a strategy, don't we? This is a chicken-and-egg problem. I have dealt with this dilemma the following way. First the organization should define its business, that is, its mission. The focus is not on strategy: That is a *how* focus. Mission is a *what* and *why* focus. *Who* do we want our clients to be, *which* of their needs do we want to satisfy? *What* is our role? That exercise leads to organizational structure. What I often find is that there is a market segmentation that calls for product differentiation and a structural representation of that differentiation.

Take the following example of a company that was introducing what I will call a new food bar. It was delicious with lots of vitamins. Sales were growing 100 percent annually. The company was structured functionally: head of Sales, head of Manufacturing, financial officer, and administration: Classical Structure 101. I asked the managers, "What's your market share?" They hesitated. "Well, it depends," they said, "how you define it. If we are talking about sports energy bars, market share is X. If we are talking about the snack market, then it is Y. And for the weight-loss market, it is Z." In other words, the company was serving a multiplicity of markets with one and the same product, one and the same promotion program, one and the same package and price delivered with one and the same functionally structured organization.

How could anyone do strategic planning? For whom do they plan if the different market segments are not represented structurally? The company should have organized itself with market-segment managers responsible for the market share of their specific markets and the profitability of those businesses. The managers should develop specific strategies for their markets. They can share Manufacturing, Accounting, Human Resources, and even the Sales force, but they need a structural focus that reflects market and product differentiation.

Only when organizations have implemented the right structure and aligned information and reward systems do we progress to strategic planning. If, after we have designed the strategic plan, we see the need for a newer structure, we adapt the latest structure to reflect those new needs. In organizations that work with the Adizes methodology, structure is continuously adapting and changing.

So why doesn't every company proceed that way? It is my belief that self-interest dominates the choices we make. It's easier to send someone for Harvard training. It's easier to hire a strategic planner to sit, smoke a pipe, write reports and get an ulcer. And it's easier to pay a very respectful consulting firm a cool million dollars for very competent recommendations than it is to put people through the pain of structural reorganization. And even if you are willing to submit to that pain, you cannot do it too often. Spending money on consulting recommendations doesn't bother management so much as spending its own time, struggling to survive political wars, and fearing the painful political repercussions of change. Once you free the genie from the bottle, who knows who will survive? So companies do not restructure or they restructure much less frequently than changing market forces dictate.

Structure affects strategy because structure reflects relative self-interests, and the interest structure affects the emerging strategy.

Structure causes behavior.

And if the structure rejects **E**, it can become the fourth factor contributing to the loss of **E**.

Growing vs. Aging Companies: The Difference

What I said above applies to aging companies. It explains how the streamlined functional structure ages them by rejecting **E**. It does not apply to growing companies which have ample, albeit personalized, **E**.

Each company should be structured to encourage and nourish the role it needs most depending on its location on the lifecycle.[4] Growing companies should structure to protect **A**, to act as a countervailing power to **E**. In growing companies, a vice president of administration to oversee accounting, personnel, legal, and information technology is recommended.

That structure would be very undesirable for aging companies, premature or not. In aging organizations you want less **A**. You should separate the **A** functions, and, to prevent aging and the loss of **E**, you should unite **E** with a vice president in charge of

Marketing, Finance, Engineering, and HRD. How can anyone manage such a diversity? How can the CEO? This is the training-wheels position for being a CEO. If the person cannot run multidisciplinary functions, it's good we identified the disability early.

Never, never, never should organizations structurally pair these functions: marketing and sales, production and engineering, finance and accounting, human resources development and human resources administration. For aging organizations it can be pathologically dangerous. In growing companies it is undesirable but bearable because the titles do not reflect what is really happening. The vice president for Sales and Marketing carries the title but does no marketing. The founder really does that. The same is true of the chief financial officer. In reality the founder monopolizes the **E** role no matter what you call it and where you put it. The problems start when the organizations are honest-to-goodness trying to find a structural solution. Then bad design causes bad behavior.

Organizational Colonialism

We have diagnosed a functional structure for a simple profit-center organization. A company with many profit centers faces an additional challenge—organizational colonialism. What is that?

We can use a single lifecycle curve to describe an organization as a whole. Such a curve, however, does not represent each of the company's component divisions or departments.

Companies comprise units, departments, or divisions, and each of those can be located in a different part of the lifecycle curve. It's not unusual for a multidivisional company to have some profit centers in Infancy, some in Go-Go, and others in Prime or Aristocracy. Frequently, such entities are organized according to the hierarchy shown in Figure 15-5.

Because Aristocracies like to take over Go-Go companies, such configurations are not unusual. The Go-Go gives the Aristocracy growth it can't otherwise achieve. Go-Go companies, on the other hand, acquire Infants because Go-Gos are promiscuous. They start or buy businesses easily. Such structures are, however, susceptible to a problem.

I define a situation in which Infants report to a Go-Go and a Go-Go reports to an Aristocracy as *organizational colonialism.*

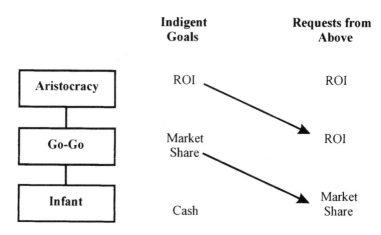

Figure 15-5: Organizational Colonialism

Analysis of the relationships among the units, in terms of their needs and the appropriate measures of performance, reveals the problem with organizational colonialism.

What is the goal of an Infant organization? To break even and get enough cash to survive. Infants are engaged in a constant fight for cash. They always need more capital. What does a Go-Go company want? Sales and sales growth are the goals they impose on those reporting to them. Moreover, because Go-Gos need capital to fund their own growth, they are not inclined to share. The request for funds annoys the Go-Go parent, who in response to the continuous requests for funding, demands, "What? More money? We gave you money four months ago. When will you stop asking? What's more, we want to know why you aren't growing so fast as we expected. We grow 35 percent a year, and your growth is nowhere near that rate. Why should we give you more money?"

What does Aristocracy want? Dividends. Return on investment. Instead of giving, an Aristocracy takes. It wants to milk the calf as well as the cow. So the Aristocracy milks the Go-Go, and the Go-Go kills the Infant by denying it resources. I call it colonialism because the higher unit imposes its goals, which reflect *its* lifecycle location, on the unit it dominates. It ignores the goals that are appropriate for the younger unit according to *its* stage on the lifecycle.

What happens is very interesting. The entire organization goes under. Every component that enables rejuvenation and growth is available, but the organization's structure causes its various units to impose nonfunctional demands on one another. Each unit suffers. The goals that the parent imposes are dysfunctional for the child's stage in the lifecycle. The demands are functional only in terms of the parent's needs, and it uses its power to impose its desires.

Summary

To summarize this and the last chapter, four factors have impact on **E**: the mental age of those in control of the organization, the functionality of the leadership style, the perceived relative market share, and the functionality of the organizational structure.

To diagnose an organization, we observe its behavior. That should indicate its location on the lifecycle. Then we analyze its managerial roles: Is **E** personalized in the leader, or is it systematically provided? If it is personalized, the organization is pre-Adolescent. If it is systematized, it is post-Adolescent.

Is **E**, as measured by the rate of change and the need for proactive response to the environment, sufficient? If the organization is aging, you need to check to see which of the four factors is contributing to **E**'s demise. That should confirm your hypothesis about the organization's location on the lifecycle and why it is there.

Where are we now?

I have stated that one's age is determined by the difference between expected and desired. Remember? As long as you wish for more and/or better than what you have, you are motivated to change. That makes you young. The day you wish for nothing more, you have aged.

But that does not describe old people. They want more, and they are old. They want more health, more youth that they have lost. Now what? Well, it depends on whether what they want is controllable. Is it wishful thinking, or do they have a potential plan of action? That brings us to our discussion of controllability and its impact on aging.

CAPI in the Lifecycle

There are internal and external forces that explain why CAPI behaves the way it does at the different stages of the lifecycle.

CAPI can break down for internal reasons. In family businesses, CAPI can break down because of deteriorating relations among family members or because other interests have started to diverge.

We have already said that prior to Adolescence, CAPI is with the founder, who, more often than not, is a dictator. Why then, if the founder has complete control, is organizational predictability low? It should be high. The reason for that unpredictability is that prior to Adolescence, CAPI is personalized. It is vested in the founder, who is a big **E**. Such founders provide continuous change, unopposed. It is predictable that their organization will behave unpredictably.

Since founders call all the shots and control their companies, they are arrogant, dictatorial, and authoritative. They make decisions in a nonparticipative way: intuitively. Founders don't articulate their strategies, and people seldom understand their decisions. Consequently, despite founders' complete control, their organizations are out of control.

The lack of organizational control is attributable to a lack of **A**—systems, rules, and policies. **A** imparts a backbone of predictabil-

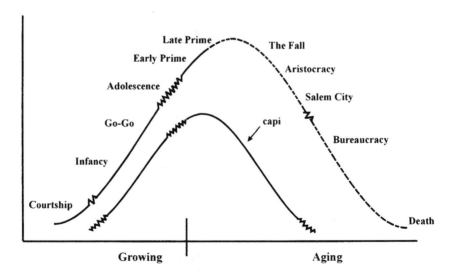

Figure 15-6: CAPI over the Lifecycle

ity to companies, controlling founders, as well. The backbone is developed during Adolescence, and organizations move to Prime where their behavior is flexible and predictable.

From Adolescence onward, control is systemic rather than personal. Incrementally, starting in Prime, the system grows stronger than the individuals who constitute it. For that reason, structure can cause the loss of **E**. That explains the increase in organizational predictability and the loss of flexibility.

When CAPI breaks down, and interest groups split in several directions, the organization is predictably stale. No one group alone can direct organizational change, and, since each group has different interests, it is difficult to coalesce and affect change. Eventually, when the form is barren, yielding no desired function, a breakdown will occur. The system will die, and a new one will emerge from the ashes.

What are the internal factors that can cause a company's CAPI to break down? Consider how personal self-interests and organizational controls interact.

In healthy, growing companies, founders control their organizations. They usually have CAPI. In Infancy, their focus is on survival. In Go-Go, the goal of those in control is to have fun: Go-Go leaders want their own personal sandboxes. All their other interests—from family needs to the demands of as-yet nonunionized labor—get only offhand attention, at best. Those interests don't yet have a chance to express themselves because the founders at that stage still have CAPI.

In the founder's trap, the self-interest of founders dominates at the expense of organizational interests. Founders' compulsion to be in control—to satisfy their own egos—prohibits their companies from developing self-control. No one else can play in a founder's sandbox. CAPI is unified and under control but because it is personalized and monopolized, it is dysfunctional to the development of the organization. Such founders are analogous to parents who refuse to allow their adolescent children freedom to mature; they want them under control, immature. This can happen in organizations comprising adult and otherwise mature people whose managerial behavior is nevertheless immature. Even the middle-aged vice presidents and members of the executive committees of such organizations exhibit immature, adolescent behavior. They are often laughing, giggling, fighting, and complaining about one another. They go to "Papa" for judgments and decisions. They refuse to accept responsibility for anything they complain about. They expect Papa to sympathize with them and solve their problems. Their biggest complaint, frequently tinged with hostility, is about Papa himself. Papa is the person who made the company grow during Go-Go. There is a love–hate relationship flourishing between Papa and the subordinates. The subordinates want Papa out, but, at the same time, they know they can't manage without him. Some organizations get stuck at this point. There is little, if any, change coming from internal sources until the founder either passes away or sells the company.

The situation of companies caught in the family trap is even more serious. The split in interests can take many forms.

Sibling rivalry is one reason companies lose CAPI in the family trap. If the reins of management are passed to an older daughter, the younger son, who might be more aggressive than his older sibling, resists his sister's control. I have observed that, depending on birth order and the style of the parents, children's style is predictable. By and large, firstborn children are not **E**s if, in the "traditional" family with the mother not working, the father was an **E**. The father burns the **E** behavior out of the child. Most firstborn children of **E**s have **A** tendencies. The second child is most likely an **I**. The third child can afford to stick out and be an **E**. Obviously, these patterns are not cast in concrete, and a lot depends on whether the family is traditional or modern.

Children who are not firstborns may object to a hierarchy of leadership determined by birth sequence. "This is not a royal succession," they claim. "Why does he or she get to be the leader?"

Family pride can easily dominate rational managerial thinking, and that can be another source of breakdown in CAPI. To maintain control, members of the family may be prohibited from selling stock. Voting stock, for instance, might be in a trust over which the patriarch or matriarch has complete control. The children clip coupons, but they have no way to affect what is going on. Eventually and inevitably, however, children grow up and patriarchs die. That's when the untrained children start fighting with the professional managers about money. There is no Papa to keep the children under control, and chaos overtakes the organizations. Management can't act professionally under those conditions. Some quit, and the family squabbles over who will assume leadership. Ego trips and personal interests dominate, overshadowing organizational needs.

For the most part, this analysis applies to companies in the western world. I have observed that birthrights are more acceptable in the eastern cultures, and, in terms of CAPI, succession there is more stable.

During Adolescence, interests diverge. **A** is risk-averse; **E** wants growth. If **A** wins, risk-averse interests dominate, and the organization drifts into premature aging. If **E** dominates, the organization returns to the Go-Go stage. If **A** and **E** move together, the organization progresses to Prime.

In Prime, interests coalesce. Management deals with a coalition of interests: stockholders' concerns about returns on their investments, management's own interests in growth, and labor's interests in security. The company is not under the control of an individual. Its plan—its strategy—unites and reflects the interests of each of the different groups.

After Prime, interests again begin to diverge. The stockholders' separation from management, when it occurred in Adolescence, was desirable. It produced Prime. But such separation has increasingly negative implications as time passes. Management becomes more self-interested than owner-interested, and its self-interest has negative impact not only on the stockholders but, over time, it has its effect on labor as well. That is not true for young companies in the Silicon Valley in which stock options make all employees stockholders, and the interest in stockholders' value is high. So how does CAPI break down after Prime? It comes with the silo syndrome. Each division or department has its goals and gets rewarded by its performance, but overall responsibility for tying everything together rests with the CEOs. They can't do it. They can't be stronger than the whole organization. They can't alone hold together the parts that are falling apart. The emperor is nude, even if he is leading by walking around.

In Aristocracy, the organization can afford the split in interests because each of those interests is milking the company. Since the company is fat, there is plenty of milk. But peaceful coexistence is over as soon as there is no more fat. Then, instead of carving up the organization, people start carving each other.

The stockholders are the first to lose. They see their investment beginning to dwindle. Next, the company starts to fire people, and labor loses. The managers are usually the last to lose, but eventually top management gets ejected too, flying away with golden parachutes.

To verify an organization's location on the lifecycle, ask who has control; not ownership, but behavioral and managerial control. Is the organization under the behavioral control of an individual or a system? If an individual is running the whole show, the organization has not yet reached Adolescence. If the organization has a system of governance that exercises control, the organization has progressed past Adolescence, and if there is a commonality of interests among the groups comprising CAPI, the organization is in Prime. If there is no commonality of the interests comprising CAPI, the organization has moved beyond Prime. Has the chronic infighting started? If not, the organization is in the Fall or Aristocracy. If there is chronic infighting, the organization has reached Salem City.

The breakdown of control can also be attributed to external causes. Such forces might be political, as when government gets involved and makes new rules or guidelines that affect control of the organization. Governments of many countries, for example, have interfered with organizations to the extent of transferring power to the workers. For political reasons, governments bring workers into decision-making positions. Management finds itself forced to negotiate with subordinates about subjects that in the past had been its exclusive prerogative. Decision-making gets stymied, and if this is part of a total anti-entrepreneurial campaign, management leaves the country, sending capital out first. Perhaps the government has legislated what and how things must be done, changing the rules of the game. In Scandinavia and Germany, workers' representatives must serve on corporate boards of directors. That requirement can lead organizations over the Adolescent hump into Prime, but if management cannot handle the diversity of interests, the company will proceed into Aristocracy.

Japan reached Prime quickly, because behaviorally, rather than legally, management tried to optimize the interests of labor, ownership, and management. Japan has a culture of mutual trust and respect and minimum internal marketing, all of which enabled Japan to reach Prime quickly. And Japan dominated the economic scene for a while. Eventually, it lost its leadership position and started aging because of the growth of **A**, which, together with the enormous culturally based **I**, caused bureaucratization. Japan's **E** is weak. Its educational system is geared to memorize, to know, not to learn and create. It will have to struggle to get out of its slump, change its educational system, or it will have to find strategic partners who can give it what it lacks in **PAEI** roles. Organizations in other Asian nations—Malaysia, Hong Kong, and Singapore, for example—are still battling their ways through Adolescence, frequently falling into the family trap. In those countries, the hierarchy of birth is not an anathema, and the family trap is not nearly so dangerous as it is in the West. CAPI, therefore, is not yet broken. In western cultures, family feuds are more common. As people of Asian countries become westernized, unless they develop formal systems to maintain **I**, they will also suffer the managerial diseases—CAPI breakdown—of the West.

We have completed our discussion of *why* things happen, the analytical part of the book. Now we will address the question of what to do. As I indicated in the introduction to this edition, I have kept this part of the book short because since the first edition of this book, I wrote *Pursuit of Prime*. That book deals exclusively with prescriptions. Readers who are interested in clinical training may address their inquiries to the Graduate School of the Adizes Institute.

Notes

1. See I. Adizes, *Corporate Lifecycles,* lst ed. (Englewood Cliffs, NJ: Prentice Hall, 1988), Chapter 11, for the theory of alignment. Because of its complexity, this chapter from the first edition has been omitted in the second edition.

2. See A.D. Chandler's well-known and influential *Strategy and Structure: Chapters in the History of Industrial Enterprise* (Cambridge: MIT Press, 1962).

3. Self-organizing systems contain component parts that are structurally coupled—they are fit together in a structure that determines what resources are exchanged with the environment. See F. Varela, *Principles of Biological Autonomy* (New York: Holland Press, 1979). Theories that address self-organization also suggest that strategy follows structure.

4. See I. Adizes, *The Pursuit of Prime* (Santa Monica: Knowledge Exchange, 1996), Chapter 2, for a discussion of "Each company should be structured to encourage and nourish the role it needs most, depending on its location on the lifecycle."

PART THREE

Raising Healthy Organizations

CHAPTER SIXTEEN

Organizational Therapy

Based on my experience as an organizational consultant and therapist, I have constructed a theory that provides a framework for
predicting change in organizational cultures: I have succeeded in
understanding why change occurs; I have developed a prescriptive
theory for managing organizational transitions on the lifecycle; and I
have tested that prescriptive theory with and through my associates.

That theory and practice provides organizations with several
distinct advantages. It enables them to discriminate between the
normal problems they can handle internally and the abnormal problems that require outside intervention. Furthermore, because the
stages of the organizational lifecycle are predictable and repetitive,
knowing their location in the lifecycle permits organizations to take
preventive measures to mitigate anticipated problems or to avoid
them altogether.

The Nature of Life
and Problems

Living means continuously solving problems. The fuller one's life,
the more complex the problems one must resolve. That is true also

for organizations. Successful management is continuously solving problems. By now you understand that an organization is without problems only when nothing is changing—when it is dead. To solve problems and have no new, increasingly complex problems emerge is equivalent to dying.

Managers who understand this theory of corporate lifecycles feel liberated by the realization that having problems is not unusual. Having problems is normal. Problems come with the territory called living and—in organizational situations—managing. What causes a person to feel inadequate is the belief that only he or she has problems. That can have a debilitating effect. Knowing which of your problems are normal and shared by others in comparable situations helps you understand that some of your problems are caused not by you but by your situation.

One day, an executive who had been attending my lectures for some time came to me for advice. He wanted to talk about his many seemingly overwhelming problems. He offered to drive me to my next appointment and, as we drove along, he described his crises. I noted that they were not all that severe. I even volunteered to describe my own managerial problems to give him a point of reference. He was surprised.

"You, of all people, have problems? You look like you have it all together."

It was my turn to be surprised. Why would he think that I had no problems? I realized that he had placed me on a no-problems pedestal just as I had done with others. But we all have problems. The people who make everything look easy are like ducks: They look calm on the surface, but underneath they are paddling frantically.

But there are problems, and there are *problems*. Not all problems are normal; and, since we must have problems, what are the right problems to have? Let me answer with an example. Suppose I describe a person with the following characteristics. He cries a lot, wakes up in the middle of the night, and drinks milk every few hours. Is this behavior a normal problem? Most people would say, yes, because they assume I am describing a newborn baby. What if I told you that I have been describing a 45-year-old CEO? What do you say? Normal?

Normal vs. Abnormal Problems

Plus ça change, plus c'est la même chose.

The more things change,
the more they remain the same.

ALPHONSE KARR, *LES GUÊPES*

The above quotation I believe applies to abnormal problems. They are chronic. You try to solve them, and you believe you did, but they reappear in a new vest. You throw them out the window, and, in the darkest hours of the night, they crawl back into your mind.

Normal problems are the lessons of life. Everyone has to learn, and we all learn by solving problems. We continue to have problems because none of us has learned everything there is to know. Since we will never know all there is to know, we should be prepared for endless normal problems. Get ready: You will have problems for the rest of your life.

Where do problems come from? What is it that organizations do not know?

As I have explained in earlier chapters, for an organization to be effective and efficient in the short and long run, it must perform four managerial roles: **PAEI**. No organization is born in Prime, so every organization needs to develop those roles. Every organization experiences problems because at any point in time at least one of the roles is not yet developed. Even in Prime, where all roles should be fully developed, organizations contend with the problem of staying in Prime, seeing to it that none of the roles decays.

Most organizations instinctively develop one managerial role at a time, following the typical path rather than working to enhance all necessary managerial roles simultaneously, in the appropriately balanced fashion I describe as the optimal path (see Figure 16-1). In developing one role—one capability—at a time, there is always the danger that if the organization runs into a difficulty, it will experience abnormal and, perhaps eventually, pathological problems.

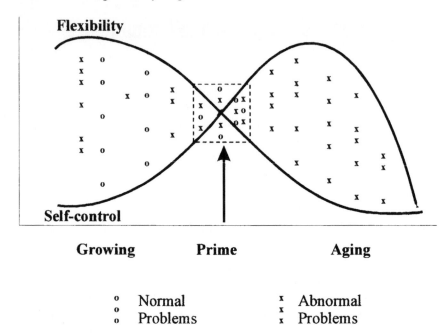

Flexibility

Self-control

| Growing | Prime | Aging |

○
○ Normal
○ Problems

x
x Abnormal
x Problems

Figure 16-1: Normal vs. Abnormal Problems

The Adizes methodology is diagnostic, discriminating among the different types of problems. As an intervention methodology, it is both curative and preventive. Its purpose is to overcome normal and abnormal problems of growing and aging, to bring an organization to Prime, and to develop an organization's internal abilities to remain there.

The Nature of Change

Change is inevitable and eternal. As I have stated already, change causes external and internal disintegration. If an organization does not adapt to external changes, it is out of step with its market and no longer satisfies the need for which it existed. In the competitive environment of the business world, its customers disenfranchise such an organization. They stop patronizing the establishment. Sales volume of product units flatten, then fall. The organization is externally disintegrated: Its capabilities don't match the needs of the marketplace.

Change also causes internal disintegration. The organization may try to adapt reactively or proactively to the changes in its external environment, but it runs into problems because all organizations, like all systems, comprise subsystems, and those subsystems do not change synchronically.[1] Some subsystems change faster than others, and that lack of coordination causes the organization to break apart, burst at the seams, come unglued. Even if an organization is not struggling to match changes in the external environment, it can still disintegrate internally. Internal changes occur independently of the external environment: People change as their individual needs change. Consequently, disintegration is inevitable, whether or not you play an active role in its cause.

Things fall apart. And unless you do something, chaos ensues. But human nature cannot accept disintegration as a permanent phenomenon. Humans strive to reintegrate. If they fail, they become psychologically, pathologically disintegrated.

Recently, I was introduced to the work of the therapists Carlos Sluzki and Sara Cobb,[2] and I came to realize that disintegration is not a steady state.[3] Humans cannot endure disintegration on an ongoing basis.[4] They need to solve, explain, and find meaning in their experience. Individually, we create scenarios to explain our problems: Our parents messed us up; our teachers or bosses are the source of all our problems; and so forth. To bring problems to closure, we need to explain them. When all fails we turn to God, assigning Him or Her all the credit or the blame. You've heard the explanations: "The devil made me do it," "It is God's will." People search for integration.[5] We need *somehow* to explain our problems and in so doing integrate what has fallen apart.

The way we "integrate" can have desired or undesired repercussions. It is that "somehow" that can generate deeper problems. In order to give meaning to their problems, organizations, societies, and people create story lines—narrative explanations that serve as *perceived* solutions. Many people assume that simply by knowing their problems, they have found the solutions. Yet we now know that the "solutions" we find often reproduce the problems we are trying to solve.[6] Religion is an integrating force, which in one form or another, grows in appeal as change and disintegration accelerate. Not all religious solutions have a unifying and healing effect. Some religions, for example, embrace racist or fascist ideologies that disintegrate people as well as societies. They are dysfunctional and destructive to humanity as a whole.[7] As change accelerates, we face more, not fewer, religious wars of global dimensions.

To repeat, not all narratives, although they integrate, are functional.[8] The story line can be functional or dysfunctional depending on what it does to the organization and what we do with it. Often, such explanations are what stand in the way of organizations' ability to address the challenges they face. Some stories stymie the capability of the person, organization, or society to keep changing and adapting.[9] They integrate, but they also freeze the status quo.[10] They are like broken arms that have been set badly. They heal, but they cannot move well or easily. A surgeon might have to break a badly set arm to reset it so that it can heal properly. As leaders of organizations or organizational therapists (historically and still identified as consultants), our task is to analyze the functionality of the existing integration. If it is dysfunctional, it is our role to dismantle it and work with the organization to develop a new functional narrative, a new framework that not only integrates but also allows future adaptations as the situation changes.[11] The organization should have inherent capabilities to reintegrate itself by itself. Or as Mary Kay, the famous and successful founder of a marketing network, expressed it best, "If you want to see the secret of my success, let me show you the scars on my knees."

Success is not the measure of how rarely you fall,
but how many times you get up.

The Role of a Therapist

If the cause for all problems is disintegration, the antidote for all problems is, by definition, integration.[12] The job of your medical doctor or family therapist is to integrate or heal, to make the system a healthy whole, capable of continuously recreating itself as one.[13] (Note that the words *whole* and *heal* are both derivatives of the Indo-European root, *kailo,* meaning whole, uninjured.)

Management, leaders of organizations, and professional consultants should be organizational therapists who cause change in the first place and then heal by reuniting the pieces that fell apart due to the change. Capable management should handle normal problems while organizational therapists should be called in to deal with the abnormal problems.

Management and management consultants should be responsible for leading the necessary and desired change, diagnosing subsequent organizational disintegration, and providing a process to reunite the parts on a new plateau. Each organizational leader is a therapist of sorts: introducing change, shattering organizationally dysfunctional old paradigms of integration, and reintegrating to a new functional whole. Of course, the newly integrated whole is subject to the same process of change, disintegration, and reintegration. When an organization's leader cannot direct this process because it is too complicated or the leader has inadequate experience, an external intervention is called for.

Successful management or therapy (so-called consulting) does not just eliminate problems. It should focus energy on removing problems the organization is experiencing in the current stage of its lifecycle, establishing foundations, and preparing the organization to deal with the problems of the next stage. An organization in Prime is not exempt from this requirement. Like an Olympic gold-medal winner, the cherished medal is not a signal to stop. To stay in Prime, an organization needs to continue training and competing. An organization in Prime has to predict the avoidable causes of its impending aging. An organization can remain in Prime so long as it continuously rejuvenates itself.

Types of Integration

There are two overlapping types of integration: external and internal cohesion.

External cohesion is the degree to which an organization is integrated with its external environment. It is a function of how well the organization integrated its capabilities with the opportunities in the marketplace. For example, product diversification should reflect market segmentation.

If, to create and maintain external cohesion, an organization dedicates functional energy to satisfying its clients' needs, I call its effort "external marketing."

Internal cohesion is a reflection of the degree of cooperation within an organization, and the energy an organization expends to achieve internal cooperation is internal integration. That is a function of mutual trust and respect within the organization's culture. Some organizations have no internal integration, no culture of cooperation, and no mutual trust and respect. In order to bring about predictable results, members of such organizations have to devote time and energy to "selling" their ideas to each other. I call such corporate politicking "internal marketing." That waste of energy is a negative phenomenon.

Dedicating energy to external marketing is a positive move. It integrates an organization with its changing environment. Internal marketing, on the other hand, is a sign of trouble. It is a waste. It usurps energy that could be devoted to external marketing. An organization characterized by mutual trust and respect has minimal, if any, internal marketing.

When there is internal cohesion—mutual trust and respect, which must be made a characteristic of the culture and nurtured continuously—the organization enjoys internal peace, and it can dedicate its limited and fixed energy to external integration.[14]

When an organization achieves and maintains both external and internal cohesion, it enjoys sustainable, desirable, and predictable results.

Physics teaches us that, at any point in time, stable systems have fixed energy. For instance, even the most energetic and productive person has no more than 24 hours in his or her day. Organizations and countries, like people, have fixed energy at a point in time.

Over the years, I have observed that organizations—and, may I suggest, all systems—allocate this fixed energy in predictable ways: Internal marketing invariably takes precedence over external marketing; the energy available and applied to external marketing is the surplus, if any, after all the needs of internal marketing have been satisfied.

Here is an example I use in my lectures:

I ask the audience, "How many of you would like to travel with me to Los Angeles at the end of my lecture? I'll show you how, in one week, you can make $100 million tax-free. It's legal. You don't need to put up any cash. And it's completely risk free. This is a serious offer," I say. Needless to say, all hands rise.

"You have raised your hand," I say, "because you have assumed something. You have assumed you are healthy. I wonder whether you would have raised your hand if during the last break someone had given you a note, saying, 'Your doctor called. You have cancer, and you must report to the hospital tomorrow to start chemotherapy or have surgery.' In that situation, you would not raise your hand. You would have responded to my offer, saying, 'I wish you had made me that offer last month.'"

Then I continue. "How many of you have been unable to make a decision or have made a very bad decision because you were suffering from a terrible cold or a terrible headache?" Again, lots of hands.

"What if you want to visit your friend who has been hospitalized after being in a car accident? Doesn't the doctor limit your visit to just a few minutes? Why, do you suppose? A sick person needs to dedicate all his energy to taking care of his body. Only then can he dedicate his remaining energy to you."

Do you see a common thread here? All systems devote the limited and fixed energy they have to "internal marketing," and only the surplus goes to "external marketing."

How much energy internal marketing needs depends on how much mutual trust and respect the system has internally.[15] Think about a highly educated young person with a Harvard Business School doctorate and $100 million dollars inherited from his parents. Will he succeed in life? It seems he has every opportunity and all the right connections. Right? What would you say if I tell you that this person has no self-respect or self-trust. Most of his limited energy dissipates between his ears. He wonders what to do. Do people really approve of him? He cannot cope with the external environment until he calms his mind first. Often such peace is won through therapy.

The same model helps us understand organizational problems and solutions. Many aging organizations have invited me to help them design strategies to increase their competitiveness. They have money, lots of it. They have the technology, most of it. They want me to help them develop their marketing orientation. Invariably, I find that the problem is not that they don't know the principles of marketing or strategic planning. They do. They can write the book on marketing and strategic planning. Their problem is that they can't address the problems of the fast-changing external environment because the members of the organization are preoccupied with internal marketing: Sales fighting Production, Engineering fighting Marketing, and Finance and Legal fighting everyone. That preoccupation with the internal environment robs everyone's energy.[16] When a customer makes a request from someone in such a company, the hapless client will hear, perhaps not in so many words, "Come back tomorrow, we're exhausted today."

It should be obvious that if an organization's energy is devoted to internal marketing, it must be at the expense of external marketing. That means the organization will be both ineffective and inefficient. Prolonged preoccupation with internal marketing can become an abnormality and, eventually, a pathological problem. In that case, the organization requires new energy from an external source: an organizational therapist to change its behavior.

Organizational Integration

The role of an organizational therapist, like all therapists, is to provide integration. Those who focus on internal integration carry such titles as organizational development facilitators, process consultants, and so forth. Those who focus on external integration are called strategic planners and management consultants. The Adizes intervention process differs from both of those approaches: It provides external *and* internal integration as a comprehensively systematic program of change. [17]

Although they are necessary conditions for organizational health, neither internal integration nor external integration per se is sufficient. If an organization works only on internal integration, the failure to achieve prompt results in external integration will cause the system to mistrust itself. People sense that they have been engaged in a "waste of time," and "all we did is feel good." Engaging exclusively in external integration, however, usually means a nicely bound, professionally presented report that almost never sees implementation. Internal marketing devours the energy necessary to support implementation. Synchronizing those two processes of integration is, in itself, a challenge the Adizes program has solved.

The Adizes Methodology

The Adizes program cues the "change leaders" so they know when to focus efforts on external integration, when to focus on internal integration, and when to work on both fronts simultaneously. The tools of the systematic program support internal, external, and simultaneous integration processes.[18] Its systemic therapeutic intervention analyzes organizations to determine, based on their location on the lifecycle, what is normal and what is not. The methodology provides lifecycle-contingent therapy that the organization itself applies. Each organization's structure, leadership style, reward system, planning process, goals, and so forth can all be desirable or destructive depending on where the organization is in the lifecycle.[19]

For years, I have struggled to find a name for the process and program I have developed. It is not consulting: Consulting, by and large, still adheres to the medical analogy, giving prescriptions. Nor is it process consultation. Process consultants focus on the process and don't necessarily dedicate attention to structure and the strategies necessary for external cohesion. And it's not a training program. Most training programs provide solutions and let the clients identify the problems.

I have named my process, *symbergetic™ methodology*. It is a *symb*iotic process that enhances the consciousness of interdependencies and the benefits derived from those interdependencies; and it is a syn*ergetic* process in which integrated and correctly interdependent diversity is rich with growth potential. I have long believed that the word "consultant" doesn't represent what we do, and the title "organizational therapist" is frightening: It implies a sick organization. We did try calling our practitioners "organizational coaches," but quite a few of our client CEOs objected, saying it connotes someone who tells them what to do. The title "integrator" is too passive because it conveys mediation, facilitation, process consultation, and we do much more than that. So, after years of wandering through the desert, I am ready to introduce *symbergy™*, and to call a practitioner of the symbergetic™ methodology an organizational *symbergist™*.

You may wonder why I have gone to the trouble of trademarking the name I have chosen to represent my concept. All too many times, I see methodologies destroyed as a result of incompetent applications. Participative management, quality of working life, quality circles, total quality management, and reengineering are a few of the more recent casualties of incompetence. People read a book, and, before you know it, they are selling their capability to apply the new theory. To protect this methodology from such premature applications, I have trademarked its name, and established a graduate school licensed by the state of California to grant degrees and provide licensing and certification training.

Successful Integration

Organizational success is a function of the disparity between external and internal marketing. The less internal marketing, the more energy is free for the external marketing that enhances the organization's integration with its external environment. Companies that are internally and externally integrated are in Prime. Organizational symbergists™ help organizations deal with the abnormal problems management can't handle alone, providing tools for auto-integration. Integration is continuously threatened by change: both changes in the external environment within which the organization operates and internal changes caused by the organization's progress or lack of progress in its lifecycle.

How to do that?[20] The next chapter introduces this subject.

Notes

1. F. Varela has argued in *Principles of Biological Autonomy* (1979) that subsystems within a system are not equivalent in the autopoisistic process; this would suggest that subsystems have varying levels of participation in the system, and that there are varying levels of permeability across subsystems.

2. C. Sluzki and S. Cobb argue in *Better-formed Stories: Managing Change Processes* (forthcoming) that problematic stories that foster disintegration of relationships function to spiral the system to increasing levels of conflict; conversely, there are stories that progressively promote the integration of the system, fostering trust.

3. See C. Sluzki, "Transformations: A Blueprint for Narrating Changes in Therapy," *Family Process* 3, 3 (1991): 217–230. He makes the point that problems escalate over time, as a function of the way they are storied.

4. See V. Frankl, *Man's Search for Meaning,* The Touchstone Edition (New York: Harper Colophon, 1984), for a powerful account of the role of meaning-making in human lives.

5. See S. Cobb, "Empowerment and Mediation: A Narrative Perspective," *The Negotiation Journal,* 9, 3: 245–261, which describes the way that narratives not only function to create coherence, but they also ward off alternative stories as a way of protecting the integration they create.

6. See D. Campbell, T. Coldicutt, and K. Kinsella, *Systemic Work with Organizations: A New Model for Managers and Change Agents,* Systemic Thinking and Practice Series (New York: Brunner/Mazel, 1995), for an excellent discussion of the way that solutions often reinforce the problem they are designed to solve.

7. Consider C. Briggs's *Disorderly Discourse: Narrative, Conflict and Inequality* (Oxford: Oxford University Press, 1996). He makes the point that there are narratives that are extremely destructive to social relationships and institutions.

8. See B. Czarniawska-Joerges, "Narrating the Organization: Dramas of Institutional Identity," *Qualitative Research Methods* 43 (New York: Sage Press, 1997), for a discussion of the role of narrative in adaptive processes.

9. See C. Sluzki and S. Cobb, *Better-formed Stories: Managing Change Processes* (forthcoming).

10. See A. Kleinman, *The Illness Narratives: Suffering, Healing and the Human Condition* (New York: Basic Books, 1988), for an excellent description of the role of illness narratives in disease processes; basically, he makes the point that health is related to the kinds of narratives that are told, just as the course of disease is a function of how illness is storied.

11. See D. Barry, "Telling Changes: From Narrative Therapy to Organizational Change and Development," *Journal of Organizational Change* 10, 1 (1997): 30–46, for an explanation of the utility of the narrative as a model for fostering evolutionary processes in organizations.

12. See F. Varela, E. Thompson, and E. Rosch, *The Embodied Mind: Cognitive Science and Human Experience* (1993).

13. J. Efran, M. Lukens, and R. Lukens, in *Language, Structure and Change: Frameworks of Meaning in Psychotherapy* (New York: W.W. Norton, 1990), note that the role of the therapist is to promote not only the resolution of existing problems, but to foster the learning that will allow the systems to maintain its well-being as new problems emerge.

14. See I. Adizes, *Mastering Change* (1992).

15. For a more in-depth elaboration of this subject, see I. Adizes, *Mastering Change* (1992).

16. See Mary Parker Follett's writings on the role of relationships in organizational processes, particularly M. P. Follett, *Dynamic Administration: The Collected Papers of Mary Parker Follett* (New York: Harper and Brothers, 1942). She was writing on this topic in the midst of the movement toward scientific management, which makes her "vision" of organizational processes even more impressive.

17. Rolfing, or so-called structural integration, is analogous to the Adizes process. Assuming there is an optimal body posture, Rolfing analyzes each patient's posture, looking to identify departures from the ideal. Through several sessions of deep muscle therapeutic massages, a Rolfer aligns a patient's body to what it should be. The Rolf therapy is founded on the theory that our physiological and psychological experiences manifest themselves in our body, causing departures from the optimal. Correct body realignment should, Rolfers maintain, change behavior. I believe that theory has merit. If I have a pain in my back, I am not likely to play basketball. Once that pain is gone, however, I am ready for even more than basketball. The ancient Greeks revered a healthy spirit in a healthy body. That paragon is congruent with my own professional bias. If my body is out of shape and in pain, I cannot think clearly. When you fix your body, your energy will flow better and you will make better use of your intelligence. For details, see I. Rolf, *Ida Rolf Talks About Rolfing and Physical Reality* (New York: Harper Colophon Books, 1978); and *Rolfing: The Integration of Human Structures* (New York: Harper & Row, 1977), among several works.

18. See I. Adizes, *How to Solve the Mismanagement Crisis* (1982), for how to compose complementary teams.

19. See I. Adizes, *The Pursuit of Prime* (1996).

20. The chapter on the Adizes Program of 11 phases that was part of the first edition has been taken out in this edition. The material is far more complex than one chapter of 15 pages or so can cover. See I. Adizes, *Corporate Lifecycles* (San Francisco: Barrett-Koehler, 1988): 303–325.

CHAPTER SEVENTEEN

Treating Organizations on the Typical Path: A Contingency Approach

Treating Infancy

What does happen and what should happen during Infancy? Organizations focus their energies on results, and creativity takes a back seat. During that period, founders are susceptible to losing their excitement and enthusiasm for their enterprises. Aside from the pride of ownership, they feel that they are gaining little for all their work. At best, during Infancy, they feel they are in control.

For Infant organizations, I strongly recommend internal, rather than external, boards of directors. Founders of Infant companies need plenty of emotional support. While it's true that Infant organizations most definitely need legal and financial advice, they can easily buy that from the outside. What is crucial, however, and not for sale, is emotional support. Lawyers and accountants who serve on boards of directors are likely to demand far too much reality. And they will test and enforce it with their votes, flattening founders' enthusiasm so efficiently, that they cause the Infant to abort innovative projects. They make founders feel they have lost control. Lawyers and accountants should participate only as paid advisors.

Infant organizations need constant and close supervision. They need attention, nurturing, support, and protection from exposure. Because Infant organizations lack systems, it's easy for them to get into trouble. Then, all their needs must be met almost simultaneously.

Organizational symbergists™ must perform at least two functions for Infant organizations. First, they must give them a sense of reality; and second, they must help the organizations secure the resources they need to make that reality happen. It is the job of such therapists to make reality-oriented cash-flow projections. Additionally, they ought to protect founders from hiring mediocre people and keep them from sharing stock prematurely. Infant organizations need to be aware of how they can grow and how to develop realistic expectations. They are inexperienced, and they often make unrealistic commitments. Because their resources are slim, they are often overworked. They lose the grand view, and their expectations of the possible are circumscribed by the limited world to which they are exposed. Because Infant organizations so often overcommit to the insignificant and the unfruitful, they squander their resources on the trivial. And the resources of Infant organizations are slim. They live a hand-to-mouth existence. Frequently, they run out of working capital. Organizational therapists need to hold their hands and help them overcome each crisis. At the same time, and equally important, symbergists™ should help them see what they should *not* do.

Consultants often counsel Infant organizations to analyze the environment, plan future cash-flow needs, and forecast sales, production, and staffing needs. While it is indispensable to do those things, those young enterprises shouldn't get too rigid about such assignments, though. Attempts to transform an Infant organization into a highly structured and predictable organization are usually harmful. The executives of most Infant organizations must do all the work themselves. Why spend time on standard operating procedures that would reduce organizational flexibility and productivity and endanger the organization's ability to survive in a highly competitive environment?

Some Infant organizations spend inordinate amounts of time trying to develop systems or buying computer systems that far exceed their needs. Others set up expensive and lavish headquarters long before they can afford such luxury. I know of a founder who, in his company's earliest days, bought fancy systems, leased beautiful office space in a prime location, and established such rigid organizational routines, that there was no room left for improvisation. The organization couldn't support the expense, and it lost its original strengths, which included flexibility and adaptability.

Organizational symbergists™ should give Infant organizations assignments designed to lead them to predict, analyze, and schedule. Infants aren't big enough to afford teamwork; therefore, individuals take responsibility for those assignments. The deadlines need to be flexible because everyone in these organizations is overworked, and as long as the companies are on the right track, there is no real need to exert time pressure.

Some Infant organizations fail to develop their capacity for **E** because their founders burn out. In such cases, the organizations find themselves in the Lone Ranger's trap, which can become a graveyard. The companies last only until their owners die or grow under new management.

For a company to advance to Go-Go, the leadership style should be **PaEi**, and the role of the symbergist™ is to facilitate style or, if not possible, leadership change.

Owners of Infant companies should be careful not to give away ownership and lose control. They should consider interlocking companies or using legal structures that allow them to control the top level of a hierarchy. Many people can join a hierarchy, becoming owners at different levels, but the owner need not lose control.

Because Infant organizations are short of cash, I suggest they prepare rolling sixteen-week cash-flow projections, and they should monitor them weekly. Profit-and-loss statements based on accrual do not provide adequate control because they ignore loss of liquidity to accounts receivable and inventory. It's crucial, therefore, for Infant organizations to keep close watch on inventory turnover and receivables. Again, it is the role of the leader of change, whether that is the CEO or the symbergist™, to see to it that these threshold **A** systems get implemented for healthy in/out growth.

Treating Go-Go

What kind of therapies is appropriate for companies in Go-Go? **E** is high. CAPI is high. The company is doing fine and the Go-Go organization feels it can tackle anything at any time. Of course that's how Go-Gos get into trouble. They make decisions and commitments they should never have made, and they get involved in activities about which they know nothing or very little.

What managers of a Go-Go organization must always keep in mind is that they are continually teetering on the brink of disaster. They should be preparing for the forthcoming move to Adolescence. They must get ready to institutionalize **E** and CAPI.

It is desirable during Go-Go to start developing teamwork. The organization must develop Integration to create an environment that will require fewer rules when they get organized later on. If they build **I**, they can reduce their need for administrative systems. The Integrative forces—the teamwork—act as a substitute for technocratic, bureaucratic, and administrative solutions; that is, they institutionalize the decision-making process in Adolescence.

The appropriate symbergetic™ intervention for Go-Go organizations is to help them realize what *not* to do. This is necessary because Go-Gos spread themselves too thin, tackling too many frontiers at once. Here's the first assignment a symbergist™ should give a Go-Go organization: Have management list all projects in the process of completion—those underway, those just being started, and those being contemplated. The next step is to have management estimate the resources and time necessary to accomplish each project. Most Go-Gos are shocked to discover that they are planning to complete a lifetime of projects in one year. The sooner the Go-Go realizes the necessity for setting priorities, the faster it will focus and become more efficient. The organization must learn, experience, and accept that resources are limited and that in a world of limited resources, the law of opportunity-costs prevails. Doing one thing means one cannot do something else; and the cost of doing one thing is the price of not doing another.

This simple law of economics, known as the law of butter or guns, was popularized by Paul Samuelson.[1] It usually comes as an unpleasant revelation to the Go-Go organization, whose members want to have both butter and guns.

After a Go-Go organization sets priorities, it needs to establish detailed objectives and guidelines. The organizational symbergist™ must do a lot of hand-holding in order to facilitate implementation of the organization's plans. The therapist must constantly watch to see how new assignments are added and make the organization realize when it violates its own priorities. Go-Gos are usually restless and jumpy.

Go-Go organizations don't like being handled, and they are always threatening to drop their therapists. Go-Go people do not appreciate having to take time away from the firing line to think things through. Clearly, these organizations need to mature. Their people are so excited with their results and their ideas that they have no patience for doomsday prophecies about the price they will pay tomorrow for today's mess.

The members of Go-Go organizations are simply too busy to spend time getting organized, and they see no *short-term* benefits to investing time in such activities. Most Go-Go organizations reward performers, are contemptuous of administrative tendencies, and show little, if any, desire to have external facilitators implement change. One simply must wait for such organizations to grow at their own pace. If, however, they fail to get themselves organized and still don't call for help from the outside, they can fall into the founder's trap.

The symbergists™ form Go-Go teams to complete their assignments, small teams of two to three people. The therapist spends lots of time assigning many small tasks in succession because people in Go-Go organizations have no patience for delayed gratification. All the assignments are short and quickly completed. If they see no immediate relevance and benefit, Go-Gos quickly lose interest and discontinue treatment.

Getting Out of the Founder's or Family Trap
—Institutionalizing E and CAPI

The difference between Go-Go and Prime is that in Go-Go, **E** and CAPI are personalized, while in Prime, they are institutionalized in the structure and the management process. In other words, in Prime they are systematized. If Go-Gos develop a culture that fosters cooperation, self-discipline, mutual trust, and respect, they can avoid the troubles of Adolescence.

Another point. Every organization has four subsystems: Client interface, **E**; transformation, **P**; human factors, **I**; and financial factors, **A**. Each subsystem has a developmental **e** and a maintenance **p** component.

The **E** function is reflected in marketing, process engineering, human resources development, and finance.

The problem with Go-Go organizations—and what can set the founder's trap—is that their leaders monopolize **E**. They monopolize

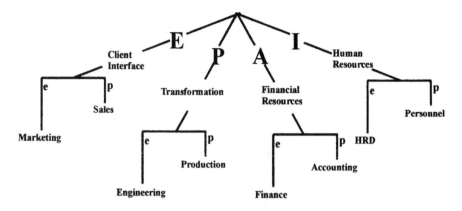

Figure 17-1: The Four Subsystems of Any Organization

all responsibility for making marketing, technology, financial, and human-resource decisions. The founders may be geniuses in one or more fields, but they are rarely brilliant in all four subsystems.

If the founders, for instance, consider themselves marketing whiz kids, they don't allow anyone else to make financial, top management, human-resource, or technological decisions or changes. All of those realms are related to **E**, which they monopolize. Although they excel only in one **E** subsystem, they won't allow anyone else to have any discretion over other **E** decisions.

In Infancy, such monopolization and unification make perfect sense. The marketing, technology, finance, and human factors are deeply interwoven. At that stage, they are nearly identical. Making a decision in one of those areas has instantaneous impact on the others. In Infancy, founders experiment, trying to identify, articulate, and formulate success. The monopolization of the four areas is normal, to be expected, and even desirable. Later, from Go-Go on, in order to institutionalize **E**, organizations need to separate those four areas and transfer them from a person into a structure—into marketing, engineering, finance, and HRD departments. That must happen even though founders resist delegation of authority for fear of losing control.

A symbergist™, as a therapist or a CEO, has to lead this transformation. It should start by identifying problems, making diagnoses, and forming a plan of action. The group agrees on the organization's location on the lifecycle and that it's time to institutionalize **E** and CAPI.

In the next therapeutic session, the group defines mission and form, agreeing on organizational priorities and what the organization will and will not do. During this process, the group clears communication, and mutual trust and respect should grow. This is the time to initiate the organization's restructuring.

First, the **P**erformance functions—sales and production—are structured to reflect geography and product lines. The **E** areas are not touched until **P** is fully stabilized. Then the four **E** functions are legitimized. The founder takes charge of all **P** and **E** departments. But, it doesn't take long for it to become clear that there is too much for one person to do. He can delegate either **P** or **E**. Most choose to delegate **P**. When a founder refuses to delegate, he must be encouraged to do so. If he still resists, the symbergist™ should not proceed. The founder may be allowed to manage **P** until he develops trust in his subordinates. When he is finally willing to delegate **P**, a chief operating officer is appointed to run the **P** functions, and the **E** functions will continue reporting to the **E** person for a while longer.

Before **E** is delegated, the organization must institutionalize its **A**dministrative function. Accounting, quality control, legal, and data processing, which serve to control **P**, should be separated from **P** and **E** as a separate division. Unification of **A** structurally is desirable in Go-Go but undesirable after Prime. It is desirable in Go-Go because it needs to counterbalance the power of **E**.

So far, the founder remains completely in charge of **E**. Later, when we work to develop an accountability control system, the

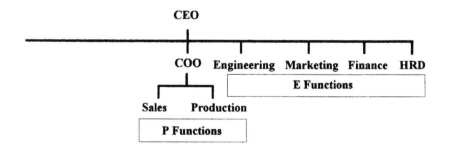

Figure 17-2: Go-Go Treatment, Bringing in the Chief Operating Officer

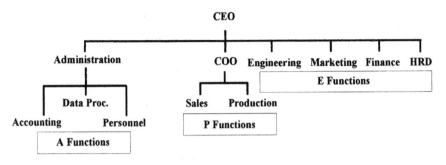

Figure 17-3: Balancing P, A, and E

founder will develop trust in **P** and **A**, and after that, we will be prepared to go to the heart of the problem: decentralization of **E**.

The first **E** department we work to establish is the one in which
the founder has the least interest. If the founder is most excited
about marketing, engineering, or product development, we focus on
finance. We then turn our attention to the next area that doesn't
interest him, and progressing through the organization, we form
departments that decentralize activities. Despite the decentralization, all departments still report to the founder. And the founder has
not lost control because the **A** function—as a process delivered by a
structure—has already been established.

The next step in this therapy is to create and institutionalize the
corporate executive committee comprising the chief operating officer, chief administrative officer, and four **E** department heads. The
president presides, and we draw up a calendar for the whole year to
ensure that meetings do take place. The symbergist™ should work
with management to establish agendas, and the group agrees to a
rule to avoid promiscuous on-the-run decision-making: No decision
is a decision until it is in writing. Minutes are taken at every meeting,
and assignments are given. For every project, the committee determines the *why, what, when, who,* and *how.* This looks mundane, but
it is important. **Es** make decisions on the fly. Often people do not
know if there is a decision or not. Maybe it was just an idea. To avoid
the confusion, it is established that decisions are in writing so all talk
is just talk. After Prime you have to reverse the rule. Too much is in
writing. They worship the written word. This rule should be abol-
ished.

The symbergist™ should teach the executive committee members the Adizes process of making decisions as a team. In this way they develop institutionalized CAPI and relatively emancipate the **E** departments from exclusive dependency on the founder. The committee learns to legitimize and functionally channel contentions and conflicts. Next, they will apply team process to develop budgets, control systems, and strategic plans, freeing the organization from exclusive dependency on the founder. Management then turns its attentions to articulating and establishing a system of incentives. By the time the structure is right and the people are working as a team with plans, controls, and incentives, both **E** and CAPI are institutionalized, the company is in Prime, and the founder is off the hook. And he hasn't lost his company.

The Problem of Premature Delegation in a Go-Go

How many times have you heard people complaining that the problem with their company's founder is that he refuses to delegate. During Go-Go, founders who don't delegate will fall into the founder's trap. The treatment for this common problem is not easily applied. For organizations in Infancy, during which founders work even harder than they do in the Go-Go stage, delegation is not only unpalatable to the founders, it is dangerous to the health of their organizations.

In Infancy, delegation is contraindicated. It is their limitless dedication to their creations that keeps founders going. At this early stage of organizational life, asking founders to delegate responsibility might threaten and alienate them from their organizations, reducing their commitment. Furthermore, consider how difficult it is to delegate nonprogrammed decisions: The decisions that will serve as precedents are only now being created without systems of controls. Delegating decision-making is equivalent to decentralizing, and in Infant organizations that means passing control from the founders to someone else. That is nearly impossible because organizations in Infancy have no managerial depth. If a consultant recommends delegating authority, it's no wonder that most founders respond with irritation, "Delegate? Fine! To whom?"

Founders should start to delegate functions during the advanced stages of Go-Go when there is too much for them to do.

They shouldn't feel that by delegating they are yielding all the fun (control). Furthermore, as Go-Gos approach Adolescence, they should be planning administrative systems and programming. Healthy Go-Gos need to make policies about what *not* to do. That is tantamount to decision programming. The more programmed the decisions, the easier it is to delegate without losing control.

So, it's important for the busy managers of small, young companies to assess the validity of recommendations to delegate. They should analyze their choices in light of their organizations' location on the lifecycle. Timing, as always, is crucial if the treatment is to succeed.

Treating Adolescence

The way to avoid the abnormal—potentially pathological—development of premature aging is to institutionalize **E**, to build it into the organizational structure as **A** grows. In that way, **E** will not disappear, and the organization will not age prematurely. If **E** remains personalized, however, the incompatibility of **E** and **A** can easily bring about premature aging. Management should spend time defining an organization chart. It should determine a corporate mission— not only what *else* it's going to do, but also what it's *not* going to do— that the organization supports. Furthermore, management needs to develop training programs, salary administration systems, and incentive systems. If this is done proactively, reorganization can avoid such future problems as haphazard salary administration, recruiting, and hiring. By consciously institutionalizing **E**, at the same time that **A** develops, a company does not have to lose **E**.

It's critical to increase **A** at just the right time. In Infancy and Go-Go, organizations become addicted to **P**. In Infancy, a worker who does not produce is fired. Companies need a functional orientation if they want to survive. Consequently, the big producers get the big promotions. In the Go-Go stage, companies focus on growth in terms of sales and market share. Again the big producers get the big emotional and financial rewards.

By the time companies reach their Adolescence, they are turning inward, needing more systems and order. It's time to change who receives recognition and appreciation. It isn't easy to switch from a sales orientation to a profit orientation. Those who are internally-oriented and those who are externally-oriented find themselves at loggerheads. It doesn't take much for people to start calling one another bureaucrats or Lone Rangers.

A company can achieve a timely move to Adolescence if management consciously determines when the organization is doing well and chooses that period to turn inward and organize. Of course, such conscious self-discipline is rare. Those who are blessed with it are the real winners. When times are good, few people think about taking challenging steps. More often, the **A**dministrative orientation emerges when companies are in trouble, losing money in the advanced stages of Go-Go. Such crises prompt movement to the Adolescent stage.

Let's consider families as analogous to other organizations. Some parents believe that they will keep their children out of trouble if they introduce strict rules when their kids become teenagers. In fact, those new rules cause the adolescents to rebel. Children who have enjoyed permissiveness throughout their early years don't take kindly to restrictions on their bids for independence. Had the parents maintained low levels of **A** and **I** when their children were still small and growing, the children would understand the boundaries, and they would feel a strong sense of family identity. The stronger the family identity, affinity, rituals, and sense of belonging—**I**—the less need there will be to impose mechanistic rules—**A**—when the children start showing independence as adolescents.

Back in the 1980s, Jim Miscole, executive vice president at Bank of America, told me that whenever his teenage sons went on dates, his wife would say to them, "Just remember who you are and whom you represent." Extra rules and controls are necessary only for those who lack a system of values to support them. The higher the Integration, the lower the need for Administration. By the same token, the more **A**dministration we use, the less **I**ntegration we will have. Note that **I** will *not* emerge unless threshold **A** exists, and **A** mushrooms if there is no **I**.

A higher Integration element mitigates the pain of children's transitions from dependency on family to independence as individuals.

Significance of Structure

Adolescence is a difficult stage. The focus on *better* versus *more* changes, and the struggle between form and function is significant.

The driving and driven forces exchange places. Through Go-Go, organizations structure themselves around people. People get appointed to roles on an ad hoc basis: Every job is temporary. Over time, the system becomes a tangled mess. When it reaches Adolescence, the organization switches the driven and the driving forces. Instead of allowing the organization to structure around people, people should structure around the organization's needs. Instead of sacrificing the needs of the organization to accommodate people, people now have to accommodate the needs of the organization.

That goal is more easily described than accomplished. Remember, if you are part of a picture, you can't see it. Consider my case. As an organizational therapist, I have structured companies with as many as 150,000 employees. I have even restructured governments. The one organization I can't seem to structure, bring out of Go-Go, and release from the founder's trap is my own company. But that is not a rare phenomenon. No surgeon performs surgery on his or her own child, and no lawyer represents himself or herself in a serious court case. Reorganizing is very serious business. Personal bias always interferes. An outsider should work with the company's leadership.

How do we handle Adolescence? Consider what's happening during this stage. Certain difficulties are compounded: Entrepreneurship and CAPI are in transition. Form and function are competing, and form is winning. There is the dangerous possibility that the founders might divorce themselves from their organizations, leaving them bereft of E and aging prematurely.

What are the appropriate therapies during Adolescence? First of all, it's essential to follow a correct sequence of therapy. Otherwise, it is almost always unsuccessful. First, after the initial steps described above, it is obvious that we must start team building in order to free organizations from their founders. Organizations have to work to free themselves from a tremendously powerful dependency syndrome. We want founders and employees to feel that, "we can work together, and we can make decisions together." Furthermore, employees should learn that they are not exclusively dependent on their companies' founders.

Once people feel more comfortable together, and they are making decentralized decisions, they need to define the organizational mission. Where is our organization going? In many cases, only the founder knows, and if he bothered to write it down, it's on the back of an envelope. The rest of the organization needs to understand and share that dream. Some founders haven't really defined their mission, or they are simply unable to articulate it. They operate with an intuitive sense that they cannot spell out. Furthermore, most Go-Gos are beset by divergent thinking. They are going in countless directions simultaneously. That tendency is enabled by their centralized decision-making, but it means that everyone depends on the founder, the only person who knows the right direction at any point in time.

After building a team and a climate of trust and respect, the mission needs articulation. When the team members know where the organization is heading, they can restructure the organization. Since **A** is the endangered role, they must build a strong **A** structure. Appointing a vice president of administration and shaping the CEO role is their next goal. Then they must work to institutionalize **E**. Up to this stage, most founders have been monopolizing **E**—marketing, technology, finance, and human-resource decisions. By and large, however, founders are unlikely to be competent or even interested in all of those realms. They simply want complete control of strategic and discretionary decisions.

Led by a symbergist™, the team institutionalizes **E** structurally by establishing organizational units in those four areas, starting with the area that the founder finds least interesting. If the founder is a marketing whiz kid with little interest in finance, the team should start by establishing a finance unit and hiring a chief financial officer. The team should let the area the founder most enjoys report to him.

Now the team has teamwork, a mission, and structure to protect **E**. It can transfer the **E** from the founder downward, and make the founder chairman of the board or chief executive officer. At this point, the team can bring in a new leader with the title of chief operating officer.

During Adolescence, organizations must transfer leadership from a **PE** to an **AE**, and it's important to make sure the timing and the sequence are right. If the company imports **A** before it has a structure and a mission, the new leader will be as irritating as a pebble in a shoe. Any time the organization moves, the **A** says, "No." And no one understands why.

Everyone goes to the founder, whining, "He's messing it up, he does not know our organization or our way of doing things."

"I knew it," the founder says. "Nobody can do right. They need me!" And, of course, he fires the **A**. It's crucial that the organization not introduce the **A** until it knows where it is going and has articulated its mission. Everyone must already know the company's direction, and there must be a structure. By then, because there is teamwork and relative independence from the founder, a new leader will be able to relate to the founder.

Next, the organization should change its information system. Why? Go-Go information systems are almost always ad hoc systems. Constructed and modified over time, they are the results of random people and situations. Rarely does a Go-Go's information system reflect where the organization is going. Instead, it is a shadow of what the organization has been. Nor does it support the information needs of the roles in the new organization chart. If organizations don't change their information structures at this time, their restructuring will erode.

Why? The structure, which is authority, power, and influence, acts in response to information.

If people don't have information, the organization has no power or authority to decide.

Eventually the new organizational structure will be jettisoned. Symbergists™, therefore, refuse to restructure companies unless they can work on who reports to whom, about what, and for what. The last *what* refers to incentive systems. Organizations must address all the three subsystems in order to change structure. A therapist might change the mission, the responsibility structure, the information system, and incentives. The treatment is similar—but not identical—to that used for advanced Go-Go.

Adolescent organizations are somewhat schizophrenic. They want stability because they yearn to escape the mess of development, the superficiality of projects, and the despair of getting involved in useless, expensive investments. They therefore seek to establish policies, routines, standards, and systems. At the same time, however, they want to keep the freedom of irresponsibility, of trying out untested methods.

Such organizations catch therapists in a double bind. If a therapist facilitates stabilization and systemization, some members are resentful. If the therapist fails to systematize, other members are resentful. Hardly anything the outsider does will be accepted gracefully by the *whole* organization. Adolescent organizations are a pain in the neck, and therapists must have enormous patience. They need to maintain the very delicate balance between flexibility and systemization, changing direction and assignments rapidly and with good timing.

For example, a symbergist™ might follow an assignment about future planning with an assignment about the system necessary to implement future planning. While maintaining optimum tension between structure and process, symbergists™ should help organizations focus on the desired results and on the process for achieving them. Thus, the schizophrenia of the Adolescent organization is, in a sense, resolved by treating the process and the desired outcomes simultaneously.

When the Adolescent organization clearly accomplishes the above, it becomes a Prime organization. Adolescents, incapable of such transformation, become Arsonists or turn very rigid. They become Arsonists when they lose all interest in systemization. They get involved in too many projects, and end up fizzling out. Those that lose **E** become rigid and, because they can't adapt and produce results, they disappear.

Prime

What do we do in Prime? Rarely do Prime organizations ask for external treatment. In their collective consciousness, managers do not sense a need. They feel they are doing fine. If this sensation creates complacency, it could be the beginning of the end. If the company is declining, nobody notices. In Prime, everyone feels as arrogant as in Go-Go. In this case, of course, people have good reason to feel confident. Everything is fine. They are doing very well. Profitability is good. Market penetration is good. They are the best. Why should they change? Prime is the stage where the decline can begin. In this stage, management must take proactive, preventive measures or, eventually, there will be call for reactive measures. It's much cheaper to act sooner than later.

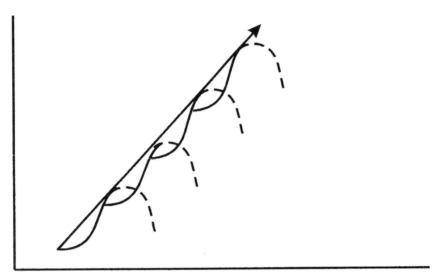

Figure 17-4: Spin-Offs for Prime

What should Primes do? They should worry about losing **E**. Primes must not allow form to take precedence over function. Form and function should be of equal importance.

A Prime organization can nurture **E** by decentralizing, spinning off satellites, and creating new lifecycle curves. By continuously creating spinoffs—experiencing continuous rebirths—Primes do not allow their organizations to enter the Fall.

What happens to an organization with decentralization? Look at the figure below.

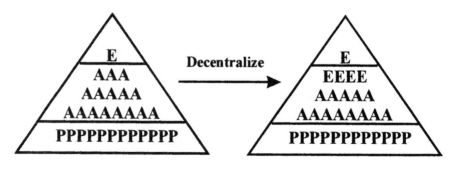

Figure 17-5: The Impact of Decentralization

Picture a modern organization as a triangle structured in layers. The **P**s, at the base of the pyramid, are the people who produce the results for which the organization exists. The administrative process **A**, in the middle, is the role of those who supervise and insure that the organization achieves desired results. This function systematizes and watches for deficiencies. At the top of the pyramid, **E**, are those who set the direction. Discretionary powers are concentrated at the top of the organization. When such an organization decentralizes, what happens to the line separating **E** from **A**? That line is pushed down, and the **A**dministrators of yesterday must become the **E**ntrepreneurs of tomorrow. They need to convert **A**s into **E**s.

Decentralization is different from delegation. Delegation is the process of transferring a task that has been articulated and systematized to someone else. Decentralization is more than just simple delegation; it includes the transfer of discretionary powers.

The more decentralization, the more the organization stimulates entrepreneurial spirit.

Prime is the right time to decentralize. For Go-Gos, because they have yet to develop good control systems and articulated missions, decentralization can be dangerous, even generating out-of-control disasters. Decentralization can begin in Prime when people know what they're doing, have some control over it, and have structure to make sure it happens correctly. Decentralization is a proactive vehicle for retarding aging through stimulation of **E**.

The symbergists'™ assignments should call for identifying boundaries for decentralization. That includes simulating the new organizational structure (so that individuals feel comfortable about the new system) and training management (so that it can perform the new tasks). The groups charged with those assignments consist of the people who will most likely lead the new profit centers. The deadlines for the completion of the assignments are neither stringent nor lenient.

Prime organizations rarely have problems with managerial transplants. Because the pie is continually growing, employees welcome newcomers. Organizations in Prime are therefore the best candidates to acquire other companies or to be acquired.

If Prime organizations don't decentralize, they slip into the Fall. This can happen as management grows older, market share grows larger, and the structure becomes more complex. The Prime organization simply becomes too heavy.

Decentralizing and Avoiding Organizational Colonialism

As I explained in my discussion covering organizational analysis, decentralization and acquisition efforts often create a problem called *organizational colonialism*. Infant and Go-Go companies end up reporting to an Aristocratic company.

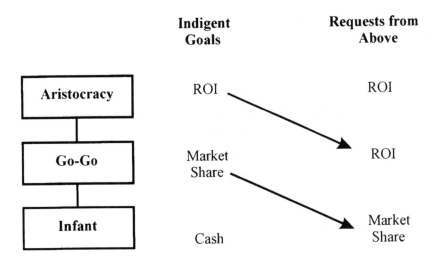

Figure 17-6: Organizational Colonialism

The demands of the parental units are not functional in terms of the offspring's capabilities. Aristocracy expects a return on investment from Go-Go, while Go-Go wants to invest for increased market share. The Infant wants cash, which Go-Go limits in response to the Infant's inability to get as much market share as its Go-Go parent. Through these dysfunctional demands, the Aristocratic company destroys the growth potential of the Go-Go and those of Infant organizations.

The Organizational Family

An effective organizational structure should look more like an extended family. If we were to snap a photo of the extended family, the grandparents would be in the middle, their children in the back, and all the little kids would be gathered in front. According to that model, the Prime or the Aristocracy ought to be in the middle, with the Go-Go not under the Aristocracy but adjacent to it. Infants and Prime units would have the same independent but interdependent relationship. By not superimposing the demands of one on the other, it's possible to protect the individuality of the organizational units. The goals are different for each unit. The Prime creates new Infants; the Aristocracy finances the Infants; and the Go-Go finances itself. Now, there is a family.

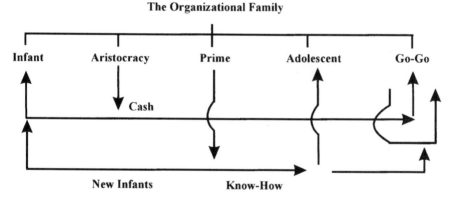

The Organizational Family

Figure 17-7: The Organizational Family

What do I mean when I say "family"? In a functional family, everybody has his own goals, and there is an interdependency among the members. Prime creates new ventures; Aristocracy finances those ventures; and the Go-Go organizations grow on their own. Eventually, the Infant becomes a Go-Go, the Go-Go becomes a Prime, and the Prime becomes an Aristocracy. Each unit is aging, but the whole does not.

The organization exists as a portfolio of units similar to a portfolio of products or stocks. A healthy organization should comprise a portfolio of business units, each at a different stage of the lifecycle. As some age, others are born, and an interdependency keeps the whole family functional.

What style of leadership should head this kind of family and each unit?

The style of the leader and the unit's place on the lifecycle should match. An Infant organization requires managers who are strong **P**s and **E**s. As the organization moves from Infancy to Go-Go, it need not change leadership. The same style should be able to take it from Infancy to Go-Go up to Adolescence. Adolescence will call for a **PA** and then **AE** style of leadership.

Aristocracy is a different story. The organization has reached the point where it needs a **PA** type to milk it for growth capital, which will support the younger offspring. I say that assuming we're dealing with an Aristocracy that is already dysfunctional or aging for the marketplace. If it needs rejuvenation, a **PE** rather than a **PA** style is called for.

A Prime unit needs a big **E** and a big **I** to lead it, and because the total family of units is also at Prime, the **EI** style for the totality is called for, too.

With a portfolio of companies and a portfolio of leaders, the Prime has a stable of horses and jockeys to ride them in different races. There is somebody to take an organization from Infancy to Go-Go and, when it reaches Adolescence, he will either change his style or transfer the organization to a different type of leader, stopping only long enough to pick up another Infant. Somebody else will take the organization from Adolescence to Prime, and when that person gets it there, he will either transfer it to another leader, or change his style.

A large organization needs different leaders for different units. That's why a large, well-structured, and competently-staffed company with many different leadership styles can do better than a small company. With only one style and a single profit center, a small company is vulnerable.

Not only should the family structure include companies at different stages of the lifecycle, each of those units should also have different goals to deliver. An Infant should be aiming to break even; a Go-Go should be striving for market penetration; and an

Aristocracy should deliver a return on investment. The goal of a company in Prime should be to produce new Infants.

The organization should reward the various activities differently and motivate each leadership style differently. I call this organizational pluralism.[2]

Good organizations are pluralistic. They allow the **E** not just to survive, but to thrive.

Time and again, I have seen organizations choose the wrong people to lead them. Although it is undesirable, many organizations select their leaders from Aristocracy, the most established unit. When that happens, the organization has an identity problem. The leader's style introduces functional—not structural—colonialism. Although we changed to a family structure, in terms of behavior and expectations, the organization will not operate as designed. Despite the structure, the Aristocracy can still dominate through the leadership's behavior. Because the leader must integrate and direct the pluralistic structure, the organization needs someone with a big **EI** at the top; bigger even than in Prime.

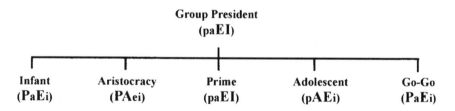

Figure 17-8: Leadership in the Organizational Family Structure

In structural pluralism, where each unit has its distinctive goals and leadership styles to thrive, the pluralistic organization should avoid the dysfunctionality of an Aristocratic culture. Aristocracies expect everybody to behave alike, and they dress up their little babies as if they are grown-ups, ready to go to a funeral. A baby is supposed to act like a baby. Adults shouldn't be expected to behave like babies, and babies shouldn't be expected to behave like adults.

The leadership must recognize and legitimize the various behaviors in terms of predictability of outcomes, functionality of rules, and how strictly the organization is expected to adhere to those rules.

Additionally, the organization must differentiate among the kinds of leadership within the structure. The organization should reward each individual and style according to its unique definition. Because each unit should perform and achieve differently, the reward system should reflect those differences. Colonialism's danger is that it recognizes but one rule, one style, one behavior, and one incentive system.

Sameness creates bureaucratization.

Treating the Fall Organization (PAeI)

What is the correct therapy for the Fall? In Prime, the organization decentralized. In the Fall, the organization should undergo the therapy we apply to Aristocracy. The difference is that the therapy should not exert so much time pressure. The Fall is the beginning of the end, but the problems are not so pronounced as in Aristocracy. The symbergist™ should feel less pressure to conduct fast interventions.

In the Fall, it's important to be aware of whether form is growing stronger than function. Is *how* becoming more important than *what*? Does the organization seem to emphasize how people appear, dress, and talk? Is *how* they do things more important than *what* they do? Note that the entrepreneurial spirit is starting to decline, and CAPI is being questioned, but these symptoms are all still mild and on the surface. What should be done?

The Fall organization needs to focus on raising its consciousness. Its members must realize by themselves and for themselves that **E** has declined.

The symbergists'™ assignments call for facilitating the organization, forecasting its future, analyzing the environment, foreseeing both threats and opportunities, and stretching when setting goals. Once the members of the Fall organization recapture a panoramic view of the future, it's important to move quickly to decentralize the company. Decentralization will stimulate and stabilize **E**. If **E** can grow without disturbing **I** or affecting **A**, then a **PAEI** organization can be achieved. This maneuver has to be periodically repeated because the organization will get out of balance again and again, due to change.

In the Fall organization, a large multidisciplinary group of people undertakes assignments, and the members must meet the stringent deadlines the symbergist™ facilitates in order to wake them up to the coming of age. The goal is to obtain **E**.

For the Fall organization and other organizations at the later stages in the lifecycle, management transplantation becomes a problem. The Fall organization is so set in its ways that a new style of management might be too trying. The older an organization becomes, the more it resents different managerial styles. The Fall organization needs a capacity for **E**. If the organization imports a **paEi** manager, she will likely experience difficulties because she is different. The difficulties, however, are not so great as to preclude integration.

In getting to the Fall, the factors that could be causing **E** to decline are: mental age, perceived relative market share, leadership style, and structure.

If the cause for aging—and the loss of **E**—is mental age, we recommend restaffing top management positions with people who are mentally younger.

If the cause is perceived relative market share, the solution lies in redefining mission. If the organization has 35 percent of a certain market, the organization needs to redefine its market scope. By redefining its markets more broadly, the company will suddenly own only 3 percent of the market and find itself facing an energizing challenge. When a climber gets to the top of a mountain, he should focus on the next ridge, identifying the next peak of another mountain. When he descends the mountain he's just climbed, he's not going down permanently. He climbs down only so that he can again be climbing to the top. If the Fall company is in the paint business with 35 percent of that market, it could redefine itself as being in the wall-protection-and-decorative services market. Now the company has 3 percent of a market that now includes wallpaper.

The nature of a business is such that it must be continually redefined, and the horizon must always be moving.

If functionality of the organizational structure is the cause of the Fall company's aging, the organization must restructure to strengthen **E**. The company should decentralize into new profit centers and structure the staff units correctly.

Treating the Aristocratic Organization

Treatment of Aristocratic organizations can involve difficulties we don't find in other stages of the lifecycle. Aristocratic organizations need to be awakened from the Finzi-Contini syndrome. The symbergist™ should start with a group diagnostic session, using a methodology of synergetic participative diagnosis. This diagnosis is a deep consciousness-raising session at which all participants talk about the company's problems. Viewed in this context, the problems seem truly overpowering, and the need for change is clear and obvious. It's necessary to conduct diagnoses at many levels of the company in order to make everyone aware of the present state of the organization and how different that is from the desired state. The symbergist™ must continually call attention to manifestations of the Finzi-Contini syndrome.

Most consultants, when they are working with Aristocratic organizations, start by saying, "First, let's define your goals." People who try to define goals while feeling hopeless about their ability to achieve them are engaging in an exercise in futility. First, they must feel confident that they can introduce change; they must feel they can work together; and they must say, "Yes, we are potent." Only then can they work on defining where they want to go.

Go-Go organizations already have so much energy that a diagnosis could be counterproductive. In an Aristocracy, however, everyone is mild, relatively passive, and complacent. When people bring all the problems out for discussion, they legitimize the need to change and that creates energy. Once they establish a strong commitment for change, the company can move promptly toward resolving the abnormal problems.

Mission definition is essential for Aristocracies because it identifies new horizons. The mission definition must be a team process, focusing on divergent thinking. The company can do much more than it is doing, and there are more opportunities than it is currently exploring. The members of the organization are not really stuck. They can affect their future. This process helps the group members analyze the organization's technological, political, economic, legal, social, and physical environments. It teaches them how to analyze their markets, product scope, and values. All of that enables them to identify the opportunities and threats that face the organization.

Identifying what they want the future to be forces them to design a structure through which they can realize that future. They design a decentralized organizational structure to implement the strategies discovered in their mission. The organization extracts any and all potential Infants and Go-Gos that are hidden in the Aristocracy and restructures horizontally as a family structure rather than the typical colonial structure.

Once they complete the structure, they turn to the redesign of information systems that support decentralized accountability. This is followed by resource allocation and redesign of the incentive systems to promote profitability and return to an achievement orientation.

It may be that the Aristocracy also needs a change in the leadership. However, it's a mistake to import a large **E** prematurely into an Aristocratic organization. The members of such an organization constitute a mutual admiration society in which detail and maintenance—not growth—are the major attractions. In such a setting, a predominantly **E** person will have trouble expressing himself and exercising creative leadership. There is a greater chance that such a transplant will succeed if the organization waits until after restructuring is complete.

If **E** must be brought in before the restructure is finished, or if **E** is required for the restructure, the symbergist™ must use a bypass system. People in Aristocratic organizations discourage the style of any newcomer whose style alienates them. The **A** rejects the **E** because the latter injects turbulence that **A** cannot control. In the end, the organization either rejects or absorbs **E** as a benign substance. In that case, **E** loses effectiveness. In other words, Aristocratic organizations develop immunities to odd, strange, or different substances. They reject pluralism that is significant and functional for their growth and survival.

To integrate **E** into an Aristocratic organization, the symbergist™ first searches the organization for anyone with an active **E**. Such people are easy to find: They are the people who are complaining. Coincidentally, they are also people the organization is trying to dump. The symbergist™ should insist that they be retained a while longer. In a sense, this stops the bleeding of **E**.

Next, the symbergist™ should establish a task force comprising the "organizational deviants" and recommends that the newly hired **E** lead the group. The group's assignment is a development project— a new product, market, or system—it can complete within a short period of time. Because the task force includes **E**s from several disciplines and levels of the organization, it constitutes a bypass of the organization's **A** channels—the people who have already developed organizational arteriosclerosis. When the "deviants" accomplish their task, **P** is created, and that somewhat rejuvenates the organization. As several such teams are established, the outsider **E** soon begins to feel comfortable, the structure changes, power centers shift, and expectations to produce results increase.

When Salem City happens, the task becomes much more difficult. The **E** has been replaced by **0**, and the organization either totally rejects and resents change or begs for it and is willing to pay any price to get it. (That, incidentally, is how dictators come to power.) The organization is on the brink of bankruptcy. Surgery—a change of management—may be the only viable alternative for such an organization. However, surgery in itself is not sufficient. Recuperation and rehabilitation—organizational therapy—is needed later on.

Treating Salem City (pAei)

The backbiting that characterizes Salem City requires prompt surgical treatment. There is no alternative to replacing the several people whose attitudes are negative, who poison the climate, or who are totally ineffective. But surgery should be conducted only once and very sparingly. If there are several surgical interventions in succession, fear might paralyze the organization. Management's suspicion and paranoia—already strong in this stage of the lifecycle—could overcome the organization. In that case, the treatment *reinforces* the neurosis, rather than *treating* it.

Management should sell unprofitable units, stop the negative cash flow, and focus on survival. For that, CAPI must be together, usually in a single individual. In Aristocracy and the Fall, because there is time for teams, CAPI is centered around teams. In Salem City, there is no time. One individual must bite the bullet and cut the company down to its profitable essence. The organization must follow the same prescription we give an Infant organization: It must prepare rolling sixteen-week cash-flow projections, conduct cost accounting to identify the real leaks in profitability, and file weekly reports on inventory turnover and accounts receivable.

After surgery, the therapeutic treatment prescribed for an Aristocracy is applied, at much higher doses. The company must cut down the *how* and pump up the *what*.

Treating Bureaucracy (OOOA) and Dead (OOOO) Organizations

More often than not, Bureaucratic organizations turn to computer consultants and auditors to increase the **A** that is already overwhelming their organizations and to solve their managerial problems. It is not difficult to see that more or different **A** is not what the organization needs. Such organizations probably need a type of bypass surgery to add **E**, followed by a long period of rehabilitation. Getting the organization to accept **E** will involve overcoming considerable resistance.

Rehabilitation is necessary in order to bring **P** back into action. Shock treatments—threats of firing, unrealistic demands, and so on—are inadvisable. They only scare people, who respond by performing their tasks frantically and ineffectively. Their results will be short-lived, and before long, the organization will fall back into apathy. In fact, a series of such treatments might spur the remaining good managers to leave, forcing the organization into a coma.

Under such circumstances, the recommended therapy requires multiple, simultaneous implementations of all aspects of the therapy applied throughout the workplace, from top management down. The symbergist™, should, of course, closely monitor the integration of the interventions.

As for restoring dead organizations to life, that is a therapy reserved for saints.

Ill-Timed and Unnecessary Surgery

Surgery—replacing top management—is the fastest way to produce change, but it is also the most painful and dangerous treatment. Companies resort to that solution because it can be done in a short time. What's more, it is highly lucrative for the executive search firms. Unfortunately, few organizational surgeons stay long enough to see the results of their work, and they accept no responsibility for post-surgical complications.

What makes a successful surgeon is not how fast she cuts, but how well she monitors the post-surgical complications that occur in weak and vulnerable bodies. Many consultants suggest a new organization chart, help locate people to fill the boxes, collect their fees, and consider their task done: But they have not completed the job. After the new structure is imposed, the organization starts to feel the real pain of adaptation. Although the pain may be acute, managers hesitate to complain publicly about their problems. They fear their complaints might occasion another surgical treatment. They would rather suffer quietly than subject themselves to another round of surgery.

While organizational change is indispensable for long-run success, changes induced as cures at the wrong time may produce almost permanent relapse. The organization may refuse to submit. If surgery has been painful, ineffective, and applied exclusively as a cure, the organization may refuse surgery for preventive purposes—especially when a problem is not yet evident. Often, for example, in Salem City, reorganization is attempted only when there is a crisis. At that stage surgery is inevitable. The treatment would have been less painful during the Prime stage of the organization's lifecycle when the organizational climate was conducive to change. Due to growth and positive expectations for the future, the perceived threats from change were much smaller and could have been minimized. In Salem City, when economic results are bad and the atmosphere is already poisoned by suspicion, change reinforces fears rather than removing them.

If the organization is an Aristocracy, I recommend a *no firing* policy. Many **E**s act like **A**s in order to survive. After six months of change, the organizational climate will start to reflect opportunities for external growth, and the **E**s will surface. There is no need to hire new **E** people. The **E**s are already there.

Can an Internal Consultant Do the Job?

It has become fashionable for large organizations to develop their own consulting departments—*organizational development* (OD) departments.

Such departments can be functional during the early stages of the organizational lifecycle. However, older organizations—the Fall organizations and their successors—will have less success with OD departments. In a young organization, **A** and **I** are the necessary ingredients. It's easy enough to provide those from within the organization, and the internal consultants would have no fear of losing their own jobs. However, as an organization approaches its zenith, it demands more **E**, and internal consultants might be unwilling or unable to make the waves necessary to create the consciousness and desire for change.

Organizational development specialists appear to have been trained for and inclined to perform only the **I** role. Most frequently they are **000Is**. At *best,* they are **paeIs**. Such styles are of no use to an organization that requires serious therapy and rejuvenation. A **paeI** or **000I** style only maintains what exists. Some OD specialists are establishment agents who make the existing fare seem palatable. They are not agents of change who create the necessary new dish.

The symbergists™ should train and develop internal integrators to act as agents of change. For at least the beginning stages of therapy, I have found that external pacing is necessary to create the impetus and direction for change and to buffer any negative short-term organizational reactions. For organizations at or beyond the Fall stage, a more potent medication than simple advice is needed, and, in most cases, that must be administered externally.

For more detail on this subject, I refer readers to my other books, *The Pursuit of Prime* and *Mastering Change.*[3]

Notes

1. See P. A. Samuelson, *Economics* (New York: McGraw Hill, 1985).

2. "Diversity," as pluralism, has been widely advocated as not only a political strategy for decreasing racism and increasing options for minorities, but it has also been advocated as a business strategy for the

next millenium. See R. Stacey's *Complexity and Creativity in Organizations* (San Francisco: Barrett-Koehler, 1996).

3. See I. Adizes, *The Pursuit of Prime* (Santa Monica: Knowledge Exchange, 1996), and *Mastering Change: The Power of Mutual Trust and Respect in Personal Life, Family, Business and Society* (Los Angeles: Adizes Institute, 1993).

CHAPTER EIGHTEEN

The Optimal Path

Typical vs. Optimal Path

Problems exist, as I have stated, when not all the **PAEI** roles are fully developed. As we solve problems, we develop the missing roles, one at a time, starting with **E**. Failure to develop a missing role means that we can't go forward until the role develops. That one-by-one approach to Prime is, of course, the typical path.

Is there a faster path to Prime? Is there a path that bypasses all—or even most—of the problems on the typical path? Is there a "road less traveled" for organizations too?[1]

There is, and I have tested that path in my work with start-ups. And it works.

I am very much aware that the following optimal-path "lecture" makes me sound like a religious preacher on the pulpit, and that makes me somewhat uncomfortable. But I feel an obligation to show that there is, in fact, an optimal path, and companies miss it on account of ignorance or because they are prisoners of their culture and experience.

What is the optimal path?

Did your mother ever tell you not to go out on a windy night after you'd had a hot bath? "You will catch a cold," she hollered after you. Right?

I have always wondered why I catch cold from the mere whiff of a wind, while, in Russia, I have read, people make holes in ice-covered rivers so they can go skinny dipping. And in Finland, the natives sit in hot saunas, sweat a lot, and then jump and roll in the snow. I have no doubt that if I ever tried that, I would die of pneumonia. What is their secret?

What gives me influenza is not the wind or the snow. My body is weak. It's not capable of handling change. As a matter of fact, I start sniffling and get a sore throat just thinking about my next trip across time zones. The Russians have been doing this ice dipping forever. The Finnish do the sauna–snow ritual from the time they are babies. They have strengthened their physical condition so that those extreme changes invigorate rather than kill them. The changes make them stronger. Their health is a reflection of their bodies and probably their minds having grown used to changes in temperature.

How can you improve an organization's ability to handle change? Have everyone start jumping into ice water daily?

Not long ago, medical researchers presented an interesting finding. People who have numerous close personal relationships are less likely to catch cold than people who are less social. In fact, diseases of all kinds are less likely to strike those who have a rich network of family and friends.[2] How about that? How about the statistical finding that married people live longer—despite the bad publicity marriages get?[3] What is going on?

As I have pointed out, integration is a factor that retards aging. That's what's going on. The more integrated the body, the stronger it is. That integration is internal and reaches into the external world. Yogis remain healthy because they subject their bodies to painful contortions every day, and meditation keeps mind, body, and spirit together. Yogis teach their bodies to remain integrated while experiencing change despite the pain of change. It becomes easy for them to handle even changes they themselves have not induced. They are used to change. Incidentally, *yoga* means unity, total integration. We need something akin to organizational yoga: We need to subject organizations to continuous change and teach people how to relax and stay "together" in spite of their pain.

If you want to have a full-grown tree in your yard, you may have trouble finding a house with the tree you want already in place. But even if you are willing to pay the price of an adult tree, you probably know that most trees don't survive transplantation. I discovered a nursery that has developed a way to grow trees that do thrive even after they have been moved. How? Every year, the workers at the nursery carefully transplant the trees into new pots, and gradually, I guess, the trees get inured to the annual change. They do not develop deep roots. When one of those trees is sold full-grown, maybe it assumes that move is just one of those annual changes—not a big deal.

Change should not be something unusual. It has to be expected, anticipated, planned for, and continuously experienced.

One organization I have observed entered the cow business at a time when owning cows was a tax shelter. Many people invested heavily in cows. It was a very big business until Congress changed the tax law. The company should have gone bankrupt. The large organization, which had enjoyed an advantage under the old tax laws, faced serious trouble. Instead of going bankrupt, however, management introduced a series of incremental changes, gradually moving into the mining business. Do the businesses of raising cows and mining have anything in common? Yes! Quality of management. Good management can always make effective changes in a controlled way.[4] The cow business died; the organization did not.

If an organization can continuously change in a planned and controlled manner, keeping itself together in spite of change, it will never die. Its business will change, but the organization as such could live forever. Aging is not an unavoidable fact of life. It can and should be averted.

It all depends on the organization's capability to integrate and remain integrated while initiating and experiencing change.

We have seen that for an organization to be effective and efficient in the short and long run, it needs four roles: **P**, **A**, **E**, and **I**.

In Chapter 11, using a square-dance metaphor, we demonstrated how, on the typical path, those roles develop one-by-one, and, in a particular sequence, they get integrated.

Once I understood the rationale and the dynamics of the lifecycle, I asked myself several questions:

1. Is there a faster way to Prime, or is the path I had observed—the typical path—the only way to develop an organization?
2. If there is a faster and better way, why don't organizations follow that alternate route?

3. If there is an optimal path, do organizations following that path behave differently from those on the typical path?

4. To get on the optimal path, what should leaders do that is different from what they do on the typical path?

The Optimal Dance: The Faster Route

Is there a faster and better route to Prime?

You bet!

Returning to the dance metaphor, the differences between the two paths start right at the beginning with the first dancer.[5]

Having **E** take the first step is what gets organizations on the typical path. My friend, the late Charles Christopher Mark, used to say, "The longest trip does not start with a single step. The Chinese are wrong. It starts with a first misstep. It takes longer!"

Who should be first then?

Let me direct your thinking back to the "rock" analogy introduced in Chapter 10. In this edition of this book, I claim that the group walking along the mountain path started to become an organization even before they encountered the rock or decided to go for a walk. In other words, there is something going on *before* there is a task—whatever that might be. That is news, isn't it? It was news to me. In the first edition, I maintained that there was *no organization and no managerial process* at all, until the group encountered the rock in the path: until it had a task, which was its purpose.

How did I change my mind?

For years I have been wondering how the group arrived on that path in the first place. Let's say the group is comprised of people who had been drinking beer together the night before, and someone had said, "Let's all go to the lake tomorrow!" Everyone agrees, and the next day, they find their path blocked by the rock. Was the organization born when they were drinking, when they decided to hike to the lake, or when they encountered the rock? Or could it have been formed even earlier? What made them get together for drinks in the first place?

The long and the short of it is that whenever there is affinity among people, something is going on. Granted, there is no managerial process, no planning, no staffing, no motivating, and so forth. But there is something going on: There is a sense of affinity. It is what we feel in a foreign country when we meet someone who comes from our hometown and went to the same high school we did. Even though we have never met before, we are excited. There is no purpose to our excitement beyond the fact that we are conscious of our common background, experiences, and upbringing. We are glad to meet each other. And if you were stranded alone on an island for years, imagine your excitement at meeting any human being even if not your buddy from high school. Humans need to affiliate. Thus it is not strange that solitary confinement is a severe punishment.

People need a sense of belonging.[6] A gang of teenagers, standing idly at the street corner, hanging out, has no specific purpose or task in mind, but observers can sense the power those kids could unleash at any moment should a passing purpose draw their attention. When it has a purpose, the gang, a social entity, is charged. The purpose gives focus to all their raw energy. But there is no action until there is a task. A task makes that interdependency, affinity, and sense of belonging realizable.

I am aware that because humans have a need to affiliate, affinity could be interpreted to be a purposeful activity, but I ask you to consider my definitions:

I define *purpose* as a result or a process one wants to achieve over time. A *task* is a result one achieves or a process one performs in the short run in order to achieve a longer-range purpose.

A constant and ongoing need is neither a purpose nor a task. We did not go traveling with the intention of looking for a fellow alumnus from our hometown. We were not wandering the streets, trying to find someone with whom we might affiliate. We did not have that as a purpose. Having met, however, we might plan to continue our travels together, and at that point, we have an emergent phenomenon—a purpose that was not originally there. That purpose is the result of our affinity that always exists.

As you can see, this sense of affinity, of belonging, this awareness of the other, precedes purpose. Affinity is a constant, and purposes emerge as a result of its existence.

Humans and, come to think of it, all living things in nature seek to relate to others.[7] Innate things, like rocks, although they are affected by the sun, cold wind, and rain, are not aware of the forces that affect them. That lack of awareness is why they are not alive.

Awareness of each other—where we are and what we are in relation to everything else, even the stones upon which we step—needs no purpose. That awareness is without a *why,* a *how,* or even a *what.* It simply is. All living things in nature are aware of the environment in which they live. For some, like rats, the awareness reaches a radius of a few yards. For a spiritual person, the awareness encompasses the universe and beyond.

Where does it take us? That sense of affinity, which is always there, is a precondition for the emergence of common purpose. The common purpose in turn, and by definition, creates a new consciousness of interdependency. If each person could, alone, accomplish his or her purpose, no new-found purpose would emerge from the sense of affinity.

The consciousness of interdependence gives rise to meaning.

Animals, although they are alive, aware of their environment, and have an emergent purpose—say, hunting for food—don't attach meaning to that awareness or purpose. They have no symbols, for instance. Have you ever seen a dog or a fish build a shrine to worship anything? What differentiates humans from all other animals is consciousness, which is not just awareness. To my mind, the difference between awareness and consciousness is that consciousness has meaning. We are driven not only by awareness. We struggle to comprehend the meaning of our awareness. We go to war for a meaning. Animals do not attach meaning to their awareness.

What makes us human is that we attach meaning to our consciousness.[8] We want to understand and to relate to this huge, vast interdependence we observe in the universe. This, for me, is where God comes in.

How about the agnostics? My definition still works. Their disbelief is their religion, and they attach themselves to it. It gives a meaning to their lives. Even people who seclude themselves in caves are trying to get closer to something else—God, who, again, gives meaning to *their* lives. And those deep in meditation are trying to get together, with themselves, seeking Integration of the body, mind, and spirit. And that, for them, has a purpose with meaning. It is their life.

We are alive by virtue of our consciousness and how we exercise our interdependence to achieve purpose that gives meaning to our lives. The more conscious we are and the more aware we are of our interdependence with what is going on around us, the more meaning we give to our lives. What's more, that "around us" can reach thousands of miles to atrocities in far-away countries. The more conscious we are, the more we recognize our interdependence, the more we realize that—in our existence—we share a common purpose. The more integrated we are with our environment, the more we feel as one, the fuller our lives will be. Living means serving and being served, being consciously interdependent, and being part of a totality. The bigger that totality is, the "bigger" we are.

Now that we have a common purpose, we are conscious of our interdependence and a meaning for that interdependence emerges. Something else emerges: the need for Integration. The more Integrated we are, the more efficient is our ability to achieve our common purpose.

I perceive the need for Integration develops in the following sequence:

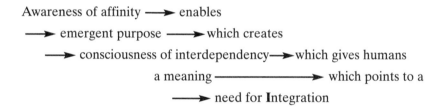

Awareness of affinity ⟶ enables

⟶ emergent purpose ⟶ which creates

⟶ consciousness of interdependency ⟶ which gives humans

a meaning ⟶ which points to a

⟶ need for Integration

The sense of affinity can give birth to different purposes. One time the purpose is to get together for a few beers; another time it is to go to the lake; and the next time it's to lift a rock. But for anything to happen, there must be the constant need to affiliate, an awareness of the potential for interdependence. Unless we feel each other and for each other, how can we ever identify a common purpose? Autism can never produce a purpose that requires teamwork.

Lack of awareness is emotional autism. And emotional autism is not life as we define it. It precludes learning, gaining, serving, and being served. It is only existence. Like a vegetable plucked from the earth, it sits on the shelf, dying.

Does anything precede that awareness or consciousness? Is there small awareness? Small consciousness? Yes, and that is preceded by a smaller awareness, which is preceded by even smaller awareness, and so forth, until there is just a kernel, the smallest seed of awareness or consciousness.[9] Tell me the magnitude of the awareness and I will tell you the magnitude of the emergent purpose. Small people have small emergent joint purpose. For example, they share gossip. People with large consciousness develop a meaning that compels them to join forces to change the face of the earth.

How big is your consciousness?

The good news is that consciousness can grow. Mine, I believe, has grown since the publication of my original edition of this book.

Now let us translate the above analogy into the **PAEI** code and the optimal dance.

Awareness, consciousness of real or potential interdependence, affinity, sense of interdependence, and integration are all different degrees of **I**. I admit that the above is sloppy, but it is the best I can do for now. And *now,* I hasten to tell you, does not mean tonight. That definition is the best my mind has been able to put together in the last 10 years. Full understanding of the **I** role has eluded me all these years, and I am aware that I am far from true comprehension. I console myself, however, by remembering that every book is, at best, a progress report. Right?

My conclusion is that **I** is not created. It always exists as a constant. Purpose, the **E**, emerges from **I**, and the stronger the **I**, the bigger the **E** that emerges.[10] Deciding to go to the lake—the purpose—is the emergent phenomenon, the **E**. True, each individual from the group could walk to the lake alone, but, in this case, they wanted to go together. That purpose emerged from their affinity. Lifting the rock, which is blocking their path, is **P**. That is the task they need to accomplish in order to realize their purpose, **E**, getting to the lake. Being efficient about meeting for a few beers, going to the lake, and lifting the rock is **A**.

Note that **E** can change. Say, instead of going to the lake, the members of the group decided to have a picnic, and, then, instead of a picnic, they decided to play softball. **P** changes depending on **E**. If the people change their minds, and instead of going to the lake, they have a picnic instead, there is no reason for them to lift the rock. For a picnic, they need to gather wood, and if they want to play softball, they need to mark the base lines. And as **E** and **P** change, **A** also has to change. **I**, however, is always there. If a person doesn't affiliate with this group, he or she will affiliate with another, or, if not with a group of people, with a living pet or a pet rock.

What if the members of the group were people who had never before met? Say, the individuals had been hiking alone, to different destinations, and each now finds it impossible to continue with the rock blocking the way. Moving the rock out of the path is still **P** if each of them, unable to lift the rock alone, needs to pass through to get to his or her own destination. Each has his or her individual and independent **E**, but nobody will be able to lift the rock until everyone is aware of each other and everyone's need for one another. If that awareness does not exist, each one will try to lift the rock alone, interfering with everyone else. A sense of awareness has to exist. The purpose will emerge, followed by the recognition of interdependence, and finally the need for integration.

And what happens if, for whatever reason, the awareness declines? Can you imagine the decline in the energy levels of the people trying to lift the rock? If that happens, the need to get to the lake will disappear. You are, I hope, getting my message. What starts a company is not Entrepreneurial energy. A company begins with mutual awareness. And it ages, not when the product line gets outdated, not when innovation, creativity, and risk-taking decline. Aging starts when awareness goes down. Old people can freeze to death without having realized that their environment had grown too cold for them.

What is this sense of affinity, consciousness, awareness of interdependency? I am describing the conditions and degrees of Integration, and I have defined Integration as the process of changing organizational consciousness from mechanistic to organic. Organic consciousness implies an internal sense of interdependency: Each part is aware that it exists to serve other parts of the whole for a *common purpose,* a common function.

Consciousness of potential Interdependency, the sense of affinity, **I**, precedes the purpose, **E**, which precedes the task, **P**, and any processes and procedures, **A**.

When is an organization born? In my first edition, I suggested the following model: An entrepreneur, walking down a busy street on a hot summer's afternoon, gets an urge for ice cream. When he's unable to find a store that sells ice cream, it occurs to him that here is an opportunity for him to open an ice cream store. The organization is conceived when he gets the idea, and is born when he signs a lease and has to pay rent—when he assumes risk.

That's what I thought then. Ten years later, the answer doesn't seem nearly so simple as it used to.

Before the entrepreneur gets his idea—before conception— there had to have been conditions that allowed the concept to form in his mind: He was interrelating, conscious, aware, interdependent, and integrated with the environment. He was conscious of where he was and how he felt. He was aware that he felt warm. He was aware of his taste buds asking for a treat. He was aware that that treat had to be ice cream, and he was aware that there were no ice cream stores in the neighborhood. Furthermore, he had enough empathy to imagine that others would also want ice cream on a hot summer's day. If he were autistic, detached, and disintegrated within himself and with his surroundings, he would have never come to the idea that there was a need for ice cream or any other cream, for that matter.

Thus, **I** precedes **E** and is the precondition for its existence. **I** is first! Whoa! How many pages has it taken me to convince you? This reminds me of a story. A teacher complains about her students. "Imagine," she says. "I explained it to them once, and they did not understand. I explained it to them a second time, and still they did not understand. I explained it to them the third time, when even I finally understood . . ."

Let's proceed. On the optimal path, **I** is first to dance, and he can dance any of the dances.[11] He just makes the rounds letting everyone know he is there and available to interrelate. **I** creates the awareness of interdependency: There is a dance for them to dance together. The emergent purpose for them to dance together is a natural progression that need not be assigned or orchestrated. As I explained in Chapter 10, each and every system aims to be effective and efficient in the short and long run. That is given. You can call it a law of organizational transformation.

Now, the second law comes into play: the law of conservation of energy. Energy is fixed and has to be used in the most efficient way. **I** does not need much energy because there is nothing for **I** to learn. *Being* is **I**'s purpose. It need not try anything. It is simply itself. The limited energy does not go to develop **I**'s dance. The energy is expended in unfreezing the other dancers, getting them ready and willing to dance together. That takes energy for a while.

So what is the difference between the typical path and the optimal path? According to what we have discussed so far, even on the typical path there is **I**, consciousness of surroundings and needs. If there weren't, the entrepreneur would not have given birth to the idea for an ice cream store. So, what is the difference?

On the typical path, **I** was both there and not there. **I** was in his corner, noticeable but quiet. The dominant dancer is **E**. It is for this reason that on the typical path, it's important to monitor **E** closely; **E** is the vital sign that tells us whether a company is growing, aging, or dead.

The optimal path uses a different "dance card." The vital sign is **I**. If there is little **I**, the company may still be conceived and born. It will even grow, but the growth will not be easy. Lots of energy will be wasted on internal marketing, internecine struggles, and politics. The company can make profits, but without **I**, it will be suboptimizing somehow. The company will adopt a what's-good-for-General-Motors-is-good-for-America point of view, and we already know that profit maximization can lead to unsustainable growth that is detrimental to the greater social good.

I introduces spirituality. There is a sense that the organization's goals encompass more than just profits. The organization is there to serve its customers, labor, management, and community. Take The Body Shop, for instance. That company tried to change the world. The Body Shop's goal was not only to sell cosmetics it developed without animal testing and sold without advertising promises of incredible beauty from a bottle. Each and every Body Shop store was an outlet for social values. Each outlet had pamphlets and other materials about the human rights of indigenous peoples. Instead of donating money to those poor and endangered people, Anita Roddick, the founder of The Body Shop, created "Trade not Aid." Under that rubric, The Body Shop bought Brazil nuts from the newly discovered tribes in the Amazon still living in the Stone Age.

The Brazil nuts were expensive, and the company lost money on that venture, but it was not an issue. The Body Shop saw itself involved in endeavors that extended beyond making money on soap and shampoo. Management was also deeply concerned about nuclear testing in the Pacific. The Body Shop delivered many hundreds of thousands of signatures to the French government. The signatures opposing the tests were collected in a worldwide campaign that included each and every Body Shop store.

And, unlike companies that reward their successful franchisees with Caribbean vacations, The Body Shop sponsored people who would go to Rumania to work in the orphanages. What does the cosmetics business have to do with orphanages in Rumania? There is no market in Rumania. And who in America—or anywhere else in the world—buys more shampoo from The Body Shop on account of its helping Rumanian orphans?

As should be obvious, The Body Shop did not engage in such activities for the sake of profit. The company funds such initiatives out of its consciousness of what should be done simply because we are human. The cries of a baby in Rumania, Albania, or Bosnia should be as painful to us as the cries of our own babies at home. They all need soothing.

That is **I**.

I is being spiritual. With love, we—humans and companies—live longer.

What I am saying, I hope, loud and clear, is that spiritually motivated business is good business. It is good for the company, for its owners, for workers, for everyone. Take Ben & Jerry's Homemade, a socially responsible company, which grew nearly 100 percent annually despite efforts to stay small.[12] Although management paid itself and the workers less than the market rate, everyone worked longer hours than the competition. The company followed a growth curve very different from many companies on the typical path.

On the typical path, many companies try to grow, yet they remain small. And frequently, management pays itself tremendous salaries, insists on keeping control, and fights to get the maximum amount of work from employees while keeping payroll as low as possible. Yet these controls result in worse results than the socially responsible business. What is going on? When people believe in what they do, they work harder. Productivity during times of war goes sky high. Like The Body Shop, at Ben & Jerry's, people believed in what they were doing. They were not laying bricks. They were building a temple where they could worship the Lord. And their Lord was saving the world from destroying itself.

In 1988, Ben & Jerry's Homemade, Inc. created a document called the Statement of Mission. I quote it here in its entirety:

Ben & Jerry's is dedicated to the creation and demonstration of a new corporate concept of linked prosperity. Our mission consists of three interrelated parts:

Product Mission: To make, distribute, and sell the finest quality, all-natural ice cream and related products in a wide variety of innovative flavors made from Vermont dairy products.

Social Mission: To operate the company in a way that actively recognizes the central role that business plays in the structure of society by initiating innovative ways to improve the quality of life of a broad community—local, national, and international.

Economic Mission: To operate the company on a sound financial basis of profitable growth, increasing value for our shareholders, and creating career opportunities and financial rewards for our employees.

Underlying the mission of Ben & Jerry's is the determination to seek new and creative ways of addressing all three parts while holding a deep respect for the individuals, inside and outside the company, and for the communities of which they are a part.

The company works to employ its Mission Statement in as many day to day business decisions as possible so that the company is profitable and the community can profit by the way Ben & Jerry's does business.

Ben & Jerry's gives away 7.5 percent of its pre-tax earnings in three ways: the Ben & Jerry's Foundation; employee Community Action Teams at the company's five Vermont sites; and through corporate grants. The company supports projects which are models for social change—projects which exhibit creative problem solving and hopefulness. The Foundation is managed by a nine-member employee board and considers proposals relating to children and families, disadvantaged groups, and the environment.

Notice the Integration of goals and the awareness that is not just Vermont-wide but international in scope. Notice that the company's goal is to increase the financial reward not only of its investors but of its employees as well. The company is dedicated to having a work place where people can experience joy—not just work, work, work. The company addresses the complete human being, community, and the world in which we live.

Are The Body Shop and Ben & Jerry's in Prime? Not at all. I believe each of them is caught in a founder's trap, and both companies have been struggling to find replacement leaders who, while sharing their values, can lead their companies forward. In my opinion, each of them has monopolized the **E** and downgraded the importance of **A**.

They downgraded the importance of **A** because of the importance they attributed to **I**. That should not be surprising. **A** and **I** substitute for one another. One is a mechanistic "organizational glue" and the other is "organic glue." Those who rely on **A** use less of **I**, and those who worship the **I** are scared to death of **A**.

But if **A** does not provide minimal infrastructure, decisions that should be standard operating procedures need to be reinvented each and every time, introducing confusion, frustration, and demoralization. **I** eventually—and necessarily so—will go down. And without **A**, it is difficult or impossible to install a new leader. Nevertheless, those two companies, and many others from Social Venture Network, demonstrate an alternate way of doing business successfully. Companies that institute not only **EI**, like they did, but true **PAEI**, will have even bigger success, both financially and politically. If there are enough such companies, they might change the world.

Being spiritual is not a luxury. It is not something only for idealists. It is most realistic.

It expedites a company's progress to Prime faster, keeping problems to a minimum. The company grows even if the founder is not looking for growth. It makes money, not despite its spirituality, but because of it.

A company does not have to be spiritual to have a spirit. Take Southwest Airlines.[13] I don't think it aims to change the world or save it. Management wants everyone to have fun at work, and everyone does work with gusto. You have experienced the companywide spirit if you have ever flown Southwest. Its spirit is like a religion, providing a unifying culture.

What other companies have such spirit? I immediately think of two hospitality chains: Four Seasons Hotels and the Ritz Carlton Hotels. Their spirit derives neither from wanting to save the world nor from wanting to have fun. Their spirit comes from their sense of pride. Once, I happened to be inside a kitchen of one of those hotels. I noticed that on the door the waiters pass through on their way out to the tables, there was a sign, cautioning them, "If you are not proud of it, don't serve it."

If you have ever had the good fortune to observe a pride of lions in nature, you can't help but notice how the lions walk. Each lion manifests the pride's pride. Just so, the employees of each hotel in those two chains—no matter where in the world, no matter what time of day—all exhibit that pride. How do they maintain that universal spirit? Sure it takes training. Sure it takes hiring the right people. But that is not enough. They have created a culture, starting from the top, that is truly dedicated to excellence, to professionalism. Every employee knows that nothing less than the best—flowers in the entrance, chocolate on your pillow, or morning wake-up call—will do.

The emergent purpose can range from saving the world and serving the community, to having a better place to work and having pride in what you do. The common denominator is a sense of purpose that exceeds profit motivation.

*The focus should be not on what you do
but on what you are.*

And you are what you stand for. What you stand for has a meaning. We must ask ourselves, what is the meaning of what we stand for and spend our lives on?

And when you expand, never expand so fast that you lose what you stand for. Never outpace your culture.

On the optimal path, before you start thinking about the market and its needs for your gadget, ask yourself what do you stand for. How will your vision make a difference for the human race? How will it help our children and grandchildren? Get a real sense of value. Any company has the potential to make a difference.

The Body Shop has a message painted on its delivery trucks and printed on T-shirts: "Don't say: I am small and insignificant. Have you ever tried sleeping with a mosquito?" No one is insignificant. What you do and who you are make a difference. Your spirit, like your smile, can be contagious. It can ignite something. Consider oil refineries. Because of current laws, regulations, and tremendous penalties, refineries don't pollute the air. At least they don't pollute so much as they used to or so much as they would if the laws did not exist. Now let's assume a refinery does its best not to pollute, within whatever the technology allows. Is that enough? No. It's acting only for **A** reasons—to comply with the law. If it had **I**, it would do something from the heart, something not required by law, something which makes it part of the human race. For example, instead of painting its refinery with the typical rust-resistant paint, management might hire an artist like a Yaacov Agam or Christo to paint it, making it a sculpture to beautify the world. Or it might hold a competition among local artists. It takes only consciousness.

Everyone, every company can do something to improve this world. Put pictures of lost kids on your milk cartons; donate time and food to food pantries that feed the hungry; bring the disadvantaged kids to see your business, and show them how, with study and some effort, they could improve their lives. Find a life's purpose that reaches beyond laying bricks. Build a temple to worship the goodness of your heart.

That is **I**, and that is where you should start if you want to be on the optimal path. But what about profits and return on investment? Can business afford such a big heart?

I don't mean to suggest that you should be so altruistic that you bankrupt your company. Just as you should establish at least minimal working conditions, you should clearly state the minimal profitability your company must achieve. Optimize your goals, and once you reach those goals, raise the optimum to higher and higher levels. Don't let yourself get stuck on a single track. Organizations have multiple stakeholders, including the universe, and your task is to optimize and integrate—not suboptimize and disintegrate.

Now that you understand and aim for values, let's think about vision.

Who should dance next? **E**. With a sense of affinity and interdependence, purpose emerges that can utilize this awareness.

Now **E** and **I** dance together in an **EI** dance. How different is that from the typical dance? The typical dance was **paEi**. The optimal dance is **paEI**. I am describing differences of degree, but cumulatively, small differences make a major difference. This is a paradigm shift from my thinking of ten years ago.

The **paEI** dance is one of integrating vision. That is not a vision of one individual that others watch, perhaps even admiring it. It's a vision which everyone shares and to which everyone is dedicated. If the initiator should die, the vision would continue. People go to war for such visions, prepared to kill or to die. The American Civil War was about states' rights, the tenth amendment of the Bill of Rights. That was an **A** issue of great significance for the South, but few from the North would die for it. By making the issue of slavery the focus of the war, the North had an issue for which its people were willing to die. Were people willing to die in Vietnam for any business interests? No way. Those who went there believed they were fighting to protect democracy.

Who dances next? Surprise! **A** is next. Plan your systems, budget, business plan, cost controls, forms, and manuals before you open your store. When you open for business, you are ready to go. With all those preparations, you can open your store and start selling and providing **P**. That readiness is borne out by the incredible, mushrooming success of the franchising movement. What a franchiser gives is: **E**—the idea, direction, concept; and **A**—the systems, all the way to the smallest detail. The newcomer has no need to experiment. If a franchiser is any good, like The Body Shop, it also gives values and a message worth working for—**I**. All that remains for the franchisee is **P**: to go and do it.

Referring to the dance again, let's see how to implement this optimal sequence and overcome the incompatibility of the roles:

$$P \qquad A$$
$$E \qquad I$$

First, **I** is there, already dancing. He's not in the corner waiting to be invited. He doesn't create his own dance because **I** has no purpose other than being there to serve others; he willingly dances with anyone. His dance is generic and works with any other dance. He even mimics all the other dancers in the square as he turns around and around. In this way, he lets all of them know that, yes, they are welcome, and there is room for each and every one of them. This dance creates a welcoming climate—an atmosphere of cooperation and good will—that makes the integration of the future dance much easier.

Does **I** have to retire when **E** gets up to dance? Certainly not. **I** can adapt easily and can dance with anyone. So **E** and **I** dance the long-term effectiveness-and-efficiency dance. During this dance, we see the emergence of the environment within which the organization will operate: The **EI** dance develops vision and values to provide the direction for the organization, and the boundaries within which it will operate.[14]

Notice that for the optimal dance, spirituality—a sense of values and vision—is a necessary condition. That integration can be human, but, unfortunately, it also can be animalistic like the Nazi movement, which did have powerful vision and values. The optimal path does not mean that you must believe in God—one way or another—or you get downgraded to the slower, second-rate, typical path. You are on the optimal path if you and your people believe in anything and have any values—even criminal values like those of the Mafia, or the Nazis. In this case you are on your own optimal path although it disintegrates society at large and puts society on a less than optimal path. Only those movements that integrate rather than disintegrate put both the organization and the society on the optimal path.

It's now **A**'s turn to join. **A** should not dance by himself, developing his own dance without **E** and **I**. That would be form for form's sake; it wouldn't serve the **E** and **P** functions that **A** needs to serve. **A**, therefore, must develop its dance in conjunction with another role. Should any of the **EI** dancers retire? Let's see. **I** can dance with anyone. Therefore, **A** has to learn to dance only with **E**, who is already dancing. But isn't that the most difficult combination? On the typical path, that combination caused the most problems. The difference, you may already have guessed, is the existence of **I**. On the typical path, **I** was either nonexistent or small. The smaller the **I** was, the more troublesome was the struggle between **E** and **A**. **I**'s presence is like having oil-lubrication—to smooth over the difficulties. So, the **pAEI** dance can take place now.

It has taken only two steps to develop a **pAEI** dance. Not bad; we are already a step ahead of those who take the typical path.

Now **P** should join. True, one should teach him the dance while the other two watch, but with the involvement of **I**, the **AEI** dance works like a dance of two, not three. **P** is really joining only **A** and **E**.

If form and function are already dancing together and doing well, it shouldn't be too difficult for **P** to join. At first, when **P** joins in, **E** will take a temporary rest, allowing short-term effectiveness to substitute for long-term effectiveness. That's the **PAeI** dance. For a short time, there should be no new ideas, and attention should be directed to getting the existing ideas working. Once that is accomplished, it's again time to look for new ideas. **E** comes back refreshed, ready to spin off new markets and/or new products. Again, the situation resembles the typical path, but with **I** as an active, leading dancer, **E**'s return is not too difficult (assuming that **A** was taken care of!). We have arrived, and we can stay in Prime. It is **PAEI** time.

On the optimal path, the transitions are easier. With the development of long-run **EI**, the systems of short-run **A** reflect the long-run purpose and the true interdependency. With values, vision, and systems, by the time **P** joins, everything is ready. **P** does not have to wonder *why, what,* or *how* to do. It's all given. Just go and do it. As I indicated above, it's easier to open a franchise fast-food restaurant than an independent, stand-alone, sit-down restaurant. The franchiser gets everything ready for the franchisee. It's all given. Just go and do it.

The Typical Path: A Comparison

Why, then, doesn't the typical path start with **I**? It does. Without it there would have been no creation. The difference is not in absolute terms but in the degree and intensity of the phenomenon. On the typical path the founder is aware and conscious of his own self and of the item that he is creating. And that is where awareness ends. On the optimal path, the **I** is much, much larger, and the larger it is, the more efficient and effective is the path. On the optimal path the organization is politically conscious, with a worldly orientation and consciousness. The organization worries not only about selling cosmetics but about the fate of the Ogoni people in Nigeria. It is concerned with the pain animals suffer if we use them to test lotions that make people perceive themselves as more sexually attractive. Tell me what you worry about and I will tell you how "big" you are. For a company to be on the optimal path, it must be really "BIG."

But why is **I** usually small? Why do companies follow the typical path rather than the optimal path? Is it because we are westerners? Is it because the western world is preoccupied with **P**?[15] Is it for that reason that the typical path starts with **E**?[16]

Does an organization really start with the **E** role? It is conceived with **E** and born with **P**, but for conception to occur, **I** is necessary. Nobody can explain why some women who have been unable to conceive become pregnant soon after they adopt a child. Might it be a question of **I**?

I have observed that all innovators are somehow integrated with their innovations. A creative-design engineer will tell you that his new machine lacks a specific part. How does he know? "I feel it," he says. The more creative he is, the more he identifies with his creation. He almost feels it in his body. He is not inventing it; he is releasing a creation from his gut. This is where intuition comes into play. And what is intuition if it is not feeling, sensing, and knowing, on a very primitive level, what the market or the client wants. An innovator is like an artist who knows, simply knows, that without a red dot in the middle of her painting, it is incomplete. How does she know that? It is as if she *is* the painting. She identifies with it.

When does an artist lose his creativity? When he loses his touch for his art, when he gets disassociated, disintegrated. Alexander Isayevich Solzhenitsyn said, "A poet who is not with his people, even the dogs do not follow."

Why is a Go-Go organization in trouble when the leader starts acting like a seagull? When the leader is gone, there is no one else to integrate. And **E** without **A** and **I** is, as the Old Testament says, "all clouds and wind but no rain."

What causes the founder's trap? First, the founder finds it difficult to transfer the **I** role, and then, he wants to monopolize **E**, introducing the one-and-only syndrome. As a matter of experience, I note that in Go-Go, founders sow disintegration rather than integration. They tell John what is wrong with Bill, complain to Bill about what is wrong with Susan, and confide to Susan how frustrated they are with both Bill and John. With such disintegration, team **E**, which is necessary to institutionalize **E**, cannot evolve.

After several years of painful experience, I have found that to transfer **E** from a single individual to several individuals and then to the structure—to institutionalize **E**—requires team cohesion. It's necessary to have group interdependency so the members can create and implement their creations. They need to cooperate. If there is no **I**, by default, the creative process retreats to a single individual. Team **E** requires team **I**. You cannot plant **E** unless **I** is already there. Entrepreneurship is based on consciousness—awareness of what is within us and outside us. That consciousness must develop before we can set Entrepreneurial spirit in motion.

How I build this **I**—this consciousness—before I decentralize **E** is a subject for another book, and I admit that as a novice, I am probably not very good at it. When I watch spiritual leaders, I am in awe. They have what organizations need, and I have recommended to many of my clients that they would do well to appoint spiritual leaders to their boards of directors.

Maybe your next human resources manager should be some-one trained not in industrial psychology. Should you consider looking for somebody with a background in religion and philosophy? A social worker? What about assigning your sales or production manager responsibility for developing this consciousness in your organization? Why not make the role of human resources manager a rotating responsibility?

E is where conception occurs. If it is individualized, it can start a company, but there will be organizational difficulties later on, in Adolescence. If the lifecycle starts with team **EI**, it nourishes the organization throughout the growing stages, and Adolescence will be easier. The companies that, from the earliest stages, grow with **EI**, are like children who have been raised in loving and supportive families. Their parents won't be forced to impose strong discipline in order to rescue them from troubled Adolescence.

Where does all that leave us?

This is the sequence of the optimal lifecycle:

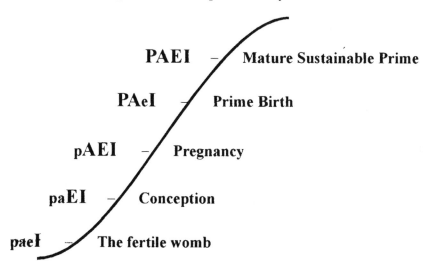

PAEI — Mature Sustainable Prime

PAeI — Prime Birth

pAEI — Pregnancy

paEI — Conception

paeI — The fertile womb

Figure 18-1: The Optimal Path

The choice is ours: typical or optimal path? And optimal for whom? Just us personally, just for our organization, or is it for society at large? And then, which society? Just our immediate community, religion, race, or creed? Is it just our country or are we talking about society worldwide? Or are we concerned about planet Earth beyond people to include flowers, birds, fish, and even moss? Does Love have boundaries? Should it?

Lift your eyes and see!

Take a deep breath and fill your heart. Awaken your spirit and nourish your love for all. For ALL. Because ALL is all there is to it.

Notes

1. See M.S. Peck, *The Road Less Traveled* (New York: Simon and Schuster Touchstone, 1978).

2. See D. Ornish, *Love and Survival: The Scientific Basis for the Healing Power of Intimacy* (New York: HarperCollins, 1998).

3. See L.S. Berger and L. Syne, "The Social Networks, Cost Resistance and Mortality: A Nine Year Follow-up Study of Alameda County Residents," *American Journal of Epidemiology* 109, 2 (1979): 186–204.

4. There is a body of research that explores the application of chaos theory to organizational processes. In this work, there is wide recognition that states of equilibrium are not productive of creative or innovative work that is necessary for organizational renewal. These theorists are advocating that organizations develop competence to work in states far from equilibrium. See R. Stacey, *Complexity and Creativity in Organizations* (San Francisco: Barrett-Koehler, 1996).

5. This notion that process is dependent on initial conditions is a central tenet of chaos theory. See R. Stacey, *Complexity and Creativity in Organizations*, for a discussion of this notion, applied to organizations.

6. The latest in psychology and psychiatry is to call this phenomenon "attachment." See J. Bowlby's *A Secure Base: Parent-Child Attachment and Healthy Human Development* (New York: Basic Books, 1988).

7. G. Bateson, in *Mind and Nature: A Necessary Unity* (New York: Dutton, 1979), has referred to this interdependence as "the pattern that connects." See R. Donaldson's edited version of Bateson's work, *A Sacred Unity: Further Steps to an Ecology of Mind* (New York: HarperCollins, 1991). This title suggests that this "integration" is a manifestation of the sacred (related to "holy," meaning whole). See

also those working on the systems planning and analysis using Gaia Theory, which postulates the fundamental integration of living and nonliving systems, particularly S. Schneider and P. Boston, *Scientists on Gaia* (Cambridge: MIT Press, 1991).

8. See V. Frankl, *Man's Search for Meaning* (New York: Harper Colophon, 1984).

9. There is a very real connection between this system for understanding the evolution of organizations and eastern philosophy that teaches that integration is the source of all compassion and holiness. See S. Rinpoche, *The Tibetan Book of Living and Dying* (San Francisco: Harper Books, 1994).

10. Here is a hypothesis. Assume that the energy for **I** is fixed. Assume that a particular human is a multifaceted individual who uses this energy to Integrate different facets of life. Now assume that for whatever reason, this human is incapable of Integrating with certain facets. If he channels all the energy to one use, the **I** would be enormous, enabling the emergence of a fantastic **E**. That, I believe, is what happens with very creative people, real geniuses. They excel creatively, but, in other aspects of their lives, they are practically handicapped. Some creative people, for example, have problems socializing with other people.

11. There is a very interesting connection between the notion that **I** has no purpose and the concept of "purposelessness" in autopeotic or self-organizing systems. F. Varela, in *Principles of Biological Autonomy* (New York: Holland Press, 1979), has described systems as purposeless and has even argued that systems driven by conscious purpose are destructive of life. This notion has contributed to a debate between system theorists who model systems on biological processes and system theorists who model systems on social or symbolic systems. The latter group has argued that human systems are purposeful systems. See F. Capra's *The Web of Life*.

12. See E. Larson, "Forever Young," *Inc. Magazine* 10, 8 (1988): 50–62.

13. See K. Freiberg and J. Freiberg, *Nuts!: Southwest Airlines' Crazy Recipe for Business and Personal Success* (Austin, TX: Bard Press, 1996).

14. However, this sequence of first **I** then **E** suggests that the role of "vision" and "values" needs to be reimagined. Currently, many experts argue that common vision and values are the source of inte-

gration, so there are many consultants who struggle to build cultural change by inserting new values in the organization, hoping that these new values will coalesce into a new organizational culture. However, if we understand that **I** preceeds **E**, we can see that the emergence of vision and values are the organic manifestation of the **IE** dance, and thus cannot be superimposed on an existing culture. From this perspective, vision/value work requires rekindling the **IE** dance and relationship.

15. Consider M. Weber, *The Protestant Ethic and the Spirit of Capitalism* (London: Unwin, 1930) as an example.

16. J. Schumpeter, the famous Austrian economist who wrote about the importance of entrepreneurship for economic growth, was captive to that bias, as was D. McClelland, the Harvard professor of psychology who studied Indian communities. He reported that those Indian villages that had entrepreneurial spirit performed better economically. I suggest, he found what he was looking for. See J. Schumpeter, *Business Cycles: A Theoretical Historical and Statistical Analysis of the Capitalist Process* (New York, McGraw-Hill, 1939); and D. McClelland, "Need Achievement and Entrepreneurship—A Longitudinal Study," *Journal of Personality and Social Psychology* 1 (1965): 389–392.

Summary

The Laws of Organizational Transformation

The whole book can be summarized into laws of transformation. The book in essence is the manifestation of these laws and the explanation of why they appear to be true.

Thus, I thought it appropriate to provide the summary as a list of laws which govern how and why organizations change. These laws serve as conclusions of the work presented in this book.

I. All living systems seek to be effective and efficient in the short and long run.

II. All living systems seek to be effective and efficient in the short and long run, using their fixed amount of energy in the most efficient way possible.

III. The factors that determine effectiveness and efficiency in the short and the long run develop and get integrated in a predictable pattern. That pattern is the lifecycle.

IV. Whether the lifecycle will follow the longer or shorter route depends on how much Integration the system has; the more Integration it has, the less energy it needs. Then, according to Law Number II, the more **I** the system has, the shorter the route to Prime will be.

V. As long as there is change, there will always be problems.

VI. All problems are created by disintegration.

VII. Disintegration occurs because the subsystems that comprise any system do not change synchronically.

VIII. The role of leaders of organizations is to lead change, integrate to solve the problems created by change, and prepare the system for the next disintegration introduced by the next change.

IX. Integration predicts development, and a system's lack of it predicts decay.

X. Never have more than ten laws.

And I hope to meet you at the next edition!

Cordially yours,
Ichak Adizes

PART FOUR

Appendices

Case Studies

I have based the following case studies on real client histories, but I have disguised the names of the people and the companies.

Before Starting: The RR Company

The following are my actual notes of a visit to RR Company, potential member for the Institute:

1. Findings

John is the vice chairman and president, 55 years old. David is his brother. He is chairman and chief executive officer, 58 years old. The company was founded 28 years ago by David who is a physicist by training. John joined his brother several years later, and they split the company in two: Engineering & Production, headed by David, and Sales & Marketing, headed by John. The two even separated geographically: John remained on the East Coast, and David moved to Silicon Valley.

Three years ago they reunited the companies. John remained on the East Coast, but in each month, he spends one week on the

West Coast, one week traveling, and two weeks on the East Coast, where the company has one plant. The company's vice president for sales and vice president for strategic alliances are also located on the East Coast.

Up until three years ago John and David led the company together. At that point, XYZ consultants reorganized them and recommended a single leader. David became chairman, and John, so far as I can see, is "in Siberia." The consultants set up a typical functional structure with one profit center at the top. RR employs 1,000 people; Annual sales, excluding sales in Japan, are $158 million. In Japan, where the company owns a 50-percent stake in a branch, sales are $75 million.

The market is consumables for manufacturing. The size of the total market in 1997 was $500 million. Anticipated for year 2000, $1 billion.

RR is in four markets according to the strategic planner:

	Year: 1997			Year: 2000			
					Company Size with Same	New	Company Revenues with New Market
Market	Market Size *(in $ millions)*	Market Share	Company Revenues *(in $ millions)*	Market Size *(in $ millions)*	Market Share *(in $ millions)*	Market Share	Market Share
D	150	33%	50	200	70	50%	100m
S	200	25%	50	300	75	20%	60m
C	120	50%	60	400	200	100%	400m
P G	?	?	?	?	?	?	
	500		160	1000	350		560m

The above figures were given to me by V.P. Sales. To John, those figures came as a surprise. Why? Is he out of it?

I believe that, by the year 2000, the sales could and should reach $560 million, with 50 percent of revenues coming from products the company does not yet sell.

2. Location on the Lifecycle

Still normal Adolescence. Normal because there is good mutual trust and respect within the CAPI group.

David and John are both **E**s. They needed **A**. They fired the chief operating officer because they believed he was not enough of an **A**, but according to the people I interviewed, it was a classic struggle: Neither David nor John allowed the former chief operating officer to add **A**. The company hired Jim, who had been their consultant, to be the chief operating officer and bring **A**. 62 years old. **PA** style. No **I**.

Classic mistake: Bringing **A** without preparing the structure first. Also, the **E**s pulled out prematurely. They gave away the keys to the store, and now they are very unhappy that they are losing control.

The Structure now:

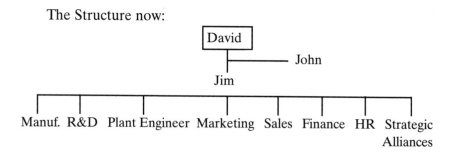

With Jim **PA**-ing, **E**s out, increased **A**, the company is turning inwards. New product development is slow, reactive, late to market; R&D is underfunded for the core businesses, D and S. Instead of a real marketing department, there is only sales support. The organization has a single profit center, and there is no organizational farm system to develop leadership succession. Jim, who is 62 years old, must retire in 3 years, and there is no internal leadership prepared to take over his role.

The direction for us to take, I believe, is:

The desired structure:

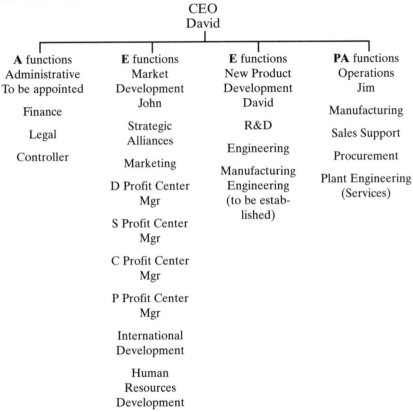

CEO
David

A functions	E functions	E functions	PA functions
Administrative	Market	New Product	Operations
To be appointed	Development	Development	Jim
Finance	John	David	Manufacturing
Legal	Strategic	R&D	Sales Support
Controller	Alliances	Engineering	Procurement
	Marketing	Manufacturing	Plant Engineering
	D Profit Center	Engineering	(Services)
	Mgr	(to be estab-	
	S Profit Center	lished)	
	Mgr		
	C Profit Center		
	Mgr		
	P Profit Center		
	Mgr		
	International		
	Development		
	Human		
	Resources		
	Development		

Process: The company needs concurrent engineering.

Financial resources: Undercapitalized for growing market. The brothers sold a 25-percent chunk of the company and then bought it back. Because of the terms of that buyback, the company cannot afford to go public until the year ——.

Made private placement in ——.

This presents problems: The market is growing, but the company is still undercapitalized and constrained from seeking equity financing in the stock market.

Moreover, because the company has no stock option plan, it has trouble attracting industry talent.

Overall:

A taking over from **E** and **I**.

Declining **E**: founders leaving, no organizational structure to nourish **E** and no incentive systems to attract and keep **E**s.

Manifestations:

- Reactive innovation
- New Product Development is second class
- Marketing function is nonexistent
- Can't get and keep talent; only now starting a stock option plan
- Succession plan nonexistent
- Problem of geographic distances for the leaders
- Disconnected, rising internal focus instead of external focus
- Company has *very strong* **I** as a culture

Barriers to Implementation:

A subsequent meeting revealed that the structure I thought would work will not be applicable because neither John nor David wants to be more active in the business. We have the following situation: The brothers don't want out, and they don't want in. And Jim has had major surgery since the last interview. The normal has now become abnormal, and very soon it will become pathological.

3. Plan of Action

We will accept the assignment if both David and John agree that they must be active for another year, giving time for **E** to grow structurally. During the year, the company should add top management talent, introduce a stock options plan, increase number of profit centers, establish a true marketing division, increase R&D spending, and focus on core competencies, while developing new markets. Finance with debt or find strategic partner. Make Jim head of operations. He can keep the chief operating officer title. **A** should continue to rise.

If above plan is accepted, start the eleven-phase program.

Reaching Prime: The ZZ Case

Now let's consider the case of ZZ, a company in deep Aristocracy. There is no need for me to describe ZZ's problems; they looked a lot like the problems described in this book's chapter on Aristocracy.

ZZ was aging because of its dysfunctional structure and dysfunctional leadership style. The company's aging was not caused by perceived market share: It was actually losing market share, and the mental age of ZZ's leadership was young and vibrant.

An unusual sequence of events preceded our invitation to ZZ. Management, unhappy with the company's information systems, had appointed a study team comprising managers from many corporate functions. One of the team members was browsing through a book store when he came across the first edition of this book. As he turned the pages, he recognized his own company's symptoms of aging. He purchased several copies of the book and distributed them to the rest of the team. Not long after that, the group invited me to make a presentation.

During that day's visit, I assembled a list of the problems the team was supposed to address. It was clear that the members couldn't possibly solve the problems of information flow until they had defined the right structure. The team hired me to help address those structural issues. It didn't take me long to see that the team lacked CAPI to solve the structural problem, and the leader who had authority—one piece of CAPI—was a **PA** type. So I took an approach that calls for starting with a small problem for which there was already CAPI. Gradually, and at the right times, we would enlarge the definition of the problem. To maintain CAPI at all times, new members would need to join the team and others would drop out. In effect, the approach allows us to climb the organizational hierarchy by gradually broadening the definition of the problem. We worked on issues for which the team had CAPI, but we always set aside a piece of the problem for which we need higher CAPI. Our approach gave the team a sense of potency and simultaneously escalated the issues to the level where we could solve the structural issue. In about one month, the team had recomposed itself as a top-level executive group assigned to review the structure of the company.

Together we realized that the structure's lack of **E** was caused by the following design: Marketing was de facto reporting to sales.

The marketing department was therefore ineffective in performing its marketing function. The names of the departments were confusing: Sales was called Marketing, and what was supposed to be the marketing function under sales was appropriately called sales support. Thus, **P** was dominating, and there was no **E** in the client interface subsystem. A second structural cause of aging was that research and development, and manufacturing, both reported to the same vice president. Third, the profit centers were managed by a central planning unit, which I called "the Kremlin." This Kremlin, a staff position, with nobody reporting to it directly, had all the authority to decide what causes profits: prices, budgets, strategies. Beyond the Kremlin no one—except for the top leader—had profit responsibility. In meetings, rather than have the manufacturing vice president report on the cost structure of manufacturing, the planner in the Kremlin made that report. It was classical by-the-book bifurcation of authority from responsibility.

In that organization, as you might expect, each decision required so many committee meetings that it was never clear who was really accountable for results.

The second cause of aging was the functionality of the leadership style. The unapproachable, decisive, command-and-control top person in the structure had the **PAeØ** style. Luckily, the person with whom we worked directly was a **paEI** type, and he took it upon himself to handle the big boss. As you can imagine, there was not much love between the **PAeØ** boss and the **paEI** subordinate, and that complicated the therapy. We had to work with a large team rather than through the **PAei** or **paEI** leaders, getting support from the **EI** while keeping the **PA** fully informed, and never sensing loss of control.

Working with ZZ's top management team, we developed a decentralized structure with multiple profit centers. We dismantled the Kremlin and united responsibility with authority. We then designed an accountability system of budgeting based on *why* the company spends money rather than on *how* it spends money. The new accountability system made it possible to redesign information systems that serve the company—the assignment that initiated the revolution.

How did the **PA** leader accept those changes? It took continuous and timely proactive briefings with presentations describing the merits of the change by all members of the CAPI team.

When it came time to implement the new structure, we ran into a problem: The reward structure didn't reward the profit-center orientation of the new structure. Clearly, that had to change, but to get that change, we had to secure the cooperation of the legal and personnel departments—big, big **A**s. Because they were afraid to alter the reward system, getting their cooperation and making the changes took an entire year.

We had reached the point where we could stretch the organization, budgets, and key performance indicators to their limits. We had formed a mission with which each and everyone could identify, a structure to deliver it, and an information system to report whether the desired is actually happening. Using the methodology, in just one year, the company improved the bottom line by millions of dollars from cutting unnecessary costs, and increasing revenues.

During the year and a half we worked with ZZ, a company whose performance had trailed behind the rest of its industry, it moved from Aristocracy to Prime, becoming its industry's leader.

BB: The Prime That Might Have Been

The following case is an example of a situation in which, I believe, we failed to deliver the necessary treatment. I present it as an illustration of the complexity involved in applying the methodology.

About twelve years ago, Kenneth and Paula Friendly, the founders of BB, opened the doors of their first store. Right from the beginning, the couple's passion for social responsibility drove their business. They were determined that their organization would create a minimum amount of waste and no pollution. Furthermore, it would be a platform for social change. They pledged to give their customers products of the highest possible value: no hype, no marketing, no manipulation. The business started in a big **I** way, and before long, people recognized it as a leader of consciously responsible business behavior.

The company grew fast through franchising. People clamored for franchises, but Kenneth and Paula franchised only to those who shared their values. Every store was more than an outlet for the BB product line: Each store was an outlet for promoting the couple's social agenda. The stores distributed a vast array of pamphlets promoting the campaign-of-the-moment: One month, BB campaigned against child abuse, the next month it was supporting the orphans of war, and always, it was defending the environment. As the company grew and its mission gained notice, Kenneth became the darling of the environmental movement. He was a frequent and popular speaker at conventions.

Kenneth approved BB's new products and innovative guerrilla marketing promotions. He provided the **EI** roles.

Paula Friendly, although she was also noted as a leader of the new business behavior paradigm, was primarily responsible for overseeing the administrative areas and the company's financing. She paid more attention to the **PA** side of the business.

BB had a special department of vision and values. Its role was to promote the agenda of social consciousness and to assure that the company never strayed from its values and vision.

All in all, BB's culture was very strongly **EI**. It had the ingredients of a company to reach Prime. The company's franchisees and employees were committed to its values with a nearly religious fervor. Employees, of their own volition, turned down their office lights in order to save on energy, and because they cared about preserving the world's forests, they watched their use of every piece of paper. This was a committed bunch if I have ever seen one. The company was growing by leaps and bounds and expanding rapidly.

So what was the problem?

A common friend referred BB's founders to us, and they called on us for help. They called us because of their apprehensions about succession planning. They wanted to insure that the people who replaced them would share their system of values. "How do we sustain the social consciousness that is the driving force of our existence?"

Our diagnosis, however, indicated that there were additional issues they needed to address. BB was excessively dependent on Kenneth, whose schedule was filled with speaking engagements that took him to meetings and conventions around the world. People throughout the company were unable to deal with the vacuum created by his absence. No decisions that involved product development, promotions, the social and political agenda, or strategic hiring could be decided without Kenneth. The company would have been suffering from a full-blown seagull syndrome if it had not been for

Paula. She screened ideas and channeled Kenneth's periodic outbursts of creativity for the organization.

In addition to having a personalized and monopolized declining **E**, the company was weak in **A** and in **P**.

A weaknesses

Supply was disorganized. Production at BB's three manufacturing facilities was not coordinated. The company lacked a common program for logistics, production planning, and purchasing. Second, there was almost no formal organizational structure. For instance, BB had designated one of its franchisees to be the company's worldwide sales manager. Not only was he supposed to do that job on a part-time basis, that so-called sales manager lived several hours' flight time away from his office at BB headquarters. Nor did the company have a vice president of marketing.

The board of directors, comprised exclusively of company insiders, posed another problem: There was no operational distinction between the executive committee and the board. Thus the governance function was weak, and there was no forum with an explicit mandate to review strategic decisions. The executive committee dealt with operational issues, and because the strategic issues were interwoven with operational discussion, they didn't get sufficient air and review time.

E weaknesses

The company started with a great innovative vision that the market really needed: honest products, honest promotion, honest manufacturing with no pollution, and a real commitment to humanity. But it didn't take long for the competition to copy that message. True, the competition's effort, offering more hype than honest action, lacked BB's spiritual foundation. Nevertheless, BB's competitors were able to promote the image of responsible behavior. BB's **I** was its biggest asset. Its enthusiasm, the commitment of its franchisees, and the innovative, truly socially responsible approach BB introduced to its industry are what made the company successful. But the company was suffering because its message of environmental consciousness and responsible manufacturing had been adopted by the competition. Several me-too chains had opened, and BB's anti-marketing values started to work against it, making it appear outdated in light of the competition's stronger marketing acumen. The company's stores were not attracting mature audiences with money to spend because BB did not innovate in its merchandising, a field in which the competition excelled.

P weakness

BB's management hadn't really decided whether BB was a retail organization with franchise outlets or a wholesale organization selling to independent outlets. There was no clarity about what BB was doing and who its real clients were. That ambiguity caused some franchisees to behave quite independently, defying headquarters on issues of promotions and merchandising. The confusion was expressed in the organizational chart, which showed the regional directors acting like coordinators, hearing the needs of the franchisees and taking orders, rather than managing the outlets and supervising franchise operations.

Our diagnosis was that the company, deep in abnormal Go-Go, was caught in the founder's trap. It needed **E** renovation (the company needed to reinvent itself, to find a strategy that will differentiate it because what it lost was its uniqueness in the marketplace) and it needed to institutionalize the **E**, provide **P** focus, and **A** structure.

A tall order indeed.

Paula was the one who called for help. In retrospect, I see that we made mistakes right from the beginning of our involvement at BB. We worked with Paula, the cofounder who wanted a solution, rather than with Kenneth, the founder whose involvement was essential to solve BB's problems. Kenneth never really bought into our involvement. He was mostly—if not exclusively—interested in **I**: in values. He really lost interest in merchandising and marketing; it was already old hat for him. His real passion was to change the world, to make a real difference. Structure and disciplined meetings were anathema to him because he believed in freedom of expression and creativity. He was a disciple of the new school of managerial thought—in which vision and values are the driving forces of organization—and he was convinced that the company needed more vision and values, certainly *no* more structure. Structure in his opinion led to bureaucracy.

Our problem, right from the start and on through the end of our involvement with BB, was that our plan of action was not adopted by Kenneth, only by Paula.

We had reason to insist on structure. BB had to reinvent itself in the marketplace. The company needed a new strategy. It needed structure to deliver the strategy and a team of people to make it work. But we needed people with whom to develop the new strategy. The company, as I have said, had no one in charge of sales, and it lacked a sales structure to deliver any strategy. We needed topnotch people for another reason. If the founders truly wanted out, if they really wanted successors, they would need to have an insider grow into the leadership position. Because of the values BB espoused, it would be impossible to import outsiders and expect that they would be ready to take over the leadership. A true successor would need to become a part of the value system, showing leadership and commitment before anybody hands him or her the "keys to the store." My plan was to place world-class leaders in marketing and sales, and after two years, we would be able to see which of them should assume the chief executive's position. We needed a structure to institutionalize **E**; to rejuvenate **E** with a new strategy that would once again distinguish the company in the marketplace, and a structure that will solve the succession problem.

Easier said than done. Kenneth felt that marketing was not at all important. Traditional marketing approaches were repugnant to him. A senior vice president from a leading retailer was introduced as a potential marketing vice president. We hoped eventually to groom that person for the role of chief executive officer. Kenneth rejected the candidate. We then took considerable time and effort to get that person appointed to the board—the first outsider to serve on BB's board. Our hope was that, over time, Kenneth would get used to that individual, learn to respect him, and accept him in an executive position.

All attempts to build a true marketing organization failed. At a certain point, Paula reluctantly took the marketing leadership role. That way, a position was created that could, later on, be filled by someone else. Paula soon begged off. Kenneth was creative, dominating, and highly opinionated. It was too difficult for anyone to stand up to him. It was not that Kenneth was no good. On the contrary, he was the best in the field. But he wasn't always available, and he claimed that he wanted out.

The problem was not only marketing. During the three years we worked with BB, we were also unable to get the company to hire a sales vice president. There was an urgent need for somebody to serve in that role, but, because management could not decide whether BB was a wholesaler or a retailer with franchisee outlets, it was impossible to know whom to hire to do what. The most qualified candidates withdrew their candidacy.

We couldn't solve that problem simply by making a resolution. The company needed to decide what its profit centers were. As a wholesaler there was only one profit center—headquarters. If the company were, however, a retailer with franchising outlets, each region could be a profit center. If the second choice was decided on, we would need to restaff the regional leadership. The regional desks had been staffed by people who were administrators and coordinators, answering questions from the franchisees, not managing them.

The company would also need to change accounting and budgeting systems. The accounting/finance department objected. Its people didn't want to change the information flow and budgeting systems. They thought that was unnecessary. They were right from their point of view: They were doing the budgeting and to continue that way, there was no need to change the system. But to change the nature of the organization—to have more **E** in the system, by having product/market managers within the regional structure accountable for profitability—it was imperative to make the change.

We could not get anyone to move on it. Paula supported the direction, but the finance people dragged their feet endlessly. They never said "no," but they never acted on it either.

We were attempting to institutionalize **E** by building a marketing department, decentralizing the company by product lines so that more than one person would be leading the company strategically, and creating a store planning and merchandising department. Our efforts, as I said, weren't very fruitful. Our initiatives moved slowly, far too slowly. We were, however, building **A** in the meantime: restructuring manufacturing, organizing and coordinating the supply function, and organizing the sales function for whoever would be heading it.

As we were working on the **A**, Kenneth was growing increasingly belligerent and resentful of our efforts. He felt that we were increasing the bureaucracy of the company. Paula, who was responsible for the **A** role, understood the value of our recommendations, and she supported us. We were getting between the two of them, and that became increasingly problematic, because they were married. Personal life and business life intermingled.

Because we were having so much difficulty stabilizing and institutionalizing **E**, we redirected more and more of our attentions to **A**, and knowing that we needed some political breathing space, we worked on the **I**. But that, too, was a problem. The methodology builds **I**, mutual trust and respect, using disciplined relations. That is to say, we build **I** the **A** way, and Kenneth's resentment focused on the growth of **A**. In some ways, he was absolutely right. Just as we were helping to build an external board of directors, hoping to demonopolize **E** by creating strategic **E**, we discovered that Paula had promised the legal vice president, the financial vice president, and the vice president of supplies that they would be members of the board. So as new members joined from the outside, so did more insiders. And each of those insiders were **A**s in role and style. With no leadership in marketing and sales, there were no inside **E** candidates to join the board. Naturally, that heavy concentration of **A** made the board highly unacceptable to Kenneth, the **E** founder, and he justifiably accused us of having increased bureaucratization of the company.

The executive committee continued to act as if it were the board. After all, except for a very few outsiders, all those on the executive committee were on the board. Everyone was confused about who decided what. Kenneth met our attempts to organize and clarify roles with hostility. He truly believed that all our talk about structure and roles was more bureaucracy for his company.

We were unable to get BB to institutionalize or rejuvenate **E**. **P** remained untended until after we'd left. We found no vice president of sales who was appropriate to succeed the founders. The **A** assignment was left incomplete; we were unable to convince the accounting people to reorganize the information to reflect the desired structure, fostering and building **E**.

Paula, the **A** cofounder, eventually decided that life has more to offer than work and, for all intents and purposes, reduced her involvement in the company. As our supporter was out, we were out.

Was it a total failure?

By my standards we failed: We did not free the company from the founder's trap.

Is there any good news? We were able to build some **A**. We helped BB clarify roles and showed management how to run meetings and work in teams to solve problems. Furthermore, we helped the company organize and integrate its supply function.

My one consolation is that without our involvement—and despite our limited success—BB's situation could have been much worse. I believe our intervention prolonged BB's life. I regret that BB, a company with the **I** ingredient that could have been on the optimal path to Prime, couldn't overcome its problems. This intervention and its disappointments does, however, confirm my theory: **I** alone is not enough although it is exciting. Although **I** alone is better than **A** alone, organizational health requires all four **PAEI** roles.

Long-term prospects? I believe that the best Paula and Kenneth can and should do is to sell their company. But, I believe they are emotionally incapable of doing that. My prognosis? Events on the typical path imply that the company will eventually isolate Kenneth, the **E** founder, and BB will lose its market dominance, becoming a Prime that might have been.

What did we learn from this case? We confirmed that if the key player does not see the problem nor is he committed to the plan of action, our intervention by definition cannot work. Kenneth never saw the problem the way we did, and Paula's commitment was not enough. It's impossible to solve a problem if the person whose cooperation you need does not share your perception of the problem and disagrees with the treatment. Kenneth was an extreme **E** with practically no **A** style. He could see no benefit to structured organization or processes. His entire focus was process and culture, vision and values. He wanted a positive culture to substitute for a managerial process. Without his trust or respect for the therapy, we were doomed to fail.

Simple, right? Why did we not see it? What should we have done? We should have resigned. That's the simple truth. But within Adizes Institute there was disagreement about what we should do. Some felt it was unprofessional to give up. And, because our relationship with Paula was so good, we felt that our resignation would be an act of treason. What we can all agree on today is that we shouldn't have accepted BB as a client in the first place until we were sure that Kenneth agreed with our definition of the problem and the treatment plan. That is where we failed. If anyone asked Kenneth he would agree: We failed, but Paula believes we succeeded beyond her expectations. She believes the company would have been much worse without our intervention.

What is success anyway? Go tell.

The CC Company: Behavior on the Optimal Path

paeI—The Fertile Womb

Consider the case of a company I identify here as CC. The founders have known each other for years. They respected each other's achievements as they advanced in their respective careers after college. Joe went to Harvard for an MBA, and following graduation, he worked for a highly respected consulting firm. He earned successive promotions, and it didn't take long for him to become a partner in the firm. Bill studied engineering at a premier university, and after graduating, he started a series of companies, all of which he sold. The two dreamed of one day working together. But they didn't know what kind of business would be right for them.

paEI—Conception

When the Internet craze took hold, they saw an abundance of opportunities. Their only question was which of all the opportunities should they take. They spent some energy considering three possibilities, eventually deciding against all of them and deciding to explore other ideas. Neither fellow left his job, but weekends and late into the night, they talked, building what-if scenarios.

Finally, they zeroed in on an idea that excited both of them. It had tremendous market potential, and both wanted to spend time on it. They were passionate about the idea, but they also recognized the potential pitfalls. After all, not all of the companies Bill had started had been remarkable successes, and Joe, having worked in a consulting firm, had seen more than a few dreams turn into nightmares.

Both men knew the new venture would take an enormous amount of time, and they wanted to be sure that they would be working on something they both truly liked. And, because they knew that for at least a few years, the venture would take them away from their families, Bill and Joe made sure to involve their wives. They told their wives about their idea, asking them whether they were willing to endure what it would take to make a success of the business. Both women requested that no matter what, one night of every week their husbands would be home for dinner with the family, and one day of every weekend, no matter what, they must spend with their children. Those were the boundaries to which everyone agreed.

pAEI—Pregnancy

Joe prepared a business plan. His plan included a market study, an assessment of the competition, projected income statements, organizational structures for the next three years, strategies for market penetration, financial forecasts of cash needs, lists of potential investors, pitches for investors, and the investors' projected returns. Joe and Bill discussed the plan extensively, bringing in advisors, venture capitalists, and marketing specialists to evaluate it.

The two agreed on their roles in the company, and they committed their job descriptions to paper. Joe would be the chief executive officer, and Bill, who would be the engineer and chairman of the board, would not be active in the day-to-day. He had many other interests. Joe realized that without Bill's full-time support, there would be too much for him to handle. So, together, they looked for a third person to be the chief operating officer. They selected another friend—a person who was already involved in an Internet company —to head up the sales effort. If he would join, they said, they would give him an equity position in their company. At the same time, they decided that every employee of their company would also have stock options.

Even though all three were still working for other companies, they wrote and agreed to descriptions of their individual responsibilities. Bill, although he was chairman of the board, took responsibility for the technology and product development. Joe, having worked for a consulting firm, took on financing and financial control. The third partner, Dave, took responsibility for sales. They designed salary plans, made a pro forma budget, and wrote a paper about their vision and the values that would form the basis of their enterprise. They pledged to enrich the communities in which they would operate and to provide a service their clients would view as exceeding their expectations.

Their next step was to design systems that would allow them to monitor their progress and ensure they did not deviate from their plans. They decided how often they would hold staff meetings and the rules by which they would reach binding decisions. For instance, any decision involving the expenditure of more than 10,000 dollars during the first three years or the appointment of anyone to a managerial position would require their unanimous agreement. They drew up a list of potential board members. Following their meetings, the entrepreneurs shared potluck suppers that evolved into a company tradition. Every Wednesday afternoon, the executive committee would meet from three until six. They would break for a dinner the executive committee members had prepared, and then they continued the meeting after together they had tidied up. "Companies where people break bread together do not fight," Bill maintained.

PAeI—Prime Birth

Finally, the day dawned when all three felt confidence in their plans. They informed their employers they would be leaving to start a company that would not be a competitor. They rented warehouse space with the capacity for expansion. The owner of the empty warehouse had agreed they could convert space for office use as they needed it, and their investment in renovation would be deducted from their rent. Before they had quit their jobs, they had secured startup financing based on their business plan. Their backers knew their background and believed in the plan. Although there were no sales, the budget allowed for hiring, because they had secured financing. They hired as many employees as the plan had specified. They did their cash-flow projections and monitored their expenses closely. They held executive meetings according to their plan, and they recorded minutes of decisions for follow up.

After the agreement of the executive committee, decisions on financing and major appointments went to the board for approval. In the early days, the three founders were the only insiders on the board. The outsiders comprised representatives of the venture capitalists and presidents of two larger high-technology companies. The founders retained a lawyer to serve as legal counsel, a public relations firm to assist their marketing efforts, and an investor-relations firm to prepare for the future public offering. The founders took their remuneration in a combination of cash and company stock and stock options.

Among the earliest hires, the company's human resources manager projected manpower needs and recruited and screened applicants well in advance of when they would be needed. In this way, the company avoided some of the pressure of growing a business. The company trained its sales people so that they weren't in the field until they had demonstrated their proficiency. And the original financial investment supported each of those expenditures because they had been included in the business plan. They also hired a young political science graduate. As community liaison, she arranged for the company to contribute free services to children and schools. She also organized visits from the chamber of commerce to the company and established a supportive network from the community.

The company did raise additional funds—bridge financing—to introduce an improved product to the market and to finance expansion. At no time—even during crises brought about by the pressures of product development deadlines and sales commitments—did anyone start flinging accusations at any other member of the organization.

The company treated everyone with respect. Those employees who did not meet management's expectations were told that the company would help them find work elsewhere. People whose productivity did not meet the company's expectations and people who complained about their jobs and failed to perform were invited to meet with the president. The president listened to their impressions of the situation, trying to see whether the complaints were legitimate and, if so, whether they could be solved organizationally. If the issue was personal, and there was no way the company could meet the complainer's aspirations, the person would be released with severance pay and help finding another job.

Management hired with extreme caution, and everyone's first six months of employment served as a trial period. New hires who did not gain the respect and trust of their fellow employees were let go. The company made many bad hires. Despite their efforts to select the best, their expectations of what *best* means were so high that only a rare few passed the test. Those who stayed were eligible for generous stock options. Long before the company went public, the company hired a lawyer to work with its accounting firm to design a stock valuation plan.

The company conducted business in an open environment, and the president and the chief executive officer shared space and a secretary. Their working space was no different from any other open space. Because their office area was at one end of the building, the farthest from the elevators, the chief executive and the president had to walk by all the other offices every time they arrived or left their desks. On their way in or out they had opportunities to talk to everyone without preparation or appointment. And, of course, the executives' visitors experienced the same route, getting a very positive picture of the company as they made their way among the employees. The open design also encouraged everyone to keep the working environment tidy and professional looking. There were closed rooms for meetings, and anyone—the chief executive officer and the president, included—who wanted to use one of the enclosed spaces had to make a reservation in advance. Parking was an issue. Because there was insufficient parking next to the premises, even the executives scurried to get parking places. There was no pecking order because there were no reserved parking spaces.

As the company developed, management wanted to form strategic alliances with local organizations that had marketing muscle. The company wanted to work with established organizations and rejected opportunities unless they were with blue-ribbon companies. Taking the long view, the executives stuck to their plans despite several aggressive offerings from entrepreneurial organizations.

PAEI—Mature, Sustainable Prime

In only five years, the company was ready to go public, and its initial public offering was oversubscribed. The company had grown to 2,000 employees, and its two organizational restructurings proceeded without a ripple, only reassuring its investors. The financial reports were always timely and accurate. The executives always realized their projections. The company's income statements showed revenues that were constantly and continuously rising. It was a company that people, employees, investors, and customers felt they could trust.

Having achieved success in one market and with one line of products, the founders decided it was time to expand. They reorganized again, making each product line a profit center with managers responsible for the profitability. A change in accounting systems enabled profit tracking for each product line. The sales organization continued to sell all the products, and each product line contributed its fair share of sales costs to support the shared sales force. In the same way, profit centers shared the costs of accounting and office services. Manufacturing and marketing acted like an internal supplier of services. The executive committee expanded to 15 members, including the product managers as well as the functional managers.

To this day, the company's original mission—the mission that many years ago, Joe, Bill, and Dave wrote when they were dreaming and planning—has a place of honor on the wall next to the company's front door.

Did we work with this company? No. They did not feel they needed us. And they were right.

Explorations of Some Eternal Questions

Now let's have some fun. We'll let our imagination soar and our intellectual curiosity take us where it will.

Creation

Some time ago, I spoke with a Hassidic Jew who had read the first edition of this book. He asked me, "Did you know that your whole lifecycle theory is in the first few verses of the Old Testament, in the story of God's creation of heaven and earth?"

I turned to the opening chapter of the Bible:

"In the beginning God created the heaven and the earth.

And the earth was without form, and void; and darkness was upon the face of the deep.

And the **spirit** of God hovered over the face of the waters.

And God said, 'Let there be **light**.' And there was light . . . And God divided the light from darkness . . . One day.

And God said, 'Let there be a firmament in the midst of the waters, and let it divide the waters from the waters.' And God made the firmament, and divided the **waters** which were under the firmament from the waters which were above the firmament . . . And God called the firmament Heaven . . . Second day.

And God said, 'Let the waters under the heaven be gathered together unto one place and let the dry land appear. And God called the dry land **Earth**; and the gathering together of the waters He called Seas. And God said, let the earth bring forth grass, the herb yielding seed, and the fruit tree yielding fruit . . . Third day."

Let me present my thoughts about that passage.

"In the beginning God created the heaven and the earth.

To me, that means that the first thing God did was to create the world. Good! But, how?

And the earth was without form, and void; and darkness was upon the face of the deep.

Note that all the ingredients were there: **earth** and **darkness**, which is the opposite of light, soon to be "created." How was it "created" if it was already there? Water was there as well. Didn't the spirit of God hover over the face of the water? How is it that God created something that was already there? Everything was, shall I say, dormant? It was there without form, or as the original in Hebrew says "Tohu va vohu." That literally means, in a total mess. The ingredients were there but without order, name, boundaries, or sequence. Remember the four dancers standing, waiting to learn their own dances and how to dance together?

*And the **spirit** of God hovered over the face of the **waters**.*

Wait, wait, wait! Where did this spirit come from? Note that this is the first time that **spirit** is mentioned. The Hebrew word from the original is "ruach." That literally means "wind," which is **air**. The spirit was not dormant. It was not created. It was there all the time. Without it, nothing would or could have happened. There is no life without air. When we look for life on other planets, we look for oxygen. If there is water there is oxygen, and it is possible that there may be life. Aren't water and air (oxygen) chemically related? The fastest way to die is to be without air. (Lack of oxygen, then, should shorten lives.)

So what did God, the spirit of Life, do first?

And God said, 'Let there be light.' And there was light.

Light comes from the sun, and the sun is heat, energy, **fire**.

We can see how God activated the elements. Fire was activated first. Please notice what I am saying. It was not created. It was not created because it was already there. It was activated, and the creation was in the act of activation. How, though, was creation activated? By giving names, boundaries, and roles.

And God said, 'Let there be a firmament in the midst of the waters and let it divide the waters from the waters.' And God made the firmament, and divided the waters which were under the firmament from the waters which were above the firmament; and it was so . . . And God called the firmament Heaven . . .

Water was activated next. It was there, and God activated it by setting boundaries and assigning names. We do not know what something is until we can name it; that is how order is made. And that is how babies learn to speak. They request names for everything.

And God said, 'Let the waters under the heaven be gathered together unto one place and let the dry land appear.

And God called the dry land Earth; and the gathering together of the waters He called Seas.

Earth—land—is last. Again note that God did not create it. It was there, he just activated it, giving it life, and now that the four elements—air, fire (energy), water, and earth—are active, He is ready for business and orders:

Let the earth bring forth grass, the herb yielding seed and tree yielding fruits.

And now that there is food, God is ready to create the fish and, later, the animals. Only when all that is ready does He create man in His own image.

Why, I wonder does God create this self-image. God started everything and ended with a replica: the beginning and the end meet. Like the burning bush, there is no beginning and there is no end.

And God saw that it was good."

Let us analyze. None of us humans creates anything new. It is all there. We just discover it, give it a name, define it, understand it, and by doing so, give it life. Even God does not create something out of nothing. Everything was there at the start, and God gave it life. How? God gave it spirit, or translated literally from the original Hebrew, God gave it a breath of air. The literal translation of the original says "ruach Elohim," wind of God. Spirit in Hebrew is "neshama," a word that comes from the same root as "neshima," which is breath. Air, which we all share, is what makes us interdependent. It is oxygen that enables life and, in doing so, causes the entropy that brings about aging and, eventually, death. Without oxygen there would be no life, and without life there would be no death. At birth, we are farther from death than we will ever be again. From that point on, we are slowly dying. Living is the process of dying.

Life starts with the first use of oxygen, and once conception occurs, the mother's blood supplies the growing embryo with oxygen-carrying blood. When a baby is born, its first act is to take a breath, but that act is like lifting the rock. Organization was born before our beer drinkers found a rock blocking their passage, and life begins long before a baby is born. Life starts not when the fetus experiences pain but when the creation starts using oxygen, when it is conceived.

Another interesting point is that God put order to the mess, and He did it one day at a time. Even God takes His job one day at a time. That's something big **E**s can learn. They act more omnipotent than God. They try to cram a year into a day.

Now, let's reconsider organizational lifecycles. Just as in God's Creation of the universe, **I** is not created, it is there. We need only to be conscious of it. Like all the other elements—air, fire, water, and earth—**I** is there. It is, however, not activated like the others. It is active by itself. It is, was, and always will be.

Who, then, is first?

The first thing that God, the life force—the Spirit that is, was, and always will be—activated was light, **fire**. The sun, the symbol of fire, is what permits us to discriminate day from night, light from darkness. Next, God activated **water** and then, **earth**.

What was going on?

Early philosophers claimed that there are four elements to creation: air, water, earth, and fire.[1] And they are not alone. Chinese medicine, thousands of years old, uses the same four elements in diagnosis and therapy. Homeopathic medicine uses those elements, too.

Let's use **PAEI** to code those elements. Visualize fire. It consumes, destroys, and, at the same time, enables life. If there were no sun there would be no life. Fire is, to me, **E**. I suggest that air is **I**, and, again we can see that without **I**, there is no **E**. Without air, the fire is extinguished.

Water is **A**; Earth is **P**. Why? I do not know, and I cannot explain except to say that just as **A** and **I** are related so are water and air.

So, how was the Creation accomplished? **I** was always there. Then **E** and **A** were activated, followed, finally, by **P**.

Is that not the optimal path?

The Meaning of Love

Some years ago Ram Dass,[2] whose work I admire, attended a lecture of mine, and told me that in the future he intends to use my definition of love. Since he liked it, let me share it with you.

What is love?[3] I am not talking about sexual passion. How does the song go?

"A bell is not a bell until you ring it;
A song is not a song until you sing it;
A tree is not a tree until you see it;
Love is not love until you give it."

Aha. Love. Giving. Let's explore this a bit more.

Why do you take your little kids to the circus? Is it so that you can write in your diary "On such and such a date I took the kids to the circus," and when you are old and feeble they can return the favor, perhaps with compounded interest? I don't think so. Nor do you take them because you love the circus, or because you couldn't get a baby sitter. You probably don't even watch the circus. You watch your children giggling, clapping their hands, laughing, and having a wonderful time. You get your joy from theirs. That is love.

Life is give *and* take—conscious interdependence. In love, give *is* take. When the act of giving is, simultaneously, the act of taking, that is love. In making your kids or spouse happy, you find your own happiness. There is no postponed gratification. It is one and the same. The happier they are, the happier you are.

Love is Integration in the highest degree.

Giving to someone you love is not giving to someone else at all. It is giving to an extension of yourself. The pain or joy of your beloved is your pain or joy. Think of how you feel when your children get hurt. You are one with the people you love.

God is ultimate love because God is the ultimate Integration. With no beginning and no end, God is the ultimate conscious Integrated Interdependency. Everything God has created has a purpose and the purpose is to serve, to do something for something else—conscious interdependency.

Integration heals. In my introduction to this book, I said that "love heals" is a popular expression. Haven't you noticed how youthful even older people look when they are in love? Love retards aging while hate accelerates it. Love integrates while hate disintegrates.

Love prolongs life. Living with love is to live life to the fullest. Every minute of it. Popular psychologists tell us that to live fuller lives we should live in the moment, in the present. Eastern philosophies have been teaching that for thousands of years.

Why live in the moment? Why live in the present? Because that is when you are integrated. Your body is not in one place, while your mind is somewhere else. And notice that at the moment of orgasm, you, all of you—body, mind, spirit, emotions—is there. If not, you will not experience orgasm.

Hate shortens life. That is why forgiveness benefits the forgiver. Forgiveness prolongs the life of the forgiver. Yogi Amrit Desai says, "When you resist nothing, you automatically experience love."

To start a company, an organization, or to create anything, you must be in love with your idea. Unless you are in love with that idea, you will be unable to build the commitment necessary to keep you going. Love is what fuels creation even if that creation is destructive. Morbid as the idea was, Hitler was in love with his idea of annihilating the Jewish people. He was passionate about it. And he created a holocaust. Without his fierce passion, it could never have happened.

Love, by definition, is selfish. The more you make your beloved happy, the happier you are. It is for your own benefit. If you try to make a person happy, for his benefit only, and you, yourself take no joy in his happiness, or, if you please only yourself, that ain't love. Starting a company with love means wanting to serve others in a way that makes you happy, too. The joy they get from your service should bring you joy. That's why disciples of eastern religions say, "Thank you for allowing me to serve you." You might be puzzled, "What the heck? He is serving me and thanking me rather than demanding that I thank him for the service? Is the guy taking something stronger than water?" The truth is that the more they serve you, bringing you happiness, the more happiness they feel.

Imagine loving the world, the trees, the air, and the water with the same intensity you love your own children. Would you pollute? Would you poison the Earth? Imagine loving people, period, whatever race, color, or religion they might be. The more you love them, the more you get from life. Mother Teresa did not have it bad. She must have been a very happy woman. (By the way, I am proud to tell you that I was born in her birth place, Skopje, Macedonia. When I met her, it was quite a thrill to speak with her in our native language.)

The Formation of a Nation

I believe that people who founded really significant enterprises never followed the typical path: I believe that Buddha, Jesus, Mohammed, and Moses all followed the optimal path. I know nothing of the lives of Buddha, Jesus, and Mohammed, and I have done no research to document my hypothesis, but having had a Jewish education, I do know a bit about Moses from the stories of the Bible.

The lifecycle of Moses's leadership began with his realization that although he had been reared as an Egyptian in the Pharaoh's palace, he was, in fact, a Hebrew. Had he not realized that, he would never have led the Hebrews out of Egypt to the promised land. His awakening was the **paeI** stage, which starts with awareness.

The conception, **paEI**, occurred when Moses encountered the burning bush and God informed him of the mission: He, Moses, was to lead the Hebrews, the people of Israel, out of Egypt to the promised land. And God tells him the *why*: It is the land I promised to your forefathers, Abraham, Isaac, and Jacob.

That is a big idea—as big an **E** as one can imagine: Take the people—the men, women, children, their flocks, and all their possessions—out of one country and lead them to new lives in another country. That would be a major assignment for any long-distance moving company. And, as it should be in the early stage, God, unlike many human **E**s, does more than just give Moses the idea, leaving him to discover his own implementation. God gives Moses a plan. It is a real Courtship of the lifecycle, a healthy one, with well-defined *why, what, how,* and *who.*

Why? The people are suffering under the Egyptians. God says, "I have heard their cry." This is the "push" strategy for change from the past. But God also includes another *why*, a "pull" strategy. He wants Moses to bring the Hebrews "unto a land flowing with milk and honey."

God also specifies the *who*—Moses and Aaron, his brother—and the *how*—will "gather the elders" and go with them to tell

Pharaoh that the Hebrews need three days to go into the desert to make sacrifices. Furthermore, God tells Moses, "I know that the king of Egypt will not give you leave to go . . . And I will put forth My hand and smite Egypt with all My wonders . . . . And it shall come to pass, that, when you go, you shall not go empty. And every woman shall ask of her neighbor...jewels of silver and jewels of gold . . ." God gives Moses specific details of how to go about getting out of Egypt.

Moses set forth, then, with a pretty good business plan: *what* to do, *why* to do it, *how* to do it, and *who* should do it. And, because the bush was burning without being consumed, there was remarkable proof that the plan did come, if not from God, at least from something very powerful. Still, Moses submits the idea to reality testing: He asks God, Why should the people believe me? And even when God reassures Moses, telling him that He will be with him, Moses continues to hesitate. God gives Moses incredible powers: Moses makes a rod into a serpent and returns it to its original state. He makes his hand leprous and returns it to health simply by placing it against his bosom. Even when God gives him the power to turn water into blood, Moses continues to doubt whether he can carry out God's instructions. Moses is submitting God to reality testing! Would you believe that? He doesn't doubt that it is God who is speaking to him. He believes it is God, but he wonders whether God has thought the idea through fully. They will not listen to me, he says. I stutter, and Pharaoh will refuse to let us go. Moses thinks of all the reasons not to go forward. That is reality testing as it should be, and it should serve as a model for entrepreneurs of the future. If Moses could challenge the reality of God's idea, shouldn't mortal entrepreneurs test their own ideas?

God solved Moses's speech problem by telling him to take Aaron, and together they would act as a complementary team. This is an interesting point. If God could heal a leprous hand, why didn't He simply cure Moses's stuttering? Because, I suggest, God wants Moses to be like the rest of us—human with frailties and deficiencies. The way to solve the problem of Moses's speech impediment is not with a miraculous cure, but with the strength of a complementary team. And that is what entrepreneurs should do, too. None of us is perfect. We all need to find our complementary team. If we work well together, we can strive for perfection, which none of us can attain alone.

In response to Moses's apprehensions, God adapts the plan, altering the original assignment. Notice that God is flexible. God learns from Moses, a mere human, changing the plan to accommodate Moses's doubts. God listens to and responds to each doubt Moses expresses. He doesn't question Moses's loyalty, and He doesn't threaten him. Shouldn't a mortal entrepreneur be at least as accommodating?

Moses accepts the assignment and leads the Hebrews out of Egypt. But the ex-slaves were undisciplined and not used to being free. The Israelite tribes, therefore, spend forty years wandering through the wilderness, during which a new generation is trained to follow a set of new rules. What rules? Moses received the Ten Commandments from God, followed by rules on top of rules. A major part of the first five books of the Old Testament is devoted to rules: what is permitted, required, and forbidden along with how to perform specified rituals. Parts of Leviticus and Numbers constitute a "manual" of rules and specifications. Now there's big **A**. Those who violated the regulations were stoned to death, or the earth swallowed them in an apparent earthquake. As we can see, even for God and his servant Moses, it's difficult to instill **A**. It took them forty years, and a whole generation had to die. Some were even executed.

In spite of the rising **A**, **E** did not recede. The Israelites were dreaming and advancing toward the promised land, and time after time, Moses reminded them of "the land of milk and honey" that awaited them. They had vision. They were learning values.

Jethro, the father-in-law of Moses, must have been the world's first management consultant. He advised Moses that it was wrong for him to exhaust himself trying to be a judge to everybody. He recommended that Moses divide the people into groups so that intermediary judges could hear their disputes. He created a hierarchy and was apparently the first to apply the principles of span of control.

As we can see, the people of Israel were getting **A**ed. That was the Adolescent stage of the lifecycle of the Israeli people, and it took forty years to start, and it continued long after they crossed the Jordan River.

Inspired and organized, **IEA** in place, the Israelites are ready for **P**—taking over the promised land. Note, please, that although God promised Canaan to the Hebrews forever and ever, they had to fight for it. Why didn't God just clean the slate and give them a clear title? Like a father trying to rear strong children, He made the Israelites earn their inheritance.

Moses, however, did not cross the Jordan River to the promised land. But, as I mentioned earlier, that, in my opinion, was not a punishment. It was God's gift to Moses: He would forever remain revered as the man who succeeded in creating the nation of Israel.

Samuel I describes the Israelites as they continued to struggle with symptoms of typical Adolescence. We read about the confrontation between Samuel and Saul. Samuel represents the **EI** stream within which God is king, and Saul represents the **PA** stream: He is the secular king. It is a struggle between church and state: values and vision, the religion as a spiritual force versus man-made rules of conduct.

When, then, was the Jewish nation in Prime? During the era of King David. At that time, the nation enjoyed full integration of the spiritual and the profane. The decline starts as expected when form takes over function. As Arnold Toynbee noted, when civilizations start to age, they start building big structures. And King Solomon built the Temple. Thereafter, we read about the nation's loss of faith, disintegration, and diaspora.

Despite 2,000 years of persecution, the Jewish nation survives with the Bible God gave to Moses. It is a book of vision and values as well as a clear-cut manual for **A**. And at least once a year, all Jews turn toward the land God promised the Israelites and say, "Be shana haba'ah beyerushalayim." Next year in Jerusalem. It is, I believe, an affirmation of **E** and the tremendous affinity that sustains the Jewish people: **I**. The secret of Jewish survival was not **P**—what they *did*— it is *who* they are—their vision, values, and sense of affinity.

It appears to me that religions have a lifecycle. They start with **I** and an emergent **E**. That is religion as a spiritual force. The process to note is how religions decay into **A**, allowing ritual without spirit to take over until a splinter group gives it new meaning.

But not only religions, nations, corporations, products, markets, technologies have a lifecycle. So does language, a marriage, people, ideas, and anything else that has a beginning, a development, and decays into stagnation.

There are more illuminations on the above subjects, but a book must end somewhere. Thank you for keeping up with me until the last page. And, as I have said already, I hope we meet again in the next edition or the next book.

Notes

1. See S.E. Stumpf, *Socrates to Sartre: A History of Philosophy*, 2nd edition (New York: McGraw Hill, 1966): 5–8.

2. Of the many books, videos, and tapes of Ram Dass, see esp.: R. Dass and L.A. Huxley, *Between Heaven and Earth: Recipes for Living and Loving* (New York: Hay House, 1991); *The Only Dance There Is; Talks given at the Menninger Foundation, Topeka Kansas, 1970, and at Spring Grove Hospital, Spring Grove, Maryland, 1972* (New York: Anchor, 1974); R. Dass (C. Trungpa), *Living Dharma: Teachings of Twelve Buddhist Masters*, J. Kornfield, ed. (Boston and London: Shambhala, 1995); *Be Here Now* (New York: Crown, 1971); *How Can I Help: Stories and Reflections on Service* (New York: Knopf, 1985).

3. See H. Maturana and F. Varela, *The Tree of Knowledge: The Biological Roots of Human Understanding* (Boston and London: Shambhala Press, 1987), which describes the self-organization or autopoesis of living systems and argues that love is the natural manifestation of integration.

References

Additional Works by the Author

Books

Adizes, I. *Industrial Democracy Yugoslav Style*. New York: Free Press, 1971.

Adizes, I. and Mann-Borgese, Elisabeth, eds. *Self-Management: New Dimensions to Democracy*. Santa Barbara, CA: ABC/CLIO, 1975.

Adizes, I. *How to Solve the Mismanagement Crisis*. 2nd printing. Los Angeles: Adizes Institute Publications, 1980. (lst printing, New York: Dow Jones Irwin, 1979.)

Adizes, I. *Corporate Lifecycles: How and Why Corporations Grow and Die and What to Do About It*. Englewood Cliffs, NJ: Prentice Hall, 1988.

Adizes, I. *Mastering Change: The Power of Mutual Trust and Respect in Personal Life, Family, Business and Society*. Los Angeles: Adizes Institute Publications, 1993.

Adizes, I. *The Pursuit of Prime*. Santa Monica, CA: Knowledge Exchange, 1996.

Adizes, I. *Managing the Performing Arts Organization*. Forthcoming publication. Los Angeles: Adizes Institute Publications, 1999.

Articles

Adizes, I. "The Role of Management in Democratic (Communal) Organizational Structures." *Annals of Public and Cooperative Economy.* Quarterly review of CIRIEC. Brussels: CIRIEC, No. 424 (1971): 399–420.

Adizes, I. "Administering for the Arts: Introduction and Overview." *California Management Review* 15, 2 (1972): 99–103.

Adizes, I. "Boards of Directors in the Performing Arts: A Managerial Analysis." *California Management Review* 15, 2 (1972): 109–117.

Adizes, I. "Economic Changes in Yugoslavia." *East Europe* 21, 10 (1972): 8–16.

Adizes, I. "Management in Der Demokratischen Organisationen." *Annalen der Gemeinwirtschaft* 41 (Januar-März, 1972).

Adizes, I. "Samoupravljanje Kao Drustveni Cilj i Organizacijski Proces [Self-Management as a Social Goal and an Organizational Process]." *Socijalizam* 11, 12 (1972): 1324–1333.

Adizes, I. "Uloga Rukovodjenja u Demokratskim Organizacionim Strukturama. [Serbo-Croatian translation of "The Role of Management in Democratic Organizational Structures"]. *Moderna Organizacija* 6 (1972): 937–951.

Adizes, I. "Vloga Vodstva v Demokraticnih (Skupnostnih) Organizacijskih Strukturah." *Moderna Organizacija* 6 (1972): 437–451. "The Role of Management in Democratic Organization"

Adizes, I, and Weston, F. "Comparative Models of Social Responsibility." *Journal of the Academy of Management* 16, 1 (1973): 112–129. Reprinted in F. Luthans and R.M. Hodgetts, *Social Issues in Business.* 2nd ed. New York: Macmillan, 1974.

Adizes, I. "Gerencia y Estructuras Comunales (I)." *Gerencia.* Instituto Peruano de Administracion de Empresas (IPAE) Lima, Peru (Noviembre/Diciembre, 1976): 23–76. "The Role of Management in Democratic Organization"

Adizes, I. "On Conflict Resolution and an Organizational Definition of Self-Management" in *Participation and Self-Management*, Volume 5 "Social System and Participation," 1–73. First International Sociological Conference on Participation and Self-Management. Zagreb, Yugoslavia (1973).

Adizes, I. "Le Rôle de la Direction Dans une Communante Organisée Sûr une Base Democratique." *Les Annales De L'Economie Collective* 1 (Jan.-Mars, 1973): 83–109. "The Role of Management in Democratic Organization"

Adizes, I. and McWhinney, W. "Arts, Society and Administration: The Role and Training of Arts Administrators, Arts and Society." *Arts and Society,* 10, 3 (1974): 40–50.

Adizes, I. "Gerencia y Estructuras Comunales (II) Management and Communal Structures" *Gerencia,* IPAE (January/February, 1974): 36–43.

Adizes, I. "Relaciones Organizativas en la Empresa Autogestionaria [The Self-Managed Enterprise]." *Apuntes* 1, 2 (1974): 21–30.

Blaine, M. and Adizes, I. "Parkview Symphony." In *Business Policy: Strategy Formation and Management Action,* ed. W. Glueck, 366–374. 2nd. ed. New York: McGraw-Hill, 1974.

Adizes, I. "Autogestion y Nciones en Dsarollo [Self-Management in Developing Nations]." *Apuntes* 4 (1975): 106–122.

Adizes, I. "The Cost of Being an Artist: An Argument for the Public Support of the Arts." *California Management Review* 17 (Summer, 1975): 80–84.

Adizes, I. "Mas Alla del 'Principio de Peter': una Tipologia de Estilos de Incompetencis Gerencial." Instituto de Administracion Cientifica de las Empresas (IACE). Monterrey, Mexico (1975).

Adizes, I. "Mismanagement Styles." *California Management Review* 19, 2 (1976): 5–20.

Adizes, I. "Seattle Opera Association." *Business Policy: Strategy Formation and Management Action,* ed. W. Glueck, 610–634. 2nd ed. New York: McGraw-Hill, 1976.

Adizes, I. and Zukin, P. "A Management Approach to Health Planning in Developing Countries." *Health Care Management Review* 2, 1 (1977): 19–37.

Adizes, I. "Industrial Democracy and Codetermination." *Encyclopedia of Professional Management.* New York: McGraw-Hill, 1978.

Zupanov, J. and Adizes, I., "Labor Relations in Yugoslavia." *Handbook of Contemporary Developments in World Industrial Relations,* ed. A. Blum. Westwood, CT: Greenwood Press, 1978.

Adizes, I. "Mismanagement." *Affarsekonomi Management.* Stockholm, Sweden, 1978.

Adizes, I. "Organizational Passages: Tools for Diagnosis and Therapy of Organizational Behavior." *Organizational Dynamics* 8, 3 (Summer, 1979): 28–46.

Adizes, I. and Turban, E., "An Innovative Approach to Group Decision Making." *Personnel,* 62, 4 (1985): 45–49.

Adizes, I. "Back to Basics: Mutual Trust and Respect and Productivity." *Executive Excellence,* 10, 10 (1993): 11–13.

Adizes, I. "Managing: The Business of Mutual Trust and Respect." *Manage* 45, 1 (1993): 26–28.

Adizes, I. "Twelve Tips on Keeping Your Growing Business at Prime." *Manage* 44, 3 (1993): 14–17.

Adizes, I. "Corporate Lifecycles: Entrepreneurship and Integration." In *Management and Entrepreneurship*, the English version, ed. I. Vaji, 168–172. Vol. II. Centar za Management i Marketing, University of Zagreb: Zagreb University Press, 1994.

Adizes, I. "How to Convert a Committee into a Team." *Successful Meetings* 43, 2 (1994): 115–118.

Adizes, I. "Integrating Innovation." *Executive Excellence.* 11, 11 (1994): 12–13.

Adizes, I. "Keeping the Fires Burning [about TQM]." *Manage* 46, 1 (1994): 12–16.

Adizes, I. "Information Superhighway: Overloading Human Potential." *Executive Excellence* 12, 4 (1995): 15.

Adizes, I. "What Comes First? Strategy or Structure?" *Executive Excellence* 2, 9 (1995): 20.

Adizes, I. "Eight Myths [about management]: Getting Right the People Dimension of Business." *Executive Excellence* 14, 9 (1997): 20.

Adizes, I. "Five Myths about Management in the 1990s." *Manage* 48 (July, 1997): 30–32.

Adizes, I. "Looking for Mr./Ms. Perfect: The Search for the Right Professional Manager in a Growing Company. *Progress* 2, 1 (1998): 14–15.

Adizes, I. "Self-Esteem: Who Cares?" *The Adizes Institute Journal of Organizational Transformation* 1, 1 (1998): 7–16.

Working Papers

Adizes, I. *Establishing a Program for Arts Administration: Summary of the UCLA Conference and a Report on Implementation.* In the Management in the Arts Research Program Publication Series, Publication 1. Division of Research, GSM. Los Angeles: UCLA, 1969.

Adizes, I. "The Roles of Art in Post-Industrial Society." Presented at the Center for the Study of Democratic Institutions Santa Barbara, CA: January, 1973.

Adizes, I. "Administering for the Arts: 'Problems in Practice.'" Management in the Arts Program Research Papers, #15. GSM. Los Angeles: UCLA, October, 1971.

Adizes, I. "A New Framework for Management Theory." Los Angeles: The Adizes Institute, June, 1987.

Adizes, I. and Haldeman, H.R. "Why Gorbachev Might Fail." Los Angeles: The Adizes Institute, January, 1988.

Adizes, I. "The Common Principles of Managing Oneself, a Family, a Corporation or a Society." Los Angeles: The Adizes Institute, September, 1990.

Video

Adizes, I. (1984). *The Adizes Program in Video.* Los Angeles: The Adizes Institute.

Program A: Overview of the Adizes Process of Management. Set of 3 videotapes.

The Adizes Process of Management. 55 min.

The Adizes Program. Questions and Answers #1

The Adizes Program. Questions and Answers # 2

Program B: The Management Process. Set of 4 videotapes.

The Roles of Management. 28 min.

Mismanagement Styles. 41 min.

The Structural Causes of Deadwood. 38 min.

What Is a Good Manager? 41 min.

Program C: Organizational Lifecycles. Set of 4 videotapes.

The Growth Phases of Organizational Lifecycles. 39 min.

The Aging Phases of Organizational Lifecycles. 38 min.

Analysis of Lifecycles. 52 min.

Treating the Growing and Aging Problems of Organizations. 56 min.

Program D: Decision Making and Implementation. Set of 2 videotapes.

CAPI: Predicting Managerial Effectiveness. 45 min.

The Adizes Process of Decision Making. 49 min.

Adizes, I. *From Entrepreneurship to Professional Management.* Speech to the Council of Growing Companies. Los Angeles: Adizes Institute Publications, 1993.

Adizes, I. *The Young Company's Lifecycle: Are You Ready for the Future?* Keynote Address to the Inc. 500 Awards. Los Angeles: Adizes Institute Publications, 1996.

Audio

Adizes, I. *Analysis of Management.* 6 audio cassettes. Los Angeles: Adizes Institute Publications, 1988.
Adizes, I. *Analysis of Lifecycles.* 6 audio cassettes. Los Angeles: Adizes Institute Publications, 1989.

CD ROM

Caric, N., Horvat, Z. and Vukic, B. *The Adizes Program: An Interactive Compilation of the Writings of Dr. Ichak Adizes and the Programs of the Adizes Institute.* Los Angeles: Adizes Institute Publications, 1998.

Additional Readings

Note: In addition to the books and articles cited in the endnotes of each chapter, the following works are suggested as supplementary sources to this book.

Books

Beck, D.E. and Cown, C.C. *Spiral Dynamics: Managing Values, Leadership, and Change.* Cambridge, MA: Blackwell Publishers, Inc., 1996.
Beckhard, R., and Harris, R.T. *Organizational Transitions: Managing Complex Change.* 2nd ed. Reading, MA: Addison-Wesley, 1987.
Behrendt, S. *Life Cycle Design: A Manual for Small and Medium-Sized Enterprises.* New York: Springer Verlag, 1997.
Bell, D.V. *Power, Influence, and Authority.* New York: Oxford University Press, 1975.
Burns, T. and Stalker, G.M. *The Management of Innovation.* London: Tavistock Press, 1961.
Capra, F. *The Turning Point: Science, Society and the Rising Culture.* New York: Bantam, 1982.
Capra, F. *Uncommon Wisdom: Conversations with Remarkable People.* New York: Bantam, 1982.
Carter, B. and McGoldrick, M. *The Changing Family Life Cycle: A Framework for Therapy.* Boston: Allyn and Bacon, 1989.

Falicov, C.J. *Family Transitions: Continuity & Change Over the Life Cycle.* The Guilford Family Therapy Series. New York: Guilford Press, 1991.

Flamholtz, E. *Growing Pains: How to Make the Transition from Entrepreneurship to a Professionally Managed Firm.* San Francisco: Jossey-Bass, 1986.

Gersick, K.E. *Generation to Generation: Life Cycles of the Family Business.* Boston: Harvard Business School Press, 1997.

Greiner, L.E. "Patterns of Organizational Change." *Organizational Change and Development* (I–II), ed. G. Dalton, P.R. Lawrence, and L.E. Greiner. Homewood, IL: Irwin, 1970.

Haire, M. "Biological Models and Empirical Histories of the Growth of Organization." *Modern Organization Theory,* ed. M.Haire. New York: Wiley, 1959.

Hales, D.R. *Family: The Life Cycle.* London: Chelsea House, 1988.

Hirschhorn, L. and Barnett, C. *The Psychodynamics of Organizations.* Philadelphia: Temple University Press, 1993.

Kets de Vries, M.F.R. "Alexitheymia in Organizational Life: The Organization Man Revisited." In *The Psychodynamics of Organizations,* ed. L. Hirschhorn and C. Barnett, 203–218. Philadelphia: Temple University Press, 1993.

Kets de Vries, M.F.R. and Miller, D. *The Neurotic Organization: Diagnosing and Changing Counterproductive Styles of Management.* San Francisco: Jossey-Bass, 1984.

Kimberly, J.R., Miles, R.H., and Associates, eds. *The Organizational Life Cycle: Issues in the Creation, Transformation, and Decline of Organizations.* San Francisco: Jossey-Bass, 1980.

Levenson, D.J., and Gooden, W. "The Life Cycle." In *Comprehensive Textbook of Psychiatry,* ed. H.L. Kaplan and B.J. Sacok. 4th ed. Baltimore: Williams and Wilkins, 1985.

Mahon, J. *Strategic Issues of Management: An Integration of Life Cycle Perspectives.* Boston University Working Paper Series. Boston University School of Management, 1991.

Miller, L.M. *Barbarians to Bureaucrats: Corporate Life Cycle Strategies.* New York: Fawcett Books, 1990.

Miller, D. and Friesen, P.H. *Organizations: A Quantum View.* Englewood Cliffs, NJ: Prentice Hall, 1984.

Miner, J.B. *Theories of Organizational Structure and Process.* Hinsdale, IL: Dryden, 1982.

Norris, J.E. *Among Generations: The Cycle of Adult Relationships.* New York: Freeman & Co., 1993.

Nystrom, P.C. and Starbuck, W.H., eds. *Handbook of Organizational Design*. New York: Oxford University Press, 1980.

Piaget, J. *The Construction of Reality in the Child*. trans. M. Cook. New York: Basic Books, 1954.

Peters, T.J. and Waterman, Jr., R. *In Search of Excellence*. New York: Harper & Row, 1982.

Redmill, F. and Dale, C., eds. *Life Cycle: Management for Dependability*. New York: Springer Verlag, 1997.

Scott, B.G. *Stages of Corporate Development*. HBS Intercollegiate Case Clearing House. Boston: HBS Press, 1971.

Sheehy, G. *Passages*. New York: Bantam, 1977.

Smith, N.R. *The Entrepreneur and His Firm: The Relationship Between Type of Man and Type of Company*. Bureau of Business and Economic Research. East Lansing: Michigan State University Press, 1967.

Starbuck, W.H. "Organizational Growth and Development." *Handbook of Organizations*, ed. J.G. March. Chicago: Rand McNally, 1965.

Stoner, J.F. "Organizational Careers and Individual Development" *Management*, Chapter 6 (1978).

Tansik, D.A. *Management: A Life Cycle Approach*. Irwin Series in Management and the Behavioral Sciences. Homewood, IL: Richard D. Irwin, 1980.

Thompson, L., Jr., and Thompson, L. *Mastering the Challenges of Change: Strategies for Each Stage in Your Organization's Life Cycle*. Washington, DC: Amacom, 1994.

Tichy, N. "Problem Cycles in Organizations and the Management of Change." In J. Kimberley, et al., eds., *The Organizational Life Cycle: Issues in the Creation, Transformation, and Decline of Organization*, 164–183. San Francisco: Jossey-Bass, 1980.

Weick, K. *The Social Psychology of Organizing*. 2nd ed. Reading, MA: Addison-Wesley, 1979.

Articles

Ansoff, I.H. "Toward a Strategic Theory of the Firm." *Business Strategy*. New York: Penguin Books, 1970: 11–31.

Argyris, C. "The Fusion of an Individual with the Organization." *American Sociological Review* 19 (1954): 145–167.

Argyris, C. "Personality vs. Organization." *Organizational Dynamics* 3, 2 (1974): 2–17.

Baron, J. and Cook, K. "Process and Outcome: Perspectives on the Distribution of Rewards in Organizations." *Administrative Science Quarterly* 37 (1992): 220–240.

Bartunek, J.M., and Louis, M.R. "The Interplay of Organizational Development and Organizational Transformation." *Research in Organizational Change and Development* 2 (1988): 97–134.

Beatty, R.W., and Ulrich, D.O. "Reenergizing the Mature Organization." *Organizational Dynamics* 20 (Summer, 1991): 16–30.

Becker, S.W. and Gordon, G. "An Entrepreneurial Theory of Formal Organizations, Part 1." *Administrative Science Quarterly* 11 (1966): 315–344.

Beckhard, R. and Dyer, W.G. "Managing Continuity in the Family-Owned Business." *Organizational Dynamics* 13, 4 (1983): 5–12.

Berenbeim, R.E. "How Business Families Manage the Transition from Ownership to Professional Management." The Conference Board. Reprinted in *Family Business Review* III, 1 (1984): 69–110.

Birley, S. and Westhead, P. "A Comparison of New Businesses Established by 'Novice' and 'Habitual' Founders in Great Britain." *International Small Business Journal* 12 (1993): 38–60.

Boulding, K.E. "The Management of Decline." Address to the Regents' Convocations of the State University of New York, Albany, September 20, 1974.

Boulding, K.E. "The Management of Decline." *Change* 6, 4 (1975): 8–9.

Breunlin, D. "Oscillation Theory and Family Development." In *Family Transitions: Continuity and Change Over the Life Cycle,* ed. C. Falicov, 133–158. New York: Guilford Press, 1988.

Brüderl, J., and Schüssel. "Organizational Mortality: The Liabilities of Newness and Adolescence [in West German firms]." *Administrative Science Quarterly* 35 (Summer, 1990): 530–547.

Cameron, K.S. "A Study of Organizational Effectiveness and Its Predictors." *Management Science* 32 (1986): 187–112.

Cameron, K.S. "Organizational Dysfunctions of Decline." *Academy of Management Journal* 30, 1 (March, 1987): 126–138.

Chakravarthy, G.S. "Adaptation: A Promising Metaphor for Strategic Management." *Academy of Management Review* 7 (1982): 35–44.

Collins, J. and Porras, J. "Organizational Vision and Visionary Organizations." *California Management Review* 34, 1 (1991): 30–52.

Davis, P. and Stern, D. "Adaption, Survival, and Growth in Family Business: An Integrated Systems Perspective." *Human Relations* 34, 4 (1980): 207–224.

Davis, S. and Davidson, B. "The Myth of the Immortal Corporation [matching organization to the same point in its lifecycle as the business it serves]." *Across Board* 28 (1991): 24–27.

Dodge, H.R. and Robbins, J.E. "An Empirical Investigation of the Organizational Life Cycle Model for Small Business Development and Survival." *Journal of Small Business Management* 30 (January, 1992): 27–37.

Drazin, R. and Kazanjian, R.K. "Research Notes and Communications: A Reanalysis of Miller and Friesen's Life Cycle Data." *Strategic Management Journal* 11 (1990): 319–325.

Fernley, G.A.T. "The Pivotal Role of an AMC [Association Management Company] in the Life Cycle of an Association." *Association Management* 48 (July, 1996): 1265–1466.

Ford, J.D. "The Occurrence of Structural Hysteresis in Declining Organizations." *Academy of Management Journal* 23 (1980): 615–630.

Freeman, J. "Organizational Life Cycles and Natural Selection Processes." *Research in Organizational Behavior* 4 (1982): 1–32.

Freeman, J. and Hannan, M.T. "Growth and Decline Processes in Organizations." *American Sociological Review* 40 (1975): 215–228.

Glick, P.C. "The Life Cycle of the Family." *Marriage and Family Living* V (1959): 3–9.

Glick, P.C. "Updating the Family Life Cycle." *Journal of Marriage and the Family* 39 (1977): 5–13.

Greiner, L.E. "Antecedents of Planned Organizational Change." *Journal of Applied Behavioral Science* 3, 1 (1967): 51–85.

Greiner, L.E. "Evolution and Revolution as Organizations Grow." *Harvard Business Review* 50 (July–August, 1972): 37–46.

Hanks, S.H. "The Organization Life Cycle: Integrating Content and Process." *Journal of Small Business Strategy* 1 (February, 1990): 1–12.

Hutchinson, J. "Evolving Organizational Forms." *Journal of World Business* 11 (Summer, 1996): 437–457.

Itzigsohn, A. "Integrating Family Therapy Concepts into Adizes' Theory of Management: Transitional Voyage OD Intervention During the Adolescence Stage." *The Adizes Institute Journal for Organizational Transformation* 1, 1 (1998): 16–34.

Kaufman, H. "The Natural History of Human Organizations." *Administration and Society* 7 (1975): 131–149.

Kepner, E. "The Family and the Firm: A Co-evolutionary Perspective." *Organizational Dynamics* 12, 1 (1983): 55–70.

Kets de Vries, M.F.R. "The Entrepreneurial Personality: A Person at the Crossroads." *Journal of Management Studies* 14 (1977): 34–57.

Kfir, A. "Using Metaphors in Organizational Diagnosis." *The Adizes Institute Journal for Organizational Transformation* 1, 1 (1998): 53–70.

Kimberly, J.R. "Issues in the Creation of Organizations: Initiation, Innovation, and Institutionalization." *Academy of Management Journal* 22 (1979): 437–457.

Kimberly, J.R. "Managerial Innovation." In *Handbook of Organizational Design,* eds. P.C. Nystrom and W.H. Starbuck, 84–85. New York: Oxford University Press, 1989.

Kuzmanovski, Z. "Organizational Revival Cycles: How to Diagnose and Treat Traumatized Organizations." *The Adizes Institute Journal for Organizational Transformation* 1, 1 (1998): 35–44 .

Lansberg, H., et al. "The Succession Conspiracy." *Family Business Review* 1, 2 (1988): 119–144.

Lavoie, D. and Culbert, S.A. "Stages of Organization and Development." *Human Relations* 31 (1978): 417–438.

Levinson, H. "Conflicts That Plague Family Business." *Harvard Business Review* 49 (March–April, 1971): 90–98.

Lipicink, B. "Building Temporary Teams in Slovenia with the Help of Adizes' Roles." *The Adizes Institute Journal for Organizational Transformation* 1, 1 (1998): 45–52.

Lippitt, G.L., and Schimdt, W.H. "Crises in a Developing Organization." *Harvard Business Review* 45 (March, 1967): 102–112.

Lorange, P. and Nelson, R.T. "How to Recognize—and Avoid—Organizational Decline." *Sloan Management Review* 28 (Spring, 1987): 41–48.

McClelland, D. "Need Achievement and Entrepreneurship—A Longitudinal Study." *Journal of Personality and Social Psychology* (1965): 1389–1392.

Miller, D. "Toward a New Contingency Approach: The Search for Organizational Gestalts." *Journal of Management Studies* 18 (1981): 257–259.

Miller, D. "The Genesis of Configuration." *Academy of Management Review* 12 (1987): 686–701.

Miller, D. and Friesen, P.H. "Archetypes of Organizational Transition." *Administrative Science Quarterly* 25 (June, 1980): 268–299.

Miller, D. and Friesen, P.H. "A Longitudinal Study of the Corporate Life Cycle." *Management Science* 30, 10 (1984): 1161–1183.

Miller, D. and Friesen, P.H. "The Longitudinal Analysis of Organizations: A Methodological Perspective." *Management Science* 28 (September, 1982): 1013–1034.

Miller, D. and Freisen, P.H. "Successful and Unsuccessful Phases of the Corporate Life Cycle." *Organization Studies* 4 (October, 1983): 339–356.

Milliman, J., et al. "Organizational Life Cycles and Strategic International Human Resource Management in Multinational Companies: Implications for Congruence Theory." *Academy Management Review* 16 (April, 1991): 318–339.

Mirvis, P.H. "Failures in Organizational Development and Change." *Organization Development: Part I—An Evolutionary Perspective*, ed. D. Berg. Boston: Wiley and Sons, 1971.

Mintzberg, H. and Westley, F. "Cycles of Organizational Change [models of change experienced by major world religions]." *Strategic Management Journal* 13 (Winter, 1992): 15–29.

O'Rand, A.M. and Krecker, M.L. "Concepts of the Life Cycle: Their History, Meanings and Uses in the Social Sciences." *Annual Review of Sociology* 16 (1990): 241–262.

Ouchi, W.G. "The Relationship Between Organizational Structure and Organizational Control." *Administrative Science Quarterly* 22 (1977): 95–113.

Penrose, E.T. "Biological Analogies in the Theory of the Firm." *American Economic Review* 42 (1952): 804–819.

Peterson, R.A. "Entrepreneurship in Organizations." *Handbook of Organizational Design*, ed. P.C. Nystrom and W.H. Starbuck. New York: Oxford University Press, 1989.

Quinn, R.E. and Cameron, K. "Organizational Life Cycles and Shifting Criteria of Effectiveness: Some Preliminary Evidence." *Management Science* 29, 1 (January, 1983): 33–51.

Schein, E.H. "The Role of the Founder in Creating Organizational Cultures." *Organizational Dynamics* 12, 1 (1983): 13–28.

Schmidt, H. and Yanay, U. "Deprofessionalization and the Organizational Life Cycle: The Case of Community Service Agencies." *Public Personnel Management*, 19 (Summer, 1990): 123–133.

Scott, W.G. "Organization Theory: A Reassessment." *Academy of Management Journal* 17 (1976): 242–254.

Smith, N.R. and Miner, J.B. "Type of Entrepreneur, Type of Firm, and Managerial Motivation: Implications for Organization Life Cycle Theory." *Strategic Management Journal* 4 (1983): 325–340.

Spanier, G.G. and Glick, P.C. "The Life Cycle of American Families: An Expanded Analysis." *Journal of Family History* (1980): 97–111.

Steinmetz, L. "Critical Stages of Small Business Growth: Why They Occur and How to Survive Them." *Business Horizons* 12, 1 (1969): 29.

Sutton, R.I. "Managing Organizational Death." *Human Resource Management* 22 (1983): 391–412.

Sutton, R.I. (1990). "Organizational Decline Processes: A Social Psychological Perspective." *Research in Organizational Behavior* 12 (1990): 205–253.

Thain, D.H. "Stages of Corporate Development." *Business Quarterly* 34 (1969): 32–45.

Tuason, R.V. "Corporate Life Cycle and the Evaluation of Corporate Strategy." *Academy of Management Proceedings* (1973): 35–40.

Weitzel, W. and Jonsson, E. "Reversing the Downward Spiral: Lessons from W.T. Grant and Sears Roebuck." *Academy of Management Ex.* 5 (August, 1991): 7–22.

Westphal, J. and Zajac, et al. "Who Shall Govern? CEO/Board Power, Demographic Similarity and New Director Selection." *Administrative Science Quarterly* 40 (1995): 60–83.

Whetten, D.A. "Growth and Decline Processes in Organizations." *Annual Review of Sociology* (1987).

Whetten, D.A. "Organizational Decline: A Neglected Topic in Organizational Behavior." *Academy of Management Review* 5 (1980): 577–588.

Zald, M.N. and Ash, R. "Social Movement Organizations: Growth, Decay and Decline." *Social Forces* 44 (1966): 327–341.

Monographs and Reports

Scott, B. "Stages of Corporate Development—Parts I and II." Working paper. Harvard Business School Boston, MA, 1970.

Whetten, D.A. "Organizational Decline: A Neglected Topic in Organizational Behavior." Working paper. College of Commerce and Business Administration, University of Illinois, 1979.

Working Papers of
the Adizes Graduate School

The following papers are available through the Adizes Institute.

Adizes, I., Chaffee, R., and Hansenfeld, Y. "Revitalizing Child Protective Services." AGS W23, 1988. 16 pp.

Axelrod, D. "A Comparison of Synerteams in the Adizes Methodology with the Concept of Self-directed Work Teams." AGS5, 1996.

Bentov, A. "Planning: Why It Fails in Organizations." AGS P20, 1981. 12 pp.

Boorn, M.L. "Urban Lifecycles According to Adizes Methodology." AGS P27, 1992. 13 pp.

Capra, M. "The Department of Energy: Infancy to Senility in Four Years." 1981.

Caric, N. "Generalized Pareto Analysis: An Advanced Deliberation Technique in the Adizes Problem Solving Method." AGS2, 1995.

Caric, N. "Civility = Constructive Conflict?" AGS3, 1995.

Chambless, D. "Goals: How They Change in an Organization Over Its Lifecycle." AGS13, 1989. 10 pp.

Dagley, E.S. "MBA Programs and the Education of Managers: An Application of the Adizes Methodology." AGS P39, 1991. 13 pp.

Denny, A. "Astrology, PAEI and the Lifecycle." AGS W24, 1988. 33 pp.

Freeman, C. "Religious Organizations and Leaders: A Comparison Utilizing the Adizes Method." AGS W11, 1983. 17 pp.

Gates. S. "Family Lifecycle and the Corporate Lifecycle: A Comparison." AGS24, 1989. 20 pp.

Gjerde, R. "Norway: Where Is It on the Lifecycle?" AGS P5, 1983. 19 pp.

Glass, C. "Men's vs. Women's Style of Management." AGS P19, 1981. 14 pp.

Green, A.J. "Color in Relation to the Adizes Theory on PAEI and Lifecycles." AGS W25, 1989. 25 pp.

Haering, P. "Civilizations and Organizations: An Analysis of Their Dynamics." AGS 9, 1988. 26 pp.

Harbaugh, K.L. "Xerox Corporation Lifecycle Analysis." AGS P24, 1981. 11 pp.

Harmon, D. "Rock Music and Adizes." AGS P37, 1991. 16 pp.

Harrison, E. "Japan: The Economic Machine." AGS W05, 1991. 16 pp.

Helfant, M. "Lifecycle of a Government Organization." AGS11, 1991. 16 pp.

Horvat. Z. "Causal Problem Analysis: Schematic Problems Diagram." AGS1, 1995.

Howe, P. "Singapore: Application of the Organizational Lifecycle to Singapore's History." AGS21, 1981. 20 pp.

Jarkow, L.C. "Applying Organization Lifecycle Theory to the American Experience." AGS30, 1992. 12 pp.

Katz, R.R. "Management and the Phenomenology of Power." AGS W15, 1983. 25 pp.

Kealy, C. "The Charismatic Leader." AGS31, 1991. 16 pp.

Kitchen, K. "Developing the 'PE' for Entrepreneurial Success." AGS8, 1983. 19 pp.

Kogus, I. "How to Set Priorities Using the Coefficient of Effort and the Coefficient of Value." AGS8, n.d.

Kogus, I. "PAEI Managerial Style Instrument." AGS9, n.d.

Kuzmanovski, Z. "Psychodiagnostics and Organizational Diagnostics." AGS11, 1996.

Labaste, S.P. "France: Where Is It on the Lifecycle?" AGS7, 1989. 20 pp.

Larsen, O.S. "Hoyanger Works and the Adizes Method." AGS W10, 1982. 23 pp.

Larsen, R. "Biogenetic Character Structure and Dr. Ichak Adizes' Decision Roles: Exploring the Relationships." AGS26, 1992. 13 pp.

Lavelle, D. "What Should be the Lifecycle Curve of a Company?" AGS P35, 1991. 12 pp.

Lehmann, F. "Hitler and Germany: The Founder's Trap." AGS W03, 1982. 20 pp.

Low, K. "Product Lifecycle: A Comparison." AGS15, 1981. 16 pp.

Mark, R. "The Reagan Revolution: A Lifecycle Analysis of the Administration." AGS W13, 1983. 14 pp.

Marshall, J. "Creativity in Organizations: Who Expresses It, What Organizations Have It, How It Can Be Stifled, How It Can Be Fostered." AGS8, 1981. 20 pp.

Meister, J. "Lifecycle of the Family. A Different Perspective." AGS10, 1981. 17 pp.

Morgan, T. "The Lifecycle of Rome." AGS W01, 1982. 24 pp.

Moskowitz, A. "Theories on Mutual Trust." AGS30, 1989. 7 pp.

Mrgdichian, L. "The Marriage Relationship and Mutual Trust and Respect." AGS45, 1991. 18 pp.

Ostlund, H. "Managing Change and Innovation." Dansk Management Center, AGS12, 1983. 11 pp.

454 References

Pellegrini, T. "Vedic Philosophy and the Adizes Methodology." AGS P25, 1981. 9 pp.

Perry, S.R. "Mutual Trust and Respect in Japanese Culture and Corporate Life." AGS W35, 1990. 11 pp.

Piper, J. "Synergetic Model of the Church." AGS36, 1988. 24 pp.

Rayner, M. "Beyond Skinner." AGS W26, 1989. 11 pp.

Recker, L. "Myers Briggs: Applying PAEI to the Myers-Briggs' Patterns." AGS P41, 1991. 16 pp.

Red, E.X., III. "A Small Company: A Practical Application of the Adizes Methodology." AGS P38, 1991. 17 pp.

Reinoud, H. "Levenscycli van Onderneingen en Directievoerders." AGS WO7, 1982.

Rojany, S. "Expert Systems in Medical Diagnosis: Comparison and Applicability to Syndags." AGS7, 1996.

Rose, S.L. "The Iran-Contra Affair, CAPI and PAEI: An Exploration of Political Decision Making and Implementation." AGS P43, 1991. 16 pp.

Scala, K.W. "E Capabilities—How to Develop Them: A Cubist Approach." AGS 18, 1981. 18 pp.

Stokes, J.W. "Mutual Trust and Respect and Basketball Team Performance." AGS W34, 1990. 16 pp.

Sullivan, A. "Developmental Therapy and Organizational Therapy: Parallels and Mutual Learning." AGS32, 1993. 32 pp.

Tanner, W.C. "Lifecycles in Government Agencies." AGS17, 1981. 14 pp.

Thye, R. "The Life and Assassination of Malcom X: An Analysis Using the Adizes Methodology." AGS48, 1991. 17 pp.

Thygesen, C. "America's Future: An Application of the Adizes Theories to the American Future." AGS49, 1991. 23 pp.

Valdesuso, C. "Alternative Diagnostic Tools: Peter Senge's *Fifth Discipline.*" AGS12, 1996.

Valdesuso, C. "Using the Adizes Model to Evaluate a Systems Development Methodology." AGS1, 1985.

Valdesuso, C. "Adizes and MIS." AGS W33, 1989. 14 pp.

Weiber, A.M. "Ross Perot as President?" AGS P33, 1991. 12 pp.

Index